Democratic Swarms

Democratic Swarms

ANCIENT COMEDY AND THE
POLITICS OF THE PEOPLE

Page duBois

THE UNIVERSITY OF CHICAGO PRESS
CHICAGO AND LONDON

The University of Chicago Press, Chicago 60637
The University of Chicago Press, Ltd., London
© 2022 by The University of Chicago
All rights reserved. No part of this book may be used or reproduced
in any manner whatsoever without written permission, except in
the case of brief quotations in critical articles and reviews.
For more information, contact the University of Chicago Press,
1427 E. 60th St., Chicago, IL 60637.
Published 2022
Printed in the United States of America

31 30 29 28 27 26 25 24 23 22   1 2 3 4 5

ISBN-13: 978-0-226-81574-9 (cloth)
ISBN-13: 978-0-226-81575-6 (e-book)
DOI: https://doi.org/10.7208/chicago/9780226815756.001.0001

Library of Congress Cataloging-in-Publication Data

Names: DuBois, Page, author.
Title: Democratic swarms : ancient comedy and the politics of the
    people / Page duBois.
Description: Chicago : University of Chicago Press, 2022. | Includes
    bibliographical references and index.
Identifiers: LCCN 2021037433 | ISBN 9780226815749 (cloth) |
    ISBN 9780226815756 (ebook)
Subjects: LCSH: Greek drama (Comedy)—History and criticism. |
Greek drama (Comedy)—Political aspects. | Drama—Chorus (Greek
    drama) | Democracy—Greece—Athens.
Classification: LCC PA3161 .D83 2022 | DDC 882/.0109—dc23
LC record available at https://lccn.loc.gov/2021037433

♾ This paper meets the requirements of ANSI/NISO Z39.48-1992
(Permanence of Paper).

For John

Contents

Preface · ix

Introduction · 1

CHAPTER 1
The Tragic Individual: The Tyranny
of Oedipus and Antigone · 17

CHAPTER 2
The Swarm · 47

CHAPTER 3
Chorus · 79

CHAPTER 4
Utopias · 117

CHAPTER 5
Parrhesia: Saying It All · 155

CHAPTER 6
Democracy, Communalism, Communism · 175

CHAPTER 7
Epilogue: The Politics of the Present · 199

*Acknowledgments · 209   Notes · 211
Selected Bibliography · 245
Index · 257*

Preface

> What is important is not an authoritarian unification, but a kind of infinite swarming of desiring machines, . . . everywhere.
>
> Félix Guattari, *Molecular Revolution*

My favorite performances of ancient Greek comedies straddle several decades. I saw a modern Greek troupe perform Aristophanes' comedy the *Acharnians* in the open-air amphitheater in Epidaurus, in Greece, many years ago with my friends Froma and George Zeitlin. It was a summer evening, warm and a little breezy. The amphitheater has been celebrated for millennia because of its extraordinary acoustics; tour guides send the guided up to the highest ranks of stone seats, and then, at the center of the orchestra, the dancing floor, drop a pin. Tourists marvel at the sound. The night we saw the *Acharnians*, the chorus was dressed in wild and brilliant colors, leapt about in slapstick and kept the audience in stitches. There were lots of references to the contemporary and messy politics of Greece in that moment, and although I didn't follow all of the modern Greek, or the jokes, I was caught up in a jubilant, mesmerizing participation in a crowd that loved the spectacle of dancing and singing and the mockery of the powerful.

Another favorite performance happened at the University of California at San Diego, where I teach. My beloved colleague William Fitzgerald invited the Aquila Theatre troupe, led by Peter Meineck, to present a version of Aristophanes' *Frogs*. The central character of this play, which concerns Greek tragedy and tragedians, is the god Dionysos, who is ridiculed for much of the action. In the Aquila troupe's presentation the god was dressed as an Elvis impersonator. In the closed space of a tiny theater, with a small group of actors making up the chorus of frogs as well as playing the other roles in the play, the performance in its own way produced hysterical laughter and delight. I remember anxiety, fearing that the students who attended might not get the Elvis thing, and the brilliantly evocative music of this display, but they were laughing as hard as I was.

This book calls for reading and watching ancient Greek comedy again, better, more. Resisting the seemingly inevitable and perennial appeal of Greek tragedy, I have wanted to set comedy alongside its companion and rival, and to consider its value to contemporary thinking on the politics of democracy. Rather than revisiting the sufferings of the nuclear family of Oedipus the king and his daughter Antigone, or tragedy's relationship to questions of sovereignty, I call for ancient comedy, its laughter, its obscenity and freedom of speech, its wild swarming animal choruses and rebellious women, to inform another model, another genealogy of democracy. Comedy has its place, even in dark days. Old Comedy continued to be performed during the plague of Athens and the Peloponnesian War, in the later fifth century BCE. In what follows, I question the privileging of tragedy in the philosophical and political theoretical tradition, and using the concepts of swarm intelligence and nomadic theory, argue for adding to a long tradition of tragic thought the resistant, utopian, libidinous, and often joyous communal legacy of comedy.

I also want to break Greek comedy out of the scholarly insularity of its study. Perhaps because of the obscenity and topicality of ancient comedy, it has in the humanities and social sciences been relatively isolated from the wider contemplation of Greek drama, and at times even by classicists themselves, trivialized or limited to a focus on historical references, individual "heroic" characters, diction, and the laborious explication of jokes. Women long did not read Greek, and the study of ancient Greek comedy and its rowdy, obscene language has often attracted an elite and gendered attention. Yet ancient Athenian comedy provides a unique perspective on everyday life, gender and sexuality, and the utopian politics of the classical period of Athenian democracy. The irrepressible energy of the comic swarm exceeds the categories of traditional analysis of the ancient city, its drama, its politics.

I have sought to make the genre accessible to contemporary readers, to coax it out of obscurity and a sometimes obscure subfield of classical studies, not a genre of ancient texts that often appeals to contemporary political theorists or culture critics. I address not only the sexual politics, the utopianism, and the political strategies concerning free speech in ancient comedy; I widen my attention to include not just Aristophanes, the best-known of ancient comic writers, but also the many other names associated with this dramatic tradition. And I locate the plays in their ritual, collective, political setting, alongside tragedy in the festivals honoring Dionysos and the city in which they were performed. Comedy opens up a line of flight that leads from the stage to the heterogeneous, lively city. I focus not so much on the *characters* of these plays, on their psychological, nuclear family struggles, but rather on the collective, the chorus, the wasps, birds, clouds, and rebellious women whose calls for change in the ancient city make this genre unique in classical Greek performance, and uniquely significant for democracy, ancient and contemporary.

Why go back to ancient comedy and its politics of the people? In part, because classics and ancient history are once again being dragged into the politics of the present. The group called "Identity Evropa" has used classicizing white sculpture to command, on American college campuses: "Protect your heritage," "Our future belongs to us," and to warn students of continuing "white genocide." As Mark Potok, an official of the Southern Poverty Law Center, which monitors extremist groups, noted, "Although you might think based on their [Identity Evropa's] propaganda that they're all about Plato and Aristotle and Socrates, in fact they're merely a gussied-up version of the Klan."[1] The Bloc Identitaire, which originated on the Far Right in France, appropriates a symbol of the LGBTQX movement, using a yellow lambda as its symbol, because, they argue, it marked the shields of the Spartans who held the pass at Thermopylae against the Persian hordes, who were, it seems, bent on white genocide. Groups recruited to fight leftist demonstrations are being recruited into "Spartan" training camps and competitions to harden them for combat.

The material of classical studies has been deployed by these alt-right, white supremacist, and other racist groups to shore up their claims for a pure, white, Aryan, and often Hellenic origin to Western civilization. It's important for classicists to denounce this instrumentalization of the ancient world.[2] To point out that ancient sculpture was not pure white. That the ancient Greek and Roman world, the Mediterranean and beyond, included Asia and Africa as well as Europe. That the societies of the classical age were not paradises of white freedom, and that they oppressed huge slave populations, excluded women from political participation, and conducted ruthless imperial campaigns. The diversity and heterogeneity of the discipline of classics, focused on ancient Greece and Rome, are finally being expanded to include more people of color, of all genders and ethnicities, and more needs to be done in this regard to dismantle the edifice of classics-as-origin-of-white-supremacy-and-the-pure-fount-of-Western civilization. Scholars begin to situate the study of Greek and Roman antiquity within a global frame. Elsewhere, I've argued for world history, for a study of antiquity all over the globe, locating classical studies in the West within a wide array of civilizations before and after the year one of the Common Era.[3] At the University of California at San Diego I teach in a general education sequence called the "Making of the Modern World," touching on not just ancient "Greece," which in fact includes parts of Europe, Asia, and Africa, but also the so-called Near East—Mesopotamia, ancient African Egypt, and the Levant—as well as ancient India, ancient China, and ancient Mesoamerica. I'm not an expert on all these regions, but the study of other societies contemporary with that of ancient Athens has greatly enriched my understanding of the specificity, even peculiarity, not always admirable by comparison, of the traditional objects of classical studies, ancient Greece and Rome.

But I also believe there is more to the ancient Greeks themselves than just a mistaken message about Euro-American superiority, the whiteness of Western civilization, the "Greek miracle," the wonders of the statesman and leader Pericles and what is seen as "his" democracy. One of the concerns that frames what I discuss in this book, as the world resists a descent in the present into human-made climate disaster, tyranny, dictatorship, and white supremacy, is the desire not to abandon hope for something different. In the face of growing tendencies to abuse history, I join with others to revive a strain of resistance that is directly opposed to monarchy, or tyranny, that is nourished by the anarchist strain of Marxism, the thinking of such ancestors as Rosa Luxembourg, with an emphasis on a relatively leaderless collective in politics. I owe much to a tradition that goes back to ancient atomist theory, to Democritus and Leucippus, to Epicurus and Lucretius, to Spinoza and his readers in modernity, Marx, Gilles Deleuze and Félix Guattari, Rosi Braidotti, Michael Hardt and Antonio Negri, Jane Bennett and Mel Chen and Judith Butler. And to the authors of the collection called *Joyful Militancy: Building Thriving Resistance in Toxic Times*.[4] We can see, in such contemporary movements as the Yellow Umbrellas, the Sunrise Movement, Occupy, and Black Lives Matter, resistance to defined leadership, to named figures who stand for the group as a whole, and by contrast, the cultivation of habits of collective decision-making and equality that could look back to ancient democracy and the wild anarchy of its choruses.

Why comedy? As someone who found inspiration, politics, and a respite from disengaged empiricism in the so-called Paris school, the reorientation of classical studies guided especially by Jean-Pierre Vernant, and including Pierre Vidal-Naquet, Nicole Loraux, and Marcel Detienne, I was drawn to the high art of Greek tragedy along with others who found their anthropological, political, and cultural contextualizing of ancient democracy and its rituals, writings, and thinking a liberating influence, given an Anglo-Saxon and Teutonic emphasis on philology and a somewhat hermetic relationship to ancient Greek society. But the privileging of Greek tragedy, in contrast to comedy, is one of the central issues of this present work; that emphasis goes beyond the discipline of classical studies to include a long history of philosophical and political theoretical and even psychoanalytic meditation on what the ancient Greeks and their tragedies established, their reception contributing to setting the terms of Western civilization.

I am greatly indebted to scholars who disregarded the implicit call to concentrate on the high art of tragedy, and whose work has been so important to my understanding of the interconnectedness of tragedy and comedy in ancient Athens. If one of the reasons for the preference for tragedy in the wider world, beyond classics per se, was the obscenity and inaccessibility and topicality of ancient Greek comedy, we all owe much to the classical scholar Jeffrey Henderson, who opened up the vocabulary of the comic poet Aristophanes, amplifying a lexicon that had long been censored in dictionaries and in commentaries on ancient authors who used "obscenity," that is, in English, diction that belongs "offstage." Comedy had been for centuries the province of male scholars who did not share their secrets with the uninitiated. Other scholars' work has inspired my engagement with ancient Athenian choruses, and the performances of Old Comedy. Mark Payne's work on the intimacy and porosity of human beings' connections with their animality, the animality of other animals, and with the so-called natural world, the universe of plants, and stones, and materiality in general, has been a revelation to me, connecting with the work of new materialists such as Jane Bennett and Mel Chen to allow a new look especially at the creatures of Old Comedy's creation—wasps and frogs and birds and clouds.[5]

As before, in this book I find myself straddling the world of high theory and that of classical studies. I have always wanted to avoid the presentism of high theory, its gaze at contemporary events or texts, its exclusive engagement with the present and the recent past, which seem to me to disregard the phenomena that have led to our present, that shape the questions we ask ourselves now. And I have continued to be fascinated by classical antiquity, especially the world of the ancient Greeks, and to see the impact of their institutions and thinking on our current-day institutions and thinking, even as we understand better how the whole globe has been implicated in the histories we study. So, as before, I find myself between two traditions, that of theory, and that of classical studies, which have very different academic protocols and imperatives, neither of which I feel I can adhere to effortlessly. I am never enough of a classicist, never enough of a theorist. But I would like to continue to insist on my right to refuse antiquarianism, the attempt to reconstruct some authentic ancient world, without acknowledging our perspective from the present, and also to refuse a theoretical stance that ignores the past, or that sees it purely as a construct of the present, denying its historicity, its material existence and specificity, its particularities.

And further, as preliminary: as I have given lectures about this project in the past few years, wanting to look again at ancient comic choruses and how they might inform the politics of the present, I have encountered two forms of objection. One finds it disturbing to look at the choruses of comedy without delineating their subordinate place in the plots of comedy, on the plays as integral literary entities, and on the intentions of the author as a conscious, strategic writer. I find it quite easy to lift the choruses to some degree from their literary situation in texts and to consider them as exemplary of collectivity and mass action. But such a strategy does violate some people's notion of the proper study of literature, of the author and the integral text. I take note of this objection, and argue against it in what follows.

And others have objected that seeing the potential in collective action, in the anarchy of leaderless and utopian protest, denies the inevitability of mob violence. I argue in what follows that while swarms are often demonized, they cannot be reduced to inevitably ferocious mobs.[6] Why should all protest be supposed to descend into chaos and destruction, into a mindless absorption in a many-headed hydra of unconscious, id-driven monstrosity?[7] I have been protesting and marching since I was a teenager, against everything from racism to the Vietnam War to police brutality and guns and bad presidents for decades, for peace and gun control and women's rights and social justice, and have never felt that in the process I had lost my reason. Rather, there was usually a sense of community and solidarity. The fear of being erased as an individual in these circumstances seems misplaced. A distinction really must be made, as we have seen in recent years, between armed protest groups bent on destruction, on racism, white supremacy, anti-Semitism, misogyny, and the erection of tyranny; and protest groups, usually nonviolent, committed to racial equality, social justice, the redistribution of wealth, and democracy. Black Lives Matter, for example, the collective organization that has led marches in the US, and stimulated massive protests against racism around the world, planned internal measures for combatting violence and maintaining peaceful presence in demonstrations and marches, and largely succeeded. The liberal internalized fear of crowds' descending into chaos may inhibit righteous protest. As Frederick Douglass wrote, at times one needs to counter force with force.

I should add too a sort of recantation: once upon a time I found a rich reservoir of the regrettable details of the everyday life of the ancient Athenians in the lines of Old Comedy, evidence of misogyny and enslavement. These features of everyday life are still there. But I also now see possibilities in the comic choruses—for utopian imagining, for free speaking against potential tyrants, for luxury and the enjoyment of food and sex, for the freedoms of animal existence, for women's desire, and democratic impulses toward equality and communalism. If tragedy is set in mythical palaces, with kings and queens and remote gods, comedy is saturated with the city on the stage and outside, porous and open, the whole city—dogs and dung beetles, wine, farts, insects, dildos, sausages, slaves, coins, pots and pans, cheese, shoemakers, aphrodisiacs—everyday life in all its intensity.

Introduction

> In his *Parts of Animals*, Chapter X, Aristotle mentions the definition of man as the "laughing animal," but he does not consider it adequate. Though I would hasten to agree, I obviously have a big investment in it, owing to my conviction that mankind's only hope is a cult of comedy. (The cult of tragedy is too eager to help out with the holocaust. And in the last analysis, it is too pretentious to allow for the proper recognition of our animality.)
>
> Kenneth Burke, *Language as Symbolic Action*

In the *Birds*, the chorus leader implicitly critiques the possible boredom induced in the spectators by tragedies, addressing the audience and celebrating the joys of having wings: "Say one of you spectators had wings, and got hungry, and grew bored with the tragic performances [literally, 'with the choruses of the tragedians']; then he'd have flown out of here, gone home, had lunch, and when he was full, flown back here to see us" (786–89). The character speaking here lays out a "line of flight," an escape from the boredom of didactic tragedies, a flight of movement out of confinement, toward the satisfactions of commensality, of appetite, material and political concerns that the choruses of the tragedians neglect. He suggests replacing and supplementing the experience of tragedy, and he does so under the aegis of becoming *animal*.

Let's laugh, at ourselves, at the powerful, the ridiculous. Laugh at comedy. And by comedy, I mean not jokes, although they figure in this book.[1] I refer rather to the comedies of ancient Greece, that is, the riotous, crude, vulgar, dancing, insulting, communal, often utopian, celebrations in honor of the god Dionysos that were performed, along with tragedies, in ancient Athens. These comedies often included choruses of men dressed as animals—insects, birds, frogs, ants, ant-men, horse-men—and as women. Birds dance, wasps sing.

In *Dancing in the Streets: A History of Collective Joy*, Barbara Ehrenreich traces the practices of many assemblies who found ecstasy and union with divinities, as well as communal solidarity, in their dancing together. She links such actions with ancient peoples' hunting in groups: "In communal hunting, the entire group—men, women, and children, advances against a herd of game animals, shouting, stamping, and waving sticks or torches. . . . One can imagine danced rituals originating as reenactments of successful animal encounters, serving both to build group cohesion for the next encounter and to instruct the young in how the human group had learned to prevail and survive."[2] Choruses, groups dancing and singing, figure in ritual and poetic practice from the very beginnings of ancient Greek culture. The choruses of ancient Old Comedy, performed in the fifth century BCE in honor of Dionysos, bear with them vestiges, perhaps, of ancient hunting practices, identification with animals, ritualization of those practices, choral celebrations of the Athenians' many gods, as well as military allusions to the democratic institution of the citizen army, in a complex synthesis of collective dance and song. And some of these choruses continue to allude to the participation of women, and the masquerade as animals, even in the fifth century BCE.

My thinking about ancient drama has led me to believe that if we abandon the Aristotelian emphases on plot, on *muthos*, on linear narrative, and the "characters," the personae, the so-called heroes of its plays, and read otherwise, ancient comedy appears unfamiliar, defamiliarized. This means reading for the *chorus*, bringing it to the foreground, at times finding two different comedies, sometimes at odds with one another. Rather than the tidy resolutions of those who seek to find all reasoned, all coming together in the dénouements of these spectacles, I discover a more ragged, uneven surface, contestation between chorus and plot/characters, where the utopian elements of the birds' life, for example, in Aristophanes' *Birds*, the pastoral, avian, airy imagination, has its own temporality, its own rhythms, not foreclosed by the assumption of tyranny of the human hero Peisetairos at the play's end. I read for suturing of differences, the irresolvable messiness, the birds with their different bodies, their capacity to fly, making them another "kind," another, different *genos*, or "tribe," from the human characters, even as they are embodied by the human actors of the chorus.[3]

A preliminary to my appreciation of these choral swarms requires a critique of the relative emphasis on tragedy, plot, and characters in modernity and postmodernity, an emphasis that follows Aristotle and the lead of European scholars of the eighteenth and nineteenth centuries, deviating from theatrical practices such as Shakespeare's, so influenced by ancient comedy, especially the romantic strain of Roman comedies by Plautus and Terence.[4] What I have to say about ancient Greek comedy and its value, its pertinence to the present, can be summed up by a bundle of arguments that concern the assertion by women of their rights to political and sexual power; freedom of speech (*parrhesia*) amid current debates; the implications of the *utopian* dimensions of ancient comedy; and the chorus, the collective, the swarm, as an entity that registers the participation of the inhabitants of a polity in communalism.

THE QUESTION OF THE "AUTHOR"

Classical scholarship on comedy has at times tended to neglect developments in the wider world of the humanities, and I go far back to the "death of the author" in the work of the late Roland Barthes. Even in such an enlightened, learned, and fascinating book as Mario Telò's *Aristophanes and the Cloak of Comedy* there is still a focus on the intention of the author, that is, "Aristophanes."[5] Trying to discern the intentions of any author, but particularly one from antiquity, seems to me a dauntingly ungrateful task.[6] And in the case of drama, where we have only the text, not the music, the choreography, the costumes of the players, the plays' embeddedness in ritual and wider celebration, the focus on intention is drastically limited by a paucity of information concerning the spectacle that was ancient Athenian festival drama.[7]

Roland Barthes's famous essay, published in English in 1967, proclaimed "the death of the author." And he pointed out that "in ethnographic societies, narrative is never assumed by a person but by a mediator, shaman, or reciter, whose 'performance' (i.e., his mastery of the narrative code) can be admired, but never his 'genius.' The author is a modern character, no doubt produced by our society as it emerged from the Middle Ages, inflected by English empiricism, French rationalism, and the personal faith of the Reformation, thereby discovering the prestige of the individual, or, as we say more nobly, of the 'human person.'"[8] The "author" is an individual with a name. And, as Barthes argues, "it is logical that in literary matters it should be positivism, crown and conclusion of capitalist ideology, which has granted the greatest importance to the author's 'person.'" He is concerned with *écriture*, with writing in the wake of Mallarmé, Proust, and surrealism, yet his words point in a direction that should change our experiences of ancient drama. We need to look at the *longue durée* before the "birth" of the author, at historical periods when the performance of poetry and drama were in the hands of the collective. The poet Alcman, for example, said to have been done to death by a swarm of fleas, or lice, apparently wrote his Partheneion for a chorus of Spartan maidens of his day. The biographical information we have concerning him, and others—Sappho, for instance—is often derived, as Mary Lefkowitz has noted, from a projection mining the poetry we have inherited, fragmentary and allusive as it is, randomly preserved, often with dubious attribution.[9] When students of classics study a list of "authors," including Homer, as well as Sappho, and Aristophanes, they are led to project authorship backward into a remote and culturally distinct past, when ideas of composition and possession differed from our own.

I also find useful the work of Pierre Macherey, who described what he called the "suturing" of the text, the ways in which texts occlude the impossible, the unknowable, what the so-called author does not say, or even cannot say, given his position within ideology. An appreciation of the unevenness, the unresolved, sometimes ragged quality of the relationship between chorus and characters in ancient comedy recalls Macherey's *Theory of Literary Production*.[10] If we cannot see Old Comedy as "literary" in his sense, nonetheless, the ways in which Macherey discussed these matters illuminates the chorus, and especially the comic chorus in its relationship to plot and character in the ancient plays:

> It is not a question of introducing a historical explanation which is stuck on to the work from the outside. On the contrary, we must show a sort of splitting within the work: this division is its unconscious, in so far as it possesses one—the unconscious which is history, the play of history beyond its edges, encroaching on those edges: this is why it is possible to trace the path which leads from the haunted work to that which haunts it. Once again it is not a question of redoubling the work with an unconscious, but a question of revealing in the very gestures of expression that which it is not. Then, the reverse side of what is written will be history itself.[11]

Macherey points to the sort of unevenness that characterizes ancient theatrical works: "A true analysis does not remain within its object, paraphrasing what has already been said; analysis confronts the silences, the denials and the resistance in the object—not that compliant implied discourse which offers itself to discovery, but that condition which makes the work possible, which precedes the work so absolutely that it cannot be found in the work."[12] What cannot be found in the work attributed to Aristophanes, his predecessors and contemporaries, includes the ritual, political, democratic context of comic performance in the fifth century BCE.[13]

This context has many dimensions, and among those that contribute to the critique of a single-author understanding of Old Comedy is the presence of what was called the *khoregos*, the wealthy Athenian, not necessarily a citizen, who financed choruses, including choruses for tragic and comic drama. These individuals were as crucial as the playwrights, as the actors and chorus members, in the production of ancient drama. Peter Wilson, in his important book on the institution of the *khoregia*, shows how these benefactors of the classical democratic city sought to inherit the brilliance and fame once attributed to the aristocrats of the archaic age. Ostentation and rivalries mark the history of the competition among *khoregoi* for victories; the volatile and charismatic aristocrat Alcibiades, who appears in Plato's *Symposium*, who was involved in a notorious incident of sacrilege in Athens, fled to the Spartans, and later the Persians, betraying the city but remaining an object of intense desire, acted as a *khoregos* greedy for victory, according to Plutarch (*Life of Alcibiades*). Wilson notes the contradictory nature of the *khoregoi*'s ambitions: "That the *khoregia* represented an expenditure on the collective legitimated the extravagance of the individual *philotimos* [one desiring honor], and domesticated such lavish expense to its democratic environment.... One could not spend too much on the demos. Yet at the same time the basic logic on which this expenditure was predicated... meant that excessive spending and victory inevitably conjured up the anti-democratic spectre of the tyrant."[14] It may be in fact that particular *khoregoi* were disposed to select particular playwrights, noted for their prize-winning abilities, and inclined to favor their names as collectives were assembled to produce the comedies. As in the complex "authorship" of a contemporary film, requiring millions of dollars of investment, a producer, a director, actors, cinematographers, editors, as well as an "author," a scriptwriter, ancient dramas entailed a complicated, politically significant network of actants, most of whom remain invisible when the surviving texts are attributed to a single author.

In an afterword, published forty years after the first appearance of Macherey's *Theory of Literary Production*, the author added:

> What do literary texts reflect? Certainly not a supposedly bare reality, but rather the contradictory ensemble of its representations, an ensemble which can be aptly designated by the concept of ideology....
>
> The argument which I was proposing was roughly as follows: the veritable object of literature is ideology in its material form, that is to say as a contradictory multiplicity of discursive and fictional complexes which render ideology in broken, laconic and decentred form. Literature does not merely offer a faithful reproduction of this object; it offers an analysis, decomposes its object, and implicitly or explicitly, exposes the internal fissures which simultaneously share and drive forwards the motion of its transformation.... All literature is, itself, though in various degrees, revolutionary, in so far as it reveals and actively contributes to certain fracture lines which run deep into historical reality and into the forms in which that reality is lived, imagined and represented.[15]

For Macherey, "literature," so called, is not only an aesthetic object, but a form of knowledge as well. His insights can contribute to a way of looking at ancient comedy liberated from a focus on individual authorship and intention.

Michel Foucault also engaged with the problem of historicizing the origins of inherited texts, and asked, "What is an author?":

> Can we say that *The Arabian Nights*, and *Stromates* of Clement of Alexandria, or the *Lives* of Diogenes Laertius constitute works? Such questions only begin to suggest the range of our difficulties, and, if some have found it convenient to bypass the individuality of the writer or his status as an author to concentrate on a work, they have failed to appreciate the equally problematic nature of the word "work" and the unity it designates. . . . Discourse that possesses an author's name is not to be immediately consumed and forgotten. . . . Rather its status and its manner of reception are regulated by the culture in which it circulates.[16]

This seems to me a particularly relevant point in relation to the name "Aristophanes" and his "work," or "works." The manner of reception, regulated by the cultures, ours and his, and all those in between, in which he, it, they, circulate, needs to be called into question more critically. Although Foucault is discussing contemporary culture, the death of the author, perhaps, in his culture, these remarks have purchase on the status of ancient "authors" as well. He asserts that "the 'author-function' is not universal or constant in all discourse. Even within our civilization, the same types of texts have not always required authors; there was a time when those texts which we now call 'literary' (stories, folk tales, epics, and tragedies) were accepted, circulated, and valorized without any question about the identity of their author" (125). And why not ancient comedies as well? It's worth noting that the prizes in the ancient Greek dramatic festivals were awarded not to an "author" of a play, but to the plays' producers, sometimes but not always what we call its "author." For Foucault, "aspects of an individual, which we designate as an author (or which comprise an individual as an author), are projections, in terms always more or less psychological, of our way of handling texts: in the comparisons we make, the traits we extract as pertinent, the continuities we assign, or the exclusions we practice" (127). Here too, the relevance to ancient comedy requires interrogation; why must we find the "intentions," the individual political stance, of something, someone, a text that we identify by the name Aristophanes?

"In literary criticism, for example," Foucault writes, "the traditional methods for defining an author—or rather, for determining the configuration of the author from existing texts—derive in large part from those used in the Christian tradition to authenticate (or to reject) the particular texts in its possession. Modern criticism, in its desire to 'recover' the author from a work, employs devices strongly reminiscent of Christian exegesis when it wished to prove the value of a text by ascertaining the holiness of its author" (127). In relation to the comedic parabasis, a special choral interlude in many comedies in which the chorus directly addresses the audience, can we not usefully apply Foucault's careful examination of the "author-function": "It does not refer, purely and simply, to an actual individual insofar as it simultaneously gives rise to a variety of egos and to a series of subjective positions that individuals of any class may come to occupy" (130–31).

If we abandon such questions as "Who is the real author?" or "What has he revealed of his most profound self in his language?" Foucault argues that "new questions will be heard: 'What are the modes of existence of this discourse?' 'Where does it come from; how is it circulated; who controls it?'" (138). Foucault ends this essay with the reiteration of a question posed by Samuel Beckett in his *Texts for Nothing*: "What matter who's speaking, someone said, what matter who's speaking."[17] Rather than asking what Aristophanes reveals of "his most profound self" in the works attributed to him, we can inquire: Where do these plays come from, how are they circulated, who controls them? This seems to me a particularly relevant point in relation to the name "Aristophanes" and his "work," or "works."

Other theorists of reading, of interpretation, share this sense of the unevenness of the text, of the collective nature of its production, and of the limitations related to authorial attribution, and these too have had their impact on my methods. Francesco Orlando, for example, author of the book exhilaratingly entitled *Obsolete Objects in the Literary Imagination: Ruins, Relics, Rarities, Rubbish, Uninhabited Places, and Hidden Treasures*, is focused on objects, and points to inassimilability, to unevenness, to the interruption of "official," conventional notions of textual integrity and authorial intention.[18] Elaine Freedgood, in *The Ideas in Things*, finds "fugitive meaning" that disrupts the novels she analyzes, meanings embedded in such objects as the "Negro head" tobacco of Magwitch in Dickens's *Great Expectations*.[19] In his *Allegory and Ideology*, Fredric Jameson presents allegorical reading as a way of gaining access to the complexity of texts:

> Allegory raises its head as a solution when beneath this or that seemingly stable or unified reality the tectonic plates of deeper contradictory levels of the Real shift and grate ominously against one another and demand a representation, or at least an acknowledgement, they are unable to find in the Schein or illusory surfaces of existential or social life. Allegory does

not reunify those incommensurable forces, but sets them in relationship with one another in a way which, as with all art, all aesthetic experience, can lead alternately to ideological comfort or the restless anxieties of a more expansive knowledge.[20]

These modes of encountering what we receive as texts, in the case of ancient drama a pale shadow of what was once living performance, allow for a richer interpretation than one that focuses on integrity, coherence, or authorial intention.

A model looking for "fracture lines," for "internal fissures," for contradictions and unruly, inassimilable objects, seems more adequate to the unevenness, the incommensurability, of elements of ancient dramatic texts, and the performances we cannot know, than studies concerned with the corpus of an author. The comic playwright cannot intend all that he wishes, cannot control all that is present, even in the limited textual version of comedy that we receive from the tradition. The roughness of the plays, the "fracturing," the ways in which the chorus may be in contradiction with the characters, working through a play of their own, imagining a utopia, or relations of their own that fly off, evading the control of the characters and the plot— all these elements strongly affect my readings. The chorus appears at times to have minds of their own, fueled by the democratic, leveling ideology of equality in the ancient city; their story cannot always be gently and easily and seamlessly integrated into the plot of the whole. The chorus has its own liveliness, parallel or veering off from the plot and its characters, establishing another vector, a "line of flight," as Gilles Deleuze and Félix Guattari call it in *A Thousand Plateaus*.[21]

In contrasting what they call "arboreal" form to the rhizome, Deleuze and Guattari describe and even celebrate a nomadic, proliferating entity more appropriate to my idea of Old Comedy than traditional conceptions of these plays as books, authored by authors:

> Once a rhizome has been obstructed, arborified, it's all over, no desire stirs; for it is always by rhizome that desire moves and produces. Whenever desire climbs a tree, internal repercussions trip it up and it falls to its death; the rhizome, on the other hand, acts on desire by external, productive outgrowths.... A rhizome may be broken, shattered at a given spot, but it will start up again on one of its old lines, or on new lines. You can never get rid of ants because they form an animal rhizome that can rebound time and again after most of it has been destroyed. Every rhizome contains lines of segmentarity according to which it is stratified, territo-

rialized, organized, signified, attributed, etc., as well as lines of deterritorialization down which it constantly flees.[22]

Comedy is a rhizome.

Especially since some of the comic choruses are constituted as animal, insect, bird, female, or cloud swarms, these can only reluctantly be harnessed and deployed as willing and obedient agents of the greater intention of the plot and the so-called comic hero(es). I think we should be looking at a more ragged, discontinuous, rougher comic object, one that allows for contradictory and disproportionate elements, not necessarily reconcilable with one another, perhaps even working against one another, with resistance to incorporation coming from the chorus, this set of creatures often not easily assimilable into the world of the human.

ARISTOPHANES, A LIFE?

While many of my examples of ancient comic choruses come from the plays attributed to Aristophanes, this book is not meant to be a study of that man as author. Although contemporary literary critics, including classicists, still often tend to focus on authorial intentions, on the politics of the poet, and on the development of the writer across decades, in fact we know very little about the lives of such ancient figures as Aristophanes. The very project of biography, a study of an individual's life from birth to death, appears relatively late in the history of genres. Although there are suggestions of the tracing of a whole life in some classical texts, as in Plato's *Apology of Socrates*, it is in the hands of the writer Plutarch (ca. 46–120 CE), a Greek who became a Roman citizen, that the practice of recounting the lives of the notable takes definitive shape.

In the case of Aristophanes, one of many Old Comedy, that is, fifth-century BCE, writers, a "vita," a life account, contains little information about his dates of birth and death, elements considered essential in our conception of a biography, the "writing" of a *bios*, a "life." As Mary Lefkowitz, who most usefully collected and commented on the various *Lives* of the Greek poets, remarks in her introduction, "The advantage of concentrating on one poet at a time is that it helps to show why the character of individual poets' works have developed in distinctive ways, and why (for example) biographies sound proportionately more like caricatures whenever biographers had access to characterizations in comedy."[23] This is all the more the case when the life in question is that of the comic poet himself. Other scholars have continued the examination of anachronism entailed in attributing a modern version of authorship to ancient names, and analyzed the instrumentalization for varied purposes of their biographies.[24]

The anonymous composer of the life of Aristophanes, writing some centuries after his death, mines the plays, ones that survive to our day, and others that do not, to which he had access, for the elements of biography. The "life" mentions Aristophanes' innovations in writing comedies, his move to producing his own plays after first relying on others, his enmity with the popular leader Cleon, especially in the comedy entitled *Knights*. There, the biographer says, taking references in the play literally: "He exposes Cleon's thefts and his tyrannical nature, and since none of the costumers had the courage to make a mask of Cleon's face, because they were too frightened, since Cleon acted like a tyrant, Aristophanes acted the part of Cleon, smearing his face with red dye" (Lefkowitz, 156). Lefkowitz notes that the red dye might be an allusion to the rope dipped in dye that was used to herd the citizens into the classical Athenians' assembly; latecomers were thus marked by Scythian slave police for their tardiness.

The details the biographer lists in relation to Aristophanes' career are frequently inaccurate, and misreport the relative dates of the plays. He also repeats the various claims that Aristophanes was not in fact an Athenian citizen, but rather from the island of Aegina, or Rhodes. The emphasis in this "biography" is, throughout, on the playwright's role as a writer of comedy, with little or no reference to family, barely sketching his political views in the debates of the city. The poet's stance is described as follows: "People praised and liked him particularly because of his determination to show in his dramas that the government of Athens was free and not enslaved by any tyrant, and that it was a democracy, and that since they were free, the people ruled themselves" (Lefkowitz, 156). The life focuses on the career of Aristophanes, on his quarrels with politicians, on his wins and losses in Dionysiac festival competitions, noting that "he won praise and a crown of sacred olive (which was considered equal in worth to a golden throne) when he spoke in the *Frogs* about the men who had been deprived of their rights: 'It is just that the sacred chorus give the city much good advice' (686–87)" (Lefkowitz, 156). The biographer also cites a metrical pattern named for Aristophanes, his fame that extended even to the Persian emperor, a detail extrapolated from the parabasis of the *Acharnians* (647–54). Plato is said to have sent Aristophanes' comedies to the Sicilian tyrant Dionysius, to instruct him about the Athenians.

The biographer notes that Aristophanes initiated the changes that led to so-called New Comedy, the work of Philemon and Alexander (the antecedents of Roman comedy), attributing the change, toward a more domestic, romantic sort of plot, to the Athenian decree that forbade the ridicule of individuals by name, and to the economic losses that diminished the power of the *khoregoi*, the funders of the city's dramas, to train choruses.[25] The biography registers the diminution of the role of the chorus in the fourth century BCE, after the Athenians' loss to the Spartans in the Peloponnesian War: "When once again the subsidies for training choruses were taken away, Aristophanes, when he wrote the *Ploutos* [*Wealth*], in order to give the actors in the scenes time to rest and change, wrote 'for the chorus' in the directions, in the places where we see the poets of New Comedy writing in 'for the chorus' in emulation of Aristophanes" (Lefkowitz, 157). This change for some readers signifies the end of the great, often rowdy, and obscene choruses of the fifth-century comedy, when Athens was free, "not enslaved by any tyrant," and a "radical" democracy. The biographer ends his account of the life of Aristophanes with this disappearance of the chorus from the comedies, when choruses do what they do, dance or sing without relying on the text of the playwright. The writer of the *bios* notes finally that with the *Ploutos* [*Wealth*] Aristophanes introduced his son Araros, "and so departed from life, leaving three sons" (Lefkowitz, 157). He sums up the whole of the life with the claim that Aristophanes wrote forty-four plays, some of which are allegedly spurious.

This account, which is called a "vita," a "life," does have some of the elements later associated with a proper biography. The writer includes the name of Aristophanes' father, his "nationality," that is, his identity as an Athenian, and the names of the three sons he left behind at his death. Otherwise, though, the vita focuses almost entirely on the poet's dramatic career, his victories and losses, his conflicts with Cleon, and his innovations in the production of comedies. If in our contemporary analyses of literary writers, the inclination remains to look for intention, for historical, social, or psychological determinants of style, narrative, and genre, then the ancient biographer fails us entirely. And as the vita assumes the individuality of Aristophanes, his sole production of the plays associated with his name, we see already the drift toward the author, the assignment of responsibility for a cultural artifact to a named single maker, an attribution that distorts the actual circumstances of such a spectacular, cultural, religious, and political performance as ancient comedy. What may seem familiar to us, the role of a single individual as author, gradually repressed the swarm of forces at play in producing ancient drama, unevenness and fissures in Attic society that are smoothed out and erased in an account such as this vita of Aristophanes. And as a theater industry began to spread throughout the Mediterranean as early as the fifth century BCE, plays began to be associated with particular poets and actors, and this phenomenon contributed to the erosion of the sense of collective production, the embeddedness of the comedies in the specific networks of democratic Athens.[26]

OTHER COMIC WRITERS

Other Old Comedy playwrights participated in the festival production of drama in the fifth and fourth centuries BCE in Athens. Although we often know less about their lives, fragments of their plays have survived, and scholars have attempted to situate them in the history of the city. Some of these poets belong to a generation earlier than that of Aristophanes, and from the fragments that survive we can possibly deduce some common themes with the later writer.

Ian C. Storey has contributed much to our knowledge and understanding of the work of Eupolis, contemporary of Aristophanes, who may have died in a sea battle during the Peloponnesian War, and whose death had the result that poets were no longer allowed to serve on active duty in the military (Suda ε 3657). In another version of the poet's death, Alcibiades is said to have thrown him in the sea for having verbally abused him, and some attribute the prohibition on comic naming of those mocked in the comic plays from this incident. Storey has translated the scant remains of this poet, including lines from his play *Demoi* (*Demes*) (412–417 BCE?), and lists the tantalizing titles associated with him, including *Poleis* (*Cities*), with a chorus of female cities subjected to the Athenians, *Heilotes* (*Helots*), *Kolakes* (*Spongers*), *Khrysoun Genos* (*Golden Race/Kind*), *Astrateutos e Androgunoi* (*Draft-Dodgers or Men-Women*). *Golden Race* or *Kind* seems to suggest a setting in the past, in the period designated by Hesiod as the golden period, at the beginning of time, utopian in the way that *Demoi* seems to have presented the return from the underworld of dead leaders, among them Pericles, with a chorus made up of the demes, the subdivisions of the ancient *polis*. Another play, *Taxiarchoi* (*Squadron Commanders*), may have included the god Dionysos, as did Aristophanes' *Frogs*. *Baptai* (*Dyers*?) contained a caricature of Alcibiades, the charismatic and erratic aristocrat mentioned earlier, who once served as a *khoregos*, financing the training of a chorus.[27]

Another contemporary of Aristophanes and Eupolis, Strattis, has recently claimed more attention as well. Christian Orth presents what is known of his work, which often involved mythic material and had a complex relationship to tragedy. Strattis alluded to tragic plots, seemingly turning them into "paratragedy," burlesques of tragedy, addressing the question of acting in drama, and playing with genre in innovative ways.[28] These poets and their work were known to ancient authors; the prominence of Aristophanes in subsequent centuries, when he is seen often as the only significant writer of Old Comedy, may be due to the excellence of his plays, but also to the filtering of a canon through millennia of loss and changing tastes.

The comic poet Cratinus rivaled Aristophanes in his reputation as one of the best at Old Comedy. *Dionysalexander* presents the god Dionysos, apparently a figure for Pericles, along with a chorus of satyrs.[29] Cratinus's most famous play, the *Wine Flask* (*Pytine*), depicted the comic writer himself, with his wife Comedy seeking a divorce on account of his drunkenness. His play *Cheirons* had a chorus of centaurs. In the *Plutuses*, the god Zeus, tyrant and usurper, has been overthrown, allowing for a return to plenty and for wealth to be redistributed, as in Aristophanes' *Wealth* (*Ploutos*). The chorus is called "Wealths, Riches," and they sing of their creation and existence in the era of Kronos, the god of the golden age.

Reading the fragmentary remains of the other Old Comedy poets can be frustrating, since we long to know more about the plays in which they were embedded, and especially, in this case, to see how the choruses of these plays performed. As well as the fragments of other comedies, there are many tantalizing lines attributed to Aristophanes himself, often without context, but nonetheless intriguing. Some of the varied fragments we have from other comic writers share themes present in the plays attributed to Aristophanes, including mockery of prominent citizens, utopian fantasies of the past or the future, animal choruses, women, even abstract entities serving as chorus members, and dreaming out loud about sexual liberty and culinary luxury. At times these playwrights won prizes when Aristophanes' plays were also in competition, and defeated. The *Wine Flask* beat *Clouds* at the City Dionysia of 423. Yet although we have a significant number of the fragments from other comic writers, and plot summaries describing performances stretching from the beginning of the fifth century BCE into the fourth, we can conclude little about their choruses' songs, and can only speculate about their membership, ranging from satyrs to centaurs to cities to helots, the enslaved serf-like laborers of Sparta. Perhaps most telling is that a vast number of these comedies, like many tragedies, were named for their *choruses* by posterity.

THE COLLECTIVE

Given their embeddedness in festival ritual, celebrating the city's god Dionysos, their support by the city and the wealthy *khoregoi*, their "producers," and the participation in the chorus by a collective of citizens and others, one might say that *the city* makes the comedies. In some ways like film in the present, comedy existed far beyond any notion of an *auteur*, just as a collective makes a movie, and the Academy Awards, like the prizes for ancient comedy, barely come to terms with the swarm of forces that unite in a performance. In the case of ancient comedy, we know only a part of a whole, not the dancing, not the music, not the singing, not the costumes, only the text, which itself has its limits, given that there are references, even words, we cannot decipher. The texts themselves have passed through many hands, and there are lacunae, fragments, much loss.

Throughout this book, I emphasize the comic chorus, and the comedies' relevance to the present, to the political concerns of our day, the sometimes vicious debates about women's power, freedom of speech, foreigners and immigration, and democracy as an ideal form. I suggest that looking at ancient Greek comedy, rather than ancient Greek *tragedy*, could offer ways of conceiving of the polity that might enrich the discourse of the present.

Chapter 1 considers what has been an intense concentration in modernity and even postmodernity on ancient Greek, ancient Athenian tragedy, as a resource for thinking about questions of identity, foreignness, the family, and sovereignty. In his *Poetics*, Aristotle, the great ancient philosopher of the fourth century BCE, presents the elements of tragedy for his day, using categories that, I argue, lose much of the context of the dramatic festivals of ancient Athens. And the fact that the second half of his *Poetics*, on comedy, has been lost for centuries, has meant that much of Western philosophy and literary and political theory has come to see *only* tragedy in considering ancient drama's contributions to the tradition. In addition, in what remains of his treatise on ancient drama, Aristotle discusses tragedy, and plot, and "character," and barely acknowledges the role of the chorus in ancient drama, whether comedy or tragedy. Considering in some detail the influential pronouncements of Hegel that focus on tragedy, and especially on Sophocles' *Antigone*, I also look at some of Hegel's heirs and their focus on tragedy alone. These thinkers have produced a version of modernity grounded in tragedy, in a tragedy for modernity that emphasizes the heroic individual and his tragic choices, serving the interests of individualism in modernity while overlooking the collective, choral dimensions of ancient drama, and all of the festival and civic ceremony surrounding it.

Chapter 2 looks at "swarms," at the possibility that a swarm, an anarchic leaderless body, can be seen not only negatively, as a threat, but also as a collective that might arrive at better solutions than would a great leader. The Greeks were interested in swarms—of bees, of wasps, of birds—as metaphors for human groups. What is the jury, if not a sort of swarm? I do a close reading of Aristophanes' *Wasps*, and take what is offered there as a clue to what emerges from an attentive look at the choral dimension of Athenian comedy. The chorus of wasps in the comedy named for these creatures dances and sings as the metaphorical swarm of elderly jurors, veterans of foreign wars who express their strong views, backed up by threats of stings, concerning matters important to the city. They are a wild, lustful, greedy, and rowdy crew.

Chapter 3 focuses on the chorus and its centrality in many forms of religious and political performance in ancient Athens, and throughout the classical Greek world. Choruses were made up of singers, dancers, celebrants of the gods. In this chapter I give special attention to the only extant "satyr" play, one of the plays added each day to the three tragedies in performance in the ancient Athenians' festivals held in honor of the god Dionysos. Enslaved satyrs make up the chorus of Euripides' *Cyclops*, one of the strange, hybrid, seriocomic plays that would end the day for the ancient spectators of tragedy. In dramatic choruses, not only the men who made up the assembly of the democratic *polis*, but outsiders to the citizen body, were often represented, embodied always by male actors, men and boys, but nonetheless marking the presence of others—female, slave, animal, foreign—in the city, inhabiting the space, as they performed before the audience. The "*comic collective*," that is, the chorus of comedy, like that of tragedy, comprised anonymous beings who danced and sang, at some moments in unison, at others led by one of their own. The comedy *Lysistrata*, also discussed in this chapter, features a strong woman leader and two choruses, one of old women. The Hellenic women in this utopian comedy, from both Athens and its enemy Sparta, succeed in achieving peace, a truce, an end to the suffering of endless war between the Greek cities.

I continue in chapter 4 to concentrate on those elements of ancient comedy that seem to me to have most to offer to thinking about politics in the present, here comedy's *utopianism*. Speculative imagining about "nowhere" or "elsewhere" survives in various forms, including speculative or "science" fiction, which includes utopian elements but also resorts often to its complement, dystopic fiction. In this chapter, I consider the utopianism of comedy, to some degree overshadowed by readerly emphasis on what are seen as the reactionary, conservative politics of Aristophanes. I look in particular at the comedy *The Birds* as a utopian text, and at its chorus as a utopian collective, with a different temporality and mode of being from the play's narrative line, which is focused on the comic hero. Moments of pastoral, idyllic luxuriating in country life, of animal existence, as well as gestures toward its constant potential for violence, alternate in this play with a plot that ends in tyranny.

Chapter 5 takes up the theme of *parrhesia*, "saying it all." Often translated as "freedom of speech," this aspect of the ancient Athenian democracy was treasured by its citizens, and referred to enviously by outsiders in tragedy.

I connect discourses about *parrhesia* with the work of Michel Foucault on this subject, to show the beginnings of these ideas in ancient society, and their working out in comedy. I find *parrhesia* to be not the dyadic form, sited in individuals, that Foucault for the most part describes in *The Government of Self and Others* and elsewhere, especially in philosophical and religious contexts, but a collective, joyous, and extravagant swing at the powerful, especially in the plays *Acharnians* and *Knights* of Aristophanes.

"Democracy, Communalism, Communism," chapter 6, considers the ways in which utopianism and *parrhesia* come together in Aristophanes' *Ecclesiazusae* (*Women at the Assembly*), where the women of Athens infiltrate the citizens' *ekklesia*, the assembly, and succeed in voting in a communistic regime. The radical nature of their solutions to the problems they see in their city, including what they see as sexual injustices, casts light on the situation of Athens at the time of the play's first production, and on the possibilities of imagining the impossible that precede philosophical deliberations on these same questions.

The epilogue, "The Politics of the Present," returns to recapitulate the ways in which the example of ancient Greek comedy can complement and refine a sense of what antiquity has to offer to our present. The emphasis on tragedy, seen as appropriate for a world in which there is the constant threat of war, impoverishment, displacement, and chaos, accompanies, it seems, a focus on individualism, the nuclear family, the private character. Comedy opens up the possibilities of laughter, of communalism, of pleasures, of ways of living more collectively. Ancient comedy confronts us with female victories, utopianism, the "saying it all" of comic *parrhesia*, and the spectacle of collectives, of singing, dancing, questioning crowds demanding their pleasures, their sexual gratification, their gourmandise, their joy in performing and in sharing the delights of material existence. I emphasize once more that a reorientation toward laughter and what Kristin Ross has called "communal luxury" might offer another sort of politics that supplements or leavens or enlivens a tragic emphasis on the character of the leader, or the sufferings of the individual. If, in a collective sense, there is still hope for particularity, for each one's enjoyment within a communal setting, then the eternal burden of tragedy might be lifted at times by a collective politics of laughter, by another, celebratory, mode of being with others, based on equality and solidarity.

[CHAPTER 1]

The Tragic Individual
The Tyranny of Oedipus and Antigone

> It is precisely laughter that destroys the epic, and in general destroys any hierarchical (distancing and valorized) distance.... Laughter has the remarkable power of making an object come up close, of drawing it into a zone of crude contact where one can finger it familiarly on all sides, turn it upside down, inside out, peer at it from above and below, break open its external shell, look into its center, doubt it, take it apart, dismember it, lay it bare and expose it, examine it freely and experiment with it. Laughter demolishes fear and piety.
>
> Mikhail Bakhtin, "Epic and Novel"

In our world, so marked by tragedy, it may seem perverse to turn to ancient Greek comedy for thinking about politics, as so many political theorists and popular commentators continue to focus on Sophocles and his tragic characters. Wounded veterans, individuals, suffering, explore and voice the words of Sophocles' *Philoktetes*, and in contemporary culture find solace in the words of the characters of ancient Greek tragedy.[1] The moving spectacle of their performance of these words calls attention to that suffering, and to their sense of betrayal by those who make the decisions for others to go to war, and then neglect their needs, physical and psychic, when they return home.

We need to hear these voices, but also to understand the ways in which tragedy not only articulates the feelings of individuals in contemporary culture, but also that certain readings and interpretations of Greek tragedy have shaped the very structures through which we understand human being in the West, as powerfully argued by Joshua Billings in his work on German philosophy and Greek tragedy.[2] Billings identifies "a concept of 'the tragic' that extended far beyond an aesthetic context, encompassing history, politics, religion, and ontology" (2). The legacy of tragedy continues to preoccupy those who think about the relationship between antiquity and the present.[3] And the foregrounding of ancient tragedy in modernity may foreclose the possibilities offered to the present by comedy.

I seek not only to locate ancient Greek drama in its own historical context, to the always limited extent possible, but also to try to come to grips with the historicity of its reception in early and later modernity, and even postmodernity. In this chapter, I consider first the presence of "the tragic" in modern Western culture, and its intense focus on Sophocles' Oedipus and Antigone. I then look at Aristotle's work on ancient Greek drama, and consider how readings of his mutilated treatise have affected the reception of both tragedy and comedy since his time. His neglect of the chorus concerns me in what follows, and I move on then to tragedy's neglect of comedy, and to comedy's constant engagement with tragedians, especially in Aristophanes' *Frogs*. I end by reiterating my claim that modernity has emphasized the individual over the collective in its evaluation and deployment of ancient drama, using a certain version of ancient tragedy to fashion modern selfhood. And I argue that study of the classical tradition has persisted in privileging tragic characters and neglected comedy in its ongoing encounter with ancient Greek drama, even though the Athenians themselves saw characters and chorus as together making up the drama, and the two forms of theater as inextricably linked to one another, to the fortunes of the city, and to the cult of the god Dionysos.

TRAGEDY, THE TRAGIC, AND MODERNITY

Miriam Leonard takes a strong stand against a current orthodoxy in the study of tragedy, especially characteristic of scholars of classical antiquity, in her important book *Tragic Modernities*.[4] The work of Jean-Pierre Vernant and Pierre Vidal-Naquet, informed as Leonard notes not just by Marxism but also, especially in the case of Vernant, by an unacknowledged debt to Nietzsche's *Birth of Tragedy*, has led to a view of ancient Athenian tragedy as irretrievably bound to its historical moment.[5] This is one version of historicism.[6] John J. Winkler and Froma Zeitlin's *Nothing to Do with Dionysos?* still very influential in the field of classics, in studies of classical reception, in the consideration of the "tragic" as such, continued to situate tragedy in a premodern world.[7] This version of historicizing of "the tragic" has, in Leonard's view, led to a failure to acknowledge the impact of the idea of tragedy in various domains of modernity.

Leonard's brilliant examination of this question opens up the discussion of "the tragic" in new directions. Going well beyond the frustrating and chaotic treatment of tragedy in Terry Eagleton's *Sweet Violence*, Leonard painstakingly reveals how the tragic, pace George Steiner, colors modernity in unexpected and sometimes paradoxical ways.[8] She shows how philosophical reflection by many modern, seemingly unrelated thinkers, committed to contradictory traditions, nonetheless meditates on the tragic irreconcilability of freedom and necessity. And in so doing, these thinkers participate in the production of modern metaphysics, history, revolution, gender, and subjectivity, at the same time changing our view of ancient tragedy.

Using the work of Raymond Williams to critique Steiner, but going well beyond, Leonard recovers the tragic for the twenty-first century. She moves from Schelling, Hegel, Nietzsche, and Heidegger to Schmitt, Adorno, and Benjamin, to Arendt, Marx, and Williams, to Freud, Lacan, Bowlby, and Butler, again to Hegel, Nietzsche, Freud, and Lacan, examining the political role of the tragic in modernity. Acknowledging the tragic does not require resignation and pessimism, Leonard shows, but rather allows for sober, tragic recognition of revolution and its failures, for example, without surrender to despair and inertia.

One of the consequences of the loss of the second part of Aristotle's *Poetics*, his treatment of comedy, to be discussed later in this chapter, is that the traditions of the West, reflecting on ancient drama, focus on tragedy to the exclusion of comedy. There was Roman comedy. There were comic performances in the Middle Ages. But the great rebirth of classical culture at the end of the medieval period rediscovered tragedy, not comedy. Even Dante's letter to Can Grande, concerning the composition of his *Divine Comedy*, looks back not to ancient comedy, but to the ascending shape, the consoling happy ending, of Christian mythology, rather than to the raucous, dancing, singing swarms and eccentric female actors in ancient Athenian comedy. And Shakespearean comedy relies more on the erotic back and forth of Roman comedy than on the ribald, obscene ruckus of the Athenians.

Later philosophers of aesthetics and the arts considered the question of drama; the most influential of these was the eighteenth-century German G. W. F. Hegel, who wrote about the arts in various contexts in his many works. Although he considers ancient comedy, he too focuses on tragedy, and locates it within a moment in his history of the human striving for freedom that defines his understanding of the progress human beings have made since time began.[9]

Greek tragedy was a phenomenon of the *polis*, the ancient city-state, the origin of the very word "politics." Hegel discusses the two sorts of "collisions" that make for satisfactory plots in the construction of tragedy, and his remarks on this question resemble those of Aristotle, whom he follows frequently in his treatment of the ancient drama. For Hegel, there are various stages of the possible "collisions" depicted in tragedy: "The principal source of opposition . . . is that of the *body politic*, the opposition, that is, between ethical life in its social universality and the family as the natural ground of moral relations. These are the purest forces of tragic representation."[10] He includes a second type of opposition, or collision, which occurs when "a man carries out with a volition fully aware of his acts . . . but unconscious of and with no intention of doing what he has done under the directing providence of the gods" (Paolucci, 69). The first sort of collision is exemplified in Sophocles' *Antigone*, the second in *Oedipus Rex* and *Oedipus at Colonus*. It is remarkable that the first sort of opposition has fascinated students of tragedy, especially those interested in the politics of the genre, and that the second sort has preoccupied the psychoanalytically oriented.

Hegel writes, modestly: "Among all the fine creations of the ancient and the modern world—and I am acquainted with pretty nearly everything in such a class, and one ought to know it, and it is quite possible—the 'Antigone' of Sophocles is from this point of view in my judgment the most excellent and satisfying work of art" (Paolucci, 73). The tradition of focusing on Antigone, the persona, and *Antigone*, the tragedy, gazes back toward this and other passages in Hegel's work that conceive the persona as the embodiment, as a personification, of a certain ethical life, and on the Sophoclean plays as the perfect depiction of the collision of one conception of human existence with another: "[The ethical consciousness] sees right only on its own side, and wrong on the other, so, of these two, that which belongs to divine law detects, on the other side, mere arbitrary fortuitous human violence, while what appertains to human law finds in the other the obstinacy and disobedience of subjective self-sufficiency" (275). Hegel understands the tragedy of the *Antigone* as the clash between these two perspectives, noting all the while that its antagonists are involved in "one whole": "Antigone, for example, lives under the political authority of Creon; she is herself the daughter of a king and the affianced of Haemon, so that her obedience to the royal prerogative is an obligation." Antigone is subject to human law. And Creon shares in her subjection to divine law: "Creon also, who is on his part father and husband, is under obligation to respect the sacred laws of relationship, and only by breach of this can give an order that is in conflict with such a sense" (73). So the collision is not a simple one; the two forces, or obligations, are mutually implicated and binding, and the result of their clashing is tragedy. How might Hegel's reading of this play, the Sophoclean *Antigone*, change if readers looked beyond the individual characters in light of the dramatic festival, chorus, processions with abundance of food, wine, revelry? Where is the city, the democracy, and the will of the chorus and the *demos* outside the text? A recognition of the play's embeddedness in its context inevitably would change the analysis of the forces at play—the support of the people for Antigone, Haimon's call for compromise, the collapse of hereditary monarchy at the play's end—but Hegel's focus on these individuals determined the shape of much speculation in the centuries that followed.

Hegel also briefly discusses comedy, the inevitable partner of tragedy when considering ancient Greek drama, in his view the highest form of art in a society, after "symbolic" architecture and "classical" sculpture. Music, painting, and poetry, especially in drama, represent the "romantic," the most developed form of art; poetry moves from epic to lyric to their synthesis in drama. He includes the role of the chorus in this progress: "The choric song expresses, among the ancients, by way of contrast to the particular characters and their more personal or more reciprocal conflict, the general or more impersonal view of the situation, and the emotion it excites, in a manner which at one time inclines to the objective style of epic narrative, at another to the impulsive movement of the Lyric" (Paolucci, 19–20). Along with this brief recognition of the role of choral song in ancient tragedy, Hegel sees the ethical totality embodied in the tragic chorus as disturbed by the actualization of the tragic characters. This sense of incommensurability, of a troubling of the surface of the drama, is an aspect of his analysis often overlooked in subsequent studies of the "tragic." And it contributes to my own desire to find turbulence and irreconcilability in comedy as well.

Hegel's view of the differences between tragedy and comedy departs from a mere classification of the features of comic plays.[11] He emphasizes the presence of the central character: "in comedy it is the purely personal experience, which retains the mastery in its character of infinite self-assuredness." This is a strangely psychological emphasis on the attitudes of the "comic hero," which refuses the sort of allegorical interpretation made of tragedy, as a collision of forces: "In comedy we have a vision of the victory of intrinsically self-assured subjectivity, the laughter of which resolves everything through the medium and into the medium of such individuality" (Paolucci, 52). Here there is no recognition of the presence or contribution of the chorus, of song and dance, of spectacle in the performances of ancient Athenian comedies. There is a psychologizing of the comic "hero" in Hegel's understanding that points toward what George Steiner called "the death of tragedy," a claim that tragedy is no longer possible in the twentieth century, although the fascination with Antigone, so apparent in contemporary culture, seems to give the lie to this portentous prophecy.[12]

In Nietzsche's *Birth of Tragedy*, we find the similar modern neglect of tragedy's partner in Dionysiac ritual, comedy.[13] The laughter of Zarathustra has not yet appeared on the scene. Nietzsche does, however, acknowledge the power of the chorus in tragedy itself: "We must understand Greek tragedy as the Dionysian chorus, disburdening itself again and again in an Apollinian image-world. The choric parts, therefore, with which tragedy is interlaced, are in a sense the maternal womb of the entire so-called dialogue, that is, of the whole stage-world, of the drama proper. . . . The *chorus* of the Greek tragedy, the symbol of the collectively excited Dionysian throng, thus finds its full explanation in our conception."[14] Nietzsche fully acknowledges the importance of the tragic chorus in this work, although he does not include comedy in his presentation of Greek drama, even as Dionysus is so central to comedy, even appearing in person in the *Frogs* and in Cratinus's now fragmentary *Dionysalexander* (in which the god, likened to Pericles, impersonates Paris and starts a "Trojan" war). Nietzsche does give some attention to the appearance of quasi-comedic satyrs, and to the poet Archilochus, singer of dithyrambs and the iambic poetry that may be connected to the origins of comedy, with its mocking, insulting elements. But he was particularly concerned with the damage done by Euripides to the magnificent synthesis of Dionysiac and Apollinian elements in classical Athenian tragedy.

Joshua Billings lists those "twentieth- and twenty-first century thinkers who have engaged with tragedy . . . : Freud, Benjamin, Heidegger, Schmitt, Camus, Lacan, Foucault, Derrida, Irigaray, Zizek, and Butler would be only a start."[15] Perhaps a Nietzschean, Sigmund Freud nonetheless followed Hegel in seeing Sophocles, and in particular his Theban plays, as exemplary of what ancient tragedy had to offer to modernity. And he saw Oedipus as an *individual* subject, an eternal son, a person who resembled those he met in his consulting room.[16] Freud memorably referred to the Oedipus myth in his *Interpretation of Dreams*, finding in Sophocles' character an unrepressed expression of the desire of all mankind to kill the father and sleep with the mother: "What I have in mind is the legend of King Oedipus and Sophocles' drama which bears his name. . . . While the poet, as he unravels the past, brings to light the guilt of Oedipus, he is at the same time compelling us to recognize our own inner minds, in which those same impulses, though suppressed, are still to be found."[17] Psychoanalysis has followed Freud's lead, and psychoanalytic journals have abounded with discussions of the individual Oedipus and his situation within what came to be called "the Oedipus complex."

Following Freud's identification of the myth of Oedipus as an unrepressed version of the destiny of the human individual, male, who desires his mother and wants to kill his father, one of the greatest, and most illuminating, books of the twentieth century on tragedy, written by the classical scholar Bernard Knox, *Oedipus at Thebes: Sophocles' Tragic Hero and His Time*, is entirely focused on the hero, the character, the individual Oedipus. Knox interprets the persona of Oedipus as a figure representing Athens, the city, the *polis tyrannos*, and also as exemplary of the intellectual revolution occurring in Athens in the fifth century BCE, observing: "Oedipus is surely the greatest single individual in Greek tragedy."[18] Writing in 1957, Knox sought to historicize the play, but was himself situated within a postwar world concerned with defending individual rights against fascist or communist collectives. For him, the ancient city had become an individual, a single subjectivity, rather than a *polis*, a swarming collectivity. While he acknowledged the presence of the chorus in *Oedipus Rex, Oedipus Tyrannos*, his analysis subordinated their song, their dance, their interventions, to the hero, the tyrant.

ANTIGONE

Oedipus long dominated many discussions of the individual, modern and ancient, but Sophocles' Antigone has captured the imagination of countless theorists and artists of contemporary culture. Billings gives a persuasive account of the turn toward Antigone: "The genealogical viewpoint on idealist thought reveals that what is often thought of as a single movement is actually composed of two distinct (though interrelated) strands: the first centers around the *Oedipus Tyrannus* (*OT*), and is elaborated mainly by Schiller, Schelling, and A. W. Schlegel from 1793 onward, then canonized in Schelling's *Philosophy of Art* and Schlegel's *Lectures on Dramatic Art and Literature*; the second is centered on the *Antigone* and seems to emerge from almost nowhere in the writings of Hölderlin and Hegel in 1804 and 1807, respectively, and is canonized by Hegel's posthumously edited and published *Lectures on Aesthetics*." The *Antigone* replaced Sophocles' *Electra*, the most influential of his plays after *Oedipus Rex* from antiquity to the earlier nineteenth century. Billings associates this new interest in the *Antigone* to "changing conceptions of genre: its central ethical conflict, political context, and foregrounding of gender relations."[19]

In some ways political theory's investment in the *Antigone* is a sort of Enlightenment trap that renders it hard to represent resistance, especially that of the collective, the swarm, as the play revolves around a royal household, a ruling family. Judith Butler, in her brilliant book *Antigone's Claim*, sought to reorient the earlier emphases by speculating about a psychoanalysis, or an idea of the family, of the grievable, based not on Oedipus but on his sister/ daughter Antigone. Butler wrote eloquently about Sophocles' Antigone, urging consideration of a psychoanalysis that focuses not on the father, not on the patriarchal family, but rather is centered on Antigone, a queer exemplar, product of incest, fixated on her brother Polyneices to the extent that she disregards her heteronormative duty as a bride, a woman who speaks boldly, with *parrhesia* even, to her uncle, the tyrant Creon.[20]

In his breezy introduction to Slavoj Zizek's translation of the *Antigone*, the contemporary novelist Hanif Kureishi, author of the play *My Beautiful Laundrette* and the novel *The Buddha of Suburbia*, among other texts, expresses a common view of the *Antigone* wrested from the context of ancient tragedy: "Antigone is a particularly modern heroine. She is a rebel, a refusenik, a feminist, an anti-capitalist (principles are more important than money), a suicide perhaps, certainly a martyr, and without doubt a difficult, insistent person, not unlike some of Ibsen's women. More decisive, less irritating, talky and circular than Hamlet—but, you might say, equally teenage—she has blazed through the centuries to remain one of the great characters of all literature."[21] This assessment, by a playwright, sets Antigone firmly in the twenty-first century. She has survived as a teenager, a "character," that is, separate, isolated from Sophocles' tragedy, from his other tragedies, from the tragic works of Aeschylus and Euripides and other lost tragedians, from the festivals of Dionysos in which their plays were performed. Antigone is set apart from the chorus of the play *Antigone*, as well as from the comedies that accompanied ancient tragic performances, and from the rituals of the democratic city, honoring the city's dead, subjecting its allies, worshipping its gods, and from its everyday life. Zizek created a "translation" of the *Antigone* that goes beyond Sophocles to locate the tragic character within the dilemmas of postmodernity. He presents three different endings for his *Antigone*, as the play reverts to a coda twice before its completion. In the first, the play ends as does Sophocles', with the character's suicide. In the second, Antigone convinces Creon to allow her to bury her brother, and the chorus concludes "the ruling class can afford to obey honour and rigid principles, while ordinary people pay the price for it." In the third choice of an ending, Zizek proposes a conclusion based on the crowd, the chorus—an ending with dire results:

> In the third version, Chorus is no longer the purveyor of stupid commonplace wisdoms, it becomes an active agent. At the climactic moment of the ferocious debate between Antigone and Creon, Chorus steps forward, castigating both of them for their stupid conflict which threatens the survival of the entire city. Acting like a kind of *comité de salut public*, Chorus takes over as a collective organ and imposes a new rule of law, installing people's democracy in Thebes. Creon is deposed, both Creon and Antigone are arrested, put to trial, swiftly condemned to death and liquidated.[22]

"Chorus," which seemed to be a single entity in Zizek's earlier discussion of the play, now proliferates into a plural being, and degenerates into a mob, reminiscent of the "people" who engaged in the Terror following the French Revolution.[23] The use of the word "liquidated" cannot but call up associations with Stalinism. This chorus exemplifies the dark, negative version of the swarm, the very mob the conception of which I argue against in this book, the conviction that a group, a collective, must turn homicidal.

In the late twentieth and twenty-first centuries, then, Antigone has survived, in the references to Hegel's understanding of her relationship to Creon, in Jacques Lacan's interpretation of her as the magnificent embodiment of the death drive, in Judith Butler's focus on her to meditate on questions of kinship and grief, in Bonnie Honig's emphasis on the sororal, in Tina Chanter's call for attention to Antigone's unqualified acceptance of and endorsement of slavery, in Anne Carson's beautiful, witty translation of Sophocles' play.[24]

Interest in Antigone as character continues. Kamila Shamsie's novel *Home Fire* (2017), a critical success, depicts a situation familiar to readers of Sophocles.[25] The novel presents a British Muslim family of Pakistani descent, an older sister Isma, and twins Aneeka and Parvaiz, as well as a British home secretary and his son Eamonn, also of Pakistani descent. The novel recounts the ways in which Parvaiz, the Polyneices character, is first recruited by a jihadi who belongs to a shadowy ISIS-like group, and goes to join them in Asia. The young man comes to regret his choice, and attempts to return to Britain. His twin sister tries to save him through intervention by her lover Eamonn and his father the government official, but her brother is gunned down by his former comrades as he approaches the British consulate in Istanbul. Aneeka, the Antigone figure, seeks to have his corpse repatriated to Britain, his home country, but the home secretary refuses. The novel ends dramatically with Aneeka, who has flown to Karachi to retrieve her brother's unburied corpse, shown on global television as she mourns him. Eamonn, her lover, defies his father and comes to her, but is overcome by hostile figures who wrap him in a suicide device that is detonated, destroying him, Aneeka, and the corpse of Parvaiz.

Filmmakers also have contributed to an ongoing set of discourses concerning Antigone as character. The South Korean director Park Chan-wook's 2003 film, *Old Boy*, alludes intermittently and tantalizingly to the Oedipus legend, the fated Theban family of Oedipus, his sons and daughters. The central character, Oh Dae-su, is mysteriously kept in a private prison for fifteen years, and then released. He seeks to know who imprisoned him, trying to solve a riddle and encountering various obstacles along the way, but also connecting with a young woman, Mi-do, who falls in love with him, and remains loyal through his many trials, even though she is much younger than he. Eventually he learns through suffering that the author of his captivity is another "old boy" from the Christian school he attended as an adolescent, and that he is being punished for spreading the rumor that his captor and that captor's sister were involved in an incestuous love affair with one another, the rumors having caused the suicide of the young girl. As he discovers the truth, Oh Dae-su cuts out his own tongue. The final moment in his punishment is revealed when he learns that his lover, Mi-do, is his daughter. The film ends with his splitting into two personae, one a monster who vanishes, the other a father/lover embraced by his daughter/lover.

The theme of incest echoes a salient feature of the Oedipus myth, and of the three Sophoclean plays that trace the history of this cursed family. Father and daughter, the mutilation of the father, the unveiling of a terrible secret, all these allusively, teasingly echo the myth of the blighted Theban family of Laius, Jocasta, Oedipus, and his children. Tropes characteristic of Asian cinema are also developed in the film: the theme of forbidden love, the freedom of adolescents to fall in love in their high school years, before paternal law becomes absolute, the tenderness between father and daughter, lover and beloved. The narrative in this film may be a tragedy, but it is also a love story.

This film was remade, as *Moebius*, a film in which no one speaks, and was also filmed by the Black American director Spike Lee, with the title *Oldboy*, in 2013. The plot follows that of Park Chan-wook very closely, but the rumors of incest concern not brother and sister, but a father who is said to have had sex with both his son and his daughter. Once again, after the central character Joe's imprisonment and subsequent search for the answer to the identity of his tormentor, he is involved in a sexual affair with a woman who, it is eventually revealed, is his long-lost daughter. In the end, Joe breaks with his daughter/lover, and chooses to return to the site of his captivity, the hotel room in which he was confined for twenty years before he was freed.

What fascinates me most about this record of engagement with the Sophoclean plot, or the myth that preceded Sophocles' use of this material, is that most of these twentieth- or twenty-first-century adaptations of the narrative of Antigone focus not on questions of sovereignty, or mourning and lamentation over burial, as does *Home Fire*, but rather on the matter of sexuality, whether it be father/daughter or brother/sister incest. Significant aspects of Sophocles' plays concerning the ruling family of Thebes— *Antigone*, *Oedipus Rex*, and *Oedipus at Colonus*—include the choruses; the engagement of the *demos*, the people, in the struggles of archaic rulership; questions of law and the role of the tyrant; the resistance of the city's women; the opinion of the city; and issues of enlightenment and philosophical humanism in a turn away from traditional religious practices. All these are ignored, or reshaped to surround the intimacies of the nuclear family, of filial relationships, to the exclusion of a politics that was recognized by Hegel but has since narrowed ever more to the question of erotic partners within the nuclear family, and the tragedies that follow from incestuous unions.

ARISTOTLE ON DRAMA

Aristotle's discussion of tragedy occurs in his *Poetics*, of which the second part, focusing on comedy, as noted earlier, has been lost. He emphasizes the fact that "the objects of representation" in tragedy are "persons doing or experiencing something" (1448a1), but that "tragedy differs from comedy. The latter sets out to represent people as *worse* than they are today, the former as better" (1448a7, emphasis mine).[26] Such a characterization of ancient comedy ignores the presence of such personae as the imposing, even noble Lysistrata, for example, who brings peace to the warring cities of Athens and Sparta, and can hardly be interpreted as "worse" than many tragic personae, such as Medea, the homicidal sorceress of Euripides.

Aristotle mentions in passing that the word "drama," referring to these sorts of representations, comes from the verb *dran*, "to do," "because they present people doing things" (1448a4). The Dorians claim to have invented both comedy and tragedy; the word for "comedy" is connected with "comedians" strolling about the villages, *komai*, a Dorian word. Aristotle begins to distinguish between tragedy and comedy, crediting their difference to the nature of the poets who compose them: "For the more serious poets represented fine (*kalas*) doings and the doings of fine men, while those of a less exalted nature represented the actions of inferior men (*phaulon*)" (1448b8). From the start, then, Aristotle denigrates comedy, measuring it against the more serious, exalted form of tragedy. He continues this comparative practice: "Comedy, as we have said, is a representation of inferior people, not indeed in the full sense of the word bad (*kakian*), but the laughable is a species of the base or ugly (*aiskhrou*) [perhaps better translated as 'shameful'?]" (1449a21). This vocabulary, difficult to put into English, communicates condescension and disdain for the people of comedy, who in fact include such enlightened characters as Praxagora, the visionary communist leader of the women in the play *Ecclesiazusae* (*Women at the Assembly*).

Aristotle emphasizes that tragedy, his subject in what remains of the extant part of the *Poetics*, is a representation of an action, *praxis* (1450a12); and continues: "The plot then is the first principle and as it were the soul (*psukhe*) of tragedy: character comes second" (1450a19). He is much less interested in "song-making," *melopoiia*, and in "spectacle," what is seen, *opsis*. "The effect of tragedy does not depend on its performance by actors," he says (1450a28). Built into his analysis is a disregard of performance, of ritual, of tragedy's embodiment as a religious-political rite in the ancient city.

Aristotle goes on at some length concerning plot, what he considers the best sort of plot, and the place of reversal and discovery as well as calamity and *pathos*, which he describes as a destructive or painful occurrence (1452b9–10). He names elements of the whole, the parts, the limbs, of tragedy, including "choral song," the "*parodos* and *stasimon*" (the first utterance of the chorus and their "stationary songs"), as well as the *kommos* (the lamentation shared by chorus and actors). But he does not elaborate on these elements, and moves immediately, notoriously, to describe the best, most complex tragedy as one that arouses pity and fear in the audience. Going into greater detail about various matters concerning the plot, the *muthos*, the philosopher has but little to say about the chorus, only this: "The chorus too must be regarded as one of the actors. It must be part of the whole and share in the action, not as in Euripides but as in Sophocles. In the others the choral odes have no more to do with the plot than with any other tragedy. And so they sing interludes, a practice begun by Agathon. And yet to sing interludes is quite as bad as transferring a whole speech or scene from one play to another" (1456a19). And that is that. Aristotle's observations make clear the insignificance he attributes to the chorus, and indicate also perhaps the decline of its importance in his day, in the fourth century, after the classical production of tragedy in the fifth century. Choruses perform mere interludes as time goes on, and these can be inserted, moved from one play to another, members lacking even a role like that of an actor in the action of the drama.

Although it may have been neglected in the debates concerning tragedy, Florence Dupont's *Aristote ou le vampire du théâtre occidental* contributes an idiosyncratic and valuable point of view to the arguments.[27] I appreciate this book not only for its lurid title, but also for the animus, the unrestrained rage that fuels its polemic, relatively rare in the Anglo-Saxon world. Dupont's aim in the project is to "deconstruct" (*déconstruire*) Aristotle's *Poetics* and his concepts, and denounce the "aesthetic postulates which poison Western theater" (7). She is concerned with a "rampant and diffuse Aristotelianism" that has invaded the entire territory of contemporary theater production. And she is especially bent on targeting the "fable," the *muthos*, the narrative of plays, arguing that everyone thinks theater is the "representation of a story, a history (*histoire*)" (8). Although her book focuses on Roman comedy, much of her argument remains pertinent for thinking about Greek drama also, tragedy as well as comedy.

Dupont argues that to read ancient comedy properly, rather than looking for a *narrative*, it is necessary to rediscover its historical reality, and to reconstitute it as cultural event, to study the context in which these plays were presented, and to recognize that these plays require *une raison [ludique]* ("a ludic logic"). She demands a change in the "habitual hierarchy" of theater production, its privileging of the text and its *muthos*. She insists on what she calls "indigenous categories" (10); in interpreting and performing these plays, we must be anthropologists. Bracingly reminding us that, as Hegel said concerning Greek civilization, we can no more "sympathize" with it, than with a dog,[28] Dupont snidely characterizes the ethnocentrism of contemporary Western thought, pointing to the presence in the European imaginary of, side by side, a dancing Dionysos, some satyrs, and Sophocles revealing to humanity his oedipal truth or the Antigonean values of democracy, as Aristotle finally delivers his edicts on the rules of mimesis (11).

In a section called "The Trap (*Le piège*) of the *Poetics*," Dupont calls for the decolonization of the theater, the revelation of its ethnocentric postulates, the recognition that the *Poetics* "entraps" contemporary practices of dramatic presentation, observing: "Aristotle has, in fact, isolated the *text* of theater to make it an object of analysis" (13, emphasis mine). As she makes abundantly clear, the ancient Greek public knew the drama of Athens only through the ritual performances of the Great Dionysia (or, as she neglects to add, at other Dionysiac festivals such as the Lenaia). But her point is well taken, that in considering only what she calls the "fable," the *muthos*, the plot, we disregard the fact that the playwrights she lists, omitting Aristophanes by the way, were known as "singers," *aoidoi*, not poets in our sense (13).

In Western thinking about theater and its performance, Dupont argues, the concept of *muthos*, of "fable," as the French call it, "plot" in English, has become the keystone. But the theory of Aristotle is inadequate not only for Greek theater, but also for Roman and traditional theaters: "Why did he, who claimed to write about Greek tragedy, arrogantly ignore its practical functioning, to begin with, by the chorus, which he makes a character like any other?" (22). In her view, Aristotelianism has progressively "colonized" European theaters. And she goes on to read closely the *Poetics*, its version of mimesis, or "representation," and its first audience. As she notes, Aristotle created his own vocabulary and categories for discussing the theater and presented a normative version of "the tragic poem," that is, tragedy, which makes little reference to the realities of Athenian theater practice.

We have the benefit of earlier work, including an important essay by Simon Goldhill on the context of the drama festivals of Athens, that sets dramatic performances in the social and political and ritual context, of which more later.[29] But much of what Dupont complains of in the Aristotelian presentation of drama remains pertinent. She recalls that the festivals opposed both tragic and comic "poet-composers," who, as noted, called themselves "singers" (*chanteurs, aoidoi*). And the theater was just one among many musical performances, often given by choruses, offered to the gods during great cult ceremonies (27). The Great Dionysia, as Goldhill also insists, comprised twenty dithyrambs in addition to dramatic presentations, the seventeen plays, tragedies, satyr plays, and comedies, stretching over five days. Tragedies took place within a "liturgical" and "epideictic" context; the great festival took place at the beginning of the season of the year when sailing became once again possible, and visitors arrived from other cities to attend the dramatic performances. As Dupont points out, at the festival the Athenians displayed the tribute from the Delian League, those allies led by Athens, initially to mount a defense against a return invasion by the Persian Empire, but eventually appropriated by the Athenians for their own use, and used in maintaining their own empire. The children orphaned by soldiers who died in war, who were supported by the Athenian state, paraded in the ceremony, which also included the announcement of honors bestowed on the benefactors of the city. Many rituals, processions, and sacrifices took place, as Dupont notes, before and during the Great Dionysia, and all these provided a context for the tragic performances and (although she omits these here) the comic performances as well.

A prize was awarded, chosen by a jury through a procedure Dupont calls "complex and democratic" (28), but victory was obtained not necessarily in terms of "beauty," but also through taking into account the *kairos*, "the right moment," that is, the timing of the matter of the play in relation to the current circumstances of the city. And "the democratic consensus [about the victors] is the occasion to reaffirm concord among the citizens" (29). The jury's decision bore not on a text, but on a ritual performance, and on the benefactor who paid for the production, financing the spectacle.[30] But "Aristotle, far from these historical realities, defines the beauty of a tragedy through objective and aesthetic criteria" (30), and entirely misses its social and religious context. He deprives the theater of its status as *an Athenian institution* (30, emphasis mine). As Dupont rather melodramatically puts it, "To objectify the theatre, to submit it to a poetic art, to substitute a text for the event, is to take away its reason for being. This is why Aristotle's *Poetics*, far from being a treatise of theatrical composition for poets, is a war machine directed against the theatrical institution" (30).

Dupont mounts further accusations against Aristotle. He was not Athenian; "he had never celebrated the Great Dionysia, never sung in the choruses, never been judged or jury, never belonged to the Athenian public which had been initiated from childhood to the musical code, celebrating every year this singular ritual, implicating identity, of the city of Athens" (32). He served those who followed, who wanted in the temporal distance from this theater, for it to be "readable," "legible," *lisible* (32). Aristotle was a foreigner, forced because of his exteriority to negotiate a status exterior to the ritual through reading. He, whom Plato called "The Reader," cites the tragedies of the fifth century BCE in the fourth century BCE, and this position of estrangement forces him to think about poetic practices as intellectual practices, with the result that he presents tragedy as "a closed discourse, coherent and structured following a narrative, the *mythos*, which is the kernel, itself organized in some necessary fashion" (33).

In his treatise the *Poetics*, therefore, Dupont concludes, Aristotle is elaborating "a system of production/reception on the model writing/reading," leaving out of account "music," and all the social, religious, and cultural dimensions of Greek theater (35). He excludes instrumental music, songs, and choreography, as "tragedy is reduced to a silent poem" (35). Neither the "enunciative" context nor the "enunciators," the actors who disappear behind the characters, are taken into account. The "plot," *muthos*, substitutes for the real performance as the object of evaluation (36). This, she says, is a rupture from all the Greek tradition that precedes. Song has become poetry, and everything that rooted tragedy in the city and in ritual practice has been eliminated (38).

The question of the chorus looms large in Dupont's critique of Aristotle. As she notes, "The chorus introduced into tragedy a different enunciation, collective, sung, tied to the ritual of the Dionysia" (50). But Aristotle, focusing on the *praxis*, on the action of the drama, cannot use "a ritual definition" of the chorus, nor does he consider the orchestra, the dancing floor in the middle of the performance space in ancient Greek theaters, because in her view he never even thinks about spatiality in this context. He turns the chorus into another character, a personage like the others, played by a single actor, which reduces the chorus to the chorus leader, and the chorus leader to an actor in the action, the *praxis*, the *muthos* of the play (51). Aristotle is critical of the choruses of Euripides (*Poetics* 56a26–32), praises Sophocles' use of the chorus, and "cannot envisage that song—that is to say, ritual song—could be the raison d'être of the chorus" (51). Nor does Aristotle understand that the audience of tragedy is Athenian, citizen, or celebrant of the Dionysia; he envisions only a reader, and as Dupont claims, his version of "reception" "presupposes a social elitism in contradiction with the democratic ideal of the Great Dionysia" (57).

Dupont is also critical of the notion of *catharsis*, generally seen after Aristotle as a crucial element of the experience of tragedy. It belongs to the medical vocabulary, and Aristotle seems to use it to suggest that certain types of music excite in listeners troubles, such as pity and fear, which are at the same time soothed and purged; the model is homeopathic, common in antiquity, the idea that difficulties are cured by what has caused them. The wounds of love, as in the *De rerum natura* of Lucretius, are cured by love.

The *muthos*, showing human beings passing from happiness to unhappiness, from unhappiness to happiness, arouses painful feelings that are immediately healed by the pleasure that the *muthos* itself offers as a shaping, a *morphe*, an "intelligible form" (65). Once again, in Dupont's view, Aristotle ignores entirely the social experience of theater in order to produce theory. And, of course, his *incivisme*, his formalism, his lack of citizenship, his lack of belief, made him unloved by the Athenians, who saw him as a collaborator and an atheist. He took refuge with the kings of Macedonia, and had to exile himself to Calchis upon the death of Alexander (65).

So the performance called tragedy, inseparable from a musical contest, "exploded" in the hands of Aristotle into diverse fragments (66). Dupont calls this "a mutilated theater" (66), bequeathed to the Greek world and taken up by those who followed, so that the text of this dramatic performance, ripped from its Athenian roots, provides a theoretical basis for modern theater, desacralized, disenchanted, deritualized, and based on text, as tragedy is identified with its *muthos*, leaving no room for spectacle, or what she calls "theatricality," or metatheatricality (76). Tragedy has become a text, and its pleasure of a purely cognitive sort, deprived of its sensual, sensuous dimensions.

Dupont's careful and meticulous denunciation of Aristotle, and of those who follow him, speaks to me of all that is missing, first of all when considerations of ancient drama treat only tragedy, and its plot, and its characters, neglecting the chorus. And when ancient comedy is left out of the picture. Comedy and tragedy are inextricably bound together in the rituals and celebrations of ancient Athens. They can be said implicitly, because of their very juxtaposition in the city's celebration of Dionysos, to critique and nourish one another. And they both feature choruses. The collective presentation of the anonymous body of the chorus may stand in for the collective body of citizens, according to some scholars, but it also brings onto the stage populations that are less often visible to the readers of high tragedy. Queens, consorts, goddesses, heroines of the epic and legendary past, appear as characters, but the chorus can be Persians, the captive and enslaved women of Troy, the ecstatic Asian worshippers of Dionysos, and in comedy, even insects and animals, varied and heterogeneous and low in comparison to tragic highborn or immortal personages.

If Dupont is correct, then the tradition of reading Greek tragedy that includes Hegel, Freud, Lacan, Terry Eagleton, Slavoj Zizek, and many others shares in the dismemberment and reduction of its ritual and spectacular elements. There are limits, and perhaps unsavory consequences, to using Aristotle to think through tragedy and then to take this notion of "tragedy" to think through modernity. And comedy, even more, has been omitted from our political or psychological or even cultural assessment of the value of Greek drama for thinking about the present.

As mentioned earlier, Dupont's work must be considered along with Goldhill's powerful and influential essay in *Nothing to Do with Dionysos?* which firmly situates tragic performance in its ritual and political context.[31] Yet, although he acknowledges the presence of comedy performances in the city's celebrations of the god, Goldhill's focus is on tragedy here. Responding to Oliver Taplin's claim that "there is nothing intrinsically Dionysiac about Greek tragedy," Goldhill frames his essay by asserting that "scholars . . . distort . . . the fundamentally questioning or agonistic nature of Greek tragedy. This article [is] . . . meant . . . to aid the understanding of Greek tragedy as a social, political, and theatrical phenomenon" (98). Goldhill points to the rituals and ceremonies that preceded the dramatic performances at the Great Dionysia, the festival in honor of the god Dionysos, which included crucial elements of political, *polis*-related matters that draw this worship, the theater, and empire, the military, and tribute into a nexus. Dionysos's statue was carried about, and there was a great procession and then sacrifice at the Dionysos precinct at the heart of the city, followed by a celebration. Poets announced the subjects of the plays they were presenting in the theatrical competition. Libations before the tragedies were poured out by the generals of the city's military, tribute from the cities of the Athenian Empire was displayed on the stage of the theatrical performances, and divided into large sums and placed in the theater's *orkhestra*, the dancing floor, and "before the tragedies the names of those men who had greatly benefited Athens in some way were read out in front of the whole city" (104). And Goldhill concludes this learned and groundbreaking essay in this way:

> Tragedy must be understood, then, in terms of the festival of which it is a constituent part and the silence of critics on the preplay ceremonies is indicative of a general unwillingness to consider both the extended context of the tragic texts and the particular difficulties involved in reading this literature of transgression and impasse. The tragic festival may at first sight seem to have little to do with our expectations of the Dionysiac religion under whose name it takes place. But in the interplay of norm and transgression enacted in the festival which both lauds the *polis* and depicts the stresses and tensions of a *polis* society in conflict, the Great Dionysia seems to me an essentially Dionysiac event. (128–29)

Note that the festival, which included comic performances as well as tragic, has become "the tragic festival." And even those performances of comedy that included the god Dionysos himself as a character, of which only Aristophanes' *Frogs* is extant, receive less notice. It is not that Goldhill does not recognize the importance of comedy, the obscenity and lampoons, "all under the aegis of the one god," but that finally the presence of comedy is subordinated to the weightier significance of tragedy.

Such an emphasis is consistent with modernity's privileging of a particular understanding of tragedy over comedy. If it is because comedy is seen as too topical, too bound up with the specific historical circumstances of the fifth and fourth centuries BCE, because comedy abounds with ridicule and abuse, often obscene, of members of the original audience, or simply because comedy addresses themes that no longer have the dignity and immensity of reference required for great literature, comedy has all but vanished from considerations of the relevance of antiquity to the present, unless it be for the exceptional performances of *Lysistrata*, the utopian antiwar play of Aristophanes. This particular comedy, to be discussed more fully in what follows, has had a significant performance history in the twentieth and twenty-first centuries, as feminists and others have seen and even enhanced a play that represents a Panhellenic women's sex strike in the name of a Panhellenic peace. This exception may prove the rule, that performances of Aeschylus's, Sophocles', and Euripides' tragedies, whether in Africa, Latin America and the Caribbean, Europe, or North America, have been seen to speak more directly to the concerns, the tragic circumstances, of the recent past.[32]

ARISTOTLE ON COMEDY

The classical scholar Richard Janko has attempted to create what he calls a "reconstruction" of Aristotle's work on comedy, the second book of the *Poetics*.[33] Relying on a document known as the *Tractatus Coislinianus*, an anonymous treatise, lacking a title, and uncovered in 1839, as well as on scattered allusions in other texts, and the documents assembled as the *Prolegomena to Comedy*, Janko argues that his reconstruction sheds considerable light on what Aristotle had to say about comedy.[34] He cites various known Aristotelian texts that comment on the genre, including the *Politics*, where the author mentions again the matter of catharsis in relation to dramatic representations. Does catharsis, then, play a role in the audience's experience of comedy? And if so, of what are they purged, or cleansed? Is it pleasure and laughter, and if so, why need they to be cleansed or removed from the spectator?

Much of Janko's reconstruction focuses on laughter, on its causes and how to produce it in the audience, through jokes or various forms of wordplay or dance. And again, there is little mention of the chorus in the restoration; the chorus is named as one of the parts of comedy, the song sung by the chorus listed in the sources, but there is no discussion of the choral participants in this form of drama. In the reconstruction, Janko proposes the following: "**A Comedy is a representation of an absurd, complete action, one that lacks magnitude, with embellished language, the several kinds of embellishment being found separately in the several parts of the play: directly represented by persons acting, and not by means of narration: through pleasure and laughter achieving the purgation of the like emotions. It has laughter**, so to speak, **for its mother**. I explained the meanings of the terms here when tragedy was defined" (93).[35] As Janko reconstructs it, the focus of this second lost part of the *Poetics* seems to be on the generation of laughter in the poet's audience, for example through the deployment of "vulgar dancing" (95). Once again, as with tragedy, discussion of the parts of the drama centers on plot; Aristotle may have listed diction and song as important elements in all comedies, "**but instances of thought, character and spectacle** [are observed] **in not a few.**" Janko adds: "Spectacle is entertaining but not germane to the art of poetry, as the effect of comedy can also be obtained from reading it." Here again we see Aristotle the reader, even as he may acknowledge that comedy must be represented, and therefore "consists of spoken diction and choral song in its separate parts" (98).

These bare bones, the survival of an extensive treatise oriented perhaps toward the composition of dramatic works, rather than to criticism in a modern sense, were known to ancient readers, and therefore had their impact on the history of drama and its interpretation in the centuries that followed. Aristotle's scant attention to the chorus, meager in the case of tragedy, almost nonexistent in this reconstruction of the treatise on comedy, may owe something to the circumstances of performance in his day. As mentioned earlier, in Middle Comedy, and in New Comedy, after the era of Old Comedy, of which we have only fragments and the few comedies of Aristophanes still extant, choruses became less significant.

THE CHORUS

In thinking about tragedy, and about its impact, its formative influence on conceptions of modern subjectivity, it is evident that the tradition, following Aristotle, neglects the presence of the chorus, and increasingly, over time, focuses on the characters of the drama. If there are remnants of the presence of a chorus in the closet tragedies of Seneca, in Shakespearean, in Racinian tragedy, the role of the chorus, if there is one, is taken up by characters, lower-class speakers, characters not central to the plot, who comment on the action or provide some sort of relief from the pained, agonized experience of such creatures as Seneca's Oedipus, of Phèdre, "la fille de Minos et de Pasiphaé," of Lear or Macbeth or Hamlet. But can we call any set of actors in such tragedy, or even the players in *Midsummer Night's Dream*, a chorus?

Looking back at Athenian tragedy, with the intention of bringing to the fore, or giving adequate weight to the chorus as well as to comedy, a reader might see a different sort of drama than someone reading for *individual characters*. In Aeschylus's *Persians*, for example, one of the earliest of Athenian tragedies, produced in 472 BCE, just eight years after the battle of Salamis, when the Greeks finally chased off the Persian navy, the chorus is made up of Persian "elders," who open the play with a song that locates its setting in the Persian capital of Susa, in the palace of the emperor Xerxes.

The Athenians agreed not to permit tragedies to refer to recent, actual events, after the poet Phrynichus presented a play in 494 BCE that depicted the fall of the city of Miletus, an Ionian city, ally of Athens, and the audience was moved to tears, the playwright fined for reminding them of their misfortunes (Herodotus 6.21.10). Aeschylus's remarkable play, which attributes humanity and pathos to the recent enemies of the Panhellenic alliance against them, the Persians, avoids referring to the catastrophe empathically suffered by the Athenian audience, setting the tragedy in the Persians' capital and making its chorus barbarians, Persians.

The Suppliants, another tragedy of Aeschylus, has a chorus of Danaids, that is, daughters of the legendary Danaus, who are fleeing from Egypt, from ethnic Egyptians who seek to possess them. They are significant figures in this tragedy, not merely commenting on the action of the characters, but beginning the play by begging for refuge from their pursuers: "Zeus Protector, protect us with care. / From the subtle sand of the Nile delta / Our ship set sail" (1–3).[36] Aeschylus's *Agamemnon*, the first play of the trilogy *The Oresteia*, features a chorus of elders of the city of Argos, who witness, sometimes passively, the speeches of the play's actors and protagonists. The chorus sings magnificent songs alluding to the haunted and cursed history of the house of Atreus, its episodes of cannibalism and child sacrifice, its entanglement with Helen, who is seen as a lion cub destroying the house, bringing destruction not only on Troy, but also on the palace of her husband's brother.

The chorus of Aeschylus's second play of the *Oresteia* trilogy is composed of female figures, the *Libation Bearers*, or *Choephoroi*, a chorus of "foreign" serving women, or slaves, who accompany Agamemnon and Clytemnestra's daughter Electra as she mourns her father and greets her brother Orestes, returned for vengeance. From the start, these slave women, veiled in black, express their terrible grief, lamenting at the bidding of their mistress:

> My cheek shows bright, ripped in the bloody furrows
> of nails gashing the skin.
> This is my life, to feed the heart on hard-drawn breath.
> (24–26, trans. Lattimore)

The last play of the trilogy features a chorus of Furies, the punishing chthonic goddesses bound on vengeance themselves, for Orestes' subsequent murder of his mother, Clytemnestra. They form a terrible, frightening, active chorus, driving the hero Orestes near to madness until they are subdued, buried under the Acropolis, and rendered benign, at least temporarily, by prayer. In Aeschylus's *Prometheus Bound*, the chorus is made of the daughters of the god Oceanus. In their engagement with the fettered Prometheus, they afford the explication of the reasons for his captivity and torture, sympathizing with his sufferings, attributing them to the great power of Zeus. They take up the female role of lamentation:

> A dirge for you came to my lips, so different
> from the other song I sang to crown your marriage.
> (556–57, trans. Grene)

Women mourn.

Nicole Loraux's work has illuminated this feature of tragedy, the ways in which women's grief and mourning resound, sometimes wordlessly, through performances of the Athenian tragic drama.[37] She points out:

> Cassandra or Antigone, Helen or Iphigeneia will borrow a song that was ordinarily intended for the dead, a deceased other, and apply it to themselves, the living. This reappropriation is important, even if those who engage in it, unlike the chorus of Aeschylus' *Suppliant Maidens*, are not always brave enough to state:
>
> *zosa goois me timo*
> "While I live, I honor myself in my dirge."
>
> In passages like these, which depict threnody as a melodic wailing, it appears impossible to reduce the lamentation to moaning. In almost every case, even if the cry dominates, music, whether it be soft or loud, is evoked at the same time; in most cases, music accompanies these evocations, which are often sung.[38]

Loraux's discussion of these moments, singing by characters or by the members of the chorus, emphasizes the role of mourning, and of music, that element lost to us in our understanding of ancient tragedy. Loraux echoes Charles Segal's observations concerning classical drama, the argument that "tragedy made weeping itself a sort of song, since, in its own music, namely, that of the flute (*aulos*), tragedy hears a weeping voice."[39] As Dupont argued as well, our experience of ancient Greek drama as "text," as written and passed on to readers, can never approach the richness of performance. And we need to try to feel our way toward tragedy's implicit expressions of mourning and lamentation, the centrality of choral dance and song in tragic performance, and, just as fully, comedy and its choruses' embeddedness in festival and performance, their audience's engagement with riotous, anarchic, collective enjoyment and laughter.

NO LAUGHING!

Something that continues to preoccupy me, nonetheless, is the modern fascination with tragedy and lamentation, the attachment to the tragic, without a concomitant gaze at laughter and the comic, the presence of comedy in the ancient city, which has been erased often from modern considerations of ancient drama and its relevance to the present. Joshua Billings cites Schlegel, and argues that "the concept of the tragic is related to the sense of 'seriousness,'" reaching for the infinite, for the sublime. Schlegel, Billings writes, "sees the tragic as prior, the quality on which tragedies are built. The tragic appears independent of its particular instances."[40] Tragedy partakes of tragic infinitude, its reach for sublimity, its seriousness, and for critics stands consistently as higher, superior, weightier, and more significant for modernity than comedy or the comic. Yet the Athenians themselves saw these two genres, tragedy and comedy, as inseparable, as bound together in worship of Dionysos. Is it an accident of transmission, the loss of the part of Aristotle's *Poetics* that was concerned with comedy, that has ensured that modernity forgets the necessity of the dialectic relationship between the two varieties of drama?

Tragedy rarely if ever acknowledges the existence of its partner, comedy, unless it be in odd moments when slaves, for example, express fear and dismay at their vulnerability to their masters' whims. Such a scene occurs, surprisingly perhaps, in Sophocles' *Antigone*, when a slave messenger anxiously hesitates to report to Creon, the new tyrant, Antigone's defiance of his threat.[41] Euripides indulges much more frequently in these games, coming close to blurring the line between tragedy and comedy, as in his tragedy *Helen*, sometimes called a "tragicomedy" or a romance, or in the *Orestes*, where a Phrygian slave speaks and sings, comically, in a dialect and to an alien new music:[42]

> Greekish sword—kill dead!
> Trojan scared, oh.
>   Run, run,
> Jump in slippers, fast, fast,
> clop-clop clamber over roof.
>   (1368–71, trans. Lattimore)

The Phrygian messenger conveys his report in language bravely translated by Richmond Lattimore, a stuttering pidgin speech that mocks the barbarian, who is implicated in a comic scene with the "hero" of the play, Orestes, then forced to beg for his life, and to say, memorably, "Slave man, free man, everybody like to live" (1524). Orestes spares his life after this scene of comical gibberish, groveling, and the assertion by the slave of his humanity. Performed in 408 BCE, near the end of the Peloponnesian War, the *Orestes* has sometimes been interpreted as revealing Euripides' exhaustion with his city, his disillusionment with self-congratulatory representations of the Hellenes, and as a prelude to his possible exile in the court of Macedonia, where it is claimed by some biographers he died a very few years later, supposedly torn apart by the royal hounds. Such an interpretation may owe more to the sorts of projections typical of biographical speculation on poets' life cycles, rather than taking account of the radical experimentation, finally foreclosed, of this play's form.

The moment of tragicomic mockery of the barbarian slave notwithstanding, with these rare Euripidean exceptions, tragedy remains the genre of high seriousness. And in post-Aristotelian interpretation, readers lay stress on the plays' characters, their subjectivity, their character, their individuality and choices, and tend to curtail their attention to the collective presence of choruses, often made up of women, barbarians, old people, beings far from Freud's exemplary human being, Oedipus the king.

TRAGEDIANS IN COMEDY

The plays of Old Comedy often refer to tragedies, and tragedians, denouncing such playwrights as Agathon, Euripides, and others. The most intense extant engagement with tragedians comes in the *Frogs*, produced around the same time as Euripides' *Orestes*, and taking on the question of tragic poets in a direct and comic vein. The play begins with the journey of Dionysos, accompanied by his slave Xanthias, into the underworld, for reasons that are not made clear until near the end of the comedy. The comic interactions between the god and his slave provide an extraordinary example of *parrhesia*, free speech, or saying it all, even about the gods, to be discussed more fully in chapter 6. In these early scenes Dionysos is revealed as cowardly, unable to control his bodily functions, willing to trade places with his slave to avoid trouble, and barely able to tolerate even the suggestion of the torture that was routinely inflicted on slaves involved in legal matters.

The critique, of the relative merits of two characters who represent opposed generations of tragic poets, proceeds after encounters of Dionysos and his slave with two separate choruses, one made up of frogs, who surround the lake that the dead must cross to enter the underworld, and another of initiates to the Eleusinian mysteries, who, because of their initiation, experience a happier, most blissful existence in the underworld. The frogs make up a sort of swarm, uttering the deathless line *brekekex koax, koax*, a noise that Dionysos himself repeats (250).

Sean Gurd, in his fascinating book *Dissonance: Auditory Aesthetics in Ancient Greece*, has this to say about Aristophanes' frog song: "*Brekekekex koax koax* is by no means meaningless (no nonsense ever is). But it derives much of its significance from the fact that it comes from the outside of human language: it paradoxically embodies both a pure music and a pure sound or noise."[43] The frog chorus includes what is outside, beyond the human, defying capture in words, while tragedy in contrast glides along smoothly, never really accommodating the politics of the swarm. Comedy makes experimental, tentative gestures, imagining froggy being in a move toward what Eduardo Viveiros de Castro calls "perspectivism," or "multinaturalism," the attribution of thinking, a point of view, to the animal.[44] Jeffrey Henderson translates the frogs' sounds, which accompany their cry: "a chorale spangled with / bubbly ploppifications" (248–49).[45] The word he translates is a *hapax legomenon*, occurring only this once, a neologism, a invented multisyllabic frog word: *pompholugopaphlasmasin*, "the noises made by bubbles rising" (LSJ).[46] Dionysos associates the sounds, the music, the noise, with farts, even as he repeats the frogs' song. The frogs exhibit a porosity with their environment; they are the song, the dance, the bubbles of their lake.

The frog chorus is contrasted with the second chorus, which appears as Dionysos and Xanthias approach their goal, the domain of Pluto and Persephone, divinities of the land of the dead. This chorus is made of a far more serious group, the initiates of the Eleusinian mysteries, devotees of Persephone and her mother, Demeter, who have achieved a more blissful afterlife than the uninitiated. They call on Iacchus, Dionysos under the name used at Eleusis, and invoke the rejuvenation that comes with their worship:

> Lo, the meadow's ablaze with flame,
> and old men's knees are aleap
> as they shed their cares
> and the longdrawn seasons of ancient years,
> owing to your worship.
>
> (341–48)

Their song summons a frequent theme of comic plays, the return of geriatric men to the gamboling and frolicking of their youth. The leader of this chorus of the dead addresses the audience, asking various categories of miscreants to stand apart from their dances, one who, for example, "shits on the offerings for Hecate while singing for dithyrambic choruses" (366). They invoke Demeter, goddess of grain, as well as Dionysos, divinity of the wet, of wine, both necessities of human existence. Dionysos, god of the theater, a character in this comedy, is thus summoned to participate and to approve the singing and dancing of choruses, as the initiates, singers and dancers, sing to him: "Iacchus lover of choruses (*philokhoreuta*), escort me on my way" (403). Although the chorus complains of being badly dressed, they thank the god for finding a way for them to perform, and lustily appreciate the tear in a young girl's dress that allows them to leer at her exposed nipple.

The choruses' role is most important in these early scenes of the comedy, when Dionysos and Xanthias, his slave, are nearing the abode of the dead. A strange moment occurs when the god takes Heracles' lionskin back from his slave, and the chorus comments on his versatility, his ability to "shift to the comfy side of the ship / and not just stand fast / in one position, like a painted (*gegrammenen*) / picture" (535–38). Dionysos is a man of *metis*, of "cunning intelligence," an opportunist like the politician Theramenes, mentioned at the end of the choral song.[47] The god responds with a speech suggesting the possibility of his voyeuristic participation in Xanthias's pleasures:

> Wouldn't it be hilarious
> if Xanthias, a mere slave (*doulos*),
> were lying all atumble
> on Milesian coverlets, and kissing
> a dancing girl, then asked for a potty,
> and I was looking over at him
> with my weenie in hand,
> and he caught me watching,
> recognizing a fellow rascal, then

punched me in the mouth and knocked out
my front row of chorus men?

(542–48)

The god likes to imagine himself watching his slave, masturbating in front of him, assaulted by his slave, losing his teeth, which are likened to the members of the chorus who have just been admiring him for his flexibility in moving between the dress of a slave, that of the god that he is, and his costume as Heracles, who has been to the underworld before him. Later he encounters Heracles himself, the mortal whom Odysseus found in the underworld, but who also dwells as an immortal on Olympus. The disruptive analogy drawn between members of the chorus and teeth (*tou khorou tous prosthious*, 548), a metatheatrical gesture of hostility, suggests a metaphorical connection between the god himself and his chorus, the celebrants of his divinity in comedy.

Dionysos is the great god in whose honor the festivals are celebrated, whose image attends the performances, who watches over the choruses, the actors, the spectacle of the drama. How can we account for the incongruities of this play, the god mocked and ridiculed, exposed as a coward willing to take the place of his slave, with the judge who appears in the later part of the play, the divinity who will choose which one of the deceased tragedians, Aeschylus or Euripides, will be conveyed back to the upper world to aid the city of Athens in its time of trouble? Perhaps the question of *parrhesia*, of saying it all, to be considered more fully in a later chapter, applies here as well as in those scenes in which the choruses of other comedies insult and taunt the politicians of the day. Dionysos is the people's god, the one who gave them the gift of wine, of forgetfulness of the pains and suffering of laboring lives. And he is the god of the theater, of transformation and possession on the floor of the orchestra, of the capacity to play the other, to enter the existence of another, slave, woman, bird, frog, in the ludic situation of the theatrical performance. Yet he is insulted, mocked, ridiculed in this comedy.

In the underworld, Sophocles, recently dead, does not challenge the preeminence of his great predecessor Aeschylus, the latter's right to hold the "chair of tragedy" among the dead. But Euripides, also recently dead, proposes to take the chair from his elder, claiming his superiority to Aeschylus. The contest that ensues, judged by Dionysos, focuses on three elements of their respective tragic legacies, and reveals perhaps what some Athenians themselves may have thought to be most significant about the plays, before the philosopher Aristotle could pronounce on the question of tragedy in his *Poetics*.

The *agon*, the contest between the two tragedians, not only concerns the sort of advice, counsel, aid that the dead playwright might bring back to the city of the living, but also focuses quite explicitly, and in some detail, on stylistic features of their plays. The arguments assume on the part of the audience a great familiarity with the varying styles of the tragedians, with their ideological orientation, but also with issues of performance and even of diction. In a world where many were illiterate, or barely literate, where so much was conveyed through hearing, the play takes for granted that a sophisticated audience, or some part of it, could recall the rhythms, the very lines of tragedies seen and heard in the past, and would bring to this play that attention and recognition that modern readers familiar with ancient texts, without the sort of aural memory skills held by ancient spectators, can only imagine. Gurd, in *Dissonance*, argues that in fact we may be more receptive to the sounds of this poetry than other recent generations have been: "The end of humanism has made us more corporeal and more subject to affective resonances (for good and ill)—in short, we are more ancient than we have been in a long time."[48]

In any case, the play clearly expects spectators to follow the mock contest between Euripides and Aeschylus, bringing some knowledge of and familiarity with the differences in orientation and style their plays exhibited. The chorus insists that members of the audience can follow the intricacies of these debates, the arguments for one tragedian pitted against the other:

> And if you're afraid
> of any ignorance among
> the spectators, that they won't
> appreciate your subtleties of argument,
> don't worry about that, because
> things are no longer that way.
> For they're veterans,
> and each one has a book (*biblion*)
> and knows the fine points;
> their natural endowments are masterful too.
> (1108–15)

This is an interesting claim. Could every spectator, or even many, have had a copy of the tragedies, or of those being discussed? Was their reliance on oral, aural performance so adept that they could follow the complexities of reference the two tragedians employ as they wrestle for the chair of excellence?

Aeschylus convinces the god Dionysos that he is the better man, winner of this contest, and that he should return to the upper world with the god. It is Aeschylus who has good sense, intelligence, who doesn't waste time sitting around chatting with Socrates, as the chorus suggests Euripides does, "ignoring the best / of the tragedian's craft" (1491–95):

> To hang around killing time
> in pretentious conversation
> and hairsplitting twaddle
> is the mark of a man who's lost his mind.
> (1496–99)

Pluto sends Aeschylus off with his blessing, and with the instruments of suicide for various characters still living in the city, who should hurry down to the underworld before he tattoos and fetters them, as he would treat slaves.[49] Aeschylus has a final word, demanding that Sophocles be given his chair in the underworld, that Euripides, criminal, liar, beggar, must never sit there in the place of honor.

Dionysos the god may be some sort of "comic hero" here, in this play, one of the first examples of literary criticism in the Western tradition. But he is, of course, also the god revealed to be a coward and a fool in the earlier part of the play. In an abrupt, jarring rupture with this earlier portrait of the divinity, he is latterly the patron of the dramatic festivals, exhibiting his concern at the end of the play to save the city of Athens, to find a thinker and writer who will offer wise counsel in its time of trouble. There is much less focus on a consistent characterization and plot in the comedy, and on the plots of the tragedies themselves, than readings of Aristotle would suggest.

The post-Aristotelian understanding of the heart of tragedy as plot and character mistakes some aspects even of the Aristotelian argument, when looked at from the point of view of this comedy. If Aristotle is principally concerned with the *muthos*, the story, the "plot," as it is usually translated, his interest in *ethos* is not necessarily in "personae," characters in our modern sense, but rather in the sort of character, that is, ethical disposition, of the persons depicted in the tragedies. And this emphasis is prefigured in the Aristophanic *Frogs*, where Aeschylus condemns his rival Euripides for presenting low, base, depraved, perverted persons who encourage base behavior in his audience. The bad examples, persons with low ethical standards or low social standing, women and slaves, drag down the city's morale and its ethical stance.[50]

COMEDY'S NEGLECT

Stephen Sondheim and Burt Shevelove wrote a version of the *Frogs*, first performed in 1974, later revised by Nathan Lane and expanded by Sondheim himself, in which Dionysos goes to hell to bring back George Bernard Shaw, who is bested by Shakespeare, chosen by the god to accompany him back to the upper world. In the original production, staged in Yale University's gymnasium, the chorus was played by the university's aquatics team, which swam around a boat crossing the pool. The production, much revised, had its day on Broadway.

But in general, in terms of scholarly interest and investment, and even entertainment, comedy has suffered. It has been seen as a poor cousin of tragedy, even though ancient performances of tragedy and comedy were intimately connected, inconceivable separated from their mutual presentation in Dionysiac festival. Tragedy has been the elite, privileged genre. And comedy studies have been more insular, more concerned with questions of authorship, of dating, of issues associated with the fragments of writers now lost to us, with the interpretation of comic vocabulary, and with the explication of historical and political references in the texts than offering opportunities for reflection on the great questions by philosophers and political theorists.

And possibly, I would argue, there has been a gendering of scholarship as well. If women for centuries had little or no Greek, they had even less access to the obscenity, the scatology, and the sexual insults rampant in the Aristophanic plays. Obscenity in Old Comedy was often not translated, elided or euphemized in generally circulated translations, or rendered into Latin, as in the standard dictionaries, so only classicists who knew the obscenities of Latin could read the obscenities of Greek. Here again, Jeffrey Henderson performed a great service in *The Maculate Muse: Obscene Language in Attic Comedy* (1975), which considered in depth the obscene vocabulary and figures of speech of Aristophanes.[51] But the masculine dominance of the study of Greek inherited from a segregated education system in Britain may have had its effect on the gendering of the study of comedy in the Anglo-Saxon world. Women may not have been present at the original performances of Aristophanes' plays in fifth-century BCE Athens, and they have been distinctly less present than men in the bibliography of studies of Attic comedy in modernity, until the important work of Edith Hall and other feminists, especially those interested in Lysistrata as a peacemonger. Are women still being sheltered from obscenity? The study of ancient Greek comedy, as opposed to Roman comedy, richly served by the scholar Amy Richlin and others, sometimes appears to be an isolate among the subdisciplines of classics, more attached to earlier modes of intellectual work.[52] The dominance of men in the field, the rejection to some degree of cultural studies approaches to the issues raised by comedy, the unwillingness at times to connect with debates within the humanities as a whole, seem to point to a more traditional methodology than has characterized other subdisciplines of classics in recent years. And the intervention of nonclassicists, as has happened in other fields of the discipline, perhaps especially in interpretation and deployment of Athenian tragedy, seems much less common.

After Aristotle, thinking about ancient Athenian drama has centered on tragedy, its plots, its personae. There has been an attempt not only to locate tragedy in its historical moment, to clarify its place within the rituals and institutions of the ancient city, but also to deploy the significance of tragedy in new historical circumstances, in the more recent past. Oedipus and his daughter Antigone have captured the imagination of modernity and postmodernity. Modern man is Oedipalized, postmodern woman Antigone. The emphasis on the individual, the agent of choice, as the subject of suffering, has taken center stage. Tragedy, with its characters, especially these personae of Oedipus and Antigone, set on stage by Sophocles, dominates the references to ancient society into the twenty-first century. The chorus, at the heart of tragedy and comedy, as well as ancient drama's setting in democratic celebration of the god Dionysos, although acknowledged in classical scholarship, has fallen away from contemporary interdisciplinary discourse. Comedy and the chorus have faded into near invisibility, and do not compel the same interest for those curious about the classical tradition, invested in philosophy and the politics of the present. And it's for this reason that in the chapters to follow I center on the possibilities comedy can offer to contemporary cultural debates, in particular what it reveals about strong, victorious women, about *parrhesia*, the freedom to speak, about utopianism, and about collectivity, communalism, and the power of the swarm in democracy.

[CHAPTER 2]

The Swarm

> To become animal is to participate in movement, to stake out the path of escape in all its positivity, to cross a threshold, to reach a continuum of pure intensities where all forms come undone.
>
> Gilles Deleuze and Félix Guattari, *Kafka*

In *The Emergence of Social Space*, her book on Arthur Rimbaud and the Paris Commune, Kristin Ross reads with a hallucinatory intensity the presence of the "swarm" in Rimbaud's poetry.[1] She points to the swarm's relationship to the anarchist notion of individual liberty, opposed to individualism: "Insect-verse. Rimbaud's poetry is the music of the swarm: quick and repeated agitation or vibration, a force field of unassigned frequencies ominous or lulling depending on the context, resounding, resonating" (105). The swarm can be coded as ominous, menacing, or full of potential as a force for liberation, although conventional, conservative thinking tends to represent it as a negative force, inevitably destined to fall into chaos or random violence, rather than as a popular force moving toward equality.

In this chapter, I consider various theoretical accounts of the swarm, negative and positive. I then look back to ancient Greek versions of swarms, from the wasplike warriors of Homer's *Iliad*, to Plato's docile and productive bees. I turn to Aristophanes' comedy *Wasps*, with an eye to its insect chorus, the role of citizen-juror-insects in that chorus, its relationship to discourses about democracy, and the stubborn tenacity of its waspish antihero.

SWARM THEORY

The liberatory potential of the swarm has been brought to the fore in *Multitude*, the work of Michael Hardt and Antonio Negri: "Recent researchers in artificial intelligence and computational methods use the term swarm intelligence to name collective and distributed techniques of problem solving without centralized control or the provision of a global model.... The swarms that we see emerging in the new network political organizations ... are composed of a multitude of different creative agents."[2] Hardt and Negri embrace what they celebrate as a benign model of "collective intelligence that can emerge from the communication and cooperation of such a varied multiplicity," and see it anticipated in Rimbaud and the Communards. Although Ross sees ambiguity in the swarm, Hardt and Negri affirm it optimistically: "Open-source, collaborative programming does not lead to confusion and wasted energy. It actually works. . . . The autonomy of the multitude and its capacities for economic, political and social self-organization take away any role for sovereignty. . . . When the multitude is finally able to rule itself, democracy becomes possible."

In a later version of their post-Deleuzian, utopian imagining of the future, *Assembly*, Hardt and Negri again emphasize the liberatory power of collective practices. The epigraph to the book's preface comes from Aimé Césaire: "Here poetry equals insurrection."[3] Hardt and Negri write: "Freedom of assembly is . . . no longer only a defense of individual liberty, or a protection against government abuse, or even a counterweight to state power. It is not a right conceded by the sovereign or the work of representation but the achievement of the constituents themselves. Assembly is becoming a constitutive right, that is, a mechanism for composing a social alternative, for taking power differently, through cooperation in social production."[4] They call for "a new Prince," alluding to Machiavelli's analysis of the politics of the early modern period: "A new Prince indicates a path of freedom and equality, a path that poses the task of putting the common in the hands of all, managed democratically by all. By Prince, of course, we do not mean an individual or even a part or leadership council, but rather the political articulation that weaves together the different forms of resistance and struggle for liberation in society today. This Prince thus appears as a swarm, a multitude moving in coherent formation and carrying, implicitly, a threat."[5] The ambiguous nature of the swarm figures in these theorists' call for resistance and equality in the present, but the threat is one directed against those forces that obstruct liberation and equality, that protest with fascist intent, as in the attack on the US Capitol by protesters seeking to overthrow the democratic state of the US. Hardt and Negri insist, as I will too in these pages, that although there is potential for menace in the swarm, that threat can also point toward equality, a wholesale condemnation of group protest and action is mistaken, and there is utopian possibility in the formation of a leaderless resistance, one that chooses disruptive and dispersed collectivity.

Feminist theorist Rosi Braidotti also addresses the swarm.[6] In her book *Nomadic Theory*, she offers a feminist, materialist version of affirmative politics, a "nomadic" theory building especially on the work of Gilles Deleuze, and on the seminal *Thousand Plateaus* of Deleuze and his comrade Félix Guattari. Braidotti states, in a sort of manifesto, that "nomadic thought rejects the psychoanalytic idea of repression and the negative definition of desire as lack inherited from Hegelian dialectics. It borrows instead from Spinoza a positive notion of desire as an ontological force of becoming" (2). Sustaining the critique of psychoanalysis found in Deleuze and Guattari's *Anti-Oedipus*, Braidotti argues: "The psychoanalytic emphasis on the role of the symbolic—or the phallogocentric code in Derrida or the heterosexist matrix in Butler—posits a master code, or a single central grid that formats and produces the subject. This social constructivist grid leaves little room for negotiation and instills loss and melancholia at the core of the subject" (5). Rejecting this emphasis on the tragic, Braidotti distinguishes some important features of nomadic thought that have influenced my understanding of the comic swarm: "Nomadic thought . . . approaches the process of subject formation in a distributive, dispersed, and multiple manner. . . . Nomadic thought rejects melancholia in favor of the politics of affirmation and mutual specification of self and other in set of relations or assemblages" (6). Braidotti joins others inspired by the paradigm of assemblages or swarms, to urge a renewed theory and politics. In an essay in *Nomadic Theory* entitled "The Cosmic Buzz of Insects," she mines insect life for insights concerning the politics of the present, and the future: "The insects/virus/parasite constitutes a model of a symbiotic relationship that defeats binary oppositions, . . . an inspiring model for a nomadic ecophilosophy" (101). She points out that insects "have a very respectable literary pedigree in European culture" (193), mentioning the locusts of the *Bible*, Aesop's ants, and, in particular, bees. (She also reminds her readers, however, that "Jacques Derrida [1997 (*Politics of Friendship*)] resorts to the metaphor of bees to express his disapproval of academic feminists and to condemn our allegedly regimented and authoritarian ways of thinking" [103].)[7]

Braidotti meditates on the positive and negative aspects of swarming insect life: "Other qualities that make insects paradigmatic are the fast rate of metamorphosis, the talents for parasitism, the power of mimetism or blending with their territory and environment, and the speed of movement" (103). Especially fascinating are her meditations on the sounds produced by insects, following the lead of Deleuze and Guattari, who remark, in a chapter of *Thousand Plateaus* titled "Becoming-Intense, Becoming Animal . . .": "Birds are . . . important, yet the reign of birds seems to have been replaced by the age of insects, with its much more molecular vibrations, chirring, rustling, buzzing, clicking, scratching, and scraping. Birds are vocal, but insects are instrumental. . . . A becoming-insect has replaced becoming bird, or forms a block with it."[8] And Braidotti, though sometimes criticized for accepting the universality of the Western philosophical tradition she follows, a unitary while still multiple notion of subjectivation, does recognize other claims: "My concern is, as always, to make sure that dissymmetry and hence power differences are not leveled out. The times and modes of women's and other marginal groups can be respected while we engage in the process of negotiations and constructive dialogue with the technocratic cultures of our days. . . . Embodiment . . . has to be thought of in the nomadic mode of a sexualized, racialized, and enfleshed complexity, not as a unity" (122). Braidotti sees a revolutionary potential in the swarm.

Some of this thinking on the swarm's possibilities may owe a debt, unacknowledged, to the thinking of Marx on "general intellect." In the *Grundrisse*, Marx discusses this combination of technological skills and social knowledge: "Nature builds no machines. . . . These are products of human industry; natural material transformed into organs of the human will over nature, or of human participation in nature."[9] Although we see here a will to power over nature that goes against the grain of recent thinking about cohabitation, coexistence, of species within a natural world, this line of thinking attributes great powers to what later thinkers have called swarm intelligence.

Yet the positive valence of the swarm has often been denied in the history of swarm theory. A "critical theory" tradition, looking back to Frankfurt school thinkers like Theodor Adorno, might interpret the swarm, like the rowers in the *Odyssey*, vulnerable to be triggered by the culture industry, zombie-like, controlled by messages administered by a repressive state, or new social media, like the Trump supporters, or the swarm as the Sirens themselves, insect-like with their hypnotic song.[10] Swarms can be roundly condemned, along with the insects, the most remote perhaps, from humankind, of animate creatures.[11] Insects, species now disappearing at an alarming rate, have been observed to approach human beings, menacingly, indifferent, covered with the exoskeletons that make them seem less vulnerable than fleshy human bodies. They obey other rules than those of their prey, often moving as a multibodied single unit through space. A friend recounted to me with amazement standing in the desert and seeing hordes of locusts crackling across his space for hours on end. Their activity excites martial metaphors, as they proceed in armies, armored, marching in battalions, flying in formation, conquering, obliviously trampling what lies before them. They appear not to see, to obey inaudible commands, to inhabit an alternate universe. A twentieth-century opera, *The Fly*, based on two earlier cinematic versions, one starring Vincent Price, the other directed by David Cronenberg, focused on the distress and horror experienced by a human protagonist whose molecules have been mysteriously fused with those of a fly, and who is gradually transformed before a horrified audience's eyes into an insect, tiny in the black-and-white film, immense on the operatic set. The creature can only cry, helplessly, "Help me," to his human lover, who in the opera finally performs what is represented as a euthanasia. Other science-fiction films depict monsters of an insect-like shape, like *Them*, where the antagonists of the gallant human beings face immense ants transformed by radioactivity into unconquerable foes.

As the work of Achille Mbembe in "Necropolitics" makes clear, the swarm can have this sinister, deadly face. He points to the development of what, again following Deleuze and Guattari, he calls "war machines," which are polymorphous, diffuse, and "characterized by their capacity for metamorphosis."[12] And the targets of these war machines, the multitudes, can themselves be reduced to swarms; "management" can "immobilize and spatially fix them," "or, paradoxically, unleash them, . . . force them to scatter."[13] The general intellect, or the resistant swarm, can be appropriated, used by neoliberalism and its theorists to limit and contain the possibilities for challenge to domination.[14] But in *Cyber-Marx*, for example, Nick Dyer-Witheford, influenced by the Italian autonomy group whose thinkers include Antonio Negri, argues for a communication strategy that counters capital's strategies of swarming commodification, globalization, and appropriation: "There are now visible signs of an emergent collectivity refusing the logic of commodification, uprising at the very moment that the world market seems to have swallowed the entire planet."[15]

The bee, an exemplary and swarming insect, serves as a vehicle for reflection on the movements of human swarms. In *Bee*, Claire Preston traces the history of reflection on bee swarms in the West. She follows the "contradictory ideas in history, where fear of the masses competes with virtuous group undertakings, where individuality and self-determination seem threatened by the collective will."[16] Up until the nineteenth century, when condemnation and alarm concerning the swarm come to dominate, philosophers and political thinkers seem in general to have admired bees, describing them as model participants in hierarchical systems of labor, and modest and retiring as individuals. Their honey was associated with "eloquence, immortality and sheer pleasure" (Preston, 13). Plato was said to have been fed with honey by bees, as an infant on Mount Hymettus, as were Pindar, Xenophon, and Vergil, and this nurturing accounts for their sweetness of style. The fourth book of Vergil's *Georgics* celebrates bees, regarding them not only as democratic, as self-effacing, subordinating themselves to the good of their state, but also as engaging in useful trade, like merchants. Vergil's view seems to contradict that of others who wrote about bees, debating whether they represented a successful monarchy led by a king, or an Amazonian kingdom with a ruling queen (61).[17]

Preston describes a shift in the valence of bees and their hives, especially after the French Revolution. The concept of the swarm became a site of ideological struggle. She recounts how "at least from the 1780s, the disobedient mob and its actions, the unruly crowd governed by political or social grievance, was particularly horrifying," and notes that "Carlyle and Burke... used *schwärmerei* (to swarm, or... rave), to describe the mob-led events of the French revolution. The sense of deathly, impersonal, and uncontrollable industrial processes combines with this fear of the crowd and its "selfless" mechanism, to be sustained and extended in the later, mechanized, electronic vision of modern social organization" (139). Yet in *Liberty Lyrics*, published in 1895 by the anarchist communists, bees are still congratulated for being free of masters, money, the press, and "property tyrants" (74).

Preston reminds her readers that "the implicit likeness of bees to the evil socialist hordes was adapted by Hollywood" (151). "Bad bees" appear in films, often racialized as "Africanized." In a 1978 film entitled *The Swarm*, "Michael Caine watches bees kill soldiers, schoolchildren and picnicking families, attack a nuclear power plant and destroy Houston" (154). When the swarm is first sighted, they are called "a moving black mass." The racial allegory is unmistakable.[18] A disclaimer projected at the end of the film maintains: "The African killer bee... bears absolutely no relationship to the industrious, hardworking American honey bee." In another film the bad bees "are finally thwarted by a hero-scientist who finds a chemical that turns bees into homosexuals" (155). In *Candyman* (1992), the ghost of a freed slave, accused of courting a white woman, stung to death by bees, haunts the Cabrini Green housing project in Chicago: "The slave's spirit lingers as 'the Candyman,' accompanied (indeed infested) by bees, to disembowel white women" (156). Bees, once benign exemplars of order, discipline, hierarchy, and the division of labor, have become a menacing swarm, racialized and dangerous. Wasps too are criminalized, and gendered: Roger Corman's 1959 film, *The Wasp Woman*, stars a deadly queen wasp, mutated from the human form of a cosmetics executive, who must be destroyed. In the final scene, her smoking head metamorphoses into a vast swarm of wasps.

ANCIENT SWARMS

In what follows, I consider more fully an earlier set of discourses concerning ancient Greek swarms, exceeding more conventional representations of citizen and barbarian, citizen and slave, citizen and city—anonymous collectivities of insects that appear ambiguously in important texts of the high classical period. I focus on the wasps of Aristophanes' eponymous comedy, unnamed and vigorous participants in the jury system of the ancient *polis*,

Athens; on the bees and cicadas of Plato; and on the natural history and biological studies of Aristotle. For the Greeks these swarms' characteristics presented an occasion for politically charged, metaphorical portraits of the city's citizens and inhabitants, another way of conceptualizing human collectivity. My inquiry concerns not just comic and philosophical representations of these creatures, especially the metamorphic potential in their "becoming-insect," but also their valence as exemplars in the political and ideological conflicts of the fifth and fourth centuries BCE.

In the Homeric epics, various metaphors and similes are based on identifications between groups of human beings and insects. Some scholars believe that the Sirens, those singers who lure human beings to their deaths on the shores of their island somewhere in a mythical sea, can be traced back to bees and bee goddesses. Gabriel Germain, in his *Genèse de l'Odyssée*, discussed the linguistic evidence for a connection among the Sirens, *melissai*, or "bee goddesses," whose name contains the word *meli*, "honey," and priestesses who served the bees.[19] Max Horkheimer and Theodor Adorno use the episode of Odysseus and the Sirens in the *Odyssey* to describe the *promesse de bonheur* permitted to the hero, allegorically read as the ruling class, who hears the Sirens' tempting song bound to his ship's mast, while the ears of his rowers, the workers, are stopped with wax, product of the bees.[20]

Bees in antiquity were associated with prophecy.[21] Dionysos/Bacchus, god of the theater, was said by Ovid (*Fasti* 3.736–63) to have discovered honey, a magical substance, an excrement of bees, neither raw nor cooked; Hesiod famously, in his account of the creation of gods and women, denounces women, descended from Pandora, for resembling the lazy (and male) drones of the hive, and he calls them a *genos*, "a tribe," a "kind," a "species," using a word that points beyond the categories of the individual and the state characteristic of political theory, especially that based on the Greek *polis*, derived from Plato and Aristotle.[22] Bees like other insects are dangerous because they sting, beloved because they provide the sweetness of honey, which is associated with the ambiguous nature of the female kind, especially in early Greek poetry.

ANTS

Another insect kind, ants, inhabits Homer's poetry, in an uncanny analogy with warriors. The soldiers of the great hero Achilles, his Thessalian "Myrmidons," have a name that suggests their ancestral link with the insect swarm, the ants, the *myrmekes*. The Myrmidons themselves were even said to have been created from ants (Hesiod frag. 76 Rzach). In one version of the myth, Aiakos, grandfather of Achilles, and a son of Zeus, ruled at a time when all of his subjects died of a plague. Zeus, answering his prayers, transformed ants into human beings, and returned life to the dead territory of Aiakos, the island of Aegina near Athens. The subjects of Peleus, Aiakos's son, father of Achilles, were then called the Myrmidons, and their name was understood to be derived from that of their insect ancestors. Ovid tells the story of transformation in his *Metamorphoses* (7.613 and following): "The ants suddenly grew, appearing larger and larger, until they rose from the ground and stood with bodies erect. Their thinness was gone, they had only two feet, and their colour no longer was black; their limbs were completely changed into human form."[23] The word for "ant" in Greek, intriguingly, figures in a verb, *mermekizdo*, "to be feeble and rapid," in a movement like that of ants, used of the pulse in medical treatises. It is as if there are ants beneath the skin, pulsing and swarming with life, measured by the physician as he touches the surface of the body.

The Myrmidons of epic are barely differentiated one from another; they have come to Troy to fight with their leader, Achilles, and form a shadowy group who move as a body with their hero. They are compared to another insect kind, the wasps, in a famed simile in the *Iliad*:

> Myrmidons,
> battalions ranged in armor with greathearted Patroclus,
> moving out now, the fury bursting inside them,
> suddenly charged the Trojans—
> They swarmed forth like wasps from a roadside nest
> when boys have made it their sport to set them seething,
> day after day tormenting them round their wayside hive—
> idiot boys! They make a menace for every man in sight.
> Any innocent traveler passing them on that road
> can stir them up accidentally—up in arms in a flash,
> all in a swarm come pouring, each one raging down
> to fight for home and children—
>   Such frenzy seized their hearts,
> Myrmidons pouring out of their ships . . .
>   (*Iliad* 16.257–66)[24]

These insect warriors provide no honey, sing no tempting songs, luring sailors to their death; they are swarming killers, exhibiting territorial aggression to defend their own, unpredictable ant-like creatures assimilated to the much more threatening wasps.

These early Greek similes and myths identify human beings intermittently with insects, see them as ancestors or as compelling examples of certain sorts of human behavior. Is it because insects lack individuation in human eyes that they eventually come to exemplify a version of the ideology of the democratic city, the notion of *isonomia*, "equality," the substitutability and equivalence of each citizen for each other citizen, brought to life in the institutions of the city, such as election to magistracies and juries by lottery? Insect swarms survive and persist in the most difficult of conditions, collectively, rather than, as do many mammals, in isolation from one another or in smaller groupings. The swarm, the horde of insects, resembles a city, a tribe, with its much greater population, often with hierarchies, duties, and internal differences, and it endures, the anonymity of its units seeming to produce that very perseverance. If the individual perishes, the collective carries on.[25]

The analogy between insects and men, the swarm of warriors, recalls another moment in the *Iliad*, where fighters on opposing sides of the Trojan War, Sarpedon and Glaukos, discuss their enmity and the friendship that binds their two families across enemy lines. Glaukos likens individual human lives to the leaves on a great tree that itself does not perish:

> Like the generations of leaves, the lives of mortal men.
> Now the wind scatters the old leaves across the earth,
> now the living timber bursts with the new buds
> and spring comes round again. And so with men:
> as one generation comes to life, another dies away.
> (*Iliad* 6.157–60)

If Achilles' warrior companions resemble ants, they will outlive him and Patroclus; they are a sturdy, indestructible, even immortal tribe, and their armor, the metal covering them as they fight, the greaves, metal coverings for their shins, make them all the more insectoid, all the more resistant to annihilation. Like a multigenerational swarm of leaves, the genealogy of warriors survives.

ART SWARMS

Michael Shanks, in his iconoclastic, inspiring work on classical archaeology, has described the swarms of animals that appear on the vases of the city of Corinth in the eighth century BCE, thus contemporaneous with the telling of the myths of Troy in epic poetry. His formally innovative collage, a reflection on the intersection of practices that result in what was called "proto-Corinthian" decoration, marks changes that occurred in the lifeworld of

Corinth: "To accept, find significance in, enjoy figured design is to enter an ideological world of masculine sovereignty, a world which determines the powers of a minority over others, and the mechanisms whereby this may be achieved. The new developments involved redefinition or reworking of the material and conceptual resources at the base of elite practice, new orientations for the energies of the propertied class and its community."[26] Some of the creatures that later appear dancing in the orchestra of the classical Athenian comic theater appear on the vases Shanks describes: "Birds are significant in this Korinthian imagery simply in terms of their numbers. Nearly half of all animate creatures on earlier friezes are birds. . . . If the designs upon the shields of painted hoplites are considered to indicate something of the soldier behind, then the bird, particularly the flying bird of prey, is the mirror of the hoplite infantryman" (90–91).[27] Shanks argues that the makers of Corinthian pots acted according to psychic and political investments, to interests, in their work: "Animals are brought to order in their stylisation on Korinthian pots, I suggest, because their contagious otherness threatens. Violence and war are of an experience where the animal erupts into the human. . . . Violence with its associated techniques of the body and material culture such as armour, allows the soldier to find identity with his bestial interior while avoiding being devoured by it. The animal interior threatens, so men upon the pots do not usually appear with the lions" (125).[28] Are the birds, wasps, frogs of comedy, dancing in unison, the bestial interiority of the human audience that is being mastered by the choreography of the chorus? The menace of the swarm is hinted at, even as the artists appropriate it for the civilization of the city.

Shanks stresses the domestication of the bestial through social practices, alluding to the distinction made by Deleuze and Guattari between the "war machine" and the state. He argues: "It is better to think of warfare and the state, of a societal (state) taming of the violence of war, bringing war within its sphere. This involves the control of otherness through armour and the phalanx, the lifestyles of hero and mercenary, and animals overcoded and tamed, their otherness controlled" (138). The situation of the classical city is very different from that of eighth-century Corinth (and Shanks chastises me for generalizing from Hesiod to Plato [106]), but his remarks are fascinating, especially since he allows himself a very wide range of comparison, from that Corinth to the Freikorps of Germany in the wake of World War I.[29] Are the animal friezes and animal choruses in classical theater efforts to control otherness, to tame and instrumentalize the bestiality of humankind, their loss of humanness in war, as seen in the frenzies of the hero Achilles in the *Iliad*? Shank's discussion of the Corinthian material, animals on pottery, hoplite armor as a kind of costume, suggests links with sixth-century

Dionysiac creatures in other vase decorations connected with the beginnings of Dionysiac festivals in Athens, depicting processions held in honor of the god and eventually resulting in the theater festivals possibly instituted by Peisistratos, the sixth-century Athenian tyrant.

FLEAS AND LICE

A wide variety of swarms, including insects, interested ancient Greek thinkers, and provided various sorts of metaphorical and analogical examples of intervention in human existence and of human collectivity, both repellent and admirable:

> The slightest quantity of putrefying matter gives rise to fleas (they are found taking shape where there is any dry moisture from living animals as it congeals outside them; lice are produced out of flesh). When lice are going to be produced, as it were small eruptions form, but without any purulent matter in them; and if these are pricked, lice emerge. Some people get this disease when there is a great deal of moisture in the body; some indeed have been killed by it, as Alkman the poet is said to have been, and Pherekydes the Syrian. (Aristotle, *Historia animalium* 556b)

Aristotle's account of the pre-Socratic Pherecydes' death by lice is repeated by the later author Aelian (second–third century CE):

> Pherecydes of Syros ended his life in the most painful way a man can, because his whole body was consumed by lice. When his appearance became hideous he withdrew from ordinary society. If anyone called to ask how he was, he would push a finger denuded of flesh through a hole in the door and say that his whole body was in a similar condition. The inhabitants of Delos say that the god of Delos brought this upon him as an act of vengeance. He was sitting with a group of pupils on Delos, they say, and after making many other remarks about his wisdom he went so far as to say that he sacrificed to no god, but still had lived no less agreeably and painlessly than men who had sacrificed hecatombs. For this lightheaded talk he paid the heaviest penalty. (Aelian, *Historical Miscellany* 4.28; Diogenes Laertius 1.118)[30]

Here infestation with insects is a punishment for atheism, the gods' vengeance on human indifference to their power. Lice figure too in the fragments of Heraclitus, this one recorded by the late author Hippolytus: "Men are deceived in their knowledge of things that are manifest, even as Homer was who was the wisest of all the Greeks. For he was even deceived by boys killing lice when they said to him: What we have seen and grasped, these we leave behind; whereas what we have not seen and grasped, these we carry away" (Hippolytus, *Refutation of All Heresies* 9.9.6). Homer failed to provide an answer to the riddle posed by the boys in their play; the insects are everywhere, and they represent an unknowable excess, a swarming supplement to human awareness.

The fleas, or lice, are generated out of putrefying matter, and lice in particular emerge out of the flesh, in Aristotle's view. They are intimates of human beings. And they are, like bees, parthenogenically produced, without interaction between genders, but emerging out of other sorts of matter as it decays. It is striking that the poet Alcman, the singer of Sparta who composed a moving and vital *Partheneion*, a choral song performed it seems by a chorus of Spartan "maidens," was also said to have been consumed by lice. Can we see the chorus of maidens, also deployed by the Lesbian poet Sappho in various songs, including *epithalamia*, "wedding songs," as a beautiful, maidenly swarm? Alcman, like Pherecydes, was killed by a swarm, generated out of the body.

CICADAS

Myth records the origin of another, more beneficent insect collectivity, the cicadas. The goddess Eos, the Dawn, became enamored of Tithonos, a son of Laomedon, king of Troy, and begged Zeus to make her mortal lover immortal, and he did. But Eos failed to ask Zeus for agelessness for her lover. The terrible ironies of this union are drawn out in greater detail by the poets, the most poignant telling of the Tithonos-Eos story coming in the *Homeric Hymn to Aphrodite*. After seducing the mortal Anchises, the goddess Aphrodite tells him the monitory tale of the union of the dawn goddess Eos and her immortalized lover, Tithonos:

> When the first gray hairs began to flow down
> From his comely head and noble chin,
> Mighty Eos did refrain from his bed,
> Though she kept him in her house and pampered him
> With food and ambrosia and gifts of fine clothing.
> But when detested old age weighed heavy on him
>
> And he could move or lift none of his limbs,
> This is the counsel that to her seemed best in her heart:
> She placed him in a chamber and shut its shining doors.

His voice flows endlessly and there is no strength,
Such as there was before, in his crooked limbs.
(228–38)[31]

The legend recurs in Sappho 58, a fragment recently supplemented by new papyrus discoveries, in which she, the poet, alludes to the immortality of Tithonos, the beloved, who differs from her in her old age, as human beings must die.[32] Later accounts report that Tithonos's thin, tiny, tinny voice finally metamorphosed into the tribe of cicadas, this in Hellanicus (ca. 480–395 BCE; *FGrH* 4 F 140), a mythographer and writer of chronicles from Sappho's own island of Lesbos.

Cicadas constitute an anonymous, collective multitude, singing ceaselessly, in a light voice, and they are associated with the aged very early, with the old men of Troy (*Iliad* 3), with legends of long life, or of immortality, as they are on the Shang bronzes of ancient China. Plato's *Phaedrus* recalls another version of their origins. Socrates and young Phaedrus walk outside Athens' wall, and stroll alongside the river Ilissos, coming upon a plane tree, and a nymphaeum. There the character Socrates recounts the myth of the origins of the cicadas, this group possessing a benign genealogy, a version of near immortality, and a link with the Muses:

> "The story is that once upon a time these creatures were men—men of an age before there were any Muses—and that when the latter came into the world, and music made its appearance, some of the people of those days were so thrilled with pleasure that they went on singing, and quite forgot to eat and drink until they actually died without noticing it. From them in due course sprang the race of cicadas, to which the Muses have granted the boon of needing no sustenance right from their birth, but of singing from the very first, without food or drink, until the day of their death, after which they go and report to the Muses how they severally are paid honor among mankind, and by whom." (259b–c)

The cicadas, then, act as spies for the gods.

The Athenians themselves, as a people, referred to this swarm of insects in their dress. The cicadas, like the Athenians, were thought to have emerged autochthonously from the earth of Attica. And one of the origin legends of the city referred to the birth of Erechtheus from that same soil; Hephaistos had impregnated the earth after attempting to force himself on the goddess Athena, who repelled his advances and caused him to ejaculate on her cloak. She wiped his semen from her garment with a bit of wool, threw it to the ground, and from this contact emerged the first Athenian. Part of the garb of the traditional, elite Athenian was a golden *tettix*, or "cicada," an ornament worn in the hair, to mark the autochthonous origin of his people. Cicadas were believed to be long-lived, perhaps immortal, emerging after burial in the earth to new life, and born from the earth itself, like the earliest Athenian.

Meleager of Gadara in the first century BCE wrote this salute to the cicada, fellow poet and singer: "Noisy cicada, drunk with dew drops, you sing your rustic ditty that fills the wilderness with voice, and seated on the edge of the leaves, striking with saw-like legs your sunburnt skin, you shrill music like the lyre's. But sing, dear, some new tune to gladden the woodland nymphs, strike up some strain responsive to Pan's pipe, that I may escape from Love and snatch a little midday sleep, reclining here beneath the shady plane-tree" (Meleager, *Greek Anthology* 7, frag. 196; Loeb trans. modified). This appeal to the benign and gifted insect singer recalls Plato's version of the cicada's origins, and its place in idyllic pastoral settings.[33]

ANCIENT BEES

Bees, in antiquity, as noted earlier, are often seen as benefactors of humankind, and as exemplary citizens of the hive. The archaic poet Semonides, in a misogynist diatribe, identifies the "bee"-woman as the exception to his catalogue of sow-, vixen-, dog-, ass-, weasel-wives: "One from a bee: he's lucky who gets her, / for she's the only one on whom no blame / alights."[34] For Xenophon too, bees function as a model for orderly and stratified life. And when they suffer from overpopulation, they send out colonies, just as the Greek cities did (*Oikonomikos* 7.34, 38; *Cyropaedia* 5.1.24). In Plato's *Phaedo*, Socrates, on the verge of drinking hemlock, discusses with his friend Cebes the nature of the soul and its fate after death:

> "I suppose that the happiest people, and those who reach the best destination, are the ones who have cultivated the goodness of an ordinary citizen, so-called 'temperance' and 'justice,' which is acquired by habit and practice, without the help of philosophy and reason."
>
> "How are these the happiest?"
>
> "Because they will probably pass into some other kind of social and disciplined creature like bees, wasps and ants; or even back into the human race again, becoming decent citizens." (82b)[35]

These human beings, though "happiest," from the point of view of the philosopher, are inferior to the lover of learning, the philosopher, who scorns the body and liberates himself from the prison bars of the senses. But they are desirable as citizens of an ideal city, pure, chaste, docile, and disciplined, accepting the hierarchy and the division of labor Plato urges in the *Republic*.[36]

ARISTOTLE ON INSECTS AND OTHER ANIMALS

By the fourth century BCE, the possibilities of analogy between animals and human beings, as often performed in Old Comedy, had diminished. After the time of Plato, the non-Athenian philosopher Aristotle, he who wrote the great treatise *The Poetics*, discussed earlier, also compiled a vast corpus of works on a variety of topics, from the history of philosophy to political history and analysis, from long-influential consideration of slaves and their nature to careful study of animals. His works, many of which were probably reconstructed from students' notes on his lectures, or from the labors of his followers, not written by "Aristotle-the-author," are among the most valuable and richest sources of our understanding of how the ancient Greeks conceived of their existence among other beings. In his works on biology and politics, Aristotle denied reason to the animals, in contrast to the Cynics, another philosophical school that developed out of the Socratic model, whose followers thought that animals, in their simplicity and abiding in nature, had a superior way of life to that of human beings.

Aristotle touches on the powers of the swarm in his work on natural history: "Plants clearly live even when divided, and some of the insects also; which implies that the parts have a soul specifically if not numerically the same as that of the whole; at any rate each of the two parts has sensation and moves in space for some time" (*On the Soul* 411b20).[37] The insects, then, can be divided and their parts survive severed from the whole; soul is attributed to these parts. Not only do insects live in collectives, in groups, but the parts of their bodies also form a collective that can break up into smaller units, in a strange configuration that recalls the formation of the chorus, from which the individual chorus leader can step forth and speak in the chorus's or the playwright's voice.

There are countless analogies made, explicit and implicit, between human beings and the animals treated in Aristotelian biological works. Aristotle categorizes as "political" (*politika*) living beings, those social animals "which all have some common activity," including "the human being, bee, wasp, ant and crane" (*Historia animalium* 488a8–13), using the adjective derived from the human community, the *polis*, the "city-state." The common activities of such beings, human and animal, distinguish them from gregarious animals (*agelaia*), which flock together and move as a community, but do not share a common project. The swarm of the bees has a special character, marked by Aristotle in the treatise *The Generation of Animals*. Here the philosopher and naturalist includes birds in his account of "blooded" animals, while insects fall into the class of "bloodless." In Greek, they are called *entoma*, which literally means "cut in pieces," like the victims of sacrifice. He refers to the shape of their bodies, in distinct and separate pieces: "I call insects those creatures which have insections (*entomas*) on their bodies" (*Historia animalium* 487a).[38] These elements of the insect body are discussed more fully in the treatise called *Parts of Animals*, where Aristotle reflects on the efficient shaping of the insect body: "Whenever it is possible to employ two organs for two pieces of work without their getting in each other's way, Nature (*phusis*) provides and employs two. Her habits are not those of the coppersmith who for cheapness' sake makes you a spit-and-lampstand combination. Still, where two are impossible, Nature employs the same organ to perform several pieces of work" (*Parts of Animals* 683a20–30).[39] In the *Generation of Animals*, which describes reproduction in all its many forms, Aristotle is said to have believed in a difference between bees and other insects, and his view corresponds with other reflections on the reproduction of bees, said, for example, by Virgil in the *Georgics* (4.284) to occur spontaneously from the blood of slaughtered bulls or oxen, a technique of reproduction learned from the Egyptians.

The Loeb editor of the *Generation of Animals* suggests that the following passage is out of place; as discussed earlier, these treatises represent, according to scholars, notes taken by students of Aristotle's teaching, and so the ordering and wording are not authoritative, authorial. But this is what the text records concerning bees: "Another piece of evidence which goes to show that bees are generated without copulation is that the brood appears to be quite small in the cells of the comb, whereas those insects which are generated by means of copulation (a) spend a long time in intercourse, and (b) quickly bring forth their offspring, which is of the nature of a larva and of considerable size" (*Generation of Animals* 760b–761a).[40] Bees are somehow reproduced without contact between male and female insects. In the following section, on bees' kin, hornets and wasps, the text says that "they contain no divine ingredient (*outhen theion*) as the tribe (*genos*) of bees does" (761a). It is not clear why Aristotle might think bees alone have an element of the divine in their makeup, unless it is their capacity for spontaneous generation. Elsewhere in the *Historia animalium* "Aristotle" argues that while other insects are reproduced from their own kind, "some, however, are not produced from animals at all, but spontaneously: some are produced out of the dew which falls on foliage, . . . others in putrefying mud and dung" (*Historia animalium* 551a1–5).

Using a category derived from human hierarchies, Aristotle describes a distinction in bees between what he calls "kings," *basileis*, and drones, *ta kephenia* (624a35), interestingly designated in the neuter case here, although Hesiod had assumed that the drones are lazy female bees who contribute nothing to the sustenance of the hive. Later Aristotle calls them *hoi kephenes*, using the masculine gender for the drones (624a). The drones remain for the most part inside the hive (as most citizen-class women in ancient Athens stayed in their homes), while the "kings" fly out with their whole swarm (*esmos*). *Esmos* is correlated with another word, *smenos*, which also means a swarm as well as the hive of the bees, and is derived from the verb *hiemi*, "to set going." The philosopher represents the swarm of insects with continuing analogies to human beings, in a practice that had found its echo in the representation of swarms in the comic choruses of the fifth century BCE.

Aristotle offers an extensive study of bees in his *Historia animalium*. He returns to the dominant bees, calling them "kings," "leaders" (*hegemones*), distinct from the "robber" (*phor*), and drone, which can damage the others' work. "When caught they are killed by the good, useful working (*khreston*) bees" (624a17). Aristotle's account of the life of the bees does not go so far as some later allegories, but he does describe a way of living for the bees that privileges good kings, or leaders, and condemns the robbers and drones, using analogies between animal and human, insect swarm and human collectivity. He appears to admire the order and productivity of the collective life of these insects: "The creatures that develop in the hives and damage the combs are cleaned out by the good working bees (*hai de khrestai melittai*) [these bees are feminine in gender]" (625b35).The word used for "cleaning out" the bad bees is *ekkathairousin*, from the same root as the well-known term Aristotle uses in the *Poetics*, *katharsis*, which has had a long history and has become an English word as well. Here the compound, with the prefix *ek-*, denotes a thorough clearing out of the bad element; the catharsis provided by tragedy would seem similarly to get rid of unwelcome emotional content in the spectator. In the description of apian life, Aristotle goes on to comment again on the moral stature of various bees; as the cleaning occurs "the other bees because of their *bad character* look on unconcerned at the destruction of the work" (626a1, emphasis mine). The word translated as "bad character" is *kakian*, a noun derived from the adjective *kakos*, which means all bad—"ill, evil, bad in its kind, worthless, ugly, evil, wicked, cowardly, mean, vile"—all these terms providing moral evaluation of the bad bees, which may be the younger and therefore ignorant members of the community (626b3-4), anthropomorphized in analogy with reckless youth like certain characters of ancient drama.

Aristotle also, in less detail, describes the life of another swarm, the wasps, those insects immortalized, metamorphosed in their human form in Old Comedy. These wasps are generated by the "mother-wasp," curiously gendered female unlike the "kings" of the bee community (628a15–20). After their generation, the "leaders," masculine *hegemones*, remain inside their comb, while the workers fly out. The "mother-wasp" is broad, heavy, not designed for flying, and "this is why they sit always in the wasp-combs, fashioning and arranging things within" (628a30–34). Clearly, wasps are less fascinating than the bees, about whom moral judgments can be made. Can all these attributes of the insects be extended to those who dressed as insects and performed, dancing and singing, in the orchestra of ancient comedy, exhibiting diligence and hostility, leadership and reckless bad character? Human behavior affects Aristotle's characterizations of the animals; animal behavior marks the performances of comic choruses.

BECOMING INSECT

The comic playwright presents insects, stinging, quite different from the bees, in Aristophanes' *Wasps*. The animal, bird, and insect choruses of classical Athenian Old Comedy, for whom the plays are named, owe something to the traditions of animal fables associated with the former slave Aesop,[41] mentioned by the character Philocleon toward the end of the *Wasps* (1401, 1445). In Aesop's fables there are crickets, a famous dung beetle, a relation of whom appears in Aristophanes' *Peace*, and of whom Philocleon starts to tell a tale (*Wasps* 1447), and other often benignly regarded instances of insects. But Aesop's creatures usually do not appear in swarms; they are more often individualized in the moralizing narratives. In the most compelling representation of human beings as insects, the *Wasps* indicted the classical Athenian jury system in this comedy known for its chorus.

In their work on Kafka, Gilles Deleuze and Félix Guattari discuss the issue of species transformation in the Czech author's work, in terms that enable a richer discussion of choral metamorphosis in ancient comedy: "To become animal is to participate in movement, to stake out the path of escape in all its positivity, to cross a threshold, to reach a continuum of pure intensities where all forms come undone, as do all the significations, signifiers, and signifieds, to the benefit of an unformed matter of deterritorialized flux, or non-signifying signs."[42] The most notorious transformation in Kafka's corpus is a "becoming-insect," as Gregor Samsa becomes a beetle, a cockroach, and some of the most painful aspects of his fate concern his exoskeleton and its vulnerability to human aggression, isolated as he is from his own kind, or trapped between these two kinds, with the consciousness of a human being and the body of the insect. It is significant that Kafka's insect-man is so fragile, so susceptible to aggression, and so silent, while the insect-men of ancient Greek comedy relish their own powers. Although aging, they still have the power to sing, to buzz, injure, sting, and convict wrongdoers in the courts of their city.

Scholars have written of the psychoanalytic dimensions of Aristophanic comedy, the struggle between fathers and sons, the regression to adolescence of its heroes, their exuberant abandonment of repression, as in the *Wasps'* old man character, Philocleon. Deleuze and Guattari see such comic phenomena differently, critical of the limiting and restrictive Oedipalization of humankind, writing of metamorphoses in Kafka: "Insofar as the comic expansion of Oedipus allows one to see these other oppressor triangles through the lens of the microscope, there appears at the same time the possibility of an escape, a line of escape. To the inhumanness of the 'diabolical powers,' there is the answer of a becoming-animal: to become a beetle, ... rather than lowering one's head and remaining a bureaucrat, inspector, judge or judged."[43] The authors trace with regret the limits, the constraints placed on Gregor become-insect: "The acts of becoming-animal cannot follow their principle all the way through, ... they maintain a certain ambiguity that leads to their insufficiency and condemns them to defeat"; "Aren't the animals still too formed, too significative, too territorialized?"[44] The wasps of fifth-century Athenian comedy, and in the works of the fourth-century philosopher Plato, become docile, socialized, productive cicadas and bees; in contrast, Aristophanes' swarm remains potent, vocal, aggressive, and capable of song and dance.

THE *WASPS*

I turn now to the wild and extravagant comic chorus of the *Wasps*,[45] with particular attention to its role in the overall drama, in order to consider how the chorus, as a swarm, becoming animal, hybrid wasp-human, figures in the play. The chorus of insect-men at some moments seems to be the whole of which one of the central characters, the old man Philocleon, is a part. They are his comrades, his collective. They also stand for a certain nostalgia concerning the past of Athens, its role in the early fifth-century war against the Persians, the Athenians' sense of victory in their response to the immense challenge from Asia, a moment of the developing democracy before the advent of what are represented as greedy, manipulative statesmen. The insectoid chorus members preserve a rowdy, swarm-like lust and greed themselves that pit them against the luxuriousness and preciosity of the other central character of the comedy, the young son Bdelycleon.

It is difficult to discern a "comic hero" in this play, although some have tried. The son, Bdelycleon, or "Loathecleon," as he is called in Jeffery Henderson's superb translation,[46] has many flaws; he is disrespectful of his unruly father, willful, and determined to smooth off his parent's rough edges and turn him into a fit companion for the son's aristocratic and cultivated friends, to such a degree that he seems neglectful and even abusive toward the old man. And that old man is unmanageable, not heroic in the least in most senses of the word, a character who can't control his own addiction to the court, to judging and convicting and carousing with his comrades, like him veterans of the old war against the Persian barbarians, and taking their pleasure in enacting what they believe to be their power and authority in jury duty.

In the *Wasps*, the insect swarm represent the stinging, dangerous kind of winged creatures. Aristotle in his *Historia animalium*, as noted earlier, devotes much less attention to wasps and hornets than to bees, which seem more amenable to allegorization. But he does observe that there are both wild and less wild wasps, that the former "all have stings and are fiercer and sting more painfully than the others" (627b24–28). The tamer sort has leaders called "mother-wasps," and workers. He records mating, but claims "the embryos do not seem to be produced by birth but to be straightaway too large to be born from a wasp" (628b18–19). Are we to understand that, like bees, the wasps have some kind of extraordinary mode of generation? The notes, or the text of Aristotle, remark that no one has seen inside the "wasperies," "nor has anyone yet been seen who has himself observed old age (*geras*) in either a mother-wasp or the wild wasps" (628a28–30). This is an interesting detail, since the wasps of Aristophanes are old men, having participated actively in the war with the Persians at the beginning of the fifth century.

These comic wasps seem to have been equipped not only with the padded buttocks and phalluses of most comedy choruses; they also call attention to a special stinger protruding from those buttocks, phallus-like but a supplement to suggest the hypervirility, superaggression, and lust of these veterans. The chorus of wasps enters the play to pick up their colleague, the old man and father Philocleon, "Lovecleon," a fellow juror whose addiction to the courts is despaired of by his son, "Loathecleon," who has locked his father in the house to prevent his going off with his friends to register for the day's court sessions. The aged veteran is guarded by two slaves who engage in characteristic humor about their sufferings, meant to amuse an audience inured to the pains of these their human possessions. One of the slaves, Xanthias, later claims that the playwright will not resort to the typical slave routines in this play, nor will a pair of slaves be "broadcasting basketfuls of nuts to the spectators" (58–59). But as the play begins, the first to speak, Sosias, warns the second, the sleeping Xanthias, that if he disobeys, "your ribs will have a bad grudge against you" (3). References to physical punishment—beating, flogging, and such—abound in these plays, and slavery, in fact, is thematized in this comedy, as Philocleon's son will later claim that his father is not a free man, but himself enslaved, virtually, to Cleon, a popular leader in the politics of the democratic city.

The play was produced in 422, and overtly attacks Cleon, represented in the comedy as a dangerous demagogue. This politician, who pushed the city toward aggressive engagement in continuing the war with the Spartans, fell in and out of favor with the people as the fortunes of antagonists in the Peloponnesian War (431–404 BCE) waxed and waned. According to the Aristophanic biography, imaginary and unreliable as noted earlier, Cleon had lost power after some setbacks when the city approved a brief treaty with the Lacedaimonians and their allies, but then, following the revolt of some subject cities of the Athenians, resumed his program of pressing for war. Cleon had earlier been a target for comedy, as will be discussed in the chapter on *parrhesia*, "free speech." Here the play dwells on the ways in which the judicial system, especially the courts where jurors were citizens representing the whole of the *demos*, succumbed in the playwright's view to manipulation by Cleon and other such politicians. The jurors are presented as victims of propaganda and coercion, and of the handouts given to them by these politicians. According to the unreliable biographical traditions, often based on the extant plays, Aristophanes himself did loathe Cleon, and they had confrontations in the courts themselves, but, as noted earlier, these fragments of biographical information must be taken with a grain of salt.

Douglas MacDowell, in his edition of the *Wasps*, contributes some nuance to the common interpretation that Aristophanes is justifiably producing a whole-hearted condemnation of the jury system, and he emphasizes the democratic nature of representation and judgment in the Athenian courts, which had no judges, only jurors:

> It is undoubtedly true that this system was democratic, and that the large juries were more representative of the Athenians than small juries or individual judges would have been. Another advantage was that a large jury was hard to bribe. But there were some serious disadvantages as well.
> One was that a jury was a crowd rather than a number of individuals. It was easily influenced by a skillful orator (like Kleon), but it could not easily give rigorous scrutiny to the details of a case or appreciate the merits of a case which was badly presented.[47]

The juries might favor Cleon, since he had increased the pay of jurors. But as MacDowell also notes, "The Athenians were people of an independent turn of mind; they were not sheep (despite *Wasps* 31–6). Probably the picture was not as black as he [Aristophanes] paints it."[48]

If we recall the comment of William Blake, that in his *Paradise Lost* Milton was unwillingly, or unbeknownst to himself, of the devil's party, on the side of Satan, then we might acknowledge a similar affection for some of the personae and chorus members of this drama that transcends, or even at times disrupts, the overt communications of characters supposedly representative of the playwright himself. In the case of the wasps, along with an overt critique of Cleon, there is also a contradictory identification with and delight in the wasp chorus's irascible, aggressive, nostalgic collective dancing and singing in opposition to "Loathecleon." The wasps make up an irrepressible swarm, a lustful, greedy, veteran collective from whose numbers the son of their comrade tries to separate him, with very limited success, as we see from the play's conclusion.

But first, who are these wasps? As they enter, the chorus leader calls attention to their advanced age, recalling Phrynichus, a writer of tragedy from the time of the Persian Wars, some fifty years before the first performance of the *Wasps*, mocking another elderly chorus member for his difficulties in walking or dancing: "I'm afraid what's here is—oh my!—all that's left of that youthful time, when we shared guard duty at Byzantium, you and I" (235–37). The city of Byzantium had been taken from the Persians more than fifty years before.

The chorus leader eagerly anticipates the court duty he and his fellow jurors will undertake today, using language appropriate to his wasp identity, looking forward to condemning the politician Laches, enemy of Cleon, as we see later in the play. An elected general, he had advocated a treaty with Sparta, and thus earned the hostility of the supposedly warmongering Cleon. Laches had led a military campaign to Sicily some years earlier, and was perhaps prosecuted for his actions there. The chorus leader, in his wasp persona, relishes the prospect of trying him, and sings, "Everybody says he [Laches]'s stuffed his hive (*simblon*) with money" (241). A *simblos* is a hive, or any kind of hoard, but the use of the word here makes Laches an insect like the members of the chorus, greedy and eager to store away treasure.

The slave Xanthias has already described the old man Philocleon as having characteristics like those of the wasps, carrying out his assignment as a member of a jury, marking a waxen tablet for punishment: "From sheer nastiness he scratches a long penalty line for all convicts, and comes with his nails caked with wax like a honeybee or bumblebee" (106–8). Using this substance derived from bees, the wax applied to a wooden tablet, the jurors recorded the degree of punishment to be assigned to a convicted defendant.[49]

Yearning to get to his task, the old man swarms like a host of insects in his attempts to escape from his son's house, crawling through gutters, through cracks in the walls, finally only confined by netting surrounding the house. He claims he is swarming like smoke, emerging from the chimney, and climbs onto the roof like a sparrow. The son, Loathecleon, characterizes his father and his comrades: "whoever riles that tribe of oldsters riles a wasps' nest. They've even got stingers, extremely sharp, sticking out from their rumps, that they stab with, and they leap and attack, crackling like sparks" (223–27). Enter the chorus.

As noted, this swarm has an extra, superphallic attachment, emerging from the backs of their costumes, not content with the padded phalluses that many comic choruses wore. When their comrade Philocleon does not emerge from his son's house to join them, the chorus leader encourages his fellow chorus members to "sing and call him out," and they comply, calling him "old man," *geron*, worrying that he's injured himself stumbling around in the dark. Once upon a time, they sing, he was the "fiercest," "keenest," *drimutatos* (275) of all. They try to tempt him with the image of a juicy victim awaiting trial. The chorus leader has a boy with him, who asks for figs, and the father pleads poverty. From the tiny allowance given to the jurors, he must get food, and wood, for his family, and if there is no court session, they will starve. This moment in the play, which in its entirety might be seen by some as an assault on the Athenians' jury system, liable as it could be to manipulation by the powerful, nonetheless reminds the spectator of the poor, those who have no part, whose livelihood is dependent on the welfare schemes of the *polis*, including payment for jury service. And the recognition of this vulnerability shows the playwright's recognition of the complexity, the varied interests of the chorus, and of the audience itself, its embeddedness in the life of the city, the porosity between comic representation and everyday life.

Philocleon yearns to join them in court, even though he is not subject to the deprivations they suffer, sustained as he is by his prosperous son. He complains that even a gnat can't escape the house, and the chorus echoes this insectoid language, singing to summon him: "It's daybreak, little honey-bee (*melittion*)" (366). Addressing him affectionately with this diminutive, they swarm around, encouraging him to defy his son and join them, and as he appears, finally threatening with their waspish rage:

Tell me, why are we waiting to launch the wrath
we feel when anyone vexes our nest?

Out now, out now
with that sharp-tempered stinger that we use to punish,
and brace it sharply.

(403–7)

The joys of phallic potency are evoked here with the summoning of their supplementary, punishing, stinging protuberance. The chorus creates a mood of rage, lust, and aggression that characterizes them throughout the earlier part of this comedy, and in which the character Philocleon longs to share. They accuse his son of tyrannical behavior (417), a frequently deployed trope of the contemporary political discourse, which seethes with claims of intended tyranny and denunciations of dictatorial behavior, anathema to the ideology of the democracy.

Xanthias the slave exclaims, shocked: "They've really got stingers (*kentr'*)!" (420). And they rejoice in these corporeal weapons: "And we'll destroy you as well with them! Now every man wheel this way, draw stingers and charge him, with ranks closed, in good order, full of rage and spirit, so he'll never forget what a swarm (*smenos*) he's angered" (421–25). Using the military vocabulary of the phalanx, the chorus leader incites his swarm to violence against the son of his comrade, recalling a former victim of their wrath. The language of the hive coalesces with the terminology of human battle. The slave Xanthias blurts out his fear as he regards the wasps' stingers, he himself threatened by the chorus leader: "Now let the man go. If you don't, I do declare you'll envy turtles their shells" (428–29). The chorus leader, as wasp, suggests that he will torment and sting the human slave, who will wish he had the animal's shell to protect him. Such threats are common in comedy; the masters allude to their power over the slaves, their willingness to resort to beating unruly slaves. The vulnerability of slaves to corporeal punishment and abuse is a constant source of amusement in these plays, and the chorus leader takes advantage of his ambiguous role as insect and citizen to remind the slave of his subjection.

In this scene, after the chorus leader's threats, the old man Lovecleon joins in with his call to military action, emphasizing the metaphorical connection between the insect swarm and a phalanx of the city's hoplites, their infantry, although this group is really an air force: "At 'em then, fellow jurors, sharp-hearted wasps! Division One get riled up and dive-bomb his arse! Division Two stab all around his eyes, and his fingers too!" (430–32). The chorus leader threatens those slaves who guard Lovecleon with the wasps' powers, their sharpness, like mustard (*kardama*). Loathecleon orders the slaves to beat the wasps off, away from the house, but the swarm transcends the power of an earthbound infantry, attacking with aerial ferocity, mobility, and military discipline.

The subsequent debate between father and son concerns the latter's claim that his father has been "enslaved" to Cleon, the dictator, the demagogue, the tyrant who controls the jurors. He argues that the jurors' leaders, their trainers, keep them waspish so they will attack the leaders' enemies, instead of providing for them as they deserve. And eventually the chorus leader is convinced; Lovecleon's son promises to provide for him, but the old man stubbornly resists the blandishments proffered. He still wants to be a juror, one of the swarm.

In the parabasis, the chorus's address directly to the audience, the chorus leader reminds the spectators and judges of the playwright's courage in attacking "the greatest monsters," including Cleon himself. Even though they failed to recognize the comic poet with a prize the year before, the chorus leader wants them to celebrate his new ideas, his fresh approach. And the chorus as a group goes on to lament their aging, pointing to the limpness of their phalluses, their white hair. They explain their appearance, their "wasp waists," and their stingers. And they recall, in the most waspish passage of the entire play, their manly exploits of the past. I cite their words at length, because their boasting reveals the history that binds them into a collective, proud swarm: "We who sport this kind of rump are the only true indigenous native (*autokhthones*) Athenians, a most virile breed and one that very substantially aided this city in battle, that time the barbarian came spewing smoke over all the city and incinerating it, intent upon forcibly eradicating our hives" (1075–80). The wasps call themselves "autochthones," born from the earth itself. True Athenians counted their lineage from this origin, like the cicadas; they claimed legitimacy as citizens, and their rights to the privileges of citizens, based on this myth of generation, which justified their place in the democracy, and protected them from enslavement according to the laws promulgated by the Athenian lawgiver of the sixth century BCE, Solon. If the aristocrats of Athens and other cities claimed superiority because of their descent from other gods and heroes, these democratic jurors, bound by equality, by *isonomia*, jointly rejoice in their autochthony.[50]

When in 480 BCE the massive Persian army invaded Greece and came down into Athens itself, burning the city and its temples, reaching the Acropolis, the height of the urban center and site of its greatest edifices celebrating the goddess Athena and the god Poseidon, these wasps fought back. At Marathon, ten years later, in the famous battle led by the Athenians, the Persians were pushed back, defeated, as the chorus recalls here, the enemy "stung in the jaws and the eyebrows" (1088). And, the swarm boastfully reminds their audience: "That's why today barbarians everywhere insist that there's nothing manlier (*andrikoteron*) than an Attic wasp" (1089–90). Their assertion of virility, of aggressive, collective, successful action has no parallel, and forms the basis, in fact, of the justifications of Athenian hegemony in the mid-fifth century, the brief but dominant phase of Attic empire over the eastern Mediterranean. The wasps claim that they alone have provided the circumstances in which Athens can exact tribute from its allies, that very tribute that the younger generation is stealing.

The chorus leader continues in this vein, explaining the nature of his cadre of wasps. I cite his speech at length, because it seems to me to serve as the essential declaration of the nature of this democratic collective, here exemplified in the form of a swarm:

> Looking at us from all sides, you'll find that in our character and lifestyle (*tous tropous kai ten diaitan*) we're in all respects most like wasps. First, no creature is more sharp-tempered than we are when irritated, or more cantankerous. Then again, we engineer everything else just like wasps: we gather in swarms (*kath'esmous*) as if into nests, some of us judging in the archon's court, some before the Eleven, and some in the Odeum, packed in tight against the walls like this, hunched toward the ground and hardly moving, like grubs in their cells. (1101–11)

His is a marvelously vivid picture both of the wasps and of the physical situation of the law courts of the Athenian *polis*. The wasps are cranky, they gather in swarms, as did the jurors of the courts of the city. There were different courts depending on what sort of case was being litigated—the archons' court, the "Eleven," the Odeum. Some of these spaces have been identified in the city plan of ancient Athens. And he describes how they group together, anonymously, huddled together like the infant worms, the larvae, of the insect mass. He evokes the experience from inside, with marvelous perspectivism, the wasps barely moving, an indistinguishable body of creatures, "becoming-insect," and then from outside, as spectators would see the jurors assembled anonymously for judgment.

The wasps make their living by stinging; they get their daily pay from the city, a subsistence wage that serves as a sort of welfare provision for the elderly and impoverished of the citizens, which for Lovecleon provides not the necessities of life, which his son offers, but the pleasure of stinging, of tormenting those on trial in the courts. The chorus leader continues in this long speech by reminding the audience that "there are drones sitting among us who have no stingers, who stay at home and feed off the fruits of the tribute (*phorou*) without toiling for it" (1114–17). The "drones" (*kephenes*) differ from these manly wasps; they are lazy and parasitic, possibly effeminate. They have appeared before in Greek texts; Hesiod, as noted earlier, differentiated between the useful manly bees, and the indolent and spoiled drones, female in his understanding, who are like women, the "race," *genos*, descended from Pandora:

> Yes, wicked womenfolk are her descendants.
> They live among mortal men as a nagging burden
> and are no good sharers of abject want, but only of wealth.
> Men are like swarms of bees clinging to cave roofs
> to feed drones that contribute only to malicious deeds;
> the bees themselves all day long until sundown
> are busy carrying and storing the white wax,
> but the drones stay inside in their roofed hives
> and cram their bellies full of what others harvest.
> So, too, Zeus who roars on high made women
> to be an evil for mortal men.
> (Hesiod, *Theogony* 594–601)[51]

This passage serves as a manifesto for misogyny, using the insect analogy to naturalize manly aversion to indolent females, even though, as we know, the drones are masculine bees, not feminine.

In the case of comedy, however, the denunciation of drones takes as its target not the women of the city, who may not even have been present in the theater, but those who reap the profits of empire but fail to engage with the duties of citizenship, such as service on juries. The chorus leader expresses his view: "I think that from now on any citizen, bar none, who doesn't have a stinger should not be paid three obols" (1120–21). This is a somewhat ironic demand, since three obols is a bare, minimum wage, when the wealthy, those who benefit most from the imperial tribute and treasure, have no need for such a paltry sum. Lovecleon's son, Loathecleon, seems so prosperous that he wants to change his father's wardrobe and replace his "ratty jacket" with a sumptuous cloak woven in the Lydian city of Ecbatana in Asia Minor, a garment that carries the Orientalizing connotations of aristocratic indulgence. He further provides his father with Laconian slippers, which the latter is meant to wear "with a sort of voluptuous swagger" (1169).

Loathecleon attempts to groom his father, and make him behave appropriately for an aristocratic symposium, an occasion of male bonding, witty storytelling, elegant reclining on sofas, drinking, and singing. The father vows, in a violent reversal, now to denounce Cleon as a potential tyrant, modeling his song on a sixth-century lyric by Alcaeus warning of tyranny:

> You there, the fellow who seeks the high authority (*to mega kratos*),
> you shall upend the city yet; it's poised to tilt.
> (1234–35)

If, however, the father has been brought to his senses concerning Cleon, in these circumstances represented as a threat to aristocratic peace and hegemony, Lovecleon nonetheless cannot abide by the rules of decorum, but remains unreformed, a wasp, a juror, a democrat, an old soldier with a stinger. He utterly fails the test imposed by his son, of behaving like a gentleman at the symposium. The slaves report that Lovecleon became drunk and disorderly, ate too much, jumped around and farted, mocking his fellow guests. He compared one to a locust, insulting them, and then drunkenly started off for home.

Lovecleon enters, staggering, leading with him a woman. He's through with jury service, but has given up none of the rowdy, lustful, aggressive behavior that characterized the wasps in their populist glory. He seems to be excited by the woman he escorts, calling her by an affectionate insect name, translated by Jeffrey Henderson as "my little blonde cockchafer" (*khrusomelolonthion*), an alliterative diminutive formed from a word for a beetle, a "cockchafer," and the adjective "golden." She seems to be blonde, unusually, like Xanthias, the "tawny one," a slave. Throughout this scene, Lovecleon seems to be reverting to the law courts, asserting his expertise in legal matters, and accepting a role as a defendant rather than juror in his changed circumstances, yet his belligerence and waspishness are unabated.

Lovecleon recalls an anecdote about Aesop, who was accused by the citizens of Delphi of stealing a bowl, and was executed for his crime.[52] Insect life reemerges here again, with a celebration of a dung beetle who took revenge on the great god Zeus. The chorus notes the change in their comrade, Lovecleon, yet also reminds the audience:

> Now he's learned different ways,
> and he'll make a really great change
> to a life of delicate luxury.
> But maybe he'll not want that;
> it's hard for anyone to depart
> from his normal and natural character.
> (1452–57)

They envy his new life of comfort and mingling with the refined leaders of the symposiastic world, but recognize that he is still a wasp, even though he has the benefit of the care of his son, who seems by now to have won over the chorus of wasps.

The final scenes of the *Wasps* bear out the wasps' suspicion that the old wasp will not have learned new tricks. Lovecleon may have turned on Cleon, but he can't stop dancing, dancing like a tragic chorus member, reverting to the old competitions, and turning toward the new. He celebrates his agility; kicking his legs high, rolling his hips, he taunts the others: "Phrynichus crouches like a rooster . . . kicking his legs sky high! The arsehole splits . . . because now my hip joints roll smoothly in their sockets!" (1490–95). Philocleon rejoices in his rejuvenation, asserting his superiority to other tragic dancers: "Any tragic performer who claims to be a good dancer, come right up here and dance against me!" (1498–99). He's a great tragic dancer, but really, in fact, a comic dancer, challenging the audience, the tragic performers, and a new entity that appears on stage, the son of Karkinos, dressed as a crab, and then another, and then a third crab. Here arrive on the dramatic stage more creatures from the nonhuman domain, creatures that swarm, that move together as a teeming collective. The comedy ends with the mad spinning of Lovecleon with this new swarm, the crabs, as the chorus joins in:

> Up, you renowned children
> of Sir Salty,
> jump along the sand
> and the shore of the barren sea
> brethren of shrimps.
>   (1518–22)

Karkinos himself, father of this swarm, enters the dancing floor, and the chorus asks him to lead them, as no one ever before has done, ending the play with the comic chorus dancing ecstatically off the stage, forecasting the desired victory celebration after the dramatic festival's contest, opening the festival stage to the city, the *polis*, the *demos*. In the process, Lovecleon has been restored, become a frisky dancer once again, aligned with a new crew of wild crabby celebrants, having refused to be assimilated into the elegant, decorous, pretentious world of his son. The waspish father remains himself, energetic, lustful, and stubbornly resistant to domestication and reterritorialization, irretrievably part of the swarm.

K. J. Dover, in his edition of the *Clouds*, another comedy with a fascinating chorus, concludes:

> In *Wasps* Philokleon, once converted from his fierce and immoderate zeal for that form of public service especially open to his age, is no less immoderate in his pursuit of pleasure. Bdelykleon begins with a lunatic of one kind on his hands, and he ends with a lunatic of a worse kind, not to mention impending prosecutions for hubris. The dancing with which the play ends simply serves to swamp and stifle with noise and excitement any inclination on our part to construct a sequence of events beyond the point to which Ar. has led us.[53]

No laughing. But if we let go of the desire for plot, and sequence, and character development, so dependent on an Aristotelian orientation toward drama, the enduring waspishness and swarming vigor of the final chorus lead to another mode of interpretation of this dramatic form, comedy, with its exuberant, riotous, untamable chorus. The noise of the dancers interrupts the linear development of the *muthos* and focus on the central character, the "comic hero," if we can even imagine such a thing here, where the lover and hater of Cleon clash without resolution, with the explicit celebration of the lover ending the festivities for now, establishing a line of flight, of further riotousness to come.

Some members of the heterogeneous audience would have been reminded by the chorus leader's insistence on the extended metaphor likening the jurors, and the chorus, to a swarm of insects, of their own collective existence as a group of equals, bound by the democratic ideology of *isonomia*, "equality of rights," equality in the laws, contrasted always with the ideology of aristocracy or *eunomia*, the ideology of "good order." This latter principle drives those set on oligarchic revolution against the democracy, and such schemes as Plato's, where there is a "geometric" rather than "arithmetic" distribution of power.[54] The gifted, the intelligent, the wealthy, the good or best, the *aristoi* in such schemes would have greater power than the many. Philocleon, the waspish old man, just wants to keep dancing with his fellow swarming creatures, the crabs.

The old man's jubilation and unwillingness to be tamed, his stubborn insistence on swarming, represent a "line of flight" in Deleuze and Guattari's terms, an opening, an escape hatch, a move away from the coherence of a tidy plot, and perhaps even from the exclusive and limited boundaries of the citizen body: "In a book, there are lines of articulation or segmentarity, strata and territories; but also lines of flight, movements of deterritorialization and destratification."[55] The play, and its transmission, its attribution to a single author, its enclosure in volumes dedicated to that author, cannot limit and contain the dancing father, who, one of the choral collective, spins out in his line of flight and represents an excess, a more, a too-much that goes beyond citizenship, the closure of the text, the literary tradition that seeks to control him.

In the ancient city of Athens, the significance of these insects lies in the potential of the swarm for conceptualizing human groups. In the *Frogs*, the chorus of initiates, a swarm in its own right, some of whom are men dressed as women, looks out at the audience and sees a swarm:

> Embark, Muse, on the sacred dance,
> And come to inspire joy in my song,
> Beholding the great multitude (*okhlon*) of people,
> Where thousands of wits are in session.
> (673–78)

The audience, the *demos*, the city itself, is a multiple, myriad-bodied swarm, *muriai*, tens of thousands of people, watching, and may include noncitizens, women, foreigners, even slaves, and the poor watching from the hill above the theater. The wisdom attributed to them resembles the "swarm intelligence" of contemporary theory, the concept that a group might arrive at a better solution to a problem than a single individual.

The comic writer, in the radical democratic period, conceives of a collectivity of insects, drawing analogies with humankind without prejudice. The wasps of his chorus present admirable qualities. They are stubborn, patriotic, and militaristic; they may be misogynists, and misled by demagogues, but the incapacity to alter his nature exhibited by Philocleon elicits, in me, at least, grudging, ambivalent admiration. He cannot be turned by his vapid son into a sycophantic symposiast, but continues to pursue little cockchafers, and to dance manically.

One of the most compelling points Kristin Ross makes about Rimbaud's metaphors is the potential for mass action on the part of a swarm. Whether in the situation of the Paris commune, or in the ambivalent relationship of Athenian poets to the *demos*, the people, the collective, there is in these texts a tense awareness of the nameless hordes, likened to insects, who mesmerize, and can threaten those who describe them: "*Bourdonnement*, the indistinct buzzing noise of the swarm that is very close to silence—that immobile background reverberation may well, with a blast, burst into the space of sound. That burst, like the adolescent lunge, is not precisely sequential, but rather 'virtual' or 'potential' (*latent*)." "The face in the crowd" is "always one step away from becoming 'people in the streets': the crowd, the demonstration, the insurrection," "always on the point of becoming 'political man.'"[56] This political man was born in the Greek *polis*; he is the *zoon politikon*, the living being of the *polis*, whom Aristotle names, who is the object of scrutiny by Giorgio Agamben, Alain Badiou, and Jacques Rancière, and before them, of Hannah Arendt and Hegel.

For Ross, Arthur Rimbaud's representation of the swarming lice of "Jeunesse" resists debasement of the worker's body into a thing on the marketplace (120). He gives instead a swarm, the more-than-human, "the transformed utopian body of infinite sensation and libidinal possibility as figure for the perfected community, for associative or collective life."[57]

In later Greek representations the wild insect chorus, threatening to break out, to sting, to dance bestially and greedily, to satisfy bodily desires and behave with erotic abandon, is eventually reterritorialized, its collective intelligence managed and repressed, the wild democratic wasps turned into a hive of orderly, socialized, hierarchical bees, especially in the works of the conservatives Xenophon and Plato. In the fourth century, the radical democracy, although always capable of regression into a stinging swarm, was domesticated and made productive of honey for its masters. Earlier, in the fifth century BCE, the time of the "radical" democracy, Old Comedy can represent the collective's desires, pleasures, voluptuosity, menace, greed, and unmanageability for a few decades. The wild erratic ludic erotic aggression of the anonymous collectivity of Aristophanes' comic wasps resists their becoming things, things that fit into the neat schemes of Plato's hierarchized world, obedient creatures like the stingless bees, the drones who feed their mistress, the queen.

The merit of the earlier visions of collective life lies in their swarming vitality, the intensity of their attention to their collective aims, and their unwillingness to be swayed or diverted from their chosen paths. In the beginnings, in the radically democratic Greek city, one could happily resemble an insect. The revulsion and distaste felt by some postmodern individuals for the anonymity of these swarms, the fear of the protest turning into a mob, are symptoms of a fetishization, perhaps, of individualism, of a comforting opposition between the individual and the masses. A delight in such swarms bespeaks a stubborn confidence in the possibility of communal intentions in a crowd bent on social justice and the redistribution of wealth, and should supplement the present-day gaze at ancient drama, extending beyond the tragic individual.

[CHAPTER 3]

Chorus

> Fortunate bridegroom, the marriage you prayed for
> has come to fruition. You have the maiden for whom you prayed.
> : : And you, your form is graceful, your eyes
> like honey. Eros pours over your beloved face
> : : Aphrodite has rewarded you extravagantly.
>
> Sappho, fragment 112, trans. John Daley

While we may have come to think of the Lesbian/lesbian poet Sappho as an individual, a solo voice singing of erotic longing, in fact many of Sappho's verses were written for choral performance. Among them are the *epithalamia*, "wedding songs," like Sappho's here. There were many forms of chorus in archaic and classical Greece, not restricted to the dancing and singing in drama, in tragedy, satyr play, and comedy. The Greek word *khoros* actually refers most literally to "dance." It can be extended to denote a group, a "choir," which dances and sings, and even a dancing floor, a place for dancing. According to one etymology, noted by Hesychius (LSJ), *khoros* means *kuklos*, "ring, or circle."

In this chapter, I first discuss the centrality of the chorus to ancient Greek ritual and performance occasions, and then argue that the work of Louis Althusser on dramatic form can contribute to the understanding of choruses in ancient Greek drama. I look at recent work on choruses, at the tragic chorus, and then turn to the only extant satyr play to consider its chorus. I recall the scholarly privileging of tragedy, and then move to comedy's choruses, especially those in which swarms of animals figure, and to scholarship on comedy.

EARLY CHORUS

Homer's *Iliad*, in perhaps the first mention of such performance in western European civilization, refers to a chorus in the description of the shield of Achilles, newly forged for the weaponless warrior by the smith god Hephaistos at the request of Achilles' mother, the goddess Thetis.[1] This marvelous defensive weapon contains a world, itself incorporating conflict, resolution, and pastoral harmony:

> On it he [Hephaistos] also fashioned a vineyard, lush with
>   clusters,
> fine and golden; black the bunched grapes, while the vines
> were propped up throughout on silver poles. Around it
> he set a ditch, done in cobalt enamel, and outside that a fence
> made of tin, with one path to the vineyard, on which
> the grape pickers went to and fro when harvesting the vines:
> and he had girls and boys, all innocently light hearted,
> carrying the honey-sweet fruit in wicker baskets,
> while in the midst of them a boy with a clear-toned lyre
> made sweet music, and accompanied his own singing—
> soft and exquisite—of the Linos Song, while they,
> stamping the beat and shouting, danced along after him.[2]

The Greek historian Herodotus connects this song with Linos, a legendary musician, the first human being given the gift of singing by the gods, and then murdered by a jealous Apollo (Herodotus 2.478). The late Alexandrian lexicographer Hesychius adds that *khoros* also means *stephanos*, "something that surrounds or encompasses," (LSJ), as in the wall that surrounds a city, and then "crown, or wreath," and so the *khoros* is thought to be a circular dance, a "ring dance."

Homer's description of the shield also refers to the "sacred circle" of the *agora*:

> There was a crowd
> of citizens drawn to the meeting place (*agora*): a dispute had
>   arisen
> between two men . . .
> the elders were sitting
> on polished seats of stone in the sacred circle.
>   (*Iliad* 496–504, trans. Green)

We might see the audience, and even the chorus, of the later classical Athenian theater as another form, a microcosm even, of this circle that becomes the assembly, in the fifth century, of the *polis*, the classical democratic city.[3]

The fact that *khoros* originally referred to a group of dancers reveals how much our understanding of the performance of the choruses of the ancient city relies on partial information. We have little or no sense of the music that accompanied the dances of the choruses, and what shreds of knowledge we have of the dancing of the choruses relies on internal references in the words that have survived, allusions to turns and counterturns, for example, or on material evidence in the archaeological remains, of dances depicted in painting on vases, or the excavation of dancing floors such as the orchestras of theaters.[4]

There are many kinds of choruses in ancient Greek performance, including the dancing implicit in Alcman's *Partheneion*, dance and song of Spartan maidens: "This our choir of ten sings as well as eleven girls: why, its song is like that of a swan on the waters of the Xanthus" (Alcman frag. 1, 98–101, trans. Campbell). Other varieties of chorus survive, the text of songs that choirs of dancers and singers performed for ritual and festival occasions. One of the most significant is the genre called "dithyramb," songs celebrating the god Dionysos. Aristotle relates that tragedy developed out of dithyrambic choruses, when a chorus leader stepped forward, out of the group, to become a single voice, and then a character in what became tragedy.[5] The chorus precedes drama as we have received it.

Choruses in drama have a special status, and although there is a wide variety of choruses, of membership, and their role in the dramas, they are often subordinated in analysis to the actions and speech of the characters who stand alone and pronounce their speeches, speak to other characters, or engage in exchanges with the members of the chorus. One of the pressing issues I want to illuminate here is that the chorus, which embodies lines of flight, of escape from the confinement of text in performance, can gesture toward a more pluralistic conception of the *polis*, the inhabited city and its territory, many varieties of spaces, and the *demos*, which included the citizens, as well as many varieties of others—slaves, foreigners, Greek and not, and women.[6] Theirs is what Althusser calls "non-dialectical time," and they occupy an alternative temporality to that of the plot, the linear narrative of the dramatic action.

ALTHUSSER ON DRAMATIC FORM

Louis Althusser's famous essay on the Piccolo Teatro relies on his views about ideology, interpellation, the "hailing" of persons, and on what seems to me a complex and illuminating model of thinking about the ways in which persons are caught up in the political structures of their present.[7] Althusser provides a model that allows for a formal analysis of the theatrical object that shows contradictions being represented theatrically, rather than as the conscious positions of a playwright, and that can cast light on the structure of ancient Athenian tragedy and comedy, characters and chorus.

Althusser describes a sort of tragedy, a melodrama in dialect, set in the nineteenth century in Milan, *El Milan Nost*, written by Carlo Bertolazzi. Althusser sets out before us a theatrical performance of the first part of the play, as directed by Giorgio Strehler, marked by two different moods, two different temporalities. The plot of the drama concerns a young woman, Nina, in love with a circus clown, who dies. She is gradually forced into prostitution, as her father attempts to save her, killing her lover; in the second part of the play, Nina enters into high society. The first part of the drama, entitled "The Poor," *La povera gent*, was staged by Strehler, and is the object of Althusser's analysis. Under Strehler's direction, it is as if the group of workers presented on stage inhabit a "chronicle," as Althusser calls it, while the characters, including the tragic heroine, Nina, live in "tragedy":

> It is precisely this opposition which gives Bertolazzi's play its depth. On the one hand, a non-dialectical time in which nothing happens, a time with no internal necessity forcing it into action; on the other, a dialectical time (that of conflict) induced by its internal contradiction to produce its development and result.... The issue here is the play's latent structure and nothing else. Bertolazzi's explicit intentions are unimportant: what counts, beyond the words, is the internal relation of the basic elements of its structure. I would go further. It does not matter whether Bertolazzi consciously wished for this structure, or unconsciously produced it: it constitutes the essence of his work.[8]

Althusser is describing, in addition to a call for disregarding "authorial" intention, an incommensurability, a lack of relation between two elements of *Il Milan Nost*. The silent proletariat performs its silent presence, while the tragedy occurs in between, in another time: "Nowhere can it [the structure] be perceived directly in the play as can the visible characters or the course of the action. But it is there, in the tacit relation between the people's time and the time of the tragedy, in their mutual imbalance, in their incessant 'interference' and finally in their true and delusive criticism. It is this revealing latent relation, this apparently insignificant and yet decisive tension that Strehler's production enables the audience to perceive without their being able to translate this presence directly into clearly conscious terms."[9] Althusser is discussing a twentieth-century theater production of a nineteenth-century drama; he describes a tragedy, not a comedy; he gives us a tragedy set in the proletariat environment of nineteenth-century workers' Milan. While this is not ancient drama, there is much of value and pertinence in this analysis, especially as Althusser describes an *incommensurability* between different elements of the staging of this tragedy, an incommensurability relevant to the presence of choruses in ancient Athenian dramatic performance. A recognition of rupture, a fracturing of the dramatic form, might begin to address what I have identified as a neglect of the chorus, not only in the *Poetics* of Aristotle, but in the theorists who come after him.

TRAGIC CHORUSES

Recent classical scholarship has tried to open up these questions, to give a fuller account of choruses, not only in tragedy, little in comedy, but in other circumstances of choral performance in the ancient city and after. In a valuable recent volume, *Choruses, Ancient and Modern*, Joshua Billings, Felix Budelmann, and Fiona Macintosh, as editors and contributors, consider the varied sorts of ancient Greek choral forms, and their descendants in modernity.[10] There are a few discussions of a few of the plays of Aristophanes, in particular the play in which Aristotle treats tragedy, the *Frogs*.[11] Yet the only entry in the index for comedy is the Comédie Française.

The introduction to the book argues, *contra* my view of Old Comedy, that the notion of choruses as revolutionary bodies is "not one at home in most accounts of ancient choruses, which, on the whole, tend to see the chorus as harmoniously aligned with cosmic, social, and political order. Even the weaker notion, which makes an appearance in various modern periods, of utopia-seeking choruses, while closer to standard models of ancient chorality, nevertheless is at odds with them because of the gap it programmatically opens up between the chorus and the current state of the world" (4). And further, "it would be productive to think through the notion that already in Archaic and Classical Greece choral songs demonstrate a hankering for the impossible (note the habit of Greek choral texts to imagine performances by other, often mythical choruses)" (5). Especially in the choruses of comedy, as I intend to show in chapters that follow.

One of the most valuable and provocative essays in this volume is Edith Hall's "Mob, Cabal, or Utopian Commune? The Political Contestation of the Ancient Chorus, 1789–1917," which does, refreshingly, take issue with the introduction's perspective on the chorus:[12] "The revolutionary potential of Greek theatrical chorality was more clearly realized than ever before in revolutionary Russia, but it was of course built into the medium from the moment of its genesis. The Greek tragic choruses that have survived are the products of democratic Athens, a society that had recently given more political power to more—and poorer—people than any previously" (283). Hall recognizes the potential of the chorus, but mentions only tragedy. She discusses the "landmark mass choruses of the French revolution, the 'voice of the cities.'" "The illiterate could learn catchy songs in which to 'express their longing for bread and security, their will to build a better social order'" (286).[13]

Hall focuses on the class identifications with the ancient tragic chorus: "The chorus did without question offer a promising paradigm in imagining a univocal Volk or compatriots within the emergent ideal of the unified nation state. But surely it is of equivalent significance that it could also look like a threatening rabble or a utopian projection of an egalitarian commune, depending on your class-political perspective?" (286).[14] Acknowledging the ambiguous nature of the choral swarm, Hall nonetheless traces an impressive and inspiring legacy of the tragic chorus of ancient Athens into modernity. The "semi-official anthem of the Russia Revolution" was Scriabin's *Prometheus: The Poem of Fire* (1910), which featured a color organ that generated light of different colors projected onto a screen, and a "wordless chorus," that sang only vowels, no consonants "that demarcate one language from another" (307).

Martin Revermann concludes his "Brechtian Chorality," in this volume, with the following caveat:[15] "Brechtian choruses remind us that chorality is, and was in the ancient Greek theatre, an enormously powerful theatrical device, capable of transforming an old traditional tale into a fresh, thought-provoking, beautiful and engaging challenge that forces, to the present day, its viewers to rethink fundamental aspects of what the world around them is, what it could be, and what it ought to be" (169). Of course, Athenian comedy does not transform "an old traditional tale," but rather invents a new world, "what ought to be," more than any tragedy. And it deploys not tales, but tails, often, possibly following on the rituals of the city, the processions of animals, beasts of various sorts, creatures connected especially with Dionysiac choral performances. The stories, animal fables, are alluded to in vases with animal processions, and offer another connection between the past of the city and its dramatic festivals, including comedy, and that, as Revermann's remarks suggest, allow us to "rethink fundamental aspects" of the present, and of the future, in utopian imaginings that include the existence of other beings among humankind, a whole global ecology.

Other scholars return principally to the tragic chorus, when surpassing the traditional philosophical focus on character. Claude Calame usefully insists on its centrality in his book *La tragédie chorale*,[16] beginning with Nietzsche, and with two twentieth-century Balinese festivals, celebrated almost forty years apart, festivals marked by long processions, sacrificial offerings, and culminating in dramatic presentations and choral dance. For him, these spectacles evoke the scenario of the Great Dionysia, marked in its turn by a long musical contest, including dithyrambs, comedies, and tragedies, ending with a satyr play: "These sung and dramatized manifestations are inserted into the long ritual sequence," including procession and sacrifice. The comparison with Balinese celebration ends here, but reminds us that an ethnographic, anthropological understanding of the fifth-century BCE Athenian festival should take note of the fact that this is similarly a ritual occasion. An eyewitness experience of Bali's festivals revealed for Calame the necessity of attempting to imagine that ritual, color, and musical rhythm to which we no longer have access in the case of ancient Athenian drama, when all we have is texts.

Calame goes on to focus on tragedy. He considers in detail the choruses of three tragedies, Aeschylus's *Persians*, Sophocles' *Oedipus Rex*, and Euripides' *Hippolytus*. Among other crucial observations, he recalls the affinities of the Persians' chorus with lamentation, and how the chorus of *Oedipus Rex* frames the figure of Oedipus himself, the principal character usually the focus of analysis, foregrounding the status of the mortal human being. His analysis of Euripides' *Hippolytus* stresses the presence of two separate choruses in the drama, one made up of the citizen-class women of the heroes' city of Troezen, the other a chorus of Hippolytus's companions. Both choruses sing in the third stasimon, the standing song of the tragedy, and in Calame's view point to the gender ambiguity of Hippolytus himself.

Tragic choruses take up varied positions in relation to the characters of the dramas in which they appear. They are often composed of older men, women, soldiers, or followers, groups too weak to offer much resistance to the demands, commands, positions of the characters, beholden to their masters. Sometimes the chorus seem to be paralyzed, static onlookers to the action, as in Aeschylus's *Agamemnon*. The later tragedian Euripides at times mocked their inaction, as they seemed to dither, and disapprove, and comment on the events or conversations conducted between the characters, without intervening in the predictably disastrous behaviors of their social superiors. At other times they seem to represent a lowest common denominator of public opinion, or some general, generic, commonsense relationship to the tragic events they witness. Some choruses seem to change course during the play, to sympathize with one character and then another as the plot unfolds. Other choruses comment soberly at the end of tragedies on the terrible spectacle they have watched. The choruses are made up of a variety of kinds of human beings in tragedy—inhabitants, bystanders, citizens, enslaved women, spectators of various sorts, or participants in the drama, and they frequently observe passively the actions of their betters.[17] Are they stand-ins for the members of the audience, paralyzed or commenting, impotent or engaged in judging or intermittently identifying with the characters and their choices as they share the stage? Comic choruses, on the other hand, often take disruptive action, act out the great refusal. And for these reasons, among others, they may be left out of the political theoretical discussions of ancient drama in modernity, which are so centered on individual choices, sovereignty, the court, and the family.

SATYR CHORUS

Satyr plays provide a bridge between tragedy and comedy. At the end of the day of classical Athens' dramatic festival celebration in honor of Dionysos, after the performance of three tragedies, sometimes linked, sometimes not, the tragic playwright also offered to his audience, judges, priests, and other spectators, a satyr play.[18] These short plays closed off the experience of tragedy with something completely different. They seem to have had comic elements, to feature satyrs often as their choruses, and like tragedy to have been based on mythic narratives, unlike comedy. Only one satyr play, *Cyclops*, by the tragedian Euripides, has survived, and its group of satyrs offers some fascinating contrasts both to tragic and to comic choruses.

The chorus in Euripides' *Cyclops* is made up of satyrs, part animal, part human creatures owned by the Cyclops Polyphemus near Mount Aetna; they are explicitly called *douloi* (24), "slaves," these sons of their satyr father, Silenus. In their first chorus, they sing, complaining of their isolation on the island of Sicily:

> No Dionysus is here, no dances (*khoroi*), no wand-bearing Bacchic worship, no ecstatic noise of drums. (63–66)

> I, your attendant, serve this one-eyed Cyclops, a slave in exile. (76–78)[19]

The Cyclops, a cannibal, or carnivore monster, reassuringly claims he would not eat them. They are creatures between human and animal, but he says: "You would be the death of me with your dance steps, leaping around inside my belly" (220–21). Laughter is tinged with horror, as we in the audience recall the scenes in Homer's *Odyssey*, where the Cyclops devours some of Odysseus's shipmates raw.

In the satyr play, the wandering hero Odysseus arrives at the Sicilian home of the Cyclops, challenging the arrangements of the site; the satyr Silenus defends himself to Polyphemus, trying to protect himself and his enslaved sons by falsely claiming that Odysseus threatened to capture Polyphemus, to pull out his guts, whip him, fetter him, make him row the ship, and then sell him as a slave (234–40). Polyphemus, an atheist, indifferent to Zeus, decides to eat Odysseus and his men straightaway.

The members of the chorus offer the flesh of the human visitors to the monster in the Cyclops's cave, but refuse to partake themselves. With some variation from the episode of Polyphemus recounted in the *Odyssey*, the hero describes the killing, cooking, and devouring of his companions, and offers to free the satyrs from their enslavement (*douleia*, 442) if they assist him in his struggle with the one-eyed creature. He will blind the Cyclops, as he did in the *Odyssey* with his human companions' help. The satyrs eagerly agree: "I could lift the weight of a hundred wagons if we are going to smoke out that cursed Cyclops' eye like a wasps' nest" (473–74). These hybrid animal-human beings share violent tendencies with their fellows the swarming wasps.

As planned, they serenade the Cyclops, already inebriated on Odysseus's wine, as he sings drunkenly in his cave, and then emerges:

Happy the man who shouts the Bacchic cry . . .
With a lovely glance he steps forth in beauty from the halls.
(495, 511–12)

The Cyclops drinks ever more, spurred to excess by Silenus and Odysseus. Polyphemus decides that Silenus is his Ganymede, the Trojan boy taken up to Olympus by Zeus to be his cupbearer. The monster declares a preference for boys over women; the two leave the stage together and enter the cave. Odysseus follows, intending to blind the Cyclops in his postcoital sleep, as the chorus joyously anticipates participating in the thrusting of the firebrand into Polyphemus's single eye (608–24), and their consequent liberation from their servitude. But they then suddenly, comically, fearfully, fall prey to doubts, claim to have become lame, to have sprained their feet, to be unable to see because of ash and dust. They deny the charge of cowardice, but purport to know an incantation of Orpheus that will cause the firebrand, on its own, to set the Cyclops on fire. Odysseus gives up on them, and they tell him to send a Carian, a mercenary, instead. The chorus is comically reluctant, but also demonstrates a commitment to pleasure, even to indolence, the workers' right to laziness that marks the difference between them and Odysseus, the "prototype of the bourgeois individual," so described by Horkheimer and Adorno in *Dialectic of Enlightenment*.[20]

As the deed is accomplished within the cave, the chorus cheers the blinders on, "Whirl and pull, whirl and pull . . . ," with an incantatory song. The blinded Polyphemus emerges from the cave as the chorus leader interrogates him. He calls out the notorious name Noman, *Outis*, which Odysseus used in Homer's *Odyssey* to trick the Cyclops. Again, "no man" has blinded him. After having punished their enemy, having taken revenge, Odysseus and his men escape, and the chorus of satyrs, freed from the Cyclops in spite of their cowardice, has the last, ironic word: "As for us, we shall be shipmates with Odysseus and ever after serve (*douleusomen*) in Dionysus' train" (708–9). *Douleusomen*: "We will be slaves to Dionysus." This is the last word of the only extant satyr play, the chorus thus trading one master for another, remaining a band of slaves, a hybrid of human being and animal enslaved to the god of the theater.

The classicist Mark Griffith, after important work on Greek tragedy, turned his attention to the satyr plays, these fourth performances given at the end of the day of three tragedies written by a single playwright. Although there is only the one surviving satyr play, the *Cyclops*, fragments of others remain. And Euripides' play *Alcestis*, which has comic elements, and is said to have been presented after three tragedies at the end of the day, has sometimes been considered as in some way a seriocomic play, a substitute for the satyr play more customarily given perhaps to relieve the anguish, or the pity and fear, excited by three tragedies in a row.

Griffith's arguments concern what he sees as a sort of "split identification," possibly characteristic of theater spectatorship in general, in which the audience responds with identification that shifts from one character or even to the chorus as a dramatic presentation proceeds. In discussing tragic performances, Griffith had previously "proposed a model (derived partly from the political sociologist David Kertzer, and ultimately from Emile Durkheim) of 'solidarity without consensus' within an Athenian theater audience."[21] Members of the tragic audience might experience a variety of "subject positions," significant for the politics of the city, identifying at one moment with aristocratic, elite, heroic characters, then with "feelings of admiration, disgust, or pity, approval or disapproval, anxiety or relief, expressed by the minor characters and chorus" (9). Griffith brings this model to the study of the satyr play, and greatly enriches the tradition of scholarship on this genre, often dismissed as crude and vulgar, a sop for the masses who needed a sort of slapstick diversion from the high seriousness of tragedy. Griffith extends his understanding of the Athenian audience to speculation about the male citizen's experience of the satyr play, using the analogy of blackface minstrelsy in nineteenth-century America, which "may provide helpful insights into the ways in which the hyper-active, musically and choreographically adventurous, sexually transgressive, and verbally impertinent satyrs may have appealed to Athenian men who were constantly subjected to expectations of good behavior, proper speech, and modest deportment in their lives outside the Theater" (11). Griffith cites Eric Lott's book, *Love and Theft: Blackface Minstrelsy and the American Working Class*.[22] Making this analogy entails some risks, of which Griffith is well aware. The history of racialized slavery in the US, and the racism that continued with Jim Crow and subsequently, make this an imperfect model. And in fact the question of slavery, the slavery of the satyrs in the *Cyclops*, seems to me to be a matter that might merit further exploration.[23]

But Griffith's description of a variety of subject positions, a changing reaction within single audience members to the spectacle of theater, complements the work of Althusser, and that of classicist David Kawalko Roselli on the heterogeneity of that audience, made up in Roselli's view not only of priests of Dionysos, city officials, and elite members of the *demos*, but also working-class citizens, the poor, even women and slaves.[24] The antics of the *Cyclops*, with its enslaved half-animal, half-human-being chorus, serve as an interval, or a link, between the sobriety and high decorum of classical tragedy, and the wild, sometimes ecstatic animal and female choruses of Greek comedy. The complexities of identification within the original audience may still be a matter of debate, but the appeal of satyr plays, comedies, and their choruses nonetheless has its potential for the politics of our present, the possibility of empathy, even, as these nontragic genres provide mockery and ridicule of the powerful as well as moments of solidarity, collective complicity, and laughter.

Tragedies' choruses, as noted, are formed by human beings of various sorts. The personae of the *Cyclops* are sketchily, comically drawn, the chorus carrying with it the hybrid quality of the human and the animal. The choruses of comedy, in contrast, are sometimes human, but often composed of other sorts of living or even inanimate creatures, such as the clouds of the play named for these meteorological phenomena, and treating comically the supposedly airy and otherworldly concerns of the philosopher Socrates and his school.

THE COMIC CHORUS

Can a reading of comedy that gives equal, or more, weight to the chorus than to the characters, especially to the so-called comic hero, alter our perception of the play as readers or viewers? Scholarship on comedy long concentrated on identifying, or even deciphering, the diction of the plays, and on references to contemporary political events and figures in the city. In 1964 Cedric Whitman published *Aristophanes and the Comic Hero*, which devoted the same kind of attention to the central character in comedy as scholarship and analysis had devoted to the tragic hero in the past. In his essay in *The Cambridge Companion to Greek Comedy*, Ralph M. Rosen reminds the reader of the mixed reception Whitman's arguments received, with their emphasis on comedy's central persona, his or her individualism, isolation from society, and "inner-directed" nature.[25] Rosen points out that Whitman's focus on a roguish, antisocial, villainous central character, although of course such a characterization does not fit a persona such as Lysistrata, who is none of the above, "was probably a response to a perceived blandness in American culture of the 1950s, and to the post-War boom in technology and science that seemed to threaten deep-rooted strains of individualism in American history."[26] As time goes on, this threat seems to have been met with an ever-increasing atomization and individualism in American culture, rather than its contrary. And the focus on the comic hero, in fact, corresponds to these developments, rather than challenging them, as the predicament, the desires and schemes of the individual "heroes" of ancient comedy appeal to readers who have come to see only individual experience as authentic. Whitman's emphasis on "the salvation of the self" in his heroes is perfectly consistent with contemporary fixations on private experience, as exemplified in best-seller lists containing memoirs and thinly disguised accounts of individuals who triumph over daunting circumstances. Whitman's discovery of the comic hero does not in fact go against the grain of American culture, but rather points the way toward an increasing individualism and narcissism in the twenty-first century, both exacerbated and at the same time compromised to some degree by new social media.

A person like Lysistrata in the comedy named for her does have heroic dimensions. She manages to effect a peace treaty between the warring enemies—the Spartans and their allies, and the Athenians and theirs, the audience of the first performance of the play.[27] Lysistrata is clever, even devious, but she is also noble, committed to peace, and an altogether non-narcissistic, non-roguish "hero." A challenge to this version of heroism lies in the potential represented by the comic chorus, which might be seen in relation to Althusser's description of the Piccolo Teatro, as a contradictory counter-presence, sometimes there to echo and support the central character, the "hero," in other cases ready to mock and ridicule and undermine the characters, and notorious inhabitants of the city. They may, in the dénouement of the comedy, become reconciled to the views of the persona central to the linear narrative of the play, if one can even discern such a thing in many comedies. But in the course of their entering, dancing, singing, they can also oppose the central character, mock audience members, speak for the playwright himself, comment on current events in the life of the city, and in general present an unruly collective body, even an alternate universe, a utopian space, as they dance and sing, often obscenely.

ANIMAL CHORUSES

Comic choruses differ in many ways from those of tragedy, although they too perform choreography and songs, and like the choruses of tragedy, often consist of females embodied by transvestite boys and men. If we assume that the chorus in some sense is representative of the citizen body, of the *demos*, like the jury standing for the whole of the community, as well as of all the residents of the city—metics, foreigners, slaves, women—then what does it mean that at times it is represented by these nonhuman beings? How can we understand the swarms of wasps, birds, clouds, frogs, clouds, or even letters in comedy?[28]

In his valuable work on animal choruses, Kenneth Rothwell discusses the brief window during which ancient Athenian comic playwrights began again to use brilliantly costumed animals in their dramas.[29] This followed an earlier period (510–480 BCE) when animals had appeared in the choruses of comedy, a practice that became less common until the final third of the fifth century, in the 420s and 410s, when the comic writers returned to them. Although the reasons for the revival are unclear, Rothwell points out that the sophists and the pre-Socratics, protophilosophers of the fifth century, made analogies between the lives of human beings and those of animals, as Aristotle did later, and that the comic writers may have been responding to their anthropologies. And attendees of symposia, elite occasions of festivity and eventually political conspiracy, sometimes included revelers dressed in animal costumes.[30]

Extant or fragmentary insect comedies include a chorus of bees, two with ants as their chorus, one with "ant-men," and two with wasps, the play attributed to Aristophanes and another by Magnes (although the evidence for this is somewhat uncertain). There seems to have been a comedy, now lost, by Pherecrates, called *Myrmekanthropoi* (*The Ant-Men*). The latter comedy may have told the tale of the flooding of the earth at the time of Deucalion and Pyrrha, and a story, recounted earlier, of the re-creation of humankind by Zeus, who turned ants into human beings, for the sake of the repopulation of the island of Aegina after its devastation.

ANIMACY

Mel Chen's fascinating work *Animacies*, although not focused on mythic representations of animal-human hybrids, calls attention to the linguistic category of "animacy," the attribution of soul, "anima," not just to human beings, or even animals, but also to things that are customarily considered to be inanimate, stone, features of the natural landscape, chemical pollutants.[31] Animals, and hybrid animal-human creatures, are given "animacy," and feature prominently in Greek art and myth. Centaurs, half human and half horse, for example, appear on temple friezes, and on innumerable Greek vases, often drinking with Heracles, attempting to carry off human women, or their most distinguished mythic character, Chiron, instructing the hero Achilles.[32] These beings may owe something to Egyptian or Mesopotamian representations of beings who share human and animal corporeal traits, like Anubis, the Egyptian jackal-headed god, assistant to Osiris in the process of judgment of the dead after mummification.

Aristotle, proponent of what A. O. Lovejoy called "the great chain of being," sees a hierarchy of creatures inhabiting the earth, with free human males at the top of a ladder.[33] And in his *Politics*, Aristotle defines animals as one of the proper objects of human beings' attention and use: "Plants exist for the sake of animals and the other animals for the good of man (*anthropon*), the domestic species both for his service and for his food, and if not all at all events most of the wild ones for the sake of his food and of his supplies of other kinds, in order that they may furnish him both with clothing and with other appliances. If therefore nature makes nothing without purpose or in vain, it follows that nature has made all the animals for the sake of men" (*Politics* 1256b15–23).[34] This is human-ism, an argument for instrumentalizing all other animate beings on earth, and subordinating them to human needs. And Aristotle justifies war here too, as a way of mastering those human beings who refuse to be subjected by others: "Even the art of war will by nature be in a manner an art of acquisition (for the art of hunting is a part of it) that is properly employed both against wild animals and against such of mankind as though designed by nature for subjection refuse to submit to it, inasmuch as this warfare is by nature just" (*Politics* 1256b23–27). Defeat of enemies, capture of slaves, those "designed by nature for subjection," and the hunting of animals all resemble one another, and the use of slaves and animals is proper to human beings. Yet the deployment of animals in comic choruses seems in some ways to contradict this understanding of the necessary and inevitable subjection and use of these other beings. In several such cases the comic chorus forms a swarm, a people (*demos*), and a city (*polis*).

Comic choruses included twenty-four members, while the choruses of tragedy had only twelve.[35] The animals chosen by comic writers to represent the group, the anonymity of the citizen body, analogous to the *demos*, including the "others" in the city, are often animals that swarm, that move collectively in groups—frogs, wasps, birds. Ritual concerns may come into play here; as noted earlier, the swarming animal and insect creatures in the comic plays may refer back to the practices of animal processions, of sacred time, cult ceremonies summoning another temporality, the suspension of linear time in collective celebration and festivity.[36]

There may be some evidence for animal choruses on extant Greek vases. For example, the *Birds*, produced in 414 BCE, won second prize at the Dionysia festival. An illustration on a vase from the fifth century BCE, owned by the J. Paul Getty Museum, shows two theater performers facing one another, dressed as birds, but they wear identical costumes, and some scholars contend they do not show actors from Aristophanes' play, although their presence on this vase is evocative of the theater.[37] Another vase (Michael C. Carlos Museum, Atlanta 2008.4.1) shows a similarly dressed figure, this time appearing alone on the vase, actively seeming to move, with his customary phallus, a bird's tail, and more phalluses attached to his boots like spurs. As Eric Csapo intriguingly remarks, "A single figure better represents the unity of a chorus than it does a confrontation."[38] Clearly this figure cannot embody a confrontation, but does the unity of a chorus emerge in such a representation? If the chorus of the *Birds* contained twenty-four dancers and singers, each dressed as a different bird, then perhaps not. The oscillation between part and whole, the metonymic stature of a single chorus member who stands for the whole of the chorus, is explored in the rhetorical moment of the parabasis, when the leader of the chorus steps forward, addresses the audience directly, breaking the illusion of the theatrical space, and when he she or it often appears to speak in the voice of the playwright himself. The *Birds*, a comedy that will be more fully discussed in chapter 4, on utopias, is unusual for many reasons, and in particular because in this play the parabasis does not break that illusion, but has the leader of the chorus continuing to speak as a bird, explaining the history of birds and justifying their claim to rule over all. Is the single bird on the vase in Atlanta the leader of a bird chorus, speaking in the name of his fellows, or of the poet who composed his speech, given animacy as human and animal by the painter?

LATER COMEDY

Later Roman and modern comedies owe much to what has been called Greek "New" Comedy, that is, the form of comedy that comes to dominate the theatrical stage of the ancient *polis* in the fourth century BCE, after the defeat of Athens' "radical" democracy of the fifth century.[39] The most successful practitioner of "New Comedy," Menander, wrote plays very different from those of Old Comedy. They lacked the scatological, abusive, free-speaking attacks on prominent individuals in the city and in the audience, and the chorus so characteristic of the strong tradition of comedy in the fifth century. Menander wrote plays about domestic life in the new circumstances of the *polis*, no longer governed by a democratic assembly, but by the Macedonians, heirs of Philip and Alexander, who had conquered the classical Greek populations of the mainland in the fourth century BCE and had left behind garrisons and governors to rule, in a regression, perhaps, to the monarchic and aristocratic forms that had preceded the institution of democracy, in Athens in particular, in the sixth and fifth centuries BCE.

Menander's plots focused on domestic life, with young couples in love whose consummation of their romances was briefly, for the course of the comedy, prohibited by circumstance, by paternal opposition to their union, to differences of status between man and woman. The eventual happy ending was brought about at times through the intervention of a wily slave, who manipulated the opposers to marital bliss, or who revealed the true status of one of the partners so that inequality of social position was no longer an obstacle to marriage. The only fully extant play of Menander, the *Dyskolos*, concerns a grumpy old man, and has no chorus.[40]

Can we interpret this absence as a symptom? A symptom of the end of "radical" democracy, of the end of the experimentation in politics that marked especially Athenian culture in the fifth century? A chorus, if it in some sense "represents," or alludes to, contains or even embodies the collective, the group, the *demos* or *polis* in the widest sense, not merely the body of citizens; then how can the absence of the chorus not signify a great shift in the ancient city's understanding of itself? Susan Lape has written about the politics of Menander, showing how even his emphasis on domestic matters, on marriage and family and a closed middle-class world, has implications for the world beyond that family, a family embedded in Mediterranean struggles, where soldiers return from war, where slave captives abound.[41] In her view, Menander defends democratic legal traditions, and argues for the independence of Greek *polis* culture even as it has been surrounded by the Hellenistic kingdoms with very different political arrangements.[42] Nonetheless, the energy and wild anarchic attacks of the choral swarm in the fifth-century comedies seem to have been tamed, domesticated, and even eliminated by the time of Menander's productions.

In fact, the performances of so-called Middle and New Comedy may have included choruses, but these fall away from the scripts passed on from antiquity, and may have been indicated simply as interludes of dance and song in the performances of these very different theatrical productions, interludes like the ballet scenes sometimes inserted into operas, no longer authored by the playwrights themselves. The parabasis, for example, the direct address to the audience, sometimes seemingly in the voice of the playwright himself and crucial to the comic practice of Aristophanes, and to almost all of his extant plays, falls away in Middle and New Comedy, in part perhaps because performances of the plays occurred eventually around the Mediterranean basin, no longer limited to the amphitheaters of mainland Greek cities, and Athens in particular.

In these later plays, including *Wealth*, attributed to Aristophanes, probably first performed in 408 BCE, the choral passages are indicated, but not recorded, not extant in the preserved text. It may be that later ancient editors considered these parts of the plays insignificant, unworthy of conservation, or that the comic playwrights themselves did not provide language for their choruses. Sometimes the surviving texts give a stage direction: "chorus," without any further indication, and it may be that these were meant to be improvised, or optional, or relying on some standard forms of dance and song that were thought not to be needed in the finished text.

The question of the parabasis touches on *parrhesia*, "freedom of speech," which will be discussed more fully in chapter 5, but its growing absence as comedy evolves after the fifth century BCE also points to its previous embeddedness in the imperial or radical phase of the Athenian democracy. Choruses that performed this direct address to the audiences were integrally bound up with the democracy, with the flourishing of its developed form in the fifth century. After the defeat of the Athenians and their allies by the coalition led by the Spartans, at the end of the fifth century, comedy, and its choruses, took on a different shape.

THE COMIC COLLECTIVE

Jean-Pierre Vernant, in his brilliant work on ancient drama, drew attention to the interactions between chorus and characters, even as his published writings rarely acknowledged ancient comedy, tragedy's festival partner. Vernant's insights into Greek drama connected its performances with the religious and political context of the Athenian *polis*, redirected scholarship away from purely formal questions, away from issues of authorship, or historical reference, or the body of a particular tragedian's production, and allowed a new generation of scholars to attend to the cultural significance of ancient drama. In an especially influential passage in a seminal essay entitled "Tensions and Ambiguities in Greek Tragedy," he discussed the dialectical relationship between choruses and characters, with the assumption that what is at stake is tragedy: "[The] debate with a past that is still alive creates at the very heart of each tragic work a fundamental distance that the interpreter needs to take into account. It is expressed, in the very form of the drama, by the tension between the two elements that occupy the tragic stage. One is the chorus, the collective and anonymous presence embodied by an official college of citizens. Its role is to express through its fears, hopes, questions, and judgments the feelings of the spectators who make up the civic community."[43] Note how Vernant begins with the chorus, this "collective and anonymous presence" of citizens. Of course, as discussed previously, the chorus appears in many other contexts in Athenian society, in the performance of hymns, dithyrambs, the songs sung in honor of Dionysos, and in comedy as well as tragedy, and may have represented not only citizens, but also other residents of the city, its foreigners, its slaves, its women, all of whom may have been present in the audience at dramatic festivals and other choral performances. Vernant continues, emphasizing the copresence with the chorus, of the characters in drama: "The other, played by a professional actor, is the individualized character whose actions form the core of the drama and who appears as a hero from an age gone by, always more or less estranged from the ordinary condition of the citizen." In the case of comedy, this "character" is not "a hero from an age gone by," but an invented character who drives forward the plot of the drama, a thinly disguised person familiar in the everyday life of the spectators, or even one of the gods, like the Dionysos of *Frogs*. Vernant goes on to comment on how the chorus uses language "that carries on the lyrical tradition of a poetry celebrating the exemplary virtues of the hero of ancient times." Can we see a similar paradox in the comic chorus, which at times reaches lyrical heights that refer back to the aristocratic past, but at other times seems to speak directly to the audience in the voice of the playwright himself?

I cite this passage at such length because it has had such an impact on the study of ancient tragedy since the essay's publication. In Vernant's formulation concerning tragedy, the characters represent the great figures of the Greeks' past, historical and legendary, characters such as Theseus, Oedipus, Ion, Athena herself. These are the beings of myth and legend, and as such emerge out of the oral tradition, laden with extrahuman significance and powers. As Vernant demonstrates, they paradoxically use a language that although metrical resembles the everyday speech of tragedy's audience, without the lyrical flourishes and elevated language of archaic poetry. It is from the mouths of the chorus, an anonymous group that dances, sings, exults, and laments, that the language of the past emerges, in another dialect, signifying archaism and the legacy of an aristocratic past. Although this passage is cited frequently as laying out the chiastic form of tragedy, that is, the X, with the chorus speaking aristocratic archaic lyrics, and the characters more contemporary prosaic language, the whole creating a sort of centripetal energy that binds the city together as it makes itself into theater, the democratic collective entwined with the archaic past, there is no such exploration of the potential for comedy to create a similar chiastic centripetal force.

Some of Vernant's most important work, profoundly influential in the field of classics, in classical literary studies, was, significantly, collected in the volume he coauthored with Pierre Vidal-Naquet entitled *Myth and Tragedy in Ancient Greece*.[44] In this work, he continued to present a progressive account of the transition from archaic to classical culture, suggesting that tragedy, then "reason," replaced myth, a position that he later revised, perhaps convinced against his will by arguments such as those of Claude Lévi-Strauss, who insisted that *pensée sauvage*, once considered "primitive" thought, was as complex and rich as philosophical reflection. But it is also important to note that in Vernant's account, the emphasis is on myth and *tragedy*, tragedy as the representative genre of the high classical age of Athens. Comedy, with its characters and choruses, does not figure in his account. In *Myth and Tragedy*, which contains essays by both Vernant and Vidal-Naquet, the comic playwrights are barely mentioned, appearing only when the authors discuss the *Frogs*, which, as remarked earlier, presents an extended commentary on the tragedians Aeschylus and Sophocles, and is an early example of the literary criticism of tragedy, and not a typical comedy.

In the work of Nicole Loraux, another brilliant historian and scholar of classical Greek culture, the *polis*, and the Athenian philosophical world, there is a similar emphasis on tragedy to the near exclusion of comedy from consideration.[45] Her work is crucial for understanding the role of the chorus, especially in tragedy, where the emphasis on lamentation, on song, on grief, and the inarticulate expression of sorrow greatly enriches our understanding of the original performances of tragedy, so remote from the disembodied and abstract presentations of the genre by moderns such as Hegel, who reduces Antigone in some work to an unnamed cipher representing the individual in the family.

The lack of interest in comedy is surprising, even though it is consistent with the long tradition of privileging tragedy in modernity, described in chapter 1. In fact the performances of comedy were even more linked to the flourishing of Athenian democracy than were tragedies, which continued to be composed after the defeat of the fifth-century imperial and radical democracy by the Spartans in the Peloponnesian War. Yet these scholars, so attentive to the context of so-called literary objects, that is, the ancient Greek dramas that were performed as religious offerings to the god Dionysos, as meditations on the politics of the *polis*, as Vernant puts it, "the city calling itself into question," curiously neglect the centrality of comedy to the ritual and political occasions of the city.[46]

Pierre Vidal-Naquet suggests that the chorus in tragedy represented the citizens of the city itself:

> The chorus was collective while heroes, whether Creon or Antigone, were individuals. Both the chorus and the heroes wore costumes and masks, but the members of the chorus, like the city hoplites, were dressed in uniform. . . . The masks and costumes of the actors were individualized. Thus, in its own way, the chorus, confronting the hero marked by his immoderation, represented a collective truth, an average truth, the truth of the city. . . . It was the chorus, the mouthpiece of the city, which through its movements paid its respects to the altar of Dionysus.[47]

Yet Vidal-Naquet also paradoxically notes that the chorus of tragedy is often composed of groups alien to the city, not citizens themselves: "It is hardly ever composed of average citizens, that is to say male adults of an age to bear arms." Women (that is, male chorus members dressed as women) frequently made up the chorus, in nine of the tragedies, and they are sometimes slave women; in other tragedies, the chorus is composed of old men. Vidal-Naquet comments: "Whether less than citizens, or more than citizens, women of Trachis or demesmen of Colonus, these figures were marginal to the city." So if, formally, the chorus represents a collective, an anonymous group, on the other hand, in tragedy at least, they are often also outsiders, not representative of the city at all.

The neglect of comedy may seem surprising for these scholars who are focused on the context, the whole, the cultural situation of the ancient Greek *polis*. After all, comedy did coexist with tragedy, comedies were presented on the same stage, at the same festivals of Dionysos, performances financed through committees of the city, priests of the god, wealthy patrons who paid for the choruses to be trained and who were honored in the case of comedy, unlike the playwrights, as only the best of the plays presented was rewarded.

SCHOLARS OF COMEDY

There is a body of invaluable and important work on comedy, an exception to the rule of the privileging of tragedy over its comic partner and rival. David Konstan's *Greek Comedy and Ideology*, published in 1995, is one major text that reflects seriously on comedy.[48] He calls his readings of several Aristophanic (and Menandrian) comedies "ideological," attentive to "the ways in which the plays respond to cultural issues, shaping the narratives by which Athenians defined and understood themselves" (4). A literary text is for Konstan "a site in which social tensions or contradictions are enacted," and he cites the work of John Frow, Fredric Jameson, Mieke Bal, and Pierre Macherey, "attending to the seams and sutures in the construction of ancient comedy, the places where the fusion of incompatible elements becomes visible" (5). Rejecting a view that the plays were aimed solely at "entertainment," he refuses also the idea, citing Simon Goldhill, that there is "an author's voice speaking out from beyond the comic interplay" (6).[49] In the plays of Aristophanes that he analyzes, *Wasps*, *Birds*, *Lysistrata*, and *Frogs*, Konstan identifies "a profoundly egalitarian or utopian impulse, which is capable of imagining an ideal of universal citizenship, the equality of women, the emancipation of slaves, or the abolition of property and class divisions" (8). Yet he finds these utopian impulses paired with conservative notions, in "a hankering for a simpler time that cannot pose a viable alternative to the hierarchies embedded in city-state life" (8). As he sums up the section of his book on Aristophanic, Old Comedy, Konstan reflects on the five plays he chooses to analyze: "The specifically literary operation of the work has been located precisely in the overdetermination of the characters' motivations and social positions, and in the hiatuses or seams in the surface narratives" (90). Significantly, his focus is on character and plot; there is no entry in his index, for example, for "chorus."[50] Yet I have found Konstan's work immensely valuable as I consider the resources of ancient Old Comedy for the present, and the place of the chorus as a model of collective energy.

More recently, in *Comic Democracies*, Angus Fletcher relies on the work of political scientists and ancient historians for his understanding of democracy, and the value of ancient comedy to debates concerning democracy in the present. He identifies the aspects of ancient *demokratia* that might be pertinent to contemporary politics, in which "new democrats" have turned away from a "liberal-electoral" model toward pluralism, pragmatism, and empiricism in efforts to change the world.[51] He identifies these same "core practices" in ancient *demokratia*, and argues that the Athenian institution evolved as a response to crisis, and continued, often successfully, to improvise pragmatic solutions to the city's difficulties, even to extend the franchise beyond the traditional citizen body in crises of the Peloponnesian War. Fletcher focuses on what he calls "the Ionian trilogy," the three Aristophanic plays performed near the end of that war.

Fletcher is interested not just in ancient Athens, but also, as a comparatist, in the legacy of Old Comedy as passed down through New Comedy, Roman and Renaissance comedies, and into the works of Cervantes, early modern novelists, Thomas Jefferson, the maker of the American Declaration of Independence, and finally, its appropriation by such figures as Washington Irving and Frederick Douglass.[52] Although Fletcher shares many of my concerns, his admirable work on ancient comedy, focusing especially on the "Ionian trilogy," *Lysistrata*, *Thesmophoriazusae*, and *Frogs*, dismisses *Ecclesiazusae* and *Wealth*, as late and lacking the pragmatism he finds in the earlier comedies: "Aristophanes' final two plays . . . are rooted in more abstract concerns: the women in *Ecclesiazusae* complain vaguely that the ship of state is adrift, while the characters of *Wealth* fret that virtue is not always materially rewarded."[53] These late plays are for me, intensely interesting, not "vague" or fretful. And furthermore, persuasive as Fletcher's arguments are, he like others neglects the chorus in the comedies, citing only the characters, mentioning the chorus only when it comments on the characters, dismissing the chorus elsewhere: "The material girls of *Lysistrata* leverage their sartorial skills to end the war."[54]

One of the most illuminating scholars on the matter of the chorus, and especially the comic chorus, is G. M. Sifakis, whose book *Parabasis and Animal Choruses* was published in 1971.[55] Sifakis is interested in the theriomorphic, animal choruses of some of Aristophanes' and other comic writers' plays. He brings to bear on this question archaeological evidence, especially vases that depict such creatures as riders on dolphins, ostriches, human beings dressed as birds, arguably depicting figures for the stage.[56] According to the lists of titles of comedies, often named for their choruses, as noted earlier, there were choruses made up of frogs, gall-flies, beasts, ant-men, goats, griffins, centaurs, fish, nightingales, and bees, as well as Aristophanic storks, and the more familiar creatures of extant comedies, frogs, birds, and wasps. Some scholars have argued for the totemic nature of these animal costumes (Sifakis, 79–80). Others suggest that the animal choruses derive from "begging-processions," in which the needy requested and expressed gratitude for gifts (81). Sifakis finds these theories unsatisfactory. Evidence from vase painting suggests that some choruses may have entered the stage covered by *himatia*, cloaks that concealed their animal costumes, and these overgarments may have been shed in a moment of surprise, to reveal the novelty of their dress and to permit freedom of movement in the dance, or that the *himatia* disguised the joining of the animal bodies to those of the human chorus members (88). Support for the former theory comes from the *Wasps*, where at line 420 the slave exclaims, after the chorus take off their cloaks: "Heracles! They really have stingers!" The chorus's animal, insectoid, swarming nature may have been concealed, then abruptly revealed to the audience.

Anton Bierl, in his important work on comic choruses, examines in detail the chorus of *Thesmophoriazusae*, and stresses the ritual origins of the dramatic chorus:

> At the core of drama lies the chorus. Its central activity, dance, is pure ritual. The chorus is in turn placed in an original, ritual context, namely, in the performances of adolescent youth on the threshold of adulthood.

> In these choral groups the performance of song and dance serves as the ritual demarcation of change of status, in particular as the foundation of an education in, and introduction to, the megatext of a traditional society, myth, and ritual practice. This megatext reflects social order, it affirms the social and theological cosmos, but it also undermines it and calls it into question. The chorus of drama is brought back to these functions diachronically in its development via choral lyric and the choruses of cultic practice.[57]

Bierl emphasizes ritual and the dramatic choruses' ties to traditional choral practices of devotion; I am more interested in the ways in which comic choruses engage, as he puts it, with the "megatext," and especially with the challenges the chorus can present to the contemporary order, in their often disruptive performance, as swarms.

Bierl embeds his analysis in metrical and cultic practices that for him locate comedy in the context of initiation rites. He tends to dismiss political readings of the comic collective: "In the view of the ancients, upon which previous scholarship was largely based until quite recently, the origin of comedy is rooted in practices involving blame and begging that were supposed to even out social tensions between city and countryside, rich and poor, powerful and politically underprivileged. . . . In the nineteenth and twentieth centuries such ideas of ancient class struggle naturally found favorable reception" (336). But he sees the themes of conflicts of this sort as subsumed under van Gennep's understanding of rites of passage that address initiation, fertility, and the coming of the new year. Under the chorus's broader "condition of marginality" (336), Bierl remarks: "One can thus not only explain the social and political tensions in political comedy between farmers and city dwellers, the poor and the rich, the disadvantaged and the powerful, but also understand practices involving ridicule and, in addition, all the phenomena of the comic and carnivalesque world, such as dressing up as animals, the staging of the Other and the foreign, phallus worship, and transvestism, all of which have their basis in so-called rites of inversion" (337). He devotes a great deal of attention to the fascinating details of the chorus in Aristophanes' *Thesmophoriazusae*, which indeed involves the rituals of a festival of Demeter and her daughter, the Thesmophoria, performed by actual citizen-class women of the ancient city. The chorus in the comedy is "transversally open," engaged with the ritual depicted in the play, but also in the ritual devoted to Dionysos, the comic performance, and with the audience participating in that theatrical setting.

Although Bierl's painstaking analyses are appealing, and stress the location of the chorus in the religious setting of the theater, I find them to be less convincing as they return to the themes of the Cambridge ritualists, and less to my taste than the readings he mentions that looked at class conflicts, and which he relegates to the nineteenth and twentieth centuries. Utopian and communalist, communist comedies such as the *Birds* and *Ecclesiazusae*, parrhesiast plays like the *Acharnians*, *Knights*, and *Wasps*, fit less neatly into his ritual paradigm than the *Thesmophoriazusae*, in any case. For example, Bierl cites "the ephebic members" of some choruses, who "temporarily return to the threshold phase of late childhood" (332). This characterization hardly suits the irascible elderly veterans of the Persian Wars who make up the chorus of the *Wasps*, and who are aggressively engaged in the politics of the city they inhabit.[58]

DEMOCRACY AND THE AUDIENCE

The thinking about democracy, and ancient Athenian democracy as its origin and invention, often focuses on the free Athenian male citizen, the only participant in the crucial institution of the democratic assembly, the voting body of the polis, the citizen-state. But the inhabitants of the city and its countryside, also part of the *polis*, the city-state, included many others: the citizen women, wives, mothers, daughters, and sisters of the citizen men; slaves, both male and female, foreign-born and domestic, Greek and barbarian; as well as free Greeks from other citizen-states, sometimes merchants who contributed to the economic life of Athens; and passersby, travelers, visitors, ambassadors from the Greek world and beyond who could, it seems, constitute part of the audiences at the Great Dionysia, one of the festivals where drama was performed.

David Kawalko Roselli has contributed a valuable new perspective on the audience of ancient Greek drama, arguing that present in the theater, and addressed, or interpellated by it in various ways, were nonelite citizens as well as women, and even slaves. And he presents evidence that in addition to a working-class, nonelite presence among the spectators in the city's amphitheater, there were unofficial spectators as well. The structure of the theater of Dionysos at Athens, as well as that of other theaters of other cities, depended on the slopes of hills, which were incorporated into an amphitheatrical shape, in which the lower slopes comprised graded steplike rows of seats, with the priests and judges of performances seated around a central circular dancing floor, the orchestra. Behind this was the *skene*, an adaptable wall in front of which the characters spoke, and onto which they arrived by means of entrance and exit provided at the edges of the *skene*. The orchestra, closest to the audience, featured the performance of the chorus, which also entered and departed, and occupied this central line of vision for the viewers. Roselli argues that above the space of the theater itself, built into the hill, in the case of Athens the very hill topped by the Acropolis, and the great Parthenon, spectators who were not invited, not welcome, unable to pay to attend, or not supported by the state through paid attendance, could assemble and watch the spectacle.[59]

In addition to the complexities of multiple subject positions, multiple identifications in the spectatorship of the ancient theater, argued for by Mark Griffith, there were multiple sorts of persons, not only the male citizens typically imagined to be the audience of Athenian festival drama, and the participants in Athenian everyday life and politics. The theater's choruses often contained representatives of such others, the women, slaves, barbarians, who made up part of the fabric of everyday life in Athens. I have discussed elsewhere the slave women of the chorus in Euripides' *Hecuba*, for example, who recall, in the first-person singular, the day of enslavement at the fall of Troy:

> I was setting my hair
> in the soft folds of the net,
> gazing at the endless light
> deep in the golden mirror,
> preparing myself for bed,
> when tumult broke the air
> and shouts and cries
> shattered the empty streets. . . .
>
> Dressed only in a gown
> like a girl of Sparta,
> I left the bed of love
> and prayed to Artemis.
> But no answer came.
> I saw my husband lying dead,
> and they took me over sea.
> Backward I looked at Troy,
> but the ship sped on
> and Ilium slipped away,
> and I was dumb with grief.
> (922–41)[60]

I return to this passage again and again, because this hauntingly beautiful tragic scene stages the threat always present in the world of the Greek cities, of war, defeat, and enslavement of the women of the defeated cities. The horror of such circumstances may seem remote, set as it is here in the time of the legendary Trojan War, but in fact in the fifth century BCE the Athenians, in their pursuit of empire and its preservation, notoriously crushed the neutral city of Melos for refusing to join them, first besieging it and starving the population, then conquering it, killing its men and enslaving its women and children in 416 BCE.

Tragic choruses, as cited above in the case of Euripides' *Hecuba*, could include groups of anonymous slave women, played of course by men in women's dress. The chorus of the *Bacchae* is made up of barbarian women, the entourage of the god Dionysos who has traveled from India, and moves with this ecstatic troupe of devotees, along with *silenoi*, satyrs, and other companions of his mysteries, as he invades the Greek world to bring them wine and other liquid delights. Myths tell of the resistance of various cities, fathers, kings, and women who refuse to fall into line with the worshippers of this god, and are punished harshly for their failure to recognize his divinity. The bacchantes of the *Bacchae* sing of their adoration of the god; they move in the dance of rejoicing in the god's presence, they admonish those who resist; as Pentheus, the ruler of Thebes, proves recalcitrant, trying to contain the Dionysiac energies, and the representative of the god himself, they demonstrate the irrepressibility of this divinity; and in some sense, as Dionysos has called the women of the city of Thebes onto the mountain to worship him, these Greek women, including Pentheus's mother, Agave, become an invisible chorus themselves, identified as part of the swarm of barbarian chorus members. A messenger describes their idyll on the mountain's top, interrupted by Theban men, as they enter the ecstatic, delirious, swarming state of a Dionysiac swarm. Agave, the mother of the king, participates energetically in the dismemberment and possible cannibalism of the swarm, as Pentheus is detected spying on the bacchantes, urged to this by the god. She enters the chorus, enters the swarm, and then gradually emerges, led by her father Cadmus, to acknowledge sorrowfully what she has accomplished. The chorus, which has celebrated many gods, including Dionysos, ends the play with a gnomic utterance, sobered as they have witnessed the tragic end of the king of Thebes, and the fragmentary final lines of the play may even seek to re-member, to reconstruct the body of the tyrant.[61]

Some readers of this play focus on its privileging of Dionysos over other gods, and see prefigurations of monotheism here. Others, including my student Tina Hyland, see a revolutionary dimension. The women, including Agave, in their pleasure and ecstasy, overthrow the king in what might be seen as a coup d'état, as the collective overpowers the monarch, and the anarchic democratic will destroys the ruling house of Thebes. The swarm accomplishes an assassination, and it far exceeds the conception of the chorus as equivalent to the *demos* defined as the male citizen body. This chorus includes barbarian women, Asiatic worshippers of the god Dionysos, and their companions in devotion and ecstasy are the women of the city of Thebes.

COMIC CHORUSES SWARMING WITH A VARIETY OF OTHERS

Old Comedy choruses, from the fifth century BCE, included women, as well as birds, insects, clouds, cities, the letters of the alphabet, and barbarian others. One of the most intriguing of the choruses performed in a lost play, the *Babylonians*, produced in 426, in which the chorus seems to have been made up of tattooed slaves, according to extant summaries. This play had as its theme the administration of the Athenian Empire, and it may be that the chorus stood for various inhabitants of the empire's subjected cities and islands. The play survives only in fragments, lines cited by other ancient authors, or preserved in commentaries or etymological texts. In his *Life of Pericles*, the same first- and second-century CE writer Plutarch wrote: "The Samians in return for an insult tattooed their Athenian prisoners of war, with an owl on their foreheads, since the Athenians had tattooed the Samians with a *samaina* [a kind of ship named after the Samians].... They say it is to these tattoos that Aristophanes alludes: 'it's the Samian demos: how many-lettered [*polygrammatos*]!'" (26.4). These prisoners, rather than complimented for their erudition, have been made slaves, who were often tattooed with marks that indicated ownership, or the fact that they had been runaways, and then captured and returned to their previous owners.

In extant comedy, there is a variety of choruses made up of barbarians, slaves, and women. I look in some detail at one of the stranger swarms of Old Comedy, made up of a meteorological phenomenon. This chorus illustrates the ways in which the categories of citizen ritual, citizen celebration, and democratic dancing and singing can extend beyond the community of human beings, or even animals—birds, frogs, wasps—to include what might be thought of as inanimate phenomena, swarms in the sky. The *Clouds*, a critique of the character Socrates and his Thinkaterium, includes a chorus of what seem to be female clouds. They arrive rather late in the play, after the character Socrates addresses them, along with Air, and Aither, seemingly alternative gods to the traditional deities of the city, his summons testimony to the sacrilegious crimes allegedly committed by the philosopher according to the "apologies," defense speeches left behind by Plato and Xenophon. The comic character Socrates convokes the swarm, and they float in, singing as they enter:

> Clouds everlasting,
> let us arise, revealing our dewy bright form,
> from deep roaring father Ocean
> onto high mountain peaks.
>   (276–79)

Strepsiades, an obstreperous father like Philocleon, the father of Bdelycleon in the *Wasps*, greets them irreverently, answering their thunder with a fart. Socrates silences him, because "a great swarm of gods is on the move in song." He uses the word deployed for other sorts of swarms, *smenos*, to describe the chorus of clouds (298). They call themselves "rainbearing maidens," *parthenoi ombrophoroi* (299). They dance, or march, into the orchestra, difficult to discern at first, according to the characters; Strepsiades mistakes them for "mist and dew and smoke" (330). But they are called "goddesses," *theas* (328). They inspire the airiest of poets, mocked by Strepsiades, as he punctures the illusion, saying these "clouds" "look like fleeces spread out, not like women. . . . And these clouds have noses!" (343–44). The chorus looks neither like clouds, nor women. Yet the comic character Socrates proclaims that they are the only real goddesses; the others are phonies. Such a claim reinforced the idea, reiterated in the lawsuit against the man Socrates that resulted in his execution by the Athenians, that he had committed impiety, failed to honor the city's gods, introduced new gods.

These clouds float onto the scene, summoned by the character Socrates from Olympus, or Ocean, or the Nile, or elsewhere. Socrates addresses them as *mega semnai*, "most revered," but the choral procession, with its grand eloquence, is undermined by Strepsiades' comic deflation; he does not fear or tremble at their appearance, but needs a shit. Socrates replies with a rebuke, and asks for silence, as the great swarm (*smenos*) of gods is moving in song. The chorus sung by these feminine clouds is a praise of Athens reminiscent of some of the most lofty choral passages of tragedy:

> Rainbearing maidens,
> let us visit the gleaming land of Pallas, to see the ravishing country
> of Cecrops with its fine men.
>   (299–301)

These maidens, men dancing and singing in the guise of women, list by allusion the divinities who watch over Attica: Pallas Athena, Demeter and Kore, goddesses of the mysteries at Eleusis, and Dionysos, here called Bromios, the noisy one, patron of the very festival at which this play is being presented. Strepsiades asks who they are, and Socrates replies that they are not female heroes, but "divine clouds, great goddesses," *ouraniai Nephelai, megalai theai*, nourishing by their mistiness various ridiculed figures who infest the city. This is a swarm like no other.

The chorus of cloud maidens provides a setting, a backdrop, a collective that nostalgically recalls these beauties, these divinities, of the physical city and its protective gods. In the year 423, when the first version of this play was performed, the Athenians had been through a plague, the death of Pericles, many deaths in war, and worse was yet to come. The comedy's ridicule of the Sophists, mistakenly including Socrates, according to Plato in his *Apology*, contrasts the newfangled excesses of education with the old ways, a lost paradise that is consistent with the image of the city presented in the airy lines of the chorus's entrance. Socrates in fact claims them for himself and for the dialectic, and their ethereal mistiness, their dew-laden smoky qualities, come to exemplify the vagueness and uselessness of the new education.

Socrates condemns himself in his own lines: "[The clouds] nourish a great many sophists, diviners from Thurii, medical experts, long-haired idlers with onyx signet rings, and tune bending composers of dithyrambic choruses, men of high-flown pretension, whom they maintain as do-nothings, because they compose music about these Clouds" (331–34). The list contains several of the frequent targets of comic scorn, including the dithyrambic musicians, seen as obsessively repeating clichés about the weather, and then fattening themselves at the banquets that followed performances. Socrates' interlocutor in the play, the uneducated and deeply skeptical Strepsiades, mocks the appearance of this chorus. Interrupting the illusion, the vulgar hero calls attention to the ridiculousness of men posing as women posing as clouds.

LYSISTRATA

Among the most militant, independent, and successful of female comic characters is Lysistrata, the male actor who leads her chorus of men posing as citizen-class women, united in resistance to the soldiers of the two opposing sides in the Peloponnesian War. The two choruses of *Lysistrata* are a group of old men, part of the military opposed to peace with the Spartan enemies in the war, and another chorus of old women. The women of the various cities of the entire Greek world, summoned by Lysistrata, seek to force their male partners to end the war and return to the pleasures of heterosexual life. They lament the difficulties of obtaining dildos during wartime shortages: "If we sat around at home all made up, and walked past them wearing only our diaphanous underwear, with our pubes plucked in a neat triangle, and our husbands got hard and hankered to ball us, but we didn't go near them and kept away, they'd sue for peace, and pretty quick, you can count on that!" (149–54).[62] Lysistrata calls for the older women to occupy the Acropolis, the height of Athens where the Parthenon, temple or treasury of the goddess Athena, stands high above the quotidian life of the city.

The first chorus, the old men of the city, plans to dislodge the old women even if it requires burning them on a pyre. The chorus of women fights back, bringing water to quench the flames, and they call on Athena for help:

> Goddess, may I never see these women aflame,
> but rather see them rescue from war and madness
> Greece and their fellow countrymen!
> (341–43)

The men express dismay at the alliance between the women who occupy the height of the city and their supporters, women assembled from all over the Greek world, including Spartan women, the enemies of the Athenians and their allies in the war. The occupiers of the Acropolis stand fast against the invaders. And the leader of the men's chorus calls this collective a swarm: "This here's a complication we didn't count on facing; this swarm (*esmos*) of women outside the gates is here to help the others!" (352–53). The swarm occupying the Acropolis, sacred to the goddess Athena, seek to refuse entry to the chorus of old men, who call it "*my* acropolis," just as the younger women plot to refuse entry into their bodies by their husbands. Like the wasps, in their comedy, these women form a nameless, anonymous collective that nonetheless is resistant, rowdy, and determined to accomplish its goals. The two choruses battle it out verbally.

In *Lysistrata*, the old women are summoned from their occupation of the Acropolis by the rebel priestess herself, who identifies them as the common people, the women of the *demos*: "Forward, you spawn of the marketplace, you soup and vegetable mongers! Forward, you landladies, you hawkers of garlic and bread!" (457–58). The comic poet uses two of his fabulous, invented, portmanteau words to describe these women: *spermagoraiolekitholakhanopolides* and *skorodopandokeutriartopolides*, mouthfuls of allusive syllables. These are women of the *demos*, of the marketplace, vendors, like the mother of Euripides, alleged to be a seller of lettuce. They are not citizens, not the reasoned actors of political theory analyzing the practices of the democratic assembly. They represent a line of flight, marking the porosity of comedy, its incorporation of the many, the poor, the women, into dramatic representation. And they scare off the police sent to remove them from their citadel.

Lysistrata herself makes a point of distinguishing her company from another sort of collective: "Did you think you were going up against a bunch of slave girls (*doulas tinas*)?" (463–64). These are free women, fully armed and ready to fight citizen men for the sake of peace. The leader of the men's chorus, nonetheless, calls them animals. The leader of the women is proud to be a wild creature, and emphasizes their affinity with the old men of the *Wasps*: "I'd rather be sitting modestly at home like a maiden, bothering no one here, stirring not a single blade of grass. But if anyone annoys me and rifles my nest, they'll find a wasp (*sphekian*) inside" (473–75). She is part of a swarm, a collective, aroused and well armed for combat with those who want to evict them. Though they are likened to wild beasts (*theriois*, 468) and to monsters (*knodalois*, 476), they promise to dance with endless energy, joining with other women to fend off danger.

These women are tough, but they have also participated in the various rites of free citizen-class women, serving Athena as little girls, working for Demeter, dancing as bears for Artemis. Their leader reminds the audience: "I have a stake in our community: my contribution is men" (651). They give the city the sons who make up its fighting forces, once upon a time cavalry, then the hoplite infantrymen, and the rowers of the fleet.[63] The men's chorus likens them to Amazons, those invaders from the East who in mythic time occupied the nearby hill, the Areopagos, seeking to retrieve their queen from the king of Athens, Theseus (678). The women compare themselves to the dung beetle that caused eagle's eggs, once set in Zeus's lap, to break, in a threat to the genitals of the men who oppose them. The women's commander braces them, when they seem to be weakening in their sex strike, by oracularly comparing them to swallows, another swarm:

> Yea, when the swallows hole up in a single hole,
> fleeing the hoopoes and leaving the phallus alone,
> then are their problems solved.
>
> (770–72)

The swarm of women must act collectively, not peeling off to return to their husbands, not arguing, flying away from the sacred Acropolis.

In one brilliant scene, the Athenian wife Myrrhine tempts and manipulates her frustrated husband, Kinesias of Paeonidae. These characters' names are significant: Myrrhine's name alludes to myrrh, an aromatic used in erotic contexts. Kinesias's name alludes to a word referring sometimes to sexual intercourse. Jeffrey Henderson, translator of the play, notes that Kinesias was "likely chosen for the pun on *kinein*, 'screw,' just as the deme name Paeonidae reminds us of *paiein*, 'bang.'" She is the temptress, he the tempted.[64]

After Myrrhine torments her husband, Kinesias, and after more comic play about the massive erections of the frustrated men, the two choruses unite in a single song. Spartan men, suffering from the same affliction as the Athenians, appear on the scene. Lysistrata ends the war with a truce, enabled by Diallage, "Reconciliation," a naked, silent female figure, and the joint chorus sings of a redistribution of wealth:

> Intricate tapestries,
> nice clothes and fine gowns,
> and gold jewellery—-all that I own
> I'll ungrudgingly provide
> to everyone....
> I now invite you all to help yourselves
> to the possessions in my house....
> If anyone's out of bread
> but has slaves to feed
> and lots of little kids,
> you can get flour from my house.
>   (1188–1206)

This seeming generosity, however, is undercut, by the warning that coming to the door of the house will excite the watchdog waiting there. The war has brought poverty to the city, and the theme of hunger and its satisfaction also draws in the circumstances of deprivation and need, the hunger for peace in some of the audience.

A Spartan delegate arrives, compelled by the shared lust and sexual deprivation of the two armies, makes peace with the Athenian delegate, and recalls the days long past when the two cities and their allies made war together against the Persians. He invites Artemis, goddess of the wild, to join in their treaty, and calls for *philia*, "love," between the two parties. The chorus, now both men and women, joins in a dance celebrating the victory and the Spartan delegate recalls his city's ritual choral traditions:

> Let's sing a hymn to Sparta,
> home of dances for the gods
> and of stomping feet,
> where by the Eurotas' banks
> young girls frisk like fillies,
> raising underfoot
> dust clouds,
> and tossing their tresses

> like maenads waving their wands and playing,
> led by Leda's daughter,
> their chorus leader pure and pretty.
>
> (1304–15)

Helen leads the chorus, and in an evocation of Alcman's famed choral song, the *Partheneion*, performed by a swarm of Spartan girls, fillies and maenads, the delegate calls on the present chorus to begin leaping like deer, to sing for the victorious goddess Athena. Panhellenism, and the utopian scheme of the priestess Lysistrata, have triumphed, and the chorus exits dancing and singing.

David Konstan observes: "At the end of the play, with the women comfortably dispersed under the authority of male heads of household, the rival Greek states stake out their territories on the body of a woman without a thought for the ideal of pan-Hellenic citizenship proposed by Lysistrata. The utopian gesture has been recontained."[65] Nonetheless, much of the utopian scheme of Lysistrata has succeeded, as peace is declared, and if the dancing and celebration of the chorus represent a "line of flight," an escape out of the play into the festival celebrating the god Dionysos, these then serve to enter the real world of the performers, the audience, the city and countryside beyond chorus and citizens.[66]

Spike Lee's controversial musical film *Chi-raq*, released in 2015, transmutes the ancient comedy *Lysistrata*, setting it in contemporary Chicago. The Spartans and the Trojans are represented by gangs; the Lysistrata figure, lover of the lord of the Trojans, enlists women across the city to participate in a sex strike to end the rivalry and violence of their gang war. This twenty-first-century Black American Lysistrata was inspired by Leymah Gbowee, a woman who tried to end a civil war in Liberia by threatening a sex strike in 2003. Lysistrata in Chicago, along with her allies, takes occupation of an armory, and arranges a duel between herself and her lover, the leader of the Spartans, Demetrius. Whoever has the first orgasm loses their duel and must accede to the terms of the other. The Trojans' leader "Cyclops" surrenders first, and eventually the women win a truce. This Lysistrata is a strong and victorious woman, inspired by her fifth-century BCE counterpart.

THESMOPHORIAZUSAE

Another comedy featuring a female chorus, and a cast of female characters as well, is *Thesmophoriazusae* (*Women at the Thesmophoria*). The Thesmophoria was a festival celebrated in honor of Demeter and her daughter Kore, or Persephone, and was bound up with the fertility of the city-state's agriculture and her citizen women.⁶⁷ The play is among other things an attack on the tragedian Euripides, ridiculed for writing tragedies about women, and slandering them. The play itself suggests that women are all in fact quite guilty of the crimes he depicts in his plays, and that they merely resent his exposure of their libidinousness and innate tendencies toward drunken lack of propriety and adultery.

Other incidental targets of this comedy include the notoriously effeminate tragedian Agathon, whose singing is compared to "ant paths" (*murmekos atrapous*, 100), a suggestive metaphor for the swarming song of an Asianizing, decadent tragic poet mocked for what are represented as effeminate and overblown tendencies in life and poetic composition.⁶⁸ Agathon sings, performing the roles of leader and chorus alternately, summoning his maidens, being his maidens; Euripides' kinsman, a central character in this play, mocks his tragic song: "How feministic and tongue-gagged and deep-kissed! Just hearing it brought a tingle to my very butt!" (131–33). The comic mockery of the adult homoeroticist calls attention not only to the alleged excesses of the tragedian, but also to the transvestism of the theater itself, which will be an issue later in the play when the kinsman himself dresses as a woman to pass as a worshipper of Demeter in the rituals of the Thesmophoria.

This comedy has its affinities with the *Ecclesiazusae* (*Women at the Assembly*), to be discussed later, since here the worshippers of Demeter, in their sacred retreat, call an assembly on the second day of their festival to punish their enemy Euripides, who has alerted husbands to the many crimes of their wives. They are suspected of having lovers, chasing men, guzzling wine, and other infractions that require intensified vigilance on the part of the men of the city. The "kinsman" of Euripides, dressed as one of the women, confirms all the accusations, and adds some more, including his/her "getting banged by the slaves and mule grooms if we haven't got anyone else" (491–92).

The kinsman justifies his free-speaking by appealing to the Athenian tradition of *parrhesia* (541), "saying it all," to be discussed in chapter 5. The kinsman says: "There is freedom of speech here, and all of us who are citizens (*astai*) are entitled to speak" (540–41). The disguised kinsman, dressed as a woman, uses the significant term *astai*; he remembers to use the feminine form of the word, which refers first of all to residents of "the city," Athens itself, or even the Acropolis itself, the *astu*, as opposed to strangers, or foreigners, or even rustic fellow countrymen. Does the kinsman betray his masculinity by alluding to this right, or were women too entitled to the city's *parrhesia*, a right to say all?

The kinsman's deception is exposed. The chorus rallies and threatens destruction to the deceiver. And the chorus leader sings a song justifying praise of women: "Well, let's step forward and sing our own praises! We'd better, because each and every man has a host of bad things to say about the female race (*phulon*), claiming that we're an utter bane to humanity and the source of all ills: disputes, quarrels, bitter factionalism, distress, war. Come on now, if we're a bane, why do you marry us?" (785–89). The woman repeats the centuries-old litany of complaints against the female kind, going back to Hesiod, who described their creation in Pandora, and the miseries that follow for mankind.

The chorus leader insists, in fact, that "we're better than you" (800). And she proposes a test (*basanos*), using the word for "touchstone" and "torture."[69] She verbally pairs a man with a woman, and demonstrates that each woman, whose name registers excellent qualities of skill in war and counsel, is superior to a man. Crimes of men are listed. Mothers who contribute useful sons to the city, she argues, should be seated front and center at the women's festivals honoring Demeter; behind the worthy mothers should sit those whose sons behave shamefully, including the mother of Hyperbolus, assassinated after this play was first produced, and whose mother had been the object of mockery as a drunken foreigner and slut.

Following these lines, the play engages in some parodies of Euripidean tragedy, before Euripides himself appears on stage, in another allusion to tragedy like those focused on so intensely in the *Frogs*. When the kinsman's transvestism is uncovered, he is condemned to death wearing his feminine garments. The chorus celebrates, praising the two goddesses, Demeter and her daughter, Apollo, Artemis and Hera, Hermes, Pan and his nymphs, and the god in whose honor the dramatic festival is held:

> This way, Lord Bacchus crowned with ivy,
> do personally be our leader:
> and with revels I will hymn you,
> who love the dance!
>
> (986–89)

Meanwhile, the Scythian archer, slave policeman for the city, has been strapping the kinsman to a plank, preparing him for torture and execution. Euripides' relative appears, in the persona of Andromeda, appealing to "dear maidens" to rescue him as the tragic heroine did, winning the aid of Perseus against a sea monster. After a lengthy exchange with the kinsman-Andromeda, Euripides himself appears above the stage, the tragedian *ex machina*, in the role of Perseus the rescuer.

The tragic parody is further sustained, the tragic mood undermined, by the obscenity of the slave archer:

EURIPIDES: Why don't you let me untie her, Scythian, that I may couch her in the nuptial bower?
ARCHER: If you're so hot to bugger the old guy, why don' you drill a hole in the backside of that there plank and buttfuck him that way?
(1121–24)

The high-flown tragic language is brought thunderingly down to earth by the obscenity of the slave, and the intrusion of everyday life into melodrama.

The chorus sings and dances on, indifferent now to the imminent demise of their enemy, the kinsman of Euripides, and they invite their goddess, Athena, to join their dance:

> Maiden girl unwedlocked,
> who alone safeguards our city (*polin*) . . .
> show yourself, you who loathe
> tyrants, as is fitting.
> The country's female people (*demos . . . gunaikon*)
> summon you: please come
> bringing peace, comrade of festivity.
>
> (1139–47)

The language the chorus of women uses here is significant; they speak of the city itself, a physical entity in need of the protection of its goddess, Pallas Athena. But they also distinguish themselves, as a *demos*, a "people," and they further specify that they are a *demos* of women.

The rule by the people, the *demos*, *democratia*, the form of polity that characterizes classical Athens, in fact excluded women from the vote, jury service, all the activities of citizen men that defined that democracy. So for the women to call themselves another *demos*, a gendered people or city, produces a hauntingly alternate, shadow polity, one that through the chorus members, as inhabitants of the *polis*, challenges the claim of the other *demos*, the *demos* of men, to be the democracy. Not just in the *Ecclesiazusae*, where the women show up to participate in the *ekklesia*, the assembly, as will be discussed in a later chapter, but also here in this play focused rather on a religious festival, the women are utopically establishing themselves as a people. There is in this claim, in the activities and words of the chorus's song, a speculative reality that undermines or exists in some imaginary space, distinct from the men's citizen body.

And in lines that echo Sappho's fragment 1, the chorus summons their two goddesses, Demeter and Persephone:

If ever before you answered our call,
now too, we beseech you,
come here to us.

(1157–59)

The voices of the women's chorus in this comedy echo the syntax, the prayer, the hymn of the Lesbian poet of the sixth century BCE. The women address their prayers to the goddesses, as they do in *Lysistrata*, and their summons may further emphasize the fact that this chorus is made up of women, or, of course, men or boys dressed as women, engaging in the same complex transvestism as does the kinsman of Euripides when he sacrilegiously invades the ceremonies of the Thesmophoria.

"Euripides" the comic character makes a separate peace with the women of the chorus of the *Thesmophoriazusae*, recalling the private treaty made between Dikaiopolis and the Spartans in the *Acharnians*, to be discussed in chapter 5. The tragedian agrees no longer to slander the women of the city, if they will release his kinsman from bondage; the ease with which the transaction is made suggests again the desire for a wider peace, that between warring Greek states. Euripides uses as a decoy, to distract the slave archer, the Scythian who is part of the Athenians' police force, another slave, a dancing girl who is sold to the archer. He buys, Euripides takes her off, and the play ends abruptly, with the archer chasing the playwright, and with the final song of the chorus:

Now it's time for each woman
to go on home. May the two Thesmophoroi
reward you with fine
thanks for this performance!

(1228–31)

Tragedy and tragedians have been mocked, the slave's satisfaction and subsequent disappointment mark the end, and we have seen the women's *demos*, another city within the city, realized by the transvestite actors.

This chorus, like others made up of women, slaves, barbarians, animals, clouds, establishes temporarily an alternative reality within the drama. The slave satyrs of the *Cyclops*, the women enslaved in Euripides' *Hecuba*, and *Trojan Women*, the women of the *Lysistrata*, *Ecclesiazusae*, and *Thesmophoriazusae*, provide an estrangement from the political, public world of some of the Athenian spectators. These transposed choral bodies show themselves capable of implicit or explicit critique of the arrangements of the polity. Given the analogies between the dramatic chorus, of satyr play, tragedy or comedy, and other choruses of the city, and between the military phalanx, the forms of order established for the ephebes, the young men of the city in their training, these dramatic choruses stretch the definition of a civic corps. Vincent Azoulay and Paulin Ismard, in *Athènes 403*, describe their account of the city itself at the end of the fourth century BCE as "une histoire chorale," a "choral history," and list Lysimakhe, the priestess after whom Lysistrata may be named, as one of the leaders of the city's choruses.[70] Singing in unison, or spoken for in the voice of the *khoruphaia*, the chorus leader, the actual members of the city's dramatic choruses destabilize the norms of the city in which power lies in the hands of the citizen men who participate in the assembly or the law courts. Although their words are composed by free, citizen, male playwrights, these choruses express various degrees of distance from the received ideas, the official norms, the hegemonic ideology of the democratic city. Even the enslaved satyrs of the only extant satyr play allow for a distance from the generally assumed acceptance of the institution of slavery. In the words of Euripides and Aristophanes, strange bedfellows, as we see from the comic persecution of the former in the *Thesmophoriazusae*, women especially are given the power of critique and provide a telling estrangement from the accepted arrangements of the democracy. The swarm has politics of its own that can veer off from the plot, the *muthos*, the stated views of the personae, the "characters" of these performances, and create imaginary, vital speculative worlds.

[CHAPTER 4]

Utopias

> There is tenderness only in the coarsest demand: that no-one shall go hungry any more.
>
> Theodor Adorno, *Minima Moralia*

From the evidence in the surviving ancient comedies, we find hunger to be on the minds of their audiences, and talk of lavish feasts everywhere. The comic poet Pherecrates wrote, perhaps about a visit to the underworld, in fragment 113, from *Metalles* (*Mine Workers*): "Abundance was what everything there oozed. . . . Rivers, filled with porridge and black broth, flowed bubbling through the canyons, croutons and all, and chunks of cheese-stuffed bread; each mouthful went slick and easy by itself down the corpses' throats. . . . Roast thrushes, seasoned to be boiled, flew round our mouths begging to be gobbled up as we lay beneath the myrtle and anemone." The scene includes girls with their pubes shaved, giving wine to the drinkers; anything consumed grew back twice its size. Pherecrates seems especially interested in utopian culinary excesses.[1] Is this a fantasy about the afterlife, trying to tempt those listening within the play? About the mines?

Old Comedies can contain radical proposals, extravagant feasts, even venturing so far as to support the freeing of slaves who participate in the defense of Athens. In his valuable survey of Aristophanic comedy, *Aristophanes and Athens*, Douglas MacDowell argues that the playwright, not aiming merely to amuse, divert, and entertain his Athenian audience, intentionally offers advice and counsel for the city.[2] For example, in 405 BCE the chorus of the *Frogs*, in the first speech of the parabasis, sings that it is their duty to present good instruction to their audience. In this speech, they argue for equality among all citizens, for amnesty for those who have made errors in the past by supporting oligarchy, citing the case that slaves who fought in the naval battle of Arginousai were made citizens, became free men instead of slaves.[3] And that this policy should be carried further, freeing all those willing to fight in the navy in the future. As MacDowell emphasizes, "All men, whether citizens, foreigners, or slaves, should be equal provided that they fight for Athens in its time of need. . . . This is, for fifth-century Greece, an astounding proposal. It echoes the proposal made six years before in *Lysistrata*. . . , but goes beyond it."[4] The radical nature of such proposals is the subject of what follows.

In this chapter, I consider contemporary calls for change that might seem "impossible," and the history of utopia, including modern theoretical work on speculative fiction. Moving on to Old Comedy's utopian passages, I review moments in fragmentary works of other playwrights, and look closely at the *Birds*, populated by a choral swarm of birds drawn into the utopian scheme of Athenians fleeing their failing city. I assess not so much the traditions of comic satire and mockery, but rather some ancient comedies' resemblance to speculative fiction. Such an argument is meant not to ignore the tragedies unfolding around us every day, here and throughout the world, nor to deny that ancient Greek tragedy addresses some of the painful issues that never cease to haunt humankind—questions of belonging, of kinship, of identity and loss, and of death. But the emphasis on the tragic, not only in relation to drama but also as an abstract element in philosophy and political theory, comes to resemble an eternal work of mourning and individual sorrow. There is little respite from human problems in tragedy, unless we consider the burial of the female Furies of Aeschylus's tragedy *Eumenides*, and the invention of the jury trial portrayed in that work, as signs of hope for democracy. But if we look to the utopian, joyful, collective mood of ancient comedy, even beyond its often explicitly utopian content, there is another side of human existence, one that is dialectically related and responsive to the somber strains of tragedy.

DEMANDING THE IMPOSSIBLE

How are laughter, and comedy, and the chorus, connected to speculation, imagination, and the future? In October 2011, Judith Butler attended Occupy Wall Street, and, in reference to calls for clarification of the protesters' demands, she said:

> People have asked, so what are the demands? What are the demands all of these people are making? Either they say there are no demands and that leaves your critics confused, or they say that the demands for social equality and economic justice are impossible demands. And the impossible demands, they say, are just not practical. If hope is an impossible demand, then we demand the impossible—that the right to shelter, food and employment are impossible demands, then we demand the impossible. If it is impossible to demand that those who profit from the recession redistribute their wealth and cease their greed, then yes, we demand the impossible.

But it is true that there are no demands that you can submit to arbitration here because we are not just demanding economic justice and social equality, we are assembling in public, we are coming together as bodies in alliance, in the street and in the square. We're standing here together making democracy, enacting the phrase "We the people!"[5]

Demand the impossible.

In their *Utopia Reader*, Gregory Claeys and Lyman Tower Sargent admirably conclude their text on utopias with "Occupy."[6] They offer no statements or manifestos, but instead summarize its utopian aspects, and then present a bibliography of writings by such thinkers as Noam Chomsky, who commented on the movement. The editors' conclusions are suggestive; they identify utopian dimensions of the group, as well as the collective's formation of utopian spaces, governed by utopian rules of procedure. They note the "horizontal" method of assembly organization, based on consensus and a variety of hand gestures to allow participants to communicate nonverbally.

The editors also call attention to the problems raised by such methods: the "crossed-arm" signal, denoting disapproval and the need to speak, "led to constant blocking by people who had no interest in building consensus but simply wanted to dominate the proceedings." The last words of the *Utopia Reader* express some regret about the problems involved in such communal practices: "Consensus is a difficult process and requires prior training and, ideally, a group united on goals and methods."[7] The contradictory, risky, and uneven process of utopian *praxis* is also evident in moments of ancient comedy, where for example the collective chorus of birds in the *Birds* witnesses the murder and feasting on rebel birds at the wedding celebration that concludes the comedy. Even their utopia of Cloudcuckooland registers the "marks and scars" of social existence. Yet utopian groups in the present, formations such as Black Lives Matter, the Movement for Black Lives, and others, nonetheless continue to engage in speculative, hopeful, and utopian practices, to attempt to put into practice versions of leaderless, collective, spontaneous political action, oriented against racism, anti-Semitism, police violence, and tyranny, toward equality, social justice, and the redistribution of wealth.[8]

UTOPIAS

The word "utopia," although based on Greek roots meaning "not a place," "nowhere," was invented by Thomas More in the sixteenth century as the name of his somewhat enigmatic and speculative fiction about a land that might be, that might or might not respond to the great changes taking place in the England of his day.⁹ Such speculative fiction existed before More named it, even in antiquity, and of course it has become a significant genre ever since, into the twenty-first century, where utopias and dystopias abound in what is now more likely to be called speculative than "science" fiction.¹⁰

Rhiannon Evans, in her *Utopia Antiqua*, discusses the presence of utopian elements in ancient Roman culture, touching on the question of Golden Age narratives and the importance of the notion of decline for Romans' attitudes toward their history.¹¹ She draws a contrast between Golden Age narratives, which look to an unblemished past, and a utopianism defined by "fictional and geographical fantasy worlds." She also argues that "looking at the utopian as 'the repository of desire' . . . allows for the investigation of Golden Age narratives as they are specifically mobilized, rather than seeing them as repetitive examples of a universal trope."¹² "Make Athens great again."

The nostalgia expressed in some of ancient Greek comedy fuses a nostalgia for a lost past, a "golden age" of democracy rather than the golden age of Hesiod, with a desire for a future that has speculative, fictional, fantastic elements marked by that past. Emphasis on hunger and its satisfaction persists. In the world of some ancient comedies fish roasting on the fire, requested to hurry it up, assert in their defense that they are done only on one side; the reply: "Turn yourselves over and baste yourselves with oil and salt" (Crates, frag. 16, from Athenaeus 267e). A jar full of aromatic oil will arrive on its own for a waiting bather (frag. 17). The desire that emerges in some comedies is not only for such a prehistoric past, for a random gratification of all hungers, but also, sometimes, for a remembered past, the age of another democracy, one that, as in Cloudcuckooland, the new colony of the *Birds*, to be discussed later in this chapter, preemptively did not permit father-beaters, sycophants, wealthy and nebulous poets, and other menaces to democratic contentment.

One of my desires in this chapter, and in this book as a whole, is to insert ancient comedy into the debates concerning utopias, especially communal, communist utopian thinking. The tendency has been, even in such a thorough, invaluable, and radical work as Doyne Dawson's *Cities of the Gods: Communist Utopias of the Greeks*, to treat ancient comedy in a few paragraphs, and then to move on to the more serious philosophical utopias that have the gravitas historians of philosophy desire.¹³ Ancient literary utopias are given short shrift. In their *Utopia Reader*, Claeys and Sargent call Aristophanes' *Ecclesiazusae* a utopian *satire*, noting: "Classical Greece provides both the earliest works we now call utopias, or descriptions of much better societies, and satires on those societies."¹⁴ They include an almost thirty-page-long excerpt from Plato's *Republic*, and then introduce Aristophanes:

"Aristophanes (448?–380 BCE), the most important Greek comedic playwright, wrote the earliest utopian satires. In addition to *Ecclesiazusae*, excerpted here, these works include *Lysistrata* and *Thesmophoriazusae*, satires on the role of women in society, and *Birds*, which presents a simple utopia of pleasure."[15] They then present three pages extracted from the *Ecclesiazusae*. Of course the authors of this valuable anthology are considering a lengthy history of utopia, from the Hebrew Bible and Hesiod to twenty-first-century utopias, but the notion of a "utopian satire" is not really prepared for in their introduction to this vast backward gaze, retrofitted for ancient texts. All depends on Thomas More's *Utopia* of 1516. A vast bibliography exists concerning this text, and all those retrospectively and subsequently added to the category. Its appropriateness for ancient Athens may need further examination.

Comic writers, before and during the time of Aristophanes—Crates and Cratinus, for example—mention previous eras of history that had more plenty, more material abundance. These golden age scenes, which include the garden of Alkinoos in Homer's *Odyssey*, presenting a constant temperate climate, with endless crops of fruit to be harvested, differ from the communalism proposed in several surviving comedies. Crates, for example, who wrote a comedy called *Beasts* (*Theria*), alludes to some sort of utopia. Later writers cite lines from this play; Athenaeus gives us the following, with lines cited earlier:

A. Then absolutely no one will get a slave man or woman,
   but an old man will have to be his own servant?
B. No! I'll make everything able to walk.
A. But what good is that to them? B. Each of the utensils
   Will come to you by itself, when you call it. "Appear beside me,
      table!
Set yourself! Grain-sack, knead the dough!
Ladle, pour! Where is the wine-cup? Go and wash yourself!
Up here, bread dough! The pot should spit out those beets!
Come here, fish." "But I'm done only on one side yet."
"Then turn yourself over, and baste yourself—with a little salt."[16]

This is animacy, soul, activity attributed to inanimate as well as animate beings, the imagining of automata that obey human commands like robots, androids, drones, or zombies. Another character promises to bring hot baths to his people, on top of pillars, with water that comes from the sea: "The water will say 'you can turn me off now,'" and the bottle of perfume will arrive along with an automatic sponge and sandals. Such fantasies resemble the dream of automata expressed by Aristotle (*Politics* 1253b), and imagined by Herbert Marcuse in his utopian projections about a future in *Eros and Civilization*, or Aaron Bastani's arguments in *Fully Automated Luxury Communism*.[17] And the arrival of such marvelous objects into daily life could not be further from the heavily laden and signifying objects of the world of ancient tragedy.[18]

Other fragmentary passages offer similarly utopian reflections. Teleclides, for example, in the *Amphictyons* (*Neighboring States*), has a character recounting the gifts once bestowed on humankind, including peace, and no diseases: "Every gutter gushed wine, breads fought each other for your mouth.... The fish delivered themselves to your house, broiled themselves up, and lay down on your table. A river of gravy flowed past the couches... ductwork for bouillabaisse.... Roast thrushes carrying crackers flew down your throat."[19] As in the utopian schemes projected in some of Aristophanes' plays, food plays a prominent role in the imagination of past or future, a symptom of hunger in the audience during the difficult years of war in the fifth century BCE.

Claeys and Sargent's characterization of Aristophanes' *Ecclesiazusae*, sadly truncated here, and classified as "utopian satire," needs more critical attention. I would recall Tom Moylan's addition to the typical vocabulary concerning utopias and dystopias, his notion of a "critical utopia," also described by Claeys and Sargent in their introduction to the *Utopia Reader*.[20] A *critical* utopia is "a nonexistent society described in considerable detail and normally located in time and space that the author intended a contemporaneous reader (*sic*) to view as better than contemporary society but with difficult problems that the described society may or may not be able to solve and that takes a critical view of the utopian genre."[21] Moylan's own formulation is somewhat different: "Utopian writing in the 1970s was saved by its own destruction and transformation into the 'critical utopia'. 'Critical' in the Enlightenment sense of critique—that is, expressions of oppositional thought, unveiling, debunking, of both the genre itself and the historical situation."[22] Might we not see the *Birds*, for example, or even the *Ecclesiazusae*, the play Claeys and Sargent include in their anthology, as fitting into this category, with some modifications? It seems more appropriate to me than the notion of satire, which is not in fact listed as one of the definitions pertinent to Claeys and Sargent's introductory discussion of the utopian genre, which includes "utopianism," "utopia," "eutopia or positive utopia," "dystopia or negative utopia," as well as the aforementioned "critical utopia."[23]

The word "satire," like "utopia," is used anachronistically to apply to the fifth century BCE. The term applies to a Roman literary genre. As my late colleague Robert Elliott commented, in his entry on satire for the *Encyclopedia Britannica*, "*Satura* (which had had no verbal, adverbial, or adjectival forms) was immediately broadened by appropriation from the Greek word for 'satyr' (*satyros*) and its derivatives. The odd result is that the English 'satire' comes from the Latin *satura*; but 'satirize,' 'satiric,' etc., are of Greek origin."[24]

And what is Aristophanes "satirizing"? He may be ridiculing Cleon in the *Acharnians*, but are the more high-flying utopian comedies such as the *Birds* and the *Ecclesiazusae* directed with irony and sarcasm at particular individual targets in this way, or at ridiculous utopian projects floating in the autopoetic universe of the democracy? The concept of "critical utopia," even if anachronistic in its own right, seems more appropriate for Aristophanes' practice in these plays. Especially with reference to Tom Moylan's "difficult problems that the described society may or may not be able to solve," the questions of redistribution of wealth, of equality, and of erotic gratification, as in the case of the utopias featuring women, touch on matters that may be treated with ridicule or sarcasm, but also with a sense of critique.[25]

Like the Monty Python sketches with their male transvestism so dear to the British, the presentation of men dressed as women in the *Lysistrata*, *Ecclesiazusae*, and *Thesmophoriazusae* may simply appeal to the funny bone of patriarchal, misogynist societies, but also smuggle in the desire to be the other, or to widen the spectrum of gratification to include the excluded. Although Mark Griffith, in his arguments concerning the shifting identifications of the audience, directs his attention primarily toward class differences, the transvestism and representation of female persons in many comedies, as well as tragedies, offer the opportunity for masculine identification with the opposite sex.[26]

Ancient Greek comedy was a complicated, multilayered performance that included not just topical reference, not just ridicule of leading politicians and decisions about war and peace, but also such speculations as we see in the philosophical deliberations on politics that follow. I am still surprised that many readers for centuries saw only mockery or satire in the communist utopian schemes of some extant comedies. Why is the perception of Aristophanes that he was a conservative satirist, rather than a wildly inventive producer of speculative fictions? Alan Sommerstein, in *The Cambridge Companion to Greek Comedy*, writes: "Our evidence indicates that from the 440s to the 400s comedy positioned itself pretty consistently on the political right."[27]

In his essay, "Utopianism," in the same volume, Ian Ruffell shares my perspective:

> Among the many paradoxes of Old Comedy, perhaps the most striking is that it combines acute social commentary and political interventions

with the expression and realization of wishes of the most thoroughly impossible kind, in the creation of a transformed world or an alternative society....

In being prepared to contemplate and explore, however humorously, notions such as economic equality, women as political agents, or, from a modern perspective, perhaps the most laughable of all, a world at peace, Old Comedy seems in its own way to have been at the forefront of public speculation, going beyond and perhaps even leading the radical edge of Greek ideas.[28]

Ruffell notes that the later comedy of the Athenians—New Comedy and the work of Menander—retreats from this sort of radical speculation.

Old comic utopia, like comedy in general, is frequently seen as trivial, bound to its own time, local, absent the philosophical purchase of such weighty tomes as Plato's *Republic*. Along with rehabilitating the idea of communism, or communalism, and setting comedy alongside tragedy as a deeply significant and still pertinent artifact from antiquity, I claim for comic utopias a central role in calling into question frustrations, desires, the worries of everyday reality, and politics in the past, present, and future.

MODERN(IST) UTOPIA

Fredric Jameson, in a chapter entitled "Utopia, Modernism, and Death," discusses the proletarian novel of Andrei Platonov, *Chevengur*, written in the 1920s but not published in full until 1988, (most of the works of Platonov, a Soviet Communist, were banned during his lifetime).[29] The book by Jameson in which this chapter appears is entitled *The Seeds of Time* and opens with an epigraph from Shakespeare: ". . . for who can look into the seeds of time / And say which grain will grow and which will not . . ." These words are fitting not just for the Soviet writer, but also for Athenian Old Comedy; one might see in its plays many "seeds," many speculative and experimental gestures tossed into the audience, some contradictory, some ironic, a sowing of ideas and thoughts and possibilities, with no claim for their realizability, their inevitability.

Some of Jameson's remarks concerning *Chevengur* and utopia, although concerned with modernism, and so-called Second World culture, the culture of the former Soviet Union, shed light on the practices of Old Comedy, especially with regard to the more utopian plays. For example, Jameson notes, with regard to the collision between daydream and reality principle: "Historically, then, this is the sense in which the vocation of Utopia lies in failure; in which its epistemological value lies in the walls it allows us to feel around our minds, the invisible limits it gives us to detect by sheerest induction, the miring of our imaginations in the mode of production itself, the mud of the present age in which the winged Utopian shoes stick, imagining that to be the force of gravity itself" (75). In the case of comic utopian imaginings, we see the oscillation among the *Birds*, in which the tattooed slave, like the bird the francolin, finds refuge in Cloudcuckooland, but which also represents a form of bird rebellion, bird cannibalism; the *Peace* (421) in which the main character, Trygaeus, flies to Mount Olympus on a dung beetle to bring an end to war; and the world of the *Women at the Assembly*, where there is communism, communal luxury for all, except for the slaves who are still ordered about with utter disregard for their humanness by characters seemingly devoted to equality.

Jameson points to the difficulties inherent in the attempt to think one's way back into another world: "[W]hatever attitude we choose, the historiographic or indeed historicist problematic of a Gadamer or even a Benjamin remains the dilemma, which is that of *Verstehen* or of contact, that of the mode of access to an era whose structure of feeling is at least substantively different from our own. This historicist dilemma poses itself, to be sure, for all the objects of the past" (81). Can postmodern, or modern, readers perceive the "structure of feeling," to use Raymond Williams's term, of an ancient Athenian democratic spectator, perceive the "seeds," the randomly sown bits of utopian thinking that Old Comedy disperses? We need both a careful reading of the past and a commitment to recognizing both disjunction and the relevance of that past.

Jameson sees the historical conditions of possibility of recognition in disjunction, in Platonov the coexistence of peasant and industrial culture, and he points to Heidegger's formulations concerning the pre-Socratics as enabled by the recognition of another such moment of transition: "Heidegger does not tell us, I believe, and perhaps he is not interested in such speculations, how one is to imagine the historical conditions of possibility of the 'original' metaphysical experiences designated as such by him—I mean the expressions and formulations of the so-called Presocratic philosophers, which nonetheless seem to have emerged from just such a secular break in life experience with the impact of nascent commerce on the elder cultures of Asia Minor" (85). One might see the transition occurring in the lifetime of Aristophanes as another such break; some of his chorus members view the world of the Persian Wars, the victory at Marathon, the democracy of the earlier part of the fifth century BCE, and are jolted by the new democracy dominated by new leaders, by the aggressive imperialism of Athens as it comes to rule over its subject allies. That disjunction, the transition between a relatively autarchic economy and one dependent on empire, calls forth in comedy utopian imaginings of a return to that earlier culture as well as recognition of the new forces at play in the late fifth century BCE.

Other remarks of Jameson in relation to Platonov illuminate comic practices in new ways. He writes of what he calls "the moment of 'world reduction'" in the work of Ursula Le Guin, and such a moment seems to be present in the imagining of Cloudcuckooland, the escape from the old world that begins with the very first words of the play, but is also part of such plans as the *Women at the Assembly*, and other utopian performances. In Platonov's novel, Jameson discerns "a fairy-tale narrative in which Sasha and other characters set forth to find that mysterious thing they lack, like the blue flower, which bears the name of 'socialism'" (94). Novalis's "blue flower," the symbol that signals a lack, could stand for all that is missing in the city of Athens but can be constructed in the new world of the birds. The search that defines the earlier scenes of the *Birds*, before the decision to build a new city, can be seen as the yearning to fulfill a lack: "In the deepest unconscious mind," writes Jameson, "the lost object, 'petit a,' is multiform, the heart's desire is both something so material and domestic as a source of oral gratification . . . and something so complex it stands as the abstraction of everything people have been able to conceive as their ideal of collective life and of the world itself" (97).

I find especially intriguing the notion that the utopian impulse does not necessarily entail a totalitarian erasure of individuality and particularity and even peculiarity, as anti-utopian debunkers might insist. Jameson connects this potential with Theodor Adorno: "I gloss here a fundamental notion of Adorno's, namely, that what we think of as individuality in the West, and what seems to us somehow to trace the outlines of an essential human nature, is little more than the marks and scars, the violent compressions, resulting from the interiorization by so-called civilized human beings of that instinct for self-preservation without which, in this fallen society or history, we would all be destroyed" (99). Individuality, or "individualism," then, is not human nature, but a consequence of our history. And the fading of the need for the instinct to survive, Jameson argues, *is* Utopia, where "the constraints for uniformization and conformity have been removed, and human beings grow wild like plants in a state of nature" (99). Viewing the utopian moments of the *Birds*, even as the birds sing in chorus, we discover the variety, the multiplicity, the swarm of difference of all the birds.[30] As in *Chevengur*, these are people, or birds "'on vacation from imperialism,'" and from war, from the Peloponnesian War that has ravaged the land of Attica.

I return to the chorus of the *Birds*, composed of twenty-four dancer-singers, each a different bird. The characters name Flamingo, Hoopoe,

Gobbler, Partridge, Francolin, Widgeon, Halcyon, Snippet, Owl, Jay, Turtledove, Lark, and many others. This collective sometimes moves as one, sometimes in countermeasures. It sings in one voice as an "I," then as "we." The chorus leader sings in the first person, then for the group, even for the playwright himself, addressing the chorus, the characters, and the audience. What I find most fascinating is the individuation of the chorus members, who are distinct and particular even as they participate in the whole. And that whole is likened to a cloud, to a swarm, to a *demos*, to a *polis*.

Jameson finds multiple ironies in the text of Platonov, and perhaps in a sense these too are relevant to the Aristophanic corpus. If there is a "wider sense of the global population brought to the metropolis by way of the new imperialisms" (118) of the twentieth century, fifth-century Athens too experienced such an opening to a wider world, through its imperialist adventures, and through the work of Herodotus, for example, who detailed the lifeways of Egyptians, Scythians, and other peoples of the Mediterranean basin. In the twentieth-century example, Jameson finds "an existential crisis in the metropolis whose effect is that radical devaluation of individual experience we call irony" (118). The chorus of the *Birds* is polymorphous, differentiated by kind, and offering an ironic perspective on the practices of the existent city, with its oraclemongers and its poets, and on the utopian dreams of the character Peisetairos as well. If Herodotus's descriptions present "a mirror" for the Greeks, they also present a variety of ways of organizing culture and society, a multiplicity of choices that relativized the Greeks' own assumptions about the proper way to live.[31]

ANCIENT UTOPIAS

Other ancient examples of invented places include, at the very beginnings of Western literary production, the island of Phaiakia in Homer's *Odyssey*, where the king's garden escapes the burden of seasonal change and is eternally productive of ripeness. There are speculative fictions in the philosophers; some would argue that the polity presented in Plato's *Republic* is such a text.[32] Alain Badiou, contemporary French philosopher, has recently published a "translation" of Plato's *Republic*, setting it in the present, making one of the interlocutors in the conversation a woman, and arguing in essence that the important burden of Plato's dialogue is not totalitarianism, as some have argued, but rather communism.[33] This idiosyncratic "translation" of Plato's *Republic*, its paperback cover (2014) adorned with a photograph of a parade in Tian'anmen Square prominently displaying a portrait of Mao Zedong, contains a rewriting of the myth of the cave:

> Imagine an enormous movie theater. Down front, the screen, which goes right up to the ceiling (but it's so high that everything up there gets lost in the dark) blocks anything other than itself from being seen. It's a full house. For as long as they've been around, the audience members have been chained to their seats, with their eyes staring at the screen and their heads held in place by rigid headphones covering their ears. Behind these tens of thousands of spectators shackled to their seats there's an immense wooden walkway, at head level, running parallel to the whole length of the screen. Still further back are enormous projectors flooding the screen with an almost unbearable white light....
>
> All sorts of robots, dolls, cardboard cut-outs, puppets, operated and manipulated by invisible puppeteers or guided by remote control, move along the walkway. Animals, stretcher-bearers, scythe-bearers, cars, storks, ordinary people, armed soldiers, gangs of youths from the *banlieues*, turtle doves, cultural coordinators, naked women, and so forth go back and forth continuously in this way. (Book 7, 514a-b; p. 212)

Other remarkable features of Badiou's translation of Plato's *Republic* include this passage in the myth of Er, describing the choice of a new life by one of the immortal souls:

> The person who'd drawn number 1 came forward and chose the life of the CEO of the biggest retail conglomerate in his country, the one whose well-known chain of giant box stores, located on the outskirts of every town, bore the names *More is Better*, *Load Your Cart*, and *Gimme more*! Carried away by his insane greed, he'd chosen this life without having bothered to look into the details. He hadn't realized that this existential fate included, among other horrors, the fact that the CEO, though of course in command of a huge fortune, married to a supermodel and the father of four sons, would only be truly sexually attracted to little girls under the age of seven. He'd bribe gangsters to procure them for him or, all in one day, he'd make round trips in his private jet to far-off Asian countries just to get a blow job on the sly from a little girl in disgusting public restrooms. Caught in the act during one of the sprees, he'd be arrested, repeatedly beaten, and handed over in prison to thugs who would turn him into a bedraggled sex slave. (619b-c; p. 350)

Plato's Greek text here—briefly—concerns a soul that chose tyranny, and the eating of his own children.

Badiou also significantly rewrites Plato's noble lie, describing three social groups: "the financiers," the intermediate professions, and the "direct producers" (109), in the Phoenician myth like different metals. But, the teller of the tale, a Phoenician sailor says:

> One day, say ... subversive preachers, a counter-god of sorts will appear, though we don't yet know in what form. ... An idea, a single spark that can set the whole prairie on fire? ... But in any event this counter-god will melt down all the Phoenicians, or maybe even humanity as a whole, and will re-make them in such a way that all without exception will hencefor-ward be made up of an undifferentiated mixture of earth, iron, gold, and silver. They'll consequently have to live indivisibly, since they'll all share identically in the equality of fate. (109–10)

(As the English translator notes, this is an allusion to Mao Zedong's 1930 essay entitled "A Single Spark Can Start a Prairie Fire" [360n3].) Badiou elsewhere, controversially, again alludes to Mao in his translation of the conversation between Socrates and Glaucon: "The communist Idea must command the gun" (110). (Mao of course notoriously wrote: "Political power grows out of the barrel of a gun ... [but] the gun must never be allowed to command the party" ["Problems of War and Strategy," published in 1938].)

Badiou also trades in Adeimantus, inventing an often annoying sister of Glaucon, Amantha, who flirts, serves to undermine Plato's pederasty and homoeroticism, and even denounces contemporary women, targeting the special pleading of feminists: "All they think about is getting ahead by stepping on men and their girlfriends. And on top of that they make everyone feel sorry for them. If the world were run by women it would be like a beehive, a nest of ants, termites!" (275). Clearly, this Amantha has not been persuaded by the comic presentation of swarms of female chorus members in the *Ecclesiazusae*.

The work of Alain Badiou is especially provoking and provocative, and relevant to the question of utopia. He declares himself to be an ardent Platonist, critical of various forms of anti-Platonism, including a Marxist anti-Platonism, "for which Plato is the origin of the notorious sensible/intelligible opposition, hence the source of idealism and the beginning of the history of ideology." Badiou frequently refers to this mode of anti-Platonism by citing the dictionary of philosophy commissioned by Stalin, where Plato is defined as "ideologue of the slave owners" (ix).

Badiou describes Spartacus, like Paul, as a Lenin-like figure who galvanizes followers, who in turn, inspired by an event, and a truth, one that authentically moves toward equality, commit themselves to that truth. Elsewhere, in his *Communist Hypothesis*, in a letter to Slavoj Zizek, Badiou argues for the productivity of failure: "The Cultural Revolution plays the role that the Paris Commune played in its Leninist sequence . . . *a terrible failure that teaches us some essential lessons*."³⁴ In the introduction to Badiou's new *Republic*, Ken Reinhard reminds the reader that "for Badiou, Plato is the first warrior in the eternal battle of philosophy against sophistry, of truth against opinion, and *the progenitor of the living idea of communism*" (vii, emphasis mine). Badiou's Socrates argues: "Private property has to be abolished. None of the members of our political community will own his own lodgings, let alone a workshop or a storehouse. Everything will be collectivized" (416d; p. 111). In the Greek text, Plato says that in the community of the *guardians* "none must possess any private property save the indispensable. Secondly, none must have any habitation or treasure-house which is not open for all to enter at will."³⁵ (The translator of the Loeb edition, Paul Shorey, noted: "Plato's communism is primarily a device to secure disinterestedness in the ruling class, though he sometimes treats it as a counsel of perfection for all men and states" [p. 310, n. a].)³⁶

Doyne Dawson, in *Cities of the Gods: Communist Utopias in Greek Thought* called attention in 1992 to the point that, "on the one hand, the way of life Plato proposes for the elite of this paradigm polis represents the most dazzling vision of human potentiality that anyone in the ancient world had ever conceived. . . . He dares to envision a truly unified community in which individual properties and families are abolished. . . . [But even as he offers us this vision of perfectibility, he seems to rob it of its force. For this radical transformation is limited to a ruling minority.]"³⁷ For Alain Badiou, the communism of Plato *is* the point. And it anticipates what Marx and Engels wrote in *The German Ideology*: "We call communism the *real* movement which abolishes the present state of things."³⁸ I am reminded of something called "cinderology," as in Cinderella, used by Stewart M. Cameron in the *British Medical Journal* to describe how "scientists frequently borrow the tale to describe the neglect of concepts or disciplines, for the positive identification of a disease or condition, or to refer to a transformation and subsequent recognition."³⁹ Besides something mysteriously named "Cinderella dermatosis," the concept of neglect seems most pertinent for the positive reading of the communist Plato.

Badiou sees Plato as a mathematician, a lover, and a communist, stressing a highly idiosyncratic and possibly cinderological reading of his works. He places greatest weight on Plato's advocacy of communism for his guardians, and writes in the preface to his translation: "We think this Plato is, and will be, a monkey wrench thrown in the machinery of Capital, a small contribution whose aim is to stop the juggernaut from crushing everything in its path" (xxx). He sees Plato as invaluable precisely because he is an idealist, not bound to the material world as it is: "Plato has been saying, and will say again, I hope, in every language, that the order of thinking can triumph over the apparent law of things, that justice can triumph over the power of money—in a word, that communism, an old word whose utter newness the old philosopher will teach us, is possible" (xxx). He refers to what he calls Plato's "fundamental intuition" on the symbiosis of communism and philosophy, his "restricted communism," which Badiou cites in order to call for "a generalized communism" (38). He likens the ancient philosopher, imagining what is not yet, to the Watchman at the beginning of Aeschylus's *Agamemnon*: "The philosopher must try to discern far into the distance, toward the horizon, whatever the glowing lights announce" (18).

Badiou is a controversial figure, denounced for sexism, idealism, anti-Semitism, Maoism, and other crimes. One reviewer of his translation of the *Republic* in *Le Point* (February 22, 2013), outraged at his tampering with a classic of the philosophical tradition, accused him of "incommensurable narcissism," and of "succumbing to the fascist temptation of the totalitarianism of the extreme left"! Yet Badiou seems to me to be enacting imprecisely what Jameson calls the Marxist solution to the dilemma of identity and difference; in the confrontation of two modes of production, the past "calls our own form of life into question," and passes judgment on us, the past points, in an allusion to Ernst Bloch, to "what we are not yet" (479).

Doyne Dawson discusses "low communism," the sort of town planning typical of Greek colonization, in which founders of new cities imagined spaces different from those of mainland, ancient *poleis*. The philosophical utopian thinking differs, incorporating thought experiments that come to include all of the known world in new forms of cosmopolitanism. There is, I would say, no "utopianism" in Greek tragedy, no speculative fiction of the sort described by Dawson. There are explorations of the mythic, legendary past, another place, perhaps hope for democracy and its law in Aeschylus's *Oresteia*, but not the imaginatively detailed creation of a better, or different, space and place that are characteristic of utopias per se.

Comic utopias offer something else, and for that reason they have particular relevance to the politics of the present. Fredric Jameson's work on utopias and science and speculative fiction argues that such writings are valuable because they reveal what is missing in the present. He explains: "I want to convey a situation in which political institutions seem both unchangeable and infinitely modifiable: no agency has appeared on the horizon that offers the slightest chance or hope of modifying the status quo, and yet in the mind—and perhaps for that very reason—all kinds of institutional variations and recombinations seem thinkable." Citing Louis Marin on utopia, Jameson reflects: "Utopia is somehow negative . . . it is most authentic when we cannot imagine it. Its function lies not in helping us to imagine a better future but rather in demonstrating our utter incapacity to imagine such a future—-our imprisonment in a non-utopian present without historicity or futurity—so as to reveal the ideological closure of the system in which we are somehow trapped and confined."[40] It is not that these texts necessarily urge the integrity of new worlds, in familiar settings or distant planets, but that their speculations are a symptom. Trying to make sense of such "nowheres," to imagine their materialization, is not the point. Rather, we can see the description, for example, of the abolition of private property, or of communism, although these may seem impossible, even at best unlikely, but the degree of likelihood of these new arrangements is not the point. Nor is the "road map," an account of what changes would have to be made to get to this new place, required of such fictions. Rather, they expose the fault lines, the fissures, the "sutures," as Pierre Macherey calls them, concealing the real relations of the culture that produced them.

UTOPIAN COMEDIES

I'm particularly interested here in the utopian plays of Athenian Old Comedy. Although much ink has been spilled trying to characterize the actual "politics" of the extant plays of comedy, it opened up questions of democracy, demagoguery, and the Athenian Empire, in imaginary settings that express some compelling critiques of the world of Athens as its poets and theatrical collectives saw it changing around them.

Earlier comic playwrights had written plays with utopian aspects, mentioned earlier. Unfortunately, all that remains of the works of Crates and Cratinus, for example, is plot summaries and fragments. Crates wrote comedies with such titles as *Feasts, Beasts, Games, Politicians*. One of his comedies, the title now lost, seems to depict a golden age society, utopia as regression to an untroubled past. According to a late writer, Stephanus of Byzantium, Cratinus refers to a city of slaves, *polin doulon* (frag. 223; Stephanus 237.5).

Discussions of the politics of Aristophanes himself often focus on the overt expressions of adherence to an antidemagogic, conservative, pacificist position, and try to trace out a stance from the utterances of characters and of the chorus, especially in the parabasis, the address to the audience by the chorus leader, who seems to speak at times in the voice of the playwright. In his work on the issue of social class in comedy, which includes consideration of Menander as well as Aristophanes, David Kawalko Roselli, cited earlier, presents a more sophisticated model of analysis.[41] He sees, implicitly at least, the staging of the contradictions of the *polis* in the work of Aristophanes, the *polis* in which there is, ideologically at least, equality, and at the same time, economic inequality. He sees the playwright as appealing to various elements in his audience, and he includes the poor as part of that audience, as recounted above, relying on the possibility that on the slopes of the hill above the theater of Dionysos, for example, the poor, even the enslaved, could enjoy theatrical spectacles without paying for the privilege of actual attendance in the city's amphitheater.

Roselli argues also that the *theorika*, the city's subsidies for viewing, at some periods allowed the poor to pay for admission to the theater. There is firm evidence for these subsidies only for a short period in the fourth century BCE; the scholarly consensus is that these were instituted in 350 BCE, long after the career of Aristophanes had ended. And, as Roselli notes, "while theoric distributions were regularized by about 350, there is some evidence that entrance fees increased . . . ; and in 322 *theorika* were most likely abolished under the oligarchs."[42] That is to say, the poor's attendance was most likely not subsidized in the fifth century BCE, and the subsidies lasted for a mere twenty-eight years in the fourth.[43] Nonetheless, Roselli's picture of the politics of Aristophanes is revealing as he mines Raymond Williams's theoretical contributions to reveal new dimensions of ancient drama. Williams described the contestation between dominant, residual, and emergent ideology, in a progressive model suggesting an almost inevitable overcoming of the past by the new.[44] Roselli looks also to Antonio Gramsci, for thinking about ideology, and in his important essay on social class in *The Cambridge Companion to Greek Comedy*, while not taking into account Althusser's important interventions on this question, very usefully points to the ways in which scholarship has failed to recognize some crucial dimensions of Old Comedy. He clarifies how, in a play such as *Wealth*, one character "accepts that communism is now the law (759) and notes that others are compliant": "Many scholarly discussions, based on a priori assumptions about the poet's conservative views, have dismissed these utopian desires as impractical and viewed Aristophanes as ridiculing such schemes. Surely it is important to note both support for and opposition to economic reforms built into these plays."[45] Such a formulation, emphasizing the *contested* presence of communism in the plays, provides a dialectical analysis of the various strains of political thinking set on stage, made into theater by the city itself, in a sense that echoes Vernant's analyses of tragedy, as the city putting itself on stage.

THE *BIRDS*

One of the most fascinating of comedy's choruses is that of the *Birds*, which I will look at in some detail here. The play has obvious utopian dimensions; here I stress the peculiarities of the constitution and performance of the *chorus* in the *Birds*. Rather than focusing on the plot and the characters of the play, as readers of Aristotle's *Poetics* are encouraged to do, even perhaps in the lost chapters of the treatise concerning comedy, I will foreground consideration of the chorus, notoriously ignored by Aristotle.

Comic choruses, as mentioned above, included twenty-four members, while the choruses of tragedy had only twelve, and there is a long tradition of animal choruses in comedy, mostly in plays that have not survived.[46] The *Birds* was produced in 414 BCE, and won second prize at the Dionysia festival. The play is unusually long for a comedy, and must have cost a great deal to produce; each of its chorus members wore a bird costume. As discussed earlier, an illustration on a vase from the fifth century BCE, owned by the J. Paul Getty Museum, shows two theater performers facing one another, dressed as birds, but they wear identical costumes, and some scholars contend they do not show actors from Aristophanes' play, although their presence on this vase is evocative of the theater.[47]

The chorus in the *Birds* forms a swarm, a people (*demos*), and a city (*polis*). The play begins with the "characters," the personae Peisetairos and Euelpides trekking away from Athens, seeking to escape the world of the *polis* and establish a utopia elsewhere, in a project that resembles the many exoduses from mainland cities in earlier centuries that resulted in the foundation of Greek colonies around the Mediterranean basin.[48] After the introduction of the individual characters, revealing their discontent with life in the earthly city of the Athenians, the chorus of birds arrives, summoned by the resident of the heavens Tereus, who in a mythic narrative was for his crimes turned into a bird.

The story was the subject of one of the tragedies of Sophocles: Tereus had married Procne, but raped her sister Philomela, and then cut out the tongue of Philomela to prevent her from telling her story. She succeeded nonetheless in communicating with her sister Procne by means of an embroidered tapestry illustrating the rape. The two sisters came together to take revenge on Tereus. They killed Procne's and Tereus's son Itys, feeding his corpse to his father. Realizing with horror what they had done, Tereus tried to pursue the sisters with his sword, but the gods metamorphosed him into a hoopoe, while Procne became a nightingale, whose song mourned the dead child; Philomela was transformed into a swallow. This is the tragic version of the birds' story. Aristophanes makes Tereus a comic hero, a help to the utopian Peisetairos, who wants to found a new city with the birds.

Tereus calls the birds to him, using a wordless song to summon them from the country, from gardens and hills and meadows, from over the sea. His utterance begins by imitating nonhuman forms of communication:

"*Epopopoi popopopoi popoi, ye ye co co co co*" (227–28). And then his call transforms into recognizable Greek, third-person imperatives that command every bird to appear. The linguistic flexibility here, moving from meaningless, coaxing noise, to meaningful, coaxing summons, provides a compelling transition between the world of the animal swarm and the human beings in bird form who appear as the chorus in the next moments of the comedy. Sean Gurd, in his fascinating book *Dissonance*, refers to these sounds. And he adds: "When song evokes sound, it becomes one means by which the enclosure of a society resonates with its environment, developing sensitivities to ambient entities and influences."[49] Comedy's porosity imbeds it in the environment.

Tereus the hoopoe's invocation of the birds, the chorus here, resembles the song of the frog chorus in the play about Dionysos's trip to the underworld to retrieve a tragedian, named for that chorus, the *Frogs*. They sing "*brek ek ek ek coax coax*," froggy sounds that make no sense in Greek, but that mimic the croaking of the swamp.[50] If human music begins as an imitation of animal sounds, and in particular of bird song, then Tereus's call erases the boundary between the bird, the birds, and the human actors, who become animal, and sing and dance as a collective in imitation of these creatures. One of the first musical instruments discovered by archaeologists is a hollowed-out bird's wing from the Paleolithic Ice Age, a simple flute, with stops for the fingers, which uses the bird's body to imitate the noise, the sound, of the animal. The chorus in this play, dressed as birds, sings and dances and in an almost totemic way expresses the kinship between human and animal.

Tereus continues his call: "*tio tio tio tio tio tio tio tio*" (237), and the birds begin to alight. "*Trioto trioto totobrix*" (243), he sings, again in wordless syllables that imitate the song of his comrades, ending with the climax: "*Torotorotorotorotix, kikkabau kikkabau, torotorotorolililix*"! (260–62). Bird after bird appears, first the red-winged bird, the "flamingo," the "mede," and then another hoopoe, like Tereus a part of the growing chorus. These birds are likened to politicians, or members of the audience, mocked for their unsavory habits. And at last a whole group of birds has assembled. Euelpides, companion of the central character, Peisetairos, compares them to a swarm, a cloud, *tou nephous* (295), which for us recalls the chorus of another Aristophanes comedy, named for that chorus, the *Clouds*, the play that ridicules Socrates and the Sophists.

The two human characters point out each bird as it arrives, and then, after noticing an owl, totemic bird of the city of Athens, Athena's bird, Euelpides utters a long list of eighteen different species, from "jay" to "woodpecker" (303–4). They dance, as Peisetairos marvels at them, wondering if they are threatening (shades of Hitchcock), and repeats as a sort of chant the word *iou, iou*, translated by Henderson as "Whooee," "Whooee."

The birds themselves first pronounce at line 310, with a sort of stuttering, noise-like sound, "*popopopopopo*," the avian preface to the Greek word *pou*, "where?" The chorus of many, varied species speaks as one here, referring to itself as "me": "Where's the one who called me?" The sliding between plural and singular in the utterances of the chorus points to the flexible indifferentiation of this group, an equality, a unity, each one a synecdochic part for the whole, indicative in some sense of the *isonomia*, the "equality" of democratic ideology. One of the beauties of this chorus is the way in which it permits individuation of the different species, while embodying at the same time the wholeness of the whole.

The members of the chorus of the *Birds*, according to Gwendolyn Compton-Engle, were variously garbed: "One of the stunning features of *Birds* is the unparalleled proliferation of animal costumes throughout the play. Each member of the twenty-four-person chorus is differentiated as a specific bird; four other mute bird-costumed characters precede the appearance of the chorus; the aulos player is represented by a bird-costumed nightingale."[51] In some sense this translation of democratic existence into the avian world recalls the famous speech of Pericles recounted by Thucydides in his history of the latter part of the fifth century BCE, an oration that celebrates the Athenian way of life, the democracy that engages men in public life, but tolerates individuality in their private existence. Democracy and the ideology of equality, in representation, do not entail the erasure of difference, but rather allow for privacy, and the inclusion of difference within a whole committed to the embrace of all its members. The birds of this chorus make up such a community.

The chorus stutters birdily as it addresses Tereus, asking him what message he has for them, "me, his friend" (*philon*), again speaking of the collective as one. And he says that it concerns their *koinon*, their "common" thing, their community. The chorus leader speaks on behalf of this communal body, or swarm, in the dialogue that follows, expressing dismay at Tereus's admission of the two foreigners, human beings, into their space. The chorus is outraged, and collectively laments, "*ea, ea*," speaking of impiety and defilement. They complain, as birds, of having been entrapped by this foreign species that has always been their enemy, and the chorus leader suggests in a violent threat that the human interlopers be dismembered. One of the human interlopers, Euelpides, the hapless sidekick of the inventive and resourceful Peisetairos, points to the audience and wishes he were back among them. Here is another line of flight, a line of escape by which the performance of the play connects with the other multiplicity that is the audience, the city outside the theater, the countryside outside the city.

The chorus moves to assault these strangers, again using a wordless cry to rally the group: "*io, io.*" Assembled like an army against an enemy, they call for an attack and are confident of victory, since the human beings have nowhere to run, nowhere to hide. The language they use to describe their plans resembles that of the chorus of wasps but is consistent with bird powers, bird bodies: they will surround the enemy with wings, pluck and peck them, level out their beaks, skin them alive. Henderson brilliantly translates the birds' reasoning: "[These men] were enemies of our very forefeathers" (374). Tereus advocates patience, caution, a willingness to learn from enemies. And as the murderous assault abates, Peisetairos observes that the birds seem to be calming and letting go of their rage.

The furious defense recedes, and the birds agree to listen to the human beings' reasons for calling them together. The comedy continues to remind us that these creatures are—birds. They begin to listen, "all aflutter," *anepteromai* (433), a verb in the first-person singular, "I'm on the wing," using the root *pteron*, "feather," to suggest a state of avian excitement. The birds solemnly promise not to attack again, as Peisetairos fears. He explains to the assembled company of many species that they once were "kings," *basileis* (467), ruling over all that exists, including the great god Zeus, including Earth, *Ge*, herself. They express amazement, as Peisetairos continues his exposition of the history of the universe, citing Aescp as a source for his version of these matters. One of the fables describes the lark (*korudos*), first of all the birds to be born, even before the earth; when her father died there was no place in which to bury him, so she placed him in her own "head" (*kephale*, also the name of a part of Attica that contained a cemetery). So if the birds came first, before *Ge* herself, first in Hesiod's almost canonical *Theogony*, then they should rule. Other evidence is adduced, to prove that the rooster, the cock, ruled over the Persians, still commanding attention as he announces the beginning of the workday. The kite ruled over the Greeks, the cuckoo reigned in Egypt and Phoenicia, and if a human being were to serve as ruler, his scepter was adorned with a bird. Portrayals of Zeus show the god with an eagle atop his head, Athena appears with an owl, Apollo with a hawk. The birds could grab the best parts of the sacrifice before the gods could make their move. Furthermore, human beings swear by the birds. Therefore it is wrong that, in the present, human beings disrespect them, throw rocks at them, set traps for them and sell them, roast them and serve them with hot sauces.

The birds understandably react with dismay to this catalogue of lost power and present torment, and surrender themselves to the scheme of

Peisetairos, as their savior. He tells them to build a city (*polis*), and to construct a wall around it that fills up all the space between the sky and the earth. Then they can reclaim sovereignty from Zeus, refuse passage to the gods who want to descend to earth with their erections, to have sex with the many human women of legend who in the past submitted to the gods and bore them children, women such as Semele, impregnated by Zeus to become mother of the god Dionysos. Human beings will henceforth have to sacrifice not to the gods, but first to the birds, with appropriate offerings for each kind.

The chorus expresses doubt concerning how the human beings would believe they are gods: "We fly around and wear wings" (573). Peisetairos points out that many of the gods, among them Hermes, Nike, Eros, Iris, themselves have wings; and in addition, if the human beings resist, the birds can send a cloud of sparrows to eat all the seeds in their fields, leaving them with no crops to harvest. The ravens can peck out the eyes of their oxen and sheep. If they do accept the birds as their gods, then good things will rain down on the human community, pests won't interfere with their farming, the swarm of locusts will be contained, and augury with birds will promise prosperity. The birds will show them where hoards of wealth have been buried, and add centuries to their lifetimes. The birds won't need temples or shrines or sanctuaries; human beings can worship them by throwing a few grains of wheat, standing in the fields.

These compelling promises persuade the chorus. Tereus and Peisetairos discuss details, Tereus claiming that if his new ally chews a certain root, he will grow wings like a bird's. The chorus requests the presence of Procne the nightingale, implicated in Tereus's dark past; they make various obscene comments about how they would like to interfere with her, as she appears dressed as a pipe player. As Henderson translates, the chorus says: "We'd like to play with her" (660). Left alone with Procne on stage, the chorus sings her praises, and asks her to lead them in their "anapests," referring to the meter and rhythm of their dance. In the long song that follows, the chorus leader gives a comical account of the creation that rivals the semi-canonical version of Hesiod's weighty *Theogony*. He begins as Hesiod does, with Chaos, Night, black Erebos and Tartaros. But he says, there was no *Ge*, Earth, no *Aer*, Air, no *Ouranos*, Sky. Instead, black-winged Night gave birth to a "wind egg," *hupenemion oon* (695). From this egg came Eros, who had golden wings, mated with winged Chaos, and hatched the "kind," the *genos*, of birds.

The rest of creation followed, including the *genos* of immortals, Sky, Ocean, Earth, and the others. Therefore, obviously, the birds are the eldest, and preceded the gods in existence, as the offspring of winged Eros: "We fly, and we keep company with lovers" (704). Boys, frequent objects of male desire in this society, give in to lovers, who "get between their thighs" because their lovers offer them love-gifts of birds. Such gift-giving appears on vases from the classical period, showing an older man, the lover, *erastes*, offering a cock, for example, to a boy, the *eromenos*, the "beloved." The birds, in this case, form part of the courtship rituals of the institution of pederasty in the ancient city. And although Aristophanes has been seen by some as homophobic, as deploring same-sex *eros*, *eros* between male persons, in fact the plays often mention man-boy love without condemning it, reserving disapproval for adult men whom comedy seems to regard as feminized, adults like Agathon, the playwright who appears in the *Frogs*. Characters and chorus mock grown men who adopt effeminate ways, or who are in the position of being penetrated in intercourse, seen to resemble women, or boys. But the chorus accepts without questioning the desire of adolescent or adult men for boys, as it does here in the birds' boast that they are on the side of lovers, that they enable courtship and amorous contact between male partners.

The chorus leader continues with his list of the benefits birds bring to humankind. They indicate the seasons of the year, helping farmers and sailors manage the changes in weather; they aid in divination. The Greeks engaged in ornithomancy, prophecy using bird flight, bird calls. In the Homeric poems, struggles between eagles prophesy conflict between the heroes Agamemnon and Achilles, for example. In the *Odyssey*, three times, an eagle appears, and flies to its right with a dead dove in its claws, this a prophecy interpreted as the return of Odysseus to his home and family, and as the killing and elimination of the suitors of his wife, Penelope. The chorus leader summarizes the benefits of bird sovereignty: "If you treat us as gods you'll have the benefit of prophets, muses, breezes, seasons" (723–26). And, they add, Zeus is far away in the clouds, but the birds on the other hand are present always among human beings, bringing them the good life——"wealthiness, happiness, prosperity, peace, youth hilarity, dances, festivities, and birds' milk"! (731–34). This is communal luxury, as Kristin Ross calls it.[52] And the chorus chimes in with their bird song: *tiotiotiotiotinx* (741), the wordless music for dancing and inaugurating a new regime of plenty for all. They sing sacred songs for Pan, for Cybele, *totototototototototinx!* (747), and recall the tragic poet Phrynichus, whom they liken to a bee; he drank the fruit of ambrosial songs, bringing sweet song, which they echo: *tiotiotiotiotinx!* (752). The pipers play the tune, the birds dance and sing.

The chorus retains the center of the stage and the action, as the comedy moves on, and the chorus leader addresses the audience directly, promising them a different life if they interweave their lives with the world of the birds.

All that is shameful (*aiskhra*) there, in the world of the spectators, for those ruled by *nomos*, "law" or "custom," are the opposite, *kala*, "good, beautiful," among the birds. This is a world upside down, a utopia, or a dystopia. You can hit your father, and what is more, in an interesting challenge to what is usually assumed to be an unquestioned acceptance of the institution of slavery in this society, "if you happen to be a runaway slave with a branded forehead, with us you'll be called a dappled francolin; if you happen to be no less a Phrygian than Spintharus, up there you'll be a pigeon of Philemon's breed; if you're a slave and a Carian like Execestides, join us and generate some forefeathers" (760–65). Some of these remarks engage in the invective typical of comic allusions to members of the audience: Spintharus is a Phrygian name, Phrygia in Asia Minor the source of many Athenian slaves. But as Henderson points out in a note, "The Spintharus teased here for foreign ancestry may be the father of the fourth-century stateman Eubulus."[53] Having slave ancestors could disqualify one from citizenship; lawsuits were brought concerning ancestry, against people accused of passing as descendants of the autochthonous Athenians.

According to a source difficult to place historically, the great opponent of Aristophanes, the so-called demagogue Cleon, had accused him in a lawsuit of being of foreign birth: "Cleon could call him a foreigner (*xenon*) inasmuch as some say he was a Rhodian from Lindos, some say an Aeginetan."[54] Passing as an Athenian citizen when one's parents were not Athenian was a crime. According to this source, Aristophanes supposedly defended himself by quoting Telemachus, son of Penelope in the *Odyssey*, who reminded his audience that no one could know who impregnated one's mother. In another passage the source says: "Some record that he [Aristophanes] was of servile birth (*apo doulon*)," literally, "from slaves."[55] This was considered a terrible slur, used at times in lawsuits to discredit opponents by denying them any citizen rights. For the chorus to suggest, in these various ways, that slaves, the dappled francolin resembling the tattooed slave, that descendants of slaves could participate in the new city, was a radical proposition.[56] We can conclude that such a policy was hilarious because of its very impossibility, as disgraceful as freely beating one's father, or that the chorus was provocatively floating a challenge to the deeply embedded institution of slavery.

This play deploys myriad possibilities, or impossibilities. These comedies, the many plays of Athenian Old Comedy, both utopian and not, continuously speculate about how members of this community might relate to one another and to their environment, in the city including the citizens themselves, non-Athenians resident in the city, foreign visitors, slaves, and animals, even the material objects that surround them.[57] Envisioning new forms of relation, as the dramas proceed, suggests the insights of what has been called the "new materialism," work that reimagines matter, its fluidity, its reconfigurability, no longer bound to the fixed categories that limit and privilege the status of human beings,[58] and that points toward the coexistence of species, the interweaving of kinds of beings, brought to the fore in contemporary theory by such thinkers as Mark Payne and Donna Haraway.[59] This is a "line of flight," away from the bounds of fixed categories.

This chorus is a *swarm* of *birds*. It reimagines human beings' relationship with these creatures, with sound and music, with slaves and foreigners, as we have seen from the passage discussed above. And perhaps the radical nature of these imaginings has been neglected, with scholarly focus on the civic politics of the man Aristophanes, his satire of leading politicians and such matters. The web of references, the moving, singing bodies on stage, the address to the crowd, invocation of gods and assault on individuals, all of this is a protean, responsive, adaptable intervention into the politics and social relations of the city, and a model for a system that tests and moves forward in part through responding to the reception of its suggestive, ironic, contradictory impulses by the audience and by the judges of the city's festivals.

The chorus of birds continues to participate vigorously in the action of the play, and also to offer a space outside the interactions of the characters to exhibit their noisy, musical selves. The singers recall the swans that "raise[d] a harmonious whoop for Apollo" (769–72), repeating their wordless call, "*tiotiotiotiotinx!*," and claiming that the Graces and Muses, those entities embodying the arts, replied in song. As cited earlier, the leader implicitly critiques the possible boredom induced in the spectators by tragic performance, addressing the crowd and celebrating the joys of having wings. In the complex interrelationship between tragedy and comedy, this chorus, or chorus leader, competitively names the possible boredom experienced by those witnessing tragedy, and the greater pleasure afforded to the audiences of comedy, which followed the tragic performances on the festival days. The playwright relies on a profound knowledge of tragedy, echoing it, mocking it, deploying it especially in a play like the *Frogs*, discussed more fully earlier. But here he allows at least one voice in the spectacle that is comedy to express a preference for the comic spirit, and a rejection of the potential ennui tragedy can impose. Further advantages accrue to being a bird, equipped with wings, according to the chorus leader: needing to shit, one could fly away, fart and return; the adulterer can leave his seat in the amphitheater, having spotted his lover's husband in the reserved seats, fly to her home and fuck her, and return with no one the wiser. Wings are a great benefit, not only for collective action, but also for the transgressive individual.

What follows in the *Birds* is a series of exchanges between the chorus leader, who speaks as a character for the chorus as a whole, and the named characters Peisetairos and Euelpides. They concur on a name for their city: *Nephelokokkugian*, traditionally translated as "Cloudcuckooland." The made-up, portmanteau word incorporates the notion of the swarm, of the cloud, *nephelo-*, and the word *kokku*, used to describe a bird's cry, "cuckoo" in English, the name of a bird as well, the cuckoo, used in Greek also to refer to a rooster, a cock. The sound echoes the birds' wordless song of the earlier choral passages, and establishes the new city as a cloudy, bird-song-filled polity. The chorus leader allusively likens it to Athens herself, calling it *liparon*, "gleaming," using an epithet often deployed to celebrate the actual city's magnificent marble edifices, the Parthenon shining on the Acropolis. But instead of the goddess Athena, matron of Athens, the city will be protected by the "Persian" bird, the cock, bird of Ares, god of war (835).

Peisetairos urges Euelpides to help with the construction of a wall between the earth and the heavens, at the midpoint of the sky; he plans to sacrifice to the new gods, the bird-gods, and a raven appears, dressed as a piper, to accompany the sacrificial ritual, as the participants address the gods, who are given new names. Apollo becomes "the Pythian and Delian swan," referring to the sites of Delphi and Delos sacred to the god. All the birds are invited, and Peisetairos objects that the tiny goat, victim of the sacrifice, can hardly feed all the predatory birds that arrive to take part in the festive meal. Suddenly new characters appear on the scene, annoying beings from the land below, first a poet, "frigid," with slavishly long hair. Peisetairos chases him off with the help of some slaves, and an interpreter of oracles follows, also repelled. Then comes a famed astronomer, Meton, who seeks to measure the air and mark it up into parcels; the citizens of Cloudcuckooland want to cast out all foreigners, even beat them, and Meton makes a hasty retreat. All the annoying stock characters of the *polis* show up in the new city, including an "overseer," someone sent from Athens to inspect and command the subject cities of the Athenian Empire. He runs away after encountering the fist of Peisetairos, who also chases off a seller of decrees.

And suddenly the chorus sings again, a lengthy song claiming the praise the birds deserve from mortals. They keep the fields and orchards safe from pests, they attack the creatures that harm human beings' agriculture. The chorus leader then puts a bounty on a seller of finches, of thrushes, of blackbirds and pigeons. Any person who keeps birds in a cage must let them go. The birds respond with a chorus that celebrates the joys of avian life:

> Happy the race (*phulon*) of feathered
> birds, who in the winter

need wear no woolen cloaks;
nor in summer's stifling heat
do the long rays roast us.
For I dwell among the flora
in the lap of flowery meadows,
when the sun-crazy cicada with voice divine
in the noonday heat intones his keen song.
                    (1088–96)

The birds lead a life of pleasure, living among the flowers, serenaded by the benign insects. The cicadas, singing like birds, are a special case of insect swarm, discussed more fully in chapter 2; as noted there, they are likened to the old-fashioned population of Attica, who wore golden cicadas as ornaments; they are compared to the elderly in Homer's *Iliad*; they are said by Plato to be favored by the Muses; the voice of the beautiful Tithonos, lover of the goddess Aphrodite, becomes cicada-like as he ages eternally, according to the singer of the *Homeric Hymn* to that goddess, according to Sappho. The birds' cicadas serenade their avian companions with a benign, divinely ordained blessing.

The birds' song continues, celebrating the pleasures of their life guided by the seasons:

I winter in hollow caverns,
frolicking with mountain nymphs;
and in spring we graze on myrtle berries,
maidenly in their white florets,
and the fruits of the Graces' garden.
                    (1097–1101)

The birds' singing moves from a description of their kind in the third person, to a first-person "I," to a "we," the first-person plural that marks the collectivity of single beings that make up a chorus. These birds inhabit the world of plants and other insects, of divine creatures, nymphs and Graces, following the rhythm of change, from winter to summer to winter to spring, safe from harm in their bird feathers, in a cyclical, circular temporality, in harmony with other beings, plant, insect, immortal. The chorus of birds thinks, acts, dances as birds, lives in the world of the performance from the perspective of birds.

The choral parabasis follows their song about the joys of bird life. The parabasis, in the voice of the chorus leader, frequently addresses the audience directly, calls out individual members for ridicule and mockery, and has been interpreted often as the voice of the poet himself, presenting political opinions as well as requesting favor from the audience and judges, their positive reactions to the play guaranteeing its author a prize in the dramatic competition. In this case, remaining true to his nature as a bird, the chorus leader asks for the judges' vote in favor of the play, and promises them swarms of owls, a metonymy for the coins of Athens, since the silver from the city's mines at Laurion bore the image of the bird, companion of Athena, who appeared on one side. She is the *glaukopis* one, "with gleaming eyes." The word *glaux* means a gleaming-eyed, glaring-eyed little owl, often used as an emblem for Athena, a sort of totemic animal, a bird representing the matron goddess of the city itself. So the chorus leader asks for owls, asks for the famous silver coins associated with his city's goddess: "They will never run out on you, no, they'll move into your house, and nest in your wallets, and hatch out small change" (1105–8). Owls don't migrate, they'll remain in the city, and keep on breeding. Other avian treats are promised to the judges—gifts associated with eagles, with a falcon—and if the judges don't come through with the vote in favor of the *Birds*, the birds will shit on their white garments. This parabasis does not insult members of the audience, nor does it propose specific political solutions to the problems of the day, as do other comedies; it remains embedded in the utopian project of bird domination even as it calls out the judges seated before the performers in the first rows of the theaters.

Birds from all over appear, from Libya, geese, herons, ducks, swallows, woodpeckers, all contributing to the construction of the city. Guardian birds attempt to protect their fortress, but the gods send their messenger, the winged goddess Iris, to complain. The chorus has little role to play in the exchange between the birdlike emissary, and the character Peisetairos, merely alerting him to the possibility of other divinities arriving to object to the birds' construction, which is blocking the sacrificial burnt offerings human beings extend to the gods. Peisetairos threatens the gods with bird retaliation, and the goddess Iris herself with rape (1255). She departs.

In *Smell and the Ancient Senses*, Ashley Clements clarifies the ways in which the scent of sacrifices nourished and placated the gods in the heavens: "In the concretizing world of Greek Comedy . . . *knise* (or *knisa*) [the burnt fat and its fragrance] is made into a sign of imminent feasting for men, and a food source for gods. . . . Old Comedy had unambiguously "carnalized" the gods into beings that do not simply enjoy, but rather, depend upon the smells of sacrifice for their sustenance."[60] The birds' new city, new fortress, in midair, has deprived the gods of deference, offerings, and sustenance, and the chorus relishes its power:

> We have barred the gods sprung from Zeus
> from any further passage through my city (*ten emen polin*),
> and no more shall any mortal on a single killing floor
> send savory smoke to the gods by this route.
> (1264–67)

Here the chorus speaks as a single entity, gliding from the first-person plural verb, "we," to the possessive adjective, "my." The old Olympian gods have been thwarted, and the chorus, oscillating between plural and singular, gloats.

Emissaries from human beings below then appear again, trying to placate the birds, and to persuade Peisetairos that human beings are now enamored of the birds, and imitate them in every way, even taking on bird names. "From sheer ornithophilia they're all singing songs with a swallow in the lyrics" (1300). As the herald leaves the scene, Peisetairos addresses someone with a slave name, "Manes," ordering him to bring him wings. *Et in Arcadia servi*. While the chorus celebrates the settlement they have created, with the verb *metoikein*, used for moving house, but also the root of the noun *metoikos*, "alien resident," "metic," their utopia still includes the presence of the enslaved Manes, who is verbally abused by Peisetairos and the chorus members.[61] He is as slow as a donkey, *deilos*, objectively "vile," subjectively "wretched" (1329). The chorus seeks to arrange the wings that have been brought by the slave, sorting them into "musical, prophetic and maritime," and then they assault Manes, wing-less, for his slowness, as he scuttles away. The call to all birds to join them, which included an invitation to the tattooed francolin, does not protect this human slave from ridicule, from being the butt of humor.

Unwelcome types from the world below, characters despised by Aristophanes, apparently, in the city, arrive to beg for residence in the new world of Cloudcuckooland. A "father-beater" shows up, and is sent off to fight in Thrace. Kinesias, a composer of dithyrambs, part of another despised group, wishes to become a nightingale, has no desire to perform as director for a chorus of flying birds, a position beneath his dignity, and he too leaves the new settlement. A "sycophant," an informer, appears on stage; he is exposed and flees. Peisetairos gathers up his silent slaves, and leaves the stage, as the chorus sings of the greater perspective flight gives them over human beings. They name the notorious, treelike, "voluminous and yellow" Cleonymos, frequently ridiculed for his effeminacy. The divine culture-bringer, advocate of humankind Prometheus appears, speaking under an umbrella so the god Zeus above can't see him from the heavens, and explains that Zeus is finished: "Since you colonized the air. Now not a single human sacrifice to the gods any more, and . . . not a whiff (*knisa*) of thigh bones" (1515–18). Prometheus uses the conventional term for the founding of a colony, *oikisate*, for the building of this new city in midair.[62] The "barbarian" gods are protesting as well. Prometheus urges a treaty, with the provisions that Zeus give his scepter back to the birds, and *Basileia*, "Queen," or "Princess," whose name in a slightly different form means "sovereignty," to Peisetairos as his wife.

Poseidon and Heracles arrive, accompanied by the barbarian god of the Triballians, Thracian allies of the Athenians, whom Poseidon proceeds to insult, implicating democracy in the gods' choice of ambassador: "Ah democracy, what will you bring us to in the end, if the gods can elect this person ambassador?" (1570–71). The assembly of the Olympian gods, usually seen as a monarchy with Zeus as the first among equals, is intriguingly seen to make up a democracy like that of the Athenians. Peisetairos returns, making preparations to devour some rebel birds who are attempting a revolution against the bird "people," the *demos*, the populace of the birds, *tois demotikoisin orneois* (1584). Are these rebellious birds seeking to resist the tyrannical hegemony of Peisetairos, reactionaries revolting against bird-led democracy, or the inevitable appearance of opposition in the Greek cities vulnerable to *stasis*, to civil war? In any case, they are set for devouring. The always hungry Heracles wants to join the feast, and eagerly urges a settlement between his fellow divinities and the birds. The other members of the embassy are persuaded eventually, Peisetairos using legal arguments concerning inheritance to convince Heracles of the plan. The butchered bird flesh will serve as the wedding feast for Peisetairos and his bride, in a sinister reversion. Are these the eggs that must be broken to make the omelet? Is civil war, bird against bird, inevitable and necessary, like money, like slaves? The utopian moment flashes up, but the polyphony and tensions of the city persist.

The chorus exults in the excising of tongues, typical of sacrifice but here aimed at various proto-philosophical, sophistic, rhetorical types, "the Gorgiases," et al. A herald congratulates the birds as a *genos*, a tribe, a "race," "thrice-blessed and winged." But he calls Peisetairos a *tyrannos*, a "[usurping] monarch," as this central character enters with his beautiful consort, his queen, carrying Zeus's thunderbolt. Democracy has vanished, as the winged Athenian, leader of the birds, has become their ruler, devouring members of the polity of the birds. The political structure of Cloudcuckooland, like that of Olympus, has oscillated, reverting from democracy to monarchy or tyranny.

Nevertheless, the chorus has the last words, leading the triumphal procession of the new ruler, and singing and dancing as they call for celebration, invoking "Hymen Hymenaios," god of marriage, with the traditional formula of the *epithalamion*, the "wedding song." They recall golden-winged Eros, who presided over the marriage of Zeus and his wife and sister, Hera. They call for celebration of Zeus, his thunder, his lightning, his thunderbolt, and ally the bridegroom Peisetairos with the great god:

> With you this man now shakes the earth,
> new master of Zeus' estate
> and of Princess, attendant of Zeus' throne.
> Hymen Hymenaeus!
> (1752–54)

Zeus cannot be neglected, yet the position of Peisetairos is somewhat ambiguous; has he displaced the great god, appropriating his queen, or is he merely allied with the great power of the universe through this connection? The chorus urges all the birds, in their *phula*, their "tribes, or kinds," to accompany the wedding party to Zeus's ground, and to the marriage bed. Is Peisetairos to cuckold the king of the gods, is he, through the treaty reached with the embassy of god ambassadors, the new ruler of Zeus's house? This possible sacrilege is greeted with hilarity and rejoicing, as Peisetairos swings his bride in the dance, and the chorus follows them offstage, singing:

> Hip hip hooray! Hail Paeon!
> Hail your success, you
> highest of divinities.
> (1763–65)

Marriage and festivity mark the end of comedy for centuries to come. Here there is a political as well as a utopian turn to the departure from the stage of the character and the chorus of brilliantly costumed birds. The highly varied collective of birds has enabled a coup d'état in heaven, even though their human advocate has been established as the new *tyrannos*, ruler in Zeus's place. Briefly, ephemerally, he set up a new kind of community, one that repelled the negative elements of the Athenian world, and that welcomed the great variety of different beings exemplified in the democratic chorus of birds.[63]

If we see the chorus not as supplementary, not as an additive to the plot, but as an operatic alternative, another mode of communicating, anonymously, collectively, democratically, if we look to this comedy as a whole, then the celebration of Peisetairos's assumption of tyranny, his wedding to

Princess, or Queen, constitutes not a continuous flow with these activities in the play, but rather a rupture. The birds in the chorus, a swarm, are volatile, change their minds as a group, fear and comply in equal measure, but their sustained obedience to a tyrant seems at best highly unlikely, their rebellion imminent. They are individualized in their different bird natures, in their bird costumes, and resistant to Peisetairos's ideas at first, reluctantly fall in with his plan, and then execute the construction of their new city because of the benefits they will receive. His assumption of tyranny seems to violate the principles in the name of which they have become a utopian site for all birds everywhere; the "hero" is winged, but not a bird. It may seem strange to resort to Althusser's formulation considering a nineteenth-century tragedy for thinking about the structure of ancient comedy, but to repeat his words on Bertolazzi's *Il Milan Nost*, in the Piccolo Teatro's production,

> Nowhere can it [the structure] be perceived directly in the play as can the visible characters or the course of the action. But it is there, in the tacit relation between the people's time and the time of the tragedy, in their mutual imbalance, in their incessant "interference" and finally in their true and delusive criticism. It is this revealing latent relation, this apparently insignificant and yet decisive tension that Strehler's production enables the audience to perceive without their being able to translate this presence directly into clearly conscious terms.[64]

The very composition of the comic chorus, its variety, the eternal, cyclical quality of avian life, following the seasons, not individuated, with the birds named by kind, not by individual names, even for the chorus leader, lends them a different sort of temporality from the linear plot of the *Birds*.

My point is that the structure of the play itself, the alternation between chorus and characters, must be taken into account, the chorus not seen as background, but rather as another reality, often pastoral and more utopian than the scheme to displace the Olympian gods voiced by the "hero." The community of birds represents a variegated unity set *against* the plot, the actions of the named characters.[65] The birds' capacity to differ from one another, to dance, to sing, to evoke the joys of their existence in songs of remarkable beauty, always consistent with their avian perspective on existence, must be seen and heard as texturally, radically different from the course of events in the comedy, and read by us as an alternative to human ambition and striving.

Eduardo Viveiros de Castro discusses the "multinaturalism" of indigenous American peoples, in ways that illuminate a point of view different from our own: "Cultural relativism, which is a multiculturalism, presumes a diversity of partial, subjective representations bearing on an external nature, unitary and whole, that itself is indifferent to representation. Amerindians propose the inverse: on the one hand, a purely pronominal representative unity—the human is what and whoever occupies the position of the cosmological subject; every existent can be thought of as thinking (it exists, therefore it thinks), as "activated" or "agencied" by a point of view—and, on the other, a real or objective radical diversity."[66] Perspectivism, he argues, is a multinaturalism. Birds will be birds. The resolution of the linear plot of the *Birds*, with Peisetairos's wedding celebration, is one kind of ending, but the world of the birds goes on, will go on, bird by bird.

The *Birds* is one of comedy's great utopian exercises. The escape from Athens, the discovery of a space between heaven and earth, the persuasion of the birds and the construction of Cloudcuckooland, all establish an elsewhere. Is it a double utopia, one with two radically different political solutions? The birds constitute a democratic entity, individuals acting in concert; Peisetairos ends as a tyrant, a monarch allied with his mate, replacing the Olympian god to rule over the cosmos. Either one, or both, seem utopian when posed against the realities of Athenian everyday life, which erupts onto the scene in the form of sycophants, oraclemongers, dithyrambic poets, father-beaters, and other menaces expelled from the ideal space of the birds' fortress. Less nostalgic than the chorus of wasps in the play called after that swarm, the birds revel in the pastoral pleasures of the countryside, singing gracefully even as they insist on their powers of destruction or vengeance on those who do not honor their omnipresence and the gifts they can bring, if they choose, to humankind.

Mark Payne's discussion of the *Birds* in his brilliant book *The Animal Part* illuminates the role of imagination and natural wonder in the utopian fantasy of Aristophanes. He links the *Birds* to other Old Comedies, now lost: "Plays like *Goats*, *Wild Animals*, and *Fish* stage heterotopian encounters between human beings and other animals in which these animals voice their own understanding of their lives and the ways in which they have been hijacked by the human culture that makes use of them for food and labor."[67] He locates the *Birds* within this "subgenre."

Payne's illuminating reflections on Old Comedy, in light of his concerns with animals, tend to support my argument that the birds' expressions of delight in their own life establish an alternative reality, in a swarming chorus that has its own being irreducible to the plot of the play, which ends with Peisetairos's domination: "The birds of *Birds* are not merely ciphers for human behavior, as the wasps of *Wasps* stand for the unrelenting quarrelsomeness of old men addicted to the law courts. They are present as birds in the earlier parts of the play, with their own forms of social organization, and this vision of zoological sociality continues to encompass and interrogate the human society that takes center stage at the end."[68] Peisetairos the near cannibal stands apart. Payne's work urges the possibilities for human self-understanding, sparked by the encounter between, among, species.

THE POLITICS OF PERFORMING THE *BIRDS*

Thousands of modern performances of ancient Greek drama have taken place, but these are usually interpretations of tragedies.[69] Comedies are the exception. Unusually, along with the *Lysistrata*, presented in concert with feminist militancy and pacifism in times of war, the *Birds* has also been performed in the twentieth and twenty-first centuries. In an essay on performance, Gonda Van Steen gives a fascinating account of the fate of the director Karolos Koun's production of the *Birds* in twentieth-century Greece. Others in modern Greece had promulgated performance of ancient theater, especially tragedy, as part of a patriotic effort sponsored by "pro-western, anticommunist, right-wing national governments," reinforced by the religious powers, and had dismissed or even banned Aristophanes' plays, on the grounds that they lacked decorum, or were notoriously immoral.[70] Koun and his Art Theatre produced Aristophanes' *Birds* in 1959, in the Herodeion at the foot of the Acropolis in Athens, and scandalized the audience. In the scene in which Peisetairos summons a priest to sacrifice a goat to the gods, Van Steen relates: "Quite unexpectedly, the actor who played the role of the priest, dressed in the robe of a modern clergyman, began chanting in the familiar notes of Byzantine ecclesiastical music, but without altering the content of Aristophanes' original mock prayer to the Olympian gods" (160). On the following day, a leading politician banned the subsequent performances of the *Birds* as "anticlerical." The outrage of the conservatives was based in part on the "boldly anti-government and anti-American translation" (160) of the play by Vasilis Rotas, a communist activist.

This performance had a profound impact on Greek cultural politics. As Van Steen notes: "Through the 1959 incident, Aristophanes himself became a powerful, stirring symbol of the resilient vitality and stubborn struggle for freedom of the suppressed Left" (163), which had been defeated in the Greek civil war following World War II. Aristophanes had become "*Aristero*-phanes," literally, "the one who reveals himself as leftist" (163). Although a revised version of the *Birds* production won international prizes, the military dictatorship of Greece (1967–74) ordered the theater company back from travel and forbade presentation of the comedy. Van Steen writes: "The comeback of the free *Birds* production [in 1975], which symbolized regained freedom of speech and fully restored democratic rights, dramatically relegated the junta era to the past" (169). In the opening scene of the Art Theatre's 1975 revival, Peisetairos and his sidekick Euelpides announced that they went looking for a "land without juntas." The scene with the priest and his parody of Orthodox liturgy was by far the most successful, and it became obligatory for this and other Greek productions of *Birds* (171). Van Steen regards the subsequent ossification of performances of the *Birds* as somewhat regrettable, yet the revolutionary, resistant, even communist associations of Aristophanes persist in the Republic of Greece.

The comedy has had similar reception in other parts of the world. As Betine van Zyl Smit describes them, performances of the *Birds* had political connotations in apartheid South Africa, a 1980 production by the University of Cape Town's Drama Department exciting a strong reaction. One apartheid-friendly critic, cited by van Zyl Smit, objected in no uncertain terms: "By using Afrikaans accents and mannerisms for the gods' delegation who come to negotiate with the birds, the play is clearly being used as an allegory for a similar usurpation of power which could arise in this country. But it is a powerless allegory, trite in its statement, and scarcely justifying the banalities used for its implementation."[71] Other South African productions of the play used its content to offer mockery of the apartheid prime minister B. J. Vorster, and deployed the colors of the African National Congress in the flag of Cloudcuckooland (237). Van Zyl Smit also lists a production of the *Birds* in the Zulu language, in which the author, Themi Gwala, "used the Aristophanic concept of creating a better society (in this case an enslaved people liberating themselves from enslavement by finding a better world) for his play called *Izinyomi*, which is the Zulu word for 'birds'" (240). Van Zyl Smit also notes that although at the time of writing, there were fourteen Afrikaans translations of Greek tragedies, only two of Aristophanes' comedies had been translated into that language.

Francesca Schironi describes a notorious incident in Italy, before a presentation of the *Frogs* in the ancient city of Siracusa in Sicily, in which the planned theater set included caricatures of leading politicians, including Silvio Berlusconi, Gianfranco Fini, and Umberto Bossi, all right-wing leaders. These were removed before the first performance after widespread objections.[72] In Britain, at a National Theatre's production of the *Birds*, anti-Americanism caused a walkout: "The wedding of Pez [the Peisetairos character] and Sovereignty was an extended dumbshow in which money rained from the ceiling. Sovereignty herself was the Statue of Liberty. It was probably just as well, at the first performance, that the two rows of American visitors had walked out at the interval."[73] The power of ancient comic productions to stimulate controversy and dissension, to produce outrage and censorship, has continued.

Some theater professionals, committed not only to inclusion of diverse actors in their performances, see the chorus as crucial to ancient comedy's impact. Martina Treu describes the work of the Italian director Marco Martinelli, who worked with young people in schools in Scampia and Naples in rewriting Aristophanes' *Peace*: "In the show the youngsters sing, dance, and move as one entity: a real comic chorus."[74] Martinelli also included references to immigrants and their suffering in a play called *All'inferno*, which featured immigrants from Senegal who travel to the underworld to look for "Wealth," and were enslaved in a hell that resembled northern Italy.[75] Treu is exceptional in emphasizing the crucial participation of the chorus of citizens in the plays of Aristophanes, and in discovering in the work of Italian directors and producers of theater a commitment to the collective, multifarious voices represented in the chorus.

Utopianism, even comic utopianism, survives in the present. See, for example, Bill McKibben's *Radio Free Vermont: A Fable of Resistance*, published in 2017. In this fable, "terrorists," that is, people who want to live sanely in an insane world, begin to foment a plot for the secession of the state of Vermont from the United States. As the author remarks in a concluding note, "An advantage to writing a fable is that you get to append a moral to the end. In this case it's not 'We should all secede.' Instead, it's that when confronted by small men doing big and stupid things, we need to resist with all the creativity and wit we can muster."[76] He points out that there have been previous attempts to persuade the citizens of Vermont to secede from the United States; these efforts echo the fantasy of escape from Athens of Peisetairos and his fellow birds.

If utopias tell us more about the undesirable, undesired limitations of the present in which they are generated, as Fredric Jameson argues, then the *Birds* might be seen to express a yearning for a rural life, for a mutuality, a reciprocity among species, for a democracy that can include a runaway slave, or, alternatively, a life of plenty and comfort and peace watched over by a benevolent dictator. As with the other utopian comedies, such as *Lysistrata, Women at the Assembly, Women at the Thesmophoria*, attention to the chorus of the *Birds* as an alternative set of voices, replete with lines of flight, not smoothly integrated into a "plot," a *muthos*, not consistent or even principally engaged with the play's characters, but establishing another reality, enriches the comic spectacle. There can be a sort of "jamming" of message, a disruption of "authorship" and of "character" that make these plays a rough and unfamiliar sort of object for readers and/or spectators accustomed to a very different sort of theater, one descended from the Aristotle of the *Poetics* on tragedy. The utopian impulses in the *Birds*, exemplified most fully in the colorful, various, wildly differentiated members of its chorus and their songs, speak to modernity and postmodernity, to a climate that demands not just mockery and laughter, but also an elsewhere defined by pastoral, eternal, paradisiac community.

[CHAPTER 5]

Parrhesia
Saying It All

> There's nothing invidious about calling bad people names; it's a way to honor good people, if you stop to think about it.
>
> *Knights* 1274–75, trans. Jeffrey Henderson

The question of "free" speech has moved to the forefront of public discussion in the contemporary United States, stimulated by the rise of social media, hate speech, and so-called cancel culture. Arguments often center on the matter of how "free" is "free," how far do the limits on the First Amendment to the US Constitution, guaranteeing freedom of speech, extend in current circumstances. One cannot shout "fire" in a crowded theater, nor incite a riot; how far are public officials, even teachers, required to control their speech? Spaces of contestation now include the university lecture hall, where instructors are in some cases supposed to warn students of possible "triggers" in their presentation of class material, to govern their own "free" speech and that of others in situations that might excite memories or negative reactions to discussion of sexual practices, or violence, or racism or xenophobia. The struggles over internet postings, questions of tolerance of abusive speech and incitement to violence, racism, and anti-Semitism, of hate speech in general, persist in the present. Who can decide what is permissible on the platforms of social media, which profit from controversy and inflammatory rhetoric? Social media of various stripes have refused to comment on or ban clearly false advertisements, and then allowed the targeting of specific groups with messages tailored to their often noxious prejudices. And how can the current sources of information, the "silos" and echo chambers of various political positions, ever communicate with one another when, again, those who own and control the silos profit from the cultivated oblivion and exclusiveness of their practices?

Here again, the performances of Old Comedy, occasions deeply embedded in the ritual and civic life of the city, with its heterogeneous and differentiated audience, offer a paradigm of greater complexity and contradiction, a politics of "frank speech" that especially targets the powerful, but also reflects on the limits of the cacophony, the swarm of "fake news" and "alternative facts." Just as in contemporary culture, in the ancient city there were limits on speaking freely, a ban, after a period of greater tolerance, on naming and abusing prominent public figures, and eventually an oath taken requiring the imposition of the death penalty on those who attempted to overthrow the Athenian democracy.

Yet *parrhesia*, the "saying of it all" in Old Comedy, can be said to make visible the social, political, and economic fissures of ancient Athenian society, and to reveal the city as a permissive and riotous space, full of heterogeneous claims, of mockery and insult, of utopian desires, of a wild variety of beings who try to call the ruling parties to account. There is criticism of unequal distribution of resources; frequently expressed desires for more sex and better food, for more family and neighborhood time; calls to depose thuggish leaders, to end needless wars, and also, at times, a recognition of the need to limit *parrhesia*, an implicit critique of unbridled speech. Scholars disagree about whether the Athenians themselves considered the comic stage to be a space immune from legal claims about abuse.[1] But certainly abuse, along with calls for change, abounded, especially in the songs of the choruses of Old Comedy, revealing the limits of the Athenian political order, and outside of that order, all those others who inhabit city and country. The plays use humor and obscenity, criticism and irony, utopian desires, to gesture parodically toward limits to *parrhesia* as well.

In this chapter I consider some modern thinkers on the question of "free" speech, as well as classicists who have studied this matter in the context of ancient Athens. I then turn to comedies full of free, frank, reckless, sometimes violent and scatological speech, and reflect on their relevance to the pressing demands of our own contemporary society. Rather than focusing on the individual, the comic hero, I see the chorus as expressing manifold points of view, providing lines of flight for the voiceless, those with no voice, outside of the confining bounds of the citizen body. I'm interested less in the culturally specific elements of ancient Athenian "free" speech, which are often homophobic, misogynist, and scatological, than in the fact that it is directed most often against the powerful—tragedians, generals, bad poets, and especially politicians.

MICHEL FOUCAULT ON *PARRHESIA*

The issue of "free" speech interested the great philosopher and intellectual historian Michel Foucault, who in his lifetime investigated and set out some principles for describing *parrhesia*, after the Greek word often translated as "free speech."[2] After his work on madness, on epistemology, on prisons, and after the first volume of his *History of Sexuality*, Foucault became interested in ancient Greece and Rome, and before his untimely death wrote several books that consider the ancient world in a prehistory of the confessional and the psychoanalytic process. Foucault looked at the place of sexual behavior in antiquity, and discussed teachings on sexual practices very different from those of modernity, focused on Greek writings advocating the mastery of the self in various domains, sexuality being only one of those opportunities, and on Rome, with emphasis on the care of the self in philosophical discourses that anticipated Christian anxiety about sexual activity and doctrine about chastity.[3]

Foucault began his discussion of *parrhesia* in his lectures at the Collège de France in 1981–82, now published in a volume entitled *The Hermeneutics of the Subject*.[4] His interest in this volume of the collected courses focused on *parrhesia* in the period of the Roman Empire, and considered in particular the works of Philodemos, Galen, and Seneca. Foucault here distinguished among *parrhesia*, flattery, and rhetoric, and his conclusions reflected this historical emphasis on Roman antiquity, remote from the role of free speech in the context of the earlier democratic city of Athens: "*Parrhesia* is free speech, released from the rules, freed from rhetorical procedures, in that it must, in one respect of course, adapt itself to the situation, to the occasion and to the particularities of the auditor. But above all and fundamentally, on the side of the person who utters it, it is speech that is equivalent to a commitment, to a bond, and which establishes a certain pact between the subject of enunciation and the subject of conduct. The subject who speaks commits himself."[5] Such observations make sense in the context in which Foucault proposed them; he was concerned to describe the role of the philosophical exemplar, the adviser, in the intimacies of Roman interaction. (Interestingly, he translated *parrhesia*, the Greek word, as *libertas* in Latin, a Roman word that suggests not just speaking without constraints, but also the juridical condition of freedom in distinction from slavery.[6] It is the free man who can speak freely. In fact the Greek word, from *pas*, "all," and *rhesis*, "speaking," means "to say all." There is no implication of "freedom" in the Greek.) Foucault seemed intent on the great man, the single politician, drawn as he is by the example of Plato, adviser of tyrants, or by the Cynic of later philosophy, the counselor of princes, or the Christian spiritual adviser. Yet Foucault did discuss certain Greek tragedies, especially the *Ion*. And he linked his analysis of the *Ion* to another tragedy that centers on "truth-telling," Sophocles' *Oedipus Rex*.

In *Fearless Speech*, a summary of his thinking about *parrhesia* published in 1983, Foucault considered in detail the tragedian Euripides' use of the concept of *parrhesia*, concentrating on this concept, and the word, in tragedy. He showed how *parrhesia* appears in the tragedian's *Phoenician Women*, *Hippolytus*, *Bacchae*, and *Electra*, but emphasized its use in the *Ion* and *Orestes*, arguing even that "*Ion* is entirely devoted to the problem of *parrhesia*, since it pursues the question: who has the right, the duty, and the courage to speak the truth?"[7] In this text, Foucault argued that we find in Euripides' later play, the *Orestes*, a moment where Athenian democracy confronts the problem of a negative as well as a positive *parrhesia*, revealed in a possibly spurious moment in Euripides' *Orestes* (902ff.), when an unnamed speaker incites others to riot, exhibiting "ignorant outspokenness" (*amathei parrhesia*). This possibility is further explored in the works of Plato, and linked to the theme of "care of the self."

These discussions of *parrhesia* are marked by their consistent attention to the question of truth, and to the individual. Rather than seeing the city as a whole, the *demos* and its assembly, its theater as sites of *parrhesia*, Foucault focused on individual tragic characters such as Ion and Oedipus, and saw in them the precursors to the sort of philosophical parrhesiast he was seeking to portray in the later texts. Even as he described a break between the political *parrhesia* of the fifth century BCE, and the philosophical parrhesia of the fourth, the courageous parrhesiast himself stands at the center of his examination of the question. I am particularly interested, rather, in the collective, in the assembly and the theater as locations for the expression of *parrhesia*, concerned not so much with the risk of death to which it might expose the individual, but rather with the establishing of a collective atmosphere of "saying all."

The discussion of *parrhesia* served Foucault as a sort of hinge, a pivot, as he swung from pagan antiquity to Christianity: "A considerable mutation took place roughly between Greco-Roman philosophy and Christianity" (*Hermeneutics*, 407). In the case of so-called pagan philosophy, he argued, the call to tell the truth "falls essentially on the master, the guide, or the friend, or anyway on the person who gives advice" (407–8). The teacher or adviser serves as a moral exemplar, often speaking aware of a genealogy that goes back to the first teacher, a figure such as Epicurus who through his personal example inspired a school of followers. "In Christianity, on the other hand . . . the truth does not come from the person who guides the soul but is given in another mode (Revelation, Text, Book, etcetera)" (408). In this very different model of access to truth, the "cost of the truth and of 'truth-telling' will be borne by the person whose soul has to be guided" (408). The role of confession in Christianity replaces the ancient idea that the truth lies in the guide, the inheritor of a philosophical truth.

Foucault did come to the matter of *parrhesia* and its role in various institutions of the ancient city, including the deliberations in the classical Athenian assembly of citizens:

> *Parrhesia* is a kind of verbal activity where the speaker has a specific relation to truth through frankness, a certain relationship to his own life through danger, a certain type of relation to himself or other people through criticism (self-criticism or criticism of other people), and a specific relation to moral law through freedom and duty. More precisely, *parrhesia* is a verbal activity in which a speaker expresses his personal relationship to truth, and risks his life because he recognizes truth-telling as a duty to improve or help other people (as well as himself). In *parrhesia*, the speaker uses his freedom and chooses frankness instead of persuasion, truth instead of falsehood or silence, the risk of death instead of life and security, criticism instead of flattery, and moral duty instead of self-interest and moral apathy.[8]

Such observations may describe the situation of later antiquity, but seem ill suited for ancient comedy. Foucault does not include Aristophanes, other comic writers, Old Comedy, the whole institution of festival comedy within his consideration of truth-telling, frank speech, free speech.[9]

These reflections on such matters have significance for our study of ancient *parrhesia* in ancient Greek comedy, not only because the appearance of this phenomenon is so different from that of later, Roman antiquity, but also because modernity has often framed considerations of such matters as the intention of an author in an anachronistic way. Aristophanes is seen as an individual, with intentions, who should be the site of his truth, the plays a confessional form that reveals that truth, when in fact the "telling all," the *parrhesia* of classical Athens, is not necessarily about "truth." If all is told, what is that all? And how many voices, how many institutions of the city are engaged in its display?

Foucault insisted on the association of *parrhesia* with risk, even risk of death, not just in the advice of the adviser to the Prince, which interested him in the later philosophical texts of the Hellenistic and Roman periods, but also in the prephilosophical, political moment of *parrhesia*. The sixth-century BCE wise man Solon was said to have appeared in the assembly of the Athenians dressed in armor, implicitly challenging the claims of the tyrant-to-be Peisistratos to need armored bodyguards to protect him against his enemies; another version of this anecdote, told in Plutarch's *Life of Solon*, reports that the lawgiver, disappointed in the Athenians' surrender to tyranny, set his armor outside his house to demonstrate his distaste for the tyrant. The late anecdote, as recounted by Foucault, alludes to but still does not develop the theme of *parrhesia* in fifth-century BCE culture, the democratic, imperial period of production of Athenian tragedies and so-called Old comedies. Nor does his retelling of the story of Socrates' execution by the Athenian state. Solon belongs to the sixth century; Socrates' death to the fourth. The tragedies Foucault analyzes in *The Government of Self and Others* and *Fearless Speech* have their place in this narrative. But the raw, abusive, satirical attacks contained in comedies of the fifth century did not figure in Foucault's account. And he focused on the relation between *parrhesia* and truth, truth which in fact is not what is at stake in the Old Comedy attacks on politicians, which spew vitriol on various prominent characters, often accusing them of deviance or crimes for which there may be little basis in "truth."[10]

PARRHESIA

While tragedy has been seen as a meditation on the individual self and on questions of kinship and sovereignty, comedy offers other potentials for political intervention, in particular in the ribald, utopian, free-speaking, insulting, and libidinous forms of the later fifth century BCE. In this chapter, I again claim the pertinence of comedy for today, with specific attention to this issue of free speech, and with reference to the comedies that demonstrate this aspect of ancient democracy and that may have caused trouble for the playwright Aristophanes, especially his play the *Acharnians*. Comic *parrhesia*, pace Foucault, is not about truth, nor about truth-telling. It may be true, but that is not the point of its expression. It is an attack on the powerful.

The Greek word *parrhesia*, used in the classical period, the fifth and fourth centuries BCE, as noted above is formed by a characteristically Greek synthesis, the union of the word for "all" and the word for "speech." The massive *Greek-English Lexicon* edited by Liddell, Scott, and Jones (LSJ) defines *parrhesia* as "outspokenness, frankness, freedom of speech, claimed by the Athenians as their privilege." The dictionary entry charts a certain history for the word, as it first appears in tragedy, beginning with Euripides' play *Hippolytus*, line 442; in this tragedy, Theseus's foreign queen, Phaidra, as she contemplates suicide, uses the word to describe what she desires for her children, and what she fears she may have lost in her unbounded passion for her stepson, Hippolytus: "My friends, it is this very purpose that is bringing about my death, [420] that I may not be detected bringing shame to my husband or to the children I gave birth to but rather that they may live in glorious Athens as free men, free of speech and flourishing (*eleutheroi parrhesia thallontes*), enjoying good repute where their mother is concerned. For it enslaves (*douloi*) a man, even if he is bold of heart, [425] when he is conscious of sins committed by his mother or father."[11] Phaidra kills herself, leaving behind a tablet accusing her stepson of sexual violence, but having expressed the wish here also to leave behind children with all the rights of citizens, free of status (*eleutheroi*), with freedom of speech (*parrhesia*), not enslaved by the memory of the shame of their mother.

Phaidra is not an Athenian, although married to the great Athenian founder, Theseus. Daughter of King Minos and Pasiphae, she comes from Crete and has become stepmother to Hippolytus, son of the Amazon Hippolyta and Theseus. Her concern to leave behind her a good name, one that will allow her own children to thrive free, with *parrhesia*, signifies an entanglement of the ancient stories, the myths, of the city of Athens, with the present of the tragedy's first audience. *Parrhesia* is a valued privilege of the citizens of the democratic city, one for which Phaidra is willing to sacrifice her own life, lying, claiming not that she desired her stepson as she did, but that he violated her. Is her letter, her tablet, denouncing him, meant to be misunderstood as an act of *parrhesia*, the "saying all," interpreted by her mourning husband as definitive proof against his own son? The lie she leaves behind destroys that son, and the father, who loses his heir through the curse he brings down on the young man, a devotee of Artemis who shuns the works of Aphrodite.[12]

We find *parrhesia* again in the same playwright's work *Ion*, an exploration of Athenian identity. The central character of this tragedy, the temple slave Ion, seeks to know his parentage, and in this speech uses the term *parrhesia*, as did Phaidra, to describe the benefits of Athenian citizenship:

> unless I find my mother,
> My life is worthless. If I may do so,
> I pray my mother is Athenian,
> So that through her I may have rights of speech (*parrhesia*).
> For when a stranger comes into a city
> Of pure blood, though in name a citizen,
> His mouth remains a slave (*doulon*): he has no right
> Of speech (*parrhesian*).
>   (669–75, trans. Willetts)[13]

One of the remarkable features of this speech is its echo of the *Hippolytus* (428) and its reliance on the great opposition in classical societies between slave and free. Lacking *parrhesia*, even the free man's mouth is enslaved. For the character Ion, *parrhesia* is an essential attribute of belonging, of participating in the city, of living freely among slave and foreign inhabitants as a privileged citizen. The discourse of *parrhesia* is grafted on to the structuring difference between freedom and slavery, which is a fact of the populations of ancient cities, but also a crucial metaphor for describing how the citizens of a free, especially a democratic polis, understand their difference from others, from, for the crucial example, the inhabitants of the Persian Empire, every one of whom is claimed ideologically to be enslaved to the sole free man, the emperor.[14]

One of the most intriguing conclusions that one can draw from these citations from tragedy, and from the plays of Euripides in particular, is that the word *parrhesia* appears in the mouths of non-Athenians, noncitizens, nonfree persons.[15] If the ability to "say all," to speak one's mind, is a privilege especially associated with the free, the citizens of the city of Athens, those who use the word in these plays express a longing, an envy, an exclusion from that entitlement that defines them as foreigners, as outsiders. There is a recognition of foreignness, as in the case of Phaidra, or even of slave status, as in the voice of the temple slave Ion. In these examples, we do not hear the Athenians themselves rejoicing in this aspect of democratic life. Phaidra, who is resident in Athens, but a Cretan, desires her sons, born to an Athenian father, to have the right of *parrhesia*, but as a woman and a foreigner, cannot exercise this freedom herself.

In tragedy, as noted especially in the texts of Euripides, *parrhesia* figures prominently in the understanding of political belonging and openness of discourse, in the creation of a boundary between those internal to the politics of the city and those who look within but cannot take part in the city's assemblies, juries, magistracies. This version of *parrhesia* differs profoundly from the tight duality Foucault described in relation to Hellenistic and Roman philosophical *parrhesia*, which he linked to the eventual development of the confessional in Christianity. In *The Government of Self and Others*, Foucault does treat the role of *parrhesia* in the politics of the fifth century, but uses it as a prelude to defining it in his own terms, as he moves from the radical democracy to the philosophers and Christians of later antiquity.[16]

PARRHESIA IN COMEDY

The conservative Attic orator Isocrates (436–338 BCE), in his speech "On the Peace," addressed to the Athenian assembly in 355, warned of the dangers inherent in democracy, of *parrhesia*: "I know that it is hazardous to oppose your views and that, although this is a democracy, there exists no 'freedom of speech' (*parrhesia*) except that which is enjoyed [here] by the most reckless orators, who care nothing for your welfare, and in the theatre by *the comic poets*" (trans. modified, emphasis mine).[17] Although Foucault and others have situated *parrhesia* almost exclusively in tragedy, in philosophical texts, and in political oratory, this ancient critic of Athenian democracy was alarmed by its appearance in *comedy*. As I see it, the *parrhesia* expressed in a play like the *Acharnians*, the first extant work of Aristophanes, produced by Kallistratos in 425 BCE, many decades before Isocrates' denunciation, comes not just from the mouth of an individual, the "author" of the text, nor from the character Dikaiopolis, the so-called hero, nor from the chorus leader who pronounces the comedy's parabasis, but rather also from the collective, that is, the chorus, the characters, the dance and song, the situation of the performance at the Lenaia, a local celebration of Dionysos. Dikaiopolis, in defense of his establishing a separate peace with the Spartans, calls attention to the fact that this performance takes place at the Lenaia, a festival no foreigners attended, and therefore Cleon, the man he considered a demagogue, a manipulator of the *demos*, cannot fault him for defaming the city in their presence.

The *Acharnians* of 425 and the *Knights*, also produced at the Lenaia, in 424, take the prominent politician Cleon as an important target, an obstacle to the enjoyment of peace, food, and sexual pleasure, which the plays celebrate as a utopian alternative to an ongoing, impoverishing, exhausting war. Dikaiopolis exposes the brutality of the war and the foolishness of its pursuit principally through the detailing of the joys that follow from his private truce. Scholars have identified Dikaiopolis as a comic "hero," and seen in him the playwright Aristophanes himself. But the chorus leader, in the parabasis, gives the most extensive defense of the ways of the city and its *parrhesia*, the right to say all, to speak frankly, collectively, against the attacks of the more powerful.

Dikaiopolis creates his own private truce with the Spartans, and utopically lives out his dream of pleasure having cut himself off from his fellow citizens. He addresses the audience in the first speech of the play, describing himself at the assembly, the heart of the democracy: "O city, city (*polis*)! I am always the very first to come to Assembly and take my seat. Then, in my solitude, I sigh, I yawn, I stretch myself, I fart. I fiddle, scribble, pluck my beard, do sums, while I gaze off to the countryside and pine for peace" (27–32).[18] A dutiful citizen, he carries out his responsibilities as part of the *demos*. Dikaiopolis's very name means "just-city," that is, perhaps one who has justice for the city, just counsel for the city. He would rather be in his country home, self-sufficient and not a victim of the urban, monetary economy.

Dikaiopolis is a parrhesiast, not a solemn adviser to a prince, or a philosopher in danger of his life, but a raucous, boisterous, hungry, thirsty rustic character yearning to go back to his farm. He establishes his own solution to the problem of war with fellow Greeks, sending off a mediator with some money to make a treaty for him and his family. Veterans of the war with the Persians, Marathonomakhai, "Marathon-Fighters," contest the treaties, wanting to continue the combat with the Spartans because their farms have suffered in the war. These are the irascible, combative, waspish veterans, resembling the old men who form the chorus of the *Wasps*. But in the *Acharnians* the mediator succeeds with Dikaiopolis, presenting a thirty-year treaty that the latter says "smells of nektar and ambrosia" (196), that is, the food and drink of the gods themselves. And the "hero," Dikaiopolis, leaves the scene as the chorus enters.

This chorus expresses its hostility to the man who has separated himself from the city as a whole, and pursued his own private truce with the Spartans. These are the Acharnians, fellow residents of a deme, one unit among those making up the Athenian *polis*. Dikaiopolis returns to the stage, ready to celebrate a festival for Dionysos, god of the theater, wine, and vines; he has with him his daughter, his wife, and slaves bearing a large phallus, one of the sacred implements used in celebration of the god. He directs his little band of celebrants, the slaves keeping the phallus erect, and sings a hymn to the phallus, friend of Dionysos:

Phales, friend of Bacchus,
revel mate, nocturnal rambler,
fornicator, pederast:
after six years I greet you,
as gladly I return to my deme,
with a peace I made for myself.
          (263–69)

Peace means sex, a neighbor's slave to be sexually assaulted, all the joys of life no longer focused on war, led by such characters as Lamakhos, the general to whom Dikaiopolis is adamantly opposed.

The chorus of Acharnian elders begins adamantly opposed to Dikaiopolis, and expresses its *parrhesia*, its right to say all, by denouncing him repeatedly. They call him "shameless and disgusting," a traitor to his fatherland (288–89); they claim to hate him more than they do Cleon, in a shift that moves from within the play to a prediction about the playwright's next comedy, the *Knights*, to be discussed later in this chapter. Dikaiopolis tries to explain, and even to defend the Spartans, accusing the chorus of having "a dark ember" in them that blazes up (321), prefiguring his taking possession of and threatening some coal, a product of the Acharnians' charcoal manufacture. The old Acharnian men agree to listen, and put down the stones with which they were preparing to "lapidate" the comic hero.

Dikaiopolis announces that he will commence to enact his *parrhesia*, saying: "I am ready to say over a butcher's block everything (*hapanth'*) I have to say on behalf of the Spartans, though I value my life" (355–57). This is "saying it all," at some risk, comically. Moving into possible identity with the playwright himself, Dikaiopolis recalls how Cleon brought him up before the Council, the administrative body of the assembly, and "soaked" him abusively, "so that I nearly died in a mephitic miasma of misadventure" (381–82). The Greek here is a long, invented word, *molunopragmonoumenos*, conveying the odor of anal filth and defilement Cleon poured over him, and playing on the common characterization of the Athenians as *polypragmones*, "restless, meddlesome busybodies."

After meeting with the tragedian Euripides, and parodying one of his tragedies, now lost, the *Telephos*, the central character calls out the members of the chorus, saying they must stand "like simpletons," and be mocked (444). Comedy can do better than tragedy what tragedy attempts in the hands of Euripides. The lines call attention, ironically, to the role of the chorus, which must be pulled into the fiction of the play from the realities available to the audience in the theater. After Euripides departs, Dikaiopolis steels himself for his speech, not in praise of the Spartans, but rather recounting the progress of the war thus far, using the example of the Trojan War to frame his story.

The chorus breaks in half to respond to his speech, naming him as the beggar he pretends to be, dressed in rags like the mythical king Telephos. The leaders of the two half choruses respond to one another, and the general, Lamakhos, enters the scene, dressed in his full armor, accompanied by his soldiers. The chorus members try to force the general on the beggar Dikaiopolis, who expresses only contempt for the blowhard soldier, and taunts him, challenging the powerful military man "to peel back my foreskin" (592). In his own defense, Dikaiopolis calls himself a good, a useful citizen, *khrestos polites* (595). And he suggests that although Lamakhos was elected general, there were very few in attendance at the assembly when this occurred, "three cuckoos" voting him general (598).

The scene includes an exchange concerning Demokratia, personified and addressed directly in a sort of lamentation. The character Lamakhos responds to Dikaiopolis, who has addressed the members of the chorus, or perhaps citizens of the audience, pointing out that they never benefit from the largesse of the city's funds. They never participate in embassies, never travel to exotic locations like Ekbatana in the Persian Empire, even though characters like Lamakhos do enjoy these perquisites of service to the city. And Lamakhos replies: "Oh, Democracy! Will such talk be tolerated?" (618). Is his addressee the city herself, its political system, a goddess personifying the city's politics? And will "Demokratia," Democracy herself, punish those who speak freely, who say all, who expose the inequalities of the city's distribution of resources? Is this not a moment of *parrhesia*, Dikaiopolis challenging the hierarchies of the democracy, and perhaps too a moment of risk, not of death, but of going out on a limb to name and denounce those who benefit most from the pleasures the city can share with its most prominent citizens? Lamakhos held the office of general, one of those few positions in Athenian governance filled through election rather than by lottery, and he insists on the justice of his rights, duties, and privileges, derived through the votes of his fellow citizens and not by pure chance.

The chorus leader speaks now on behalf of the playwright, in a defense speech that insists on *parrhesia*. The chorus has been convinced by Dikaiopolis's arguments against war and for peace, and the chorus leader claims the poet's right to continue his practices: "Since he has been accused by his enemies before Athenians quick to make up their minds, as one who makes comedy of our city (*polin*) and outrages the people (*demos*), he now asks to defend himself before Athenians just as quick to change their minds" (630–32). The chorus leader claims too that the playwright has alerted them to flattery by foreigners, who praise the city by calling it "violet-crowned," or "gleaming," when in fact, the audiences will come to see and hear the spectacles presented in Aristophanes' name. And he alleges that the Persian emperor, interrogating ambassadors from Sparta, demanded which side in the Peloponnesian War was stronger in ships, the Spartans or the Athenians, and then "which side this poet profusely abused" (*eipoi kaka polla*, 649), literally, about which side the poet said many bad things: "So far has the renown of his [Aristophanes'] boldness already spread that even the King, in questioning the envoys from Sparta, asked them first which side was stronger in ships, and then which side this poet profusely abused; because those folks, he said, have become far better and far likelier to win the war, with him as an adviser" (647–51). The matter of *parrhesia*, saying all, here concerns not tragedy, but comedy, and is one of the reasons why the consideration of comedy and its choruses seems so relevant in our current discussions of democracy. *Parrhesia* strengthens the democracy, increases its chances of survival. Comedy toughens and energizes its fellow citizens, by saying bad things, things the powerful, or the audience, do not want to hear, often presented in the songs of the chorus. This, to my mind, is *parrhesia*, more appropriate to the role Mario Telò sees in the author Aristophanes, a concerned figure who wants to nurture or protect his fellow Athenians, than to Foucault's parrhesiast.[19]

Although the speech of the chorus leader here in the parabasis does seem based in the notion of a single person leading the city toward better practices, it is embedded in the play as a whole, differs from the character Dikaiopolis, and is located within the ongoing spectacle of chorus, dance, and song. The chorus leader, instead of speaking in the voice of the playwright himself, speaks as an advocate for him, advising the city never to let him go, to allow him to continue to make comedy and to lead them toward good fortune, rather than, as the demagogues do, tricking them, bribing, and flattering. He will teach (*didaskein*) many good things, so that they will be happy, fortunate (*eudaimonas*, 656).

The chorus leader ends with a smack at Cleon, defying him to prosecute Aristophanes once more; justice will be his ally (*summakhon*), will fight alongside him. And suddenly the chorus leader shifts to the first-person singular: "Never will I be caught behaving toward the city as he does, a coward and a punk-arse (*lakatapugon*)" (662–64). The insult is a telling one, *lakatapugon* meaning "extra assy," or, as LSJ puts it, "given to unnatural lust," "lecherous," "lewd," in the lexicon's evasive and bowdlerizing way. *Puge* means "ass." Henderson comments on the word in a list of those "attacked by comic poets as pathics," that is, as the penetrated in homosexual intercourse, with the further implication that Cleon is a dung collector, a shit gatherer. He adds that, using language that is unenlightened at best, "these references do not mean that Cleon was actually a pathic; they are merely scabrous insults brought on by the poet's personal dislike of Cleon."[20] This is *parrhesia*.

And Dikaiopolis proceeds to establish the terms of his separate peace, his private truce with the Spartans. He does business, the chorus congratulates him, and remarks that he will encounter none of the undesirable and annoying characters of Athenian urban life in his new capacity as the sole administrator of his private market. Theban pipers arrive, also enemies, here called *sphekes*, "wasps," a swarm that Dikaiopolis wants to chase away from his space. In this situation, the wasps, a chorus in the later comic production, cause annoyance in their swarming, are Theban, that is, foreign to Athens, and annoying because of noisemaking, because of the sound made by their flutes as their leader asks them to pipe an obscene song, "The Asshole of the Dog."

The chorus leader, persuaded of the excellence of Dikaiopolis's negotiations, sings a song of praise, now abruptly rejecting war in favor of the joys of peace: "To this man all bounties are supplied spontaneously. I will never welcome the War God (*Polemon*) into my house, nor will he ever recline at my side and sing the Harmodius song" (978–79). War is to be excluded, and the line here refers to the great hero of the democracy, Harmodius, who, with his lover Aristogeiton, assassinated the son of the tyrant Peisistratos in the sixth century BCE, and according to Athenian lore, ushered in the era of democracy to the city.

In the comedy, war has disrupted festivities, crashing the party and ruining the grape harvest and the making of wine. With Dikaiopolis's actions, the restoration of peace and a truce with the Spartans, Reconciliation (Diallage), companion of the goddess Aphrodite and the Graces, has appeared with her lovely face, and excited the desire of the chorus leader, who lustily imagines he could possess her three times in a row. A theatrical machine, the *ekkyklema*, was probably used at this point, to show the feast being readied for the celebration of peace by the women of Dikaiopolis's household, including his slaves. Delicious treats are prepared. When a victim of the war appears, asking for help, Dikaiopolis retorts that he is not a city doctor (*demosieuon*), one of the physicians supported by the city to give free health care to the poor, just another of the ways in which the democracy extended its benefits to all the *demos*. But Dikaiopolis won't share, won't dab some peace into the eyes of the war victim.

The "author-function," the representation of the comic poet himself, is split among various voices in this text, including the central character, Dikaiopolis, but also including the chorus leader, and the chorus itself, which may express the desires of the playwright and at least some of the spectators for peace and plenty. Cleon is the object of their contempt and vitriolic critique, but the form of the play itself is a plea for expressing all, that loathing and critique, but also the yearning for a utopian solution to an increasingly painful present of war, deprivation, and enmity not only among the Greek cities, but inside the city of Athens itself.

THESMOPHORIAZUSAE

Discussions of *parrhesia* such as that of Foucault, which leads to a portrait of Socrates, and to philosophers, as heroic parrhesiasts, risking death through truth-telling, and guiding the souls of their interlocutors, barely touch on the role of *parrhesia* in this other important genre of fifth-century drama, comedy. *Parrhesia* figures explicitly in a comedy discussed earlier, *Thesmophoriazusae*, when one of the characters, the kinsman of Euripides, secreted among women celebrating a women's festival, and disguised as one of them, uses the term in the context of forced depilation.

After a long speech on behalf of Euripides, in which he argues that the tragedian, who has a reputation among them for slandering women, is only portraying them as they really are, in her transvestite person the kinsman claims that he was deflowered at the age of seven by someone who continued to enjoy her after her marriage, in a scene that recapitulates the claims in a famous lawsuit argued by a forensic orator. S/he reminds his internal audience, the chorus of female worshippers of Demeter and her daughter Kore, that they "get banged by their slaves and mule grooms" (491–92), that a wife sneaked her lover out of her house by distracting her husband, another purchased a baby after pretending to be in labor for ten days. The chorus is outraged at the kinsman's words (*eipein ten panourgon*), using a word that prepares for the *pan*, the "all," of *parrhesia*, the "telling all." Mica, one of the women, demands that they find a hot coal somewhere to singe the hair of the "woman"'s pubis. Echoing the *pan* of *panourgon*, their readiness to do "all," with a connotation of deviousness, or rascality, he in turn claims the right of *parrhesia*, in order to avoid punishment: "Please, no, ladies, not my pussy! There is freedom of speech (*parrhesias*) here, and all of us who are citizens are entitled to speak, so if I merely said on Euripides' behalf what I know to be fair, am I to be punished by depilation at your hands?" (540–43). Does the right of *parrhesia* extend to women, or does the disguised kinsman betray his gender here?

The right to "say all" was a valuable attribute of the Athenian democracy, as noted especially in tragedy, a feature of civic life that distinguished it from tyrannies or monarchies or oligarchies, in which the powerful could silence the people. But here the exercise of *parrhesia*, in this comic context, begins to turn, and becomes the object of implicit critique. The women certainly object to the kinsman's disparaging account of their deceptions, and want to punish *his parrhesia*, which no longer has the authorization of the political, democratic setting, the customary attack on the powerful, here an exposure of the secretive practices of women. The play is a site of contestation concerning freedom of expression, opening to the possibility of abuse of *parrhesia*; it allows for the ambivalence of its audience toward the saying of all, if that all gores one's own ox.

KNIGHTS

According to the biographical tradition, the Acharnians' attack on the so-called demagogue Cleon did seem to have provoked, if not threats to the life of Aristophanes, at least prosecution and attempts to avenge the insults, or to silence the comic playwright.[21] The play was said to have excited such a reaction; how is its *parrhesia* consistent with other comic representations of this aspect of Athenian democracy, for example in the play *Knights*, which Aristophanes presented the year after the *Acharnians*?

The *Knights* again viciously attacks the politician Cleon, whom the play presents as a danger to the democracy. In the *Acharnians*, the chorus has threatened to use its *parrhesia* to destroy him. Addressing Dikaiopolis, they sing:

> I hate you even more
> than Cleon, whom
> I intend to cut up
> as shoeleather for the Knights.
> (299–302)

These "knights," the cavalrymen, form the chorus of the next year's comedy, which again attacks the demagogue. It is emphatically parrhesiast, not in the sense of Foucault's careful philosophical advice to the initiate, but as a rowdy, obscene, and thoroughgoing condemnation of the playwright's alleged enemy.

One of the characters of this play is in fact Demos, the personification of the people, who has purchased a new slave, a Paphlagonian tanner. He, by profession resembling the citizen Cleon, has deceived and manipulated his master while keeping goods for himself, even as he alienates the native slaves, born in the household of Demos. Oracles reveal that Paphlagon will be succeeded by a sausage seller, who then outdoes the Cleon figure in various contests, and rejuvenates Demos, the people, returning him to his past glories of victory in the Persian Wars, in the battles of Marathon and Salamis. Demos rejoices.

The *parrhesia* of denunciation of Cleon includes, from the very first lines of the *Knights*, condemnation by the slaves of Paphlagon's administration of the household. The slaves born to the household (*tois oiketais*, 5) have been beaten mercilessly since he arrived. The split between the barbarian Paphlagonian and the house-born slaves reveals the potential for discrimination among different kinds of slave, those of Greek origin, house-born, indigenous Greek-speakers, a different category of unfree compared to the barbarian imports.[22]

The chorus of this play is "knights," cavalrymen, and they enter the scene as a swarm, reminding the modern spectator, or reader, and possibly the ancient spectators as well, of the ways in which the chorus, drilled and moving usually as a unit in its dancing and singing, has affinities with a military unit, a block of horsemen or a phalanx of hoplites, or even a group of battleships in formation. (Sappho says she prefers her lover to any of these.) The swarm of comic horsemen in this comedy might be compared to the magnificent ranks of the cavalry, riders, on the Parthenon frieze, horsemen in a different register.[23]

The chorus leader exhorts his troops to attack Paphlagon as if he were an enemy force, rousing them as the wasp leader does his swarm: "Come on, hit him, pursue him, shake him up, mix him up, loathe him as we do, give out with a war cry as you attack him!" (251–52). Their denunciation of Paphlagon/Cleon exemplifies the *parrhesia* so prized in other texts as an attribute of the Athenian democracy:

> You filthy disgusting shout-downer, your brazenness
> fills the whole land, the whole Assembly,
> the taxes, the indictments and the lawcourts,
> you muckraker, you who have thrown our whole city
> into a sea of troubles,
> who have deafened our Athens with your bellowing,
> watching from the rocks like a tuna fisher for shoals of tribute!
> (303–12)

The exchange of insults between this Paphlagon and the Sausage Seller similarly resounds with accusations of greed, lust, and depredations. One of the slaves indulges in a fantasy of violent abuse: "We'll jam a peg in his mouth like butchers, and yank out his tongue and take a good brave look down to his gaping arsehole, to see if he's measly" (375–81). That is, we'll see if he's pimply or has tubercles down there, making him less fit for butchering. This, again, is "saying it all," a far cry from the polite conversation between adviser and advisee described by Foucault, or even from the representation of *parrhesia* in tragedies, where it connotes the social, legal, and political invulnerability of the rhetoric of a citizen in the city of Athens.

The chorus reacts to the imagination of violence put into the mouth of the slave, just cited, with a sense too that their duty is to combat the likes of Paphlagon: "So there really are temperatures hotter than fire, and speeches more brazen (*anaidesteroi*) than the brazen speeches heard in the city" (382–85). The word Henderson translates as "brazen," *anaidesteroi*, means "reckless," literally, "shameless." The speeches in the city's assembly may be shameless, but comedy, and the slave, exceed even their shamelessnesss.

In the parabasis of this play, the address to the audience sometimes voiced in the person of the poet himself, the chorus leader recalls another comic writer, Magnes, who was booed off the stage when he reached old age. But the chorus leader recalls the vigor of his youthful choruses, using language that invokes the swarm: "He vocalized all kinds of sounds, strumming, flapping, singing Lydian, buzzing himself, dying himself green as a frog" (522–23). The swarming froggy sounds of Magnes, once his hair grew gray, no longer satisfied his audience. The work of the comic playwright Cratinus too once flowered but is no longer in favor (although he was in fact in competition with Aristophanes in the festival at which this play was produced, and won second prize after Aristophanes).[24]

The dance and song of the knights emphasize the military aspect of this chorus; as swarms, their ancestors fought in infantry and in naval expeditions, and they invite Poseidon, the god of horses, master of dolphins, to come and dance with them. A vase painting may show these half men, half horses, not centaurs, but military figures of the cavalry. The chorus members in the *Knights* are not animals, like the wasps and the birds, but, as knights, as a swarm of cavalrymen, they praise their horses, who bravely jumped aboard ships and, according to the chorus leader, "sat to their oars like we [sic] humans, dipped their blades, and raised a snort of 'Heave Horse! . . . Stroke harder'" (601–4). These horses recall the centaurs, so identified with their human riders that they become one with their fellow soldiers.

Demos toys with his various lovers, his *erastai* (1163); Paphlagon is exposed as a thief, Demos eventually decides, after the rivals offer various tantalizing benefits, to award the reins of the Pnyx, the site of the democratic city's assembly, to the sausage seller. And the chorus leader defends the practice of *parrhesia*: "There's nothing invidious about calling bad people names; it's a way to honor good people, if you stop to think about it" (1274–75). He takes the occasion to say very rude things about the brother of the talented Arignotus, Ariphrades "the sleazy" (*poneros*) (1281): "He pollutes his own tongue with disgraceful gratifications, licking the detestable dew in bawdyhouses, besmirching his beard, disturbing the ladies' hotpots" (1284–86). These insults, piled on, seem to justify the insults hurled at the Cleon figure in the play, and legitimate the obscenity by claiming that it provides a contrast to the proper praise of excellent men.

The play ends with the transformation of Demos, from ugly to handsome, setting him "in the violet-crowned Athens of former, ancient times" (1323). Having been boiled, like the king killed by Medea, but truly rejuvenated, Demos, ruler of all Greece, reappears, wearing the emblem of the old Athens, the cicada, part of the legendary heroic swarm of the past: "Here he is for all to see, wearing a golden cricket (*tettigophoras*), resplendent in his old-time costume, smelling not of ballot shells but peace accords, and anointed with myrrh" (1331–32). This new Demos promises to pay the wages owed to the rowers in the fleet, the poorest of citizens, when they land, and to perform other reforms, expelling decadent and pretentious youths from the *agora*. He's rewarded with a slave boy who will serve him sexually if he desires. And two girls, "Treaties," Spondai, arrive, as Paphlagon is demoted to selling sausages made of dog and ass meat, insulting prostitutes, and drinking the runoff from the public baths. The wild and raucous invective of the chorus seems to have been domesticated, the *demos* returned, with some concessions, to the ancient ways, but if we read for this chorus, for its rage and language flying off in all directions, the dénouement, like that of the *Birds*, may seem like a compromise formation, a "psychic horse-trading," as Fredric Jameson calls it, that allows for the contradictory and anarchic energy at its heart.[25]

The obscenity, insults, and ferocious hostility inflicted on Cleon, presented on stage as demagogue and enemy of the people in both the *Acharnians* and the *Knights*, supposedly excited his wrath and provoked attempts to take revenge on the playwright.[26] Cleon may have been an advocate of the people at times, a favorite of some of the *demos*. Yet the energy of denunciation, even though it may have been recontained, as Demos bears the golden cicada of the aristocracy, has its own power, giving voice to the contestations and struggles of a heterogeneous population in the ancient city. The stage of comedy was, at least for some years, a privileged space, a site of freedom of speech, where chorus and characters could say all. Stephen Halliwell discusses condemnation of *aischrologia*, "shameful speech, 'foul' language, abuse," by conservative and elite authors. And he claims "Old Comedy's aischrologic imperative brought with it at least an implicitly recognized legal immunity (αδεια) in relation to the Athenian law(s) of slander (*kakêgoria*)."[27] "Comedy," says Halliwell, "can say and do what cannot otherwise be said or done with impunity in public life, and the behavior of its audience is part of that special contract. Comedy plays by different rules."[28] Halliwell argues that this aspect of Old Comedy is not democratic, but "pre- or sub-democratic": "Old Comedy exploits an unruly license for mockery that is no more respectful of democratic controls than of any other."[29] Alan Sommerstein argues that, concerning the question of Aristophanes' legal liability for slander, especially of Cleon, who is ridiculed and insulted in several comedies, "comedy's privileged access to a vast (and, at the City Dionysia, an international) audience did not require it to be held to any higher or more restrictive standards than the law imposed on all alike."[30]

The *Knights* was produced, performed, won a prize, and throughout demonstrates the permissiveness inherent in the fifth-century city's idea of itself, the right to insult, to say it all, to free speech, a right that belongs to the riotous legacy of ancient Athenian Old Comedy. Robert W. Wallace, in "The Power to Speak—and Not to Listen," discusses "hubbub," *thorubos*, the vociferous, rowdy, shouting crowd reaction to speech in the city.[31] *Thorubos*, "uproar, clamor, noise, applause, cheers, groans, tumult, confusion," is the language of the swarm, a roar without words, the voice of those who, as Jacques Rancière might say, have no voice, have no part.

In Greek ideology and practice, the obligation to sit quietly without speaking, to listen silently to whatever someone said, was a hated characteristic of monarchy, tyranny, and oligarchy.[32] The crowd, the audience, became part of the performance, in the assembly, in the law courts, and in the theater, especially in the comic theater. There may be so-called structured silences in these plays, the avoidance of topics, perhaps related to the playwright himself, who exempts himself from the variety of insults paraded before the audience. Nonetheless, much can be said, much is said, many are insulted and splashed with the mud of invective in the course of the plays, in a display of freedom of speaking rarely available to our own contemporary audiences, where the vocabulary of obscenity is still policed in the United States. And although insults to people of color, LGBTQX people, women, and others vulnerable to abuse take up much of the discussion in these days of trigger warnings and self-censoring, the insults and ridicule directed at those in power, in particular the former US president Donald J. Trump, from the mouths of late-night comedians Trevor Noah, John Oliver, and Stephen Colbert, as well as the comedians of *Saturday Night Live*, demonstrate a willingness, an eagerness, to say all that, and although limited by corporate television, still have some power to provoke laughter and to encourage resistance, as do the efforts of other comics, accessible on social media, who rally the contempt and rage of the masses to disrespect those who abuse their power. The *Guardian* newspaper's political cartoonist Steve Bell represented the former president Trump as an orange pumpkin-head topped with a golden toilet seat, lid open.

On the other hand, violent insurrection in defense of inequality, racism, anti-Semitism, anti-immigration sentiment, and misogyny, in defense of tyrannical seizure of power, can also be incited through speech, through lies, especially in these days of social media that refuse to discriminate among varieties of political rhetoric. One's evaluation of *parrhesia*, of free speech, of saying it all, depends on what is being said, on what the aims of the speaker are. Speech that mocks the abusers, that calls for equality, should not be conflated in a false equivalence with speech that encourages hatred and the concentration of power in the hands of white supremacists, and exploiters of others, national and international.

As the philosopher Judith Butler puts it so well in her book *Excitable Speech*, "Insurrectionary speech becomes the necessary response to injurious language, a risk taken in response to being put at risk, a repetition in language that forces change."[33] The example from Athenian democracy's comedy points toward greater liberty, toward a resistance to repression, to tyrants, to those who manipulate their followers, toward a tolerance for different points of view on difference that continues to be, and should be, the subject of passionate debate in democracies.

[CHAPTER 6]

Democracy, Communalism, Communism

> There is a moment in Camaraderie
> when interruption is not to be understood.
> I cannot bear an interruption.
> This is the shining joy;
> the time of not-to-end.
>
> On the street we smile.
> We go
> in different directions
> down the imperturbable street.
>
> Gwendolyn Brooks, Riot

Movements like Occupy and Black Lives Matter have challenged the assertions of white supremacy and neoliberalism through peaceful protest, organized democratically, in recent years. Two twenty-first-century political theorists comment on the legacy of ancient Athenian democracy, which seems at present to be threatened by antidemocratic tendencies, generated by the waves of supposedly "populist," really white supremacist, anti-Semitic, misogynist, nativist politics in the US and Europe. The French theorist Jacques Rancière, in books including *Hatred of Democracy*, has responded to this growing tendency to turn neoliberal states into technocratic oligarchies.[1] In a book titled *Against Democracy*, Jason Brennan, professor of strategy, economics, ethics, and public policy at Georgetown University, calls into question the practices of democracy in the US.[2] In contrast to Rancière, Brennan's treatment of democracy focuses on voting. He divides the voting population in the US into three categories: "hobbits," "hooligans," and "Vulcans." He defines the first category in this way: "*Hobbits* are mostly apathetic and ignorant about politics. They lack strong, fixed opinions about most political issues. . . . They have little, if any, social scientific knowledge; they are ignorant not just of current events but also of the social scientific theories and data needed to evaluate as well as understand these events" (4). His second category thus: "*Hooligans* are the rabid sports fans of politics. They have strong and largely fixed worldviews.... They may have some trust in the social sciences, but cherry-pick data and tend only to learn about research that supports their own views. They are overconfident in themselves and what they know" (5). Note that the criterion for these classifications is knowledge of the social sciences; Professor Brennan is himself a social scientist. His third category: "*Vulcans* think scientifically and rationally about politics. Their opinions are strongly grounded in social science and philosophy. They are self-aware, and only as confident as the evidence allows. Vulcans can explain contrary points of view in a way that people holding those views would find satisfactory. They are interested in politics, but at the same time, dispassionate, in part because they actively try to avoid being biased and irrational. They do not think everyone who disagrees with them is stupid, evil, or selfish" (5). In other words, Vulcans resemble Professor Brennan.

Brennan proposes abolishing democracy as we know it. He argues that democracy, or voting, doesn't work, citing numerous social scientific studies. Based on their findings, he concludes that political participation "corrupts" people, making them more dogmatic, and more ignorant (chapter 3, pp. 54–74). One vote in a democracy has no significance, so people don't bother to be informed. Voting does not empower people (chapter 4). Democracy is incompetent (chapter 6). And in a democracy people who *do* know, people like him, are controlled by those who do *not* know (chapter 6).

In place of democracy, Brennan proposes what he calls "epistocracy," that is, rule by those who know: "As noted in chapter 2, political knowledge is not evenly dispersed among all democratic groups. Whites on average know more than blacks, people in the Northeast know more than people in the South, men know more than women, middle-aged people know more than the young or old, and high-income people know more than the poor. In general, people who are already advantaged are much better informed than the disadvantaged. Most poor black women, as of right now at least, would fail even a mild voter qualification exam" (226). Furthermore, he writes: "The disadvantaged citizens ... might know what kinds of outcomes would serve their interests, but unless they have tremendous social scientific knowledge, they are unlikely to know how to vote for politicians or policies that will produce these favored outcomes" (227). ("Tremendous" there, "tremendous social knowledge," language very reminiscent of former US president Donald Trump.) As a consequence of these findings, Brennan proposes that only social scientists should vote, and rule. Or, that those who are permitted to vote would need to pass a qualifying examination to vote. Or that those who perform well on such a test should have more votes than those who receive lower marks on the examination. Or that random selection would occur, of panels of citizens who would spend many hours being educated on the issues of the day, and who would then be allowed to vote and decide on all questions.

Brennan acknowledges that there are some problems with the solutions he proposes. For example, during the Jim Crow era, he notes, "governments deprived blacks of the rights to vote by requiring them to pass nearly impossible literacy tests" (223). He does not take account of the myriad obstacles to voting we continue to see in elections. But his response to the Jim Crow era deprivations is that "governments claimed these tests had an epistocratic purpose, when in fact they only had a racist purpose. These tests were administered in bad faith. They were designed to be impossible to pass, and whites were not required to take them." But, he adds, "the fact that governments used to hide their racism beneath an epistocratic disguise does not show us that epistocratic exams are inherently objectionable. Instead, the question we would need to ask about any such exam is just how badly it would be abused today" (224). This is the thinking of a naive, cunning, or willfully ignorant political theorist, who assumes that objectionable racist motives might not now determine how such tests would be administered.

This scholar's work has been widely read and taken seriously in the academic and popular press. And his argument was followed up in a more recent book, the cover of which bears an endorsement by Brennan, entitled *10% Less Democracy: Why You Should Trust Elites a Little More and the Masses a Little Less*. The author, Garett Jones, articulates his "central idea: that in most of the rich countries, we've taken democracy, mass voter involvement in government, at least a little too far."[3] One of the reforms he advocates echoes Brennan's: "Giving a little more weight to more informed groups of voters, especially in the upper house of a national legislature, might be just the epistocratic nudge that representative democracy needs" (179). He relies on the ancient thinkers Aristotle and Polybius, as well as Machiavelli, who he believes preferred "Democracy Plus Oligarchy" (181). A reform that Jones's readers might consider: "Requiring college degrees to vote in elections—but only to the upper house of parliament" (188). Turning toward oligarchy, perpetuating and even increasing racist, gender, and class discrimination, appeals to a growing body of propagandists in Western so-called democracy, who seek to turn back even the most modest of democratic procedures in their countries, which in fact have never instituted the direct democracy of the ancient city at the origins of this political form, nor its filling of political and administrative offices in the city through the drawing of lots.

In this chapter, I describe the ancient democracy, discuss its legacy, and point to the ways in which contemporary antidemocratic thinkers share some of the assumptions of ancient writers about the democratic swarm. I look also to a wider range of participants in the life of the ancient city, who brought new forms of knowledge to the polity, comic poets as well as statesmen, shoemakers as well as philosophers, as exemplified in the comedy *Women at the Assembly*, which depicts a communist takeover of Athens by its women, who redistribute sexual pleasure and the economic resources of their city.

ATHENIAN DEMOCRACY

Ancient Old Comedy and its comic choruses intervened in moments of political crisis in classical Athens, and in some instances promoted a radical democracy, a communism that extended even to women. Such comedy allowed for laughter, laughter at the powerful, at the *demos* itself, at the audience itself, a welcome instrument in troubled times, including our own, and in our case, disrupting the norms of condescending sociological debate. It is too easy to "cancel" Old Comedy for its hostile and demeaning remarks about women, about slaves, and targeted sexual practices, and ignore the fact that ancient comedy makes fun of everyone in sight and enjoys collective laughter as well as the presence in the city of others, slaves, farmers, women, foreigners. The ancient democracy took advantage of the complexity of the composition of the city's population, not relying on "experts."

Robert Sobak, in an article entitled "Sokrates among the Shoemakers," offers a telling critique of the antidemocratic propagandists, based on his analysis of the richness of association, in the assembly and in "free spaces," in a "collective, emergent intelligence refined through usage in and outside of the institutions of the state," among all the classes in Athenian democracy:[4]

> Telling any citizen-shoemaker within a strongly democratic system to "stick to his last" is a fundamentally political criticism. It is an attempt to short-circuit democratic knowledge production and dispersal, first by undermining the way nonelite knowers are evaluated, and then by excluding them from the epistemic system altogether. It is the first step on the road from a robust and diverse epistemic polyculture to a carefully crafted and tight controlled managerial monoculture. This disregard for and disaggregation of the socially constructed common knowledge of common people strikes at the very foundation of a truly democratic conception of *politike techne*, and thence at the ultimate success of *demokratia* as a governing system.[5]

The debate about democracy in the present should look back to this more multiplicitous understanding of the ancient city, its comic theater included.

The classical democratic Athenian *polis* of the fifth century BCE was fundamentally different from the great nearby empires of Egypt, Persia, and eventually Rome.[6] Greek citizens of democratic cities knew their leaders, they had no divine emperors, no extensive imperial bureaucracies or standing armies. The average *polis* relied on its own citizens for protection. The richest citizens in the classical period served as cavalry, because they could afford the maintenance of horses; a heavily armed infantry was an important force in warfare, and its hoplites, or foot soldiers, provided their own equipment, and were of "middling" status.[7] These soldiers were amateurs, a militia that defended their territory. The poorest of citizens, along with some slaves, rowed in the navy's fleet and contributed to some important victories of the classical age, the fifth and fourth centuries BCE.[8]

A *polis* could be governed in any of several ways: monarchy, Greek for "rule by one man," meant a king, who inherited his hegemony over the city; aristocracy denoted rule by "the best," as they called themselves, rule by hereditary nobles; in oligarchies, control was held by "a few," *oligoi*, often a small group of the wealthy. Tyranny was rule by a monarch who had usurped rule, taken power by illegal means. And then there was democracy, rule by the *demos*, "the people." This brings us to Athens itself, where, from the sixth to fourth century BCE, its citizens conducted a radical experiment in governance. Instead of creating an oligarchy, as did the Spartans, through a period of class struggle, conflicts between the rich and the poor, the Athenians extended to all citizens the right and duty of governing their *polis*. Their democracy, "rule by the people," has different connotations for different thinkers. *Demos*, the crucial word, can mean either "all the people," that is, all the citizens, or, alternatively, the "poor," for some, "the mob," "the rabble." This distinction becomes crucial, especially in the work of antidemocratic thinkers.

In a fascinating argument concerning the ontological status of ancient Athens, Greg Anderson presents an alternative understanding of *demos*, one that refuses the imposition of contemporary and anachronistic social scientific categories of analysis:

> This communion [*koinonia*] known as "the Athenians" was a unitary, freestanding agency in its own right. Unlike, say, liberal civil society, it was not merely an aggregate of pregiven individuals. In the thought and practice of the Athenians, their *koinonia* was an ontologically autonomous thing-in-itself, a polyadic person or self that existed prior to and apart from themselves as discrete persons. As the human personality or essence

of the *polis*, it was a kind of ageless primordial superorganism, one that had been continually present in Attica since the time of those first earthborn kings. As such, it had a certain subjectivity, a life, will, and an interest all its own. The Athenians called this living persona of their *polis* simply *ho Demos*, "the People."[9]

Is the comic chorus, a "polyadic" swarm, not a better way of representing this multiple, heterogeneous, active being than the abstractions of political science?

The Athenians understood themselves mythically, as Anderson notes, to be autochthonous, that is, to have sprung from their land themselves, like plants, as recounted earlier, and claimed that this autochthony gave some residents the right to citizenship and to privileges denied to slaves and foreigners, privileges such as *parrhesia*. Such myths justified landownership and the distinction of citizens from other residents of the city.

In Athens, by the early sixth century BCE, there seem to have been intense social conflicts based on economic differences. The city was dominated by its aristocrats, who traced their ancestry back to heroes and gods. They owned the best land, met in an assembly to govern, and interpreted the laws as they saw fit. Noble landowners forced poorer farmers into sharecropping; some of these people, falling into debt, were sold into slavery. The poet and lawmaker Solon, mentioned in the chapter preceding on *parrhesia*, asked to help the city to avoid tyranny, the seizure of power by a strong man, was chosen to reform the state. Debt bondage remained a feature of the *polis*, but Solon freed former citizens from slavery, brought back enslaved Athenians who had been sold to other cities, made enslavement of citizens illegal, and reformed the structure of the governance of the *polis*, paving the way for democracy.[10] Other reforms followed, as did a tyrant, Peisistratos. The Athenians told an inspiring and anachronistic fictional account of the end of the tyranny and the advent of democracy. Hippias, son of the tyrant, inherited tyrannical rule, his brother insulted the sister of an aristocrat, Harmodius; he along with his male lover, Aristogeiton, assassinated the tyrant's son and were tortured and killed. The Athenians looked to their courageous act and their martyrdom as the foundation of democracy, and set up a monument to the two lovers in the *agora*, the central civic space of the city.[11]

There were further developments eroding the old kinship and tribal hierarchies of the Athenian *polis*, and eventually the central government included an assembly of all the citizens. Various offices were set up to administer the business of the city-state. Most officers of the city were eventually chosen by lot, that is, by lottery, by a drawing, by chance. These procedures proved very important for another of the twenty-first-century thinkers

I mentioned earlier, Jacques Rancière, because it meant that any citizens who so desired had to be prepared to govern, to be magistrates, treasurers, tax collectors, to be equal to the tasks necessary for the city-state to function. All these officers of the state were assumed to be equal, to be *equal* to all other citizens, in the governance model called *isonomia*, "equality in law," as opposed to *eunomia*, "excellence in law," the justification of aristocratic or elite rule.

Officeholders underwent an audit automatically at the end of their service. Jurors for the legal system of the city were also chosen by lot, were understood to be equal to all other citizens, and were paid by the state, as we saw in the comedy *Wasps*. Eventually citizens were paid to attend performances of tragedy and comedy, as noted earlier. In various ways, the city distributed funds to its citizens.[12] The wealthy were required to contribute to various institutions of the city, including the fleet and the dramatic festivals.[13] The Athenian democracy, with its various instruments of governance by the people, was an anomalous institution, especially in light of other neighboring societies of this period, such as various Mesopotamian regimes, and Egypt, ruled by the pharaoh, a god on earth. The Athenians *were* their government.

There were exclusions to this rule by the people. Some of the residents in the ancient city of Athens were not descended from the ancestors who themselves had sprouted from the land. There were residents who had moved to Athens from other Greek cities, citizens in their own land but not in Athens. "Metics," those non-Athenian free persons who lived in the city, were not eligible to participate in deliberations in the assembly, but were required to serve in person in the military.[14] All women, even if born into the citizen class, were excluded from the democracy, had no role in the political life of the city, could not attend the assembly, nor speak, nor vote, nor testify in legal cases, nor serve on juries.

And there was a large body of slaves. Some of these slaves were born in Athenian households to slave mothers, although their fathers might have been their citizen-masters; they could be citizen-class infants, especially daughters, exposed to die or to be claimed by strangers, as was Oedipus. The slaves were sometimes prisoners of war, or people of any status captured by kidnappers and sold. In the later fourth century, after the conquest of the Greeks by the Macedonians, between 317 and 307 BCE, a later tyrant, Demetrius of Phaleron, is said to have ordered a general census of Attica, which arrived at the following figures: 21,000 citizens, 10,000 metics or foreign, non-Athenian residents, and 400,000 slaves. These figures are disputed; in fact no one knows precisely how many slaves there were in the city, and what percentage of its residents were free persons, or citizens.

A famous and curmudgeonly Athenian citizen objected to the resemblance of arrogant Athenian slaves to free citizens and the annoying difficulty of determining who was slave and who free, although wealthier Athenians tried to set theirs apart from the "common" slaves and even poorer citizens, with finer clothing, representations of domestic intimacy, and more heroic physiognomy on funeral monuments. Slaves could often be differentiated ethnically from Athenian citizens; they bore names that identified them as "other," referring for example to red hair, Xanthias, or "barbarian" descent, Thratta, of Thracian origin. Such naming recalls Orlando Patterson's description of slavery as "social death." And the Athenian legal system required that slaves, when their evidence was required in a legal trial, be tortured, as made clear by the scene in the *Frogs* in which the god Dionysos is threatened with such treatment.[15]

CONTRADICTIONS OF ANCIENT DEMOCRACY AND ITS AFTERLIFE

The legacy of ancient Athens is contradictory, including not just a radical and extraordinary insistence on equality among all citizens, but also a de facto oligarchic shape, as described above, and colonialism and engagement in imperialist adventures.[16] For a brief period in the fifth century BCE the city-state of Athens dominated many other cities and enforced its hegemony over the eastern Mediterranean. Historians record episodes of savagery conducted against disobedient allies and enemies—the crucifixions of rebels, resisters clubbed to death in the marketplace of the Milesians, "now spectators as well as beneficiaries of imperial repression," according to Plutarch in his *Life of Pericles* (28.2). Citizens of the island of Melos were massacred, their women and children enslaved.

Yet even the mutilation or drowning of enemy rowers did not prevent the Athenians from composing, performing, and sharing with allies, subjects, and foreigners the tragedies in which they emphasized Athenian mercy and hospitality toward the needy, and the benefits that these others should provide to the city and its empire in exchange.[17] Yet classical historian John Ma, in discussing the ambitions of the fifth-century Athenian *polis*, insists: "I still believe in the usefulness of the concept of 'empire' [for Athens]: coercion, centralization, economic exploitation all characterize the Athenian *arche*"; and adds: "Empires cannot exist without torture, atrocities, and self-conscious, spectacular violence."[18]

The Athenian state, as noted, relied internally on slaves. The philosopher Aristotle, long resident in Athens, made arguments in his *Politics* in favor of "natural slavery"; these principles were used for millennia to justify slavery. In his *Politics* he says: "One that can foresee with his mind is naturally ruler and naturally master, and one that can carry out labour with his body is subject and naturally a slave" (1252a32–34). "One who is a human being belonging by nature not to himself but to another is by nature a slave, and a person is a human being belonging to another if being a man he is an article of property, and an article of property is an instrument for action" (1254a15–18). "He is by nature a slave who is capable of belonging to another (and that is why he does so belong), and who participates in reason so far as to apprehend it but not to possess it . . . ; the usefulness of slaves diverges little from that of the animals" (1254b21–28). These concepts, once applied to a great variety of enslaved persons, and especially to those the Athenians and other Greeks called "barbarians," were racialized in the early modern era, as Africans and indigenous Americans were denoted as "natural slaves," needing the governance of white masters.

These ideas were embraced and developed in the United States, especially in antebellum slaveholding states, and pro-slavery ideologues often made reference to the example of classical antiquity, a period of freedom for some enabled by the slavery of others. William Harper, in his *Memoir on Slavery*, argued for the great republics of the past as models for the US. Another pro-slavery polemicist wrote: "How came the distinguished heathen Republics of Greece and Rome to flourish, having the Institution of slavery as the foundation of their Constitution? The institution of slavery ever has been and ever will be the only sure foundation of all republican governments."[19] The naming of Athens, Georgia, site of the University of Georgia, in 1801, confirmed the imagined kinship of two slaveholding polities.

The afterlife of ancient democracy is complex: there was radical equality, offices held only by lot, by sortition, all citizens equal, officeholders audited at the end of their terms of office. But democracy was also a de facto oligarchy, based on nativism, in which only the autochthonous participated, where women, foreigners, and slaves were excluded, and where the economy relied on the labor of the slaves, the judicial system on the torture of slaves. The founders of the American state based their model of government not on Athenian democracy, which was seen as dangerously populist, but rather on the Roman republic, which protected itself against what was seen as the unruly mob, the *demos*, and throughout the republican period resisted any such developments as were seen in Athens in the fifth and fourth centuries BCE. The Romans maintained a group of senators, or elders, wiser heads, who prevented their state from falling into the hands of the people and of such popular reformers as the Gracchi.

The constitution of the American state preserved the ancient and time-honored institution of slavery, established a senate that was not based on arithmetic representation but, geometrically, on individual state's power, two members, per state. And as we have seen in recent elections, the popular, democratic vote does not determine the winner of the presidency. In other ways, the US has perpetuated some of the worst elements of the ancient Athenian state, relying on slavery, even after abolition, and on torture to achieve its ends.

Lisa Lowe's book *The Intimacies of Four Continents* argues that the abolition of legal slavery in the British Empire, and eventually throughout the Americas, long sought after, and supported by some Christian groups in Britain and the United States, in fact resulted in the virtual enslavement of new populations.[20] The liberal narrative of "freedom" relied on the extension of unfreedom to others. Chinese "coolies," for example, were brought to the Caribbean in the nineteenth century, after the slave trade with Africa was abolished, and after the reproduction of the slave population in such sites as Jamaica failed, in order to replace the workforce. These new workers, although not technically "slaves" in the sense that they were the private property of their masters, retained many of the features of enslaved persons. In his seminal work on world slavery, Orlando Patterson discusses some of these phenomena, situations of limited slavery, of indentured servitude, and the like.[21] In the context of the American South, in *Slavery by Another Name*, Douglas Blackmon shows how its criminal justice system, which targeted African American men, former slaves and descendants of slaves, arresting them for petty crimes and then selling them for enforced labor to mine owners, construction companies, and other corporations, simply perpetuated the slave system in another form.[22] Those caught in these circumstances never achieved their freedom from confinement and forced labor, as they were condemned for resistance within the prisons, labor camps, and workforces of the postwar South, and as the fines they were assessed mounted and could never be paid.

Scholars such as Blackmon and Edward Baptist, who wrote *The Half Has Never Been Told: Slavery and American Capitalism*, have detailed slavery's long shadow over the present. Along with the filmmaker Ava Duvernay, my colleague Dennis Childs, in his book *Slaves of the State: Incarceration from the Chain Gang to the Penitentiary*, has examined how the criminal justice system of the present perpetuates slavery, how the Thirteenth Amendment of the US Constitution abolished slavery for all with the notable exception of those held in penal institutions. The US military has continued to torture people overseas, in such sites as Abu Ghraib and Guantanamo Bay, and there is now an archive at the University of Chicago containing over 10,000 documents that detail two decades of torture of black men by Chicago police officers.[23] Evidence from that archive proves that "over 100 black men were tortured by officers in order to force confessions, drive them to incriminate co-defendants, or to intimidate possible witnesses to police brutality."

There is no reason to think that such practices were confined to Chicago, and the record of continuing killings of African Americans by police officers throughout this country stands as an extreme example of racialized torture, provoking international protest. An article in the *Washington Post* published on March 5, 2017, describes a lawsuit claiming that "tens of thousands of immigrants detained by U.S. Immigration and Customs Enforcement (ICE) were forced to work for $1 a day, or for nothing at all—-a violation of federal anti-slavery laws.... The lawsuit, filed in 2014 against one of the largest private prison companies in the country, reached class-action status... after a federal judge's ruling. That means the case could involve as many as 60,000 immigrants who have been detained."[24] Nativism, white supremacy, racism, slavery, and torture persist, and there is no reason to believe that these practices will cease.

Recent history, the rise of so-called populism, votes for Brexit in the UK, for Marine Le Pen in France, for Donald Trump in the US, have resulted from and reawakened antidemocratic sentiments. The distinction I cited earlier, between *demos* meaning "all the people," or *demos* meaning "the poor," had affected antidemocratic theory even in antiquity. Here is Socrates in Plato's *Republic*, before Alain Badiou's rewriting, as he condemns democracy for leading inexorably to tyranny: "Then in democracy, there's no compulsion either to exercise authority if you are capable of it, or to submit to authority if you don't want to; you needn't fight if there's a war, or you can wage a private war in peacetime if you don't like peace; and if there's any law that debars you from political or judicial office, you will none the less take either if they come your way. It's a wonderfully pleasant way of carrying on in the short run, isn't it?" (558a) "Democracy ... doesn't mind what the habits and background of its politicians are; provided they profess themselves the people's friends, they are duly honoured." (558c). A young man's "internal oligarchy starts turning into a democracy." "[His desires] lead in a splendid garlanded procession of indolence, licence, extravagance, and shamelessness. They [these desires] praise them all extravagantly and call insolence good breeding, licence liberty, extravagance generosity and shamelessness courage" (559e). "[The democratic man] lives from day to day, indulging the pleasure of the moment. One day it's wine, women and song, the next water to drink and a strict diet; one day it's hard physical training, the next indolence and careless ease, and then a period of philosophic study. Often he takes to politics and keeps jumping to his feet and saying or doing whatever comes into his head" (561c-d). His interlocutor replies: "A very good description of the life of one who believes in liberty and equality."

So, what is to be done? Is the answer the abolition of democracy, the antidemocratic changes urged by Jason Brennan, following in Plato's footsteps? As Sobak notes, "Plato's complaint about the rudeness of donkeys on the streets of the democratic polis (*Resp* 563c) . . . is a smear directed at workmen in particular and the *demokratia* in general. But if read from a different, nonelite perspective, it hints at the existence of a cultural landscape where freedom of speech, equality under the law, and a robust, diverse economy, in which men and women of all statuses and classes participated and mingled, helped fashion the city of Athens into an especially fluid 'free space.'"[25] Ancient Greek comedy puts on stage the range of these participants, men and women of all statuses and classes, even animals, in rowdy association, and challenges the complacencies of Western liberalism based on ancient models.

ECCLESIAZUSAE

The comedy *Ecclesiazusae*, translated as *Women at the Assembly*, sometimes *Assemblywomen*, is a fine example of ancient comedy's speculative staging of "politics."[26] It doesn't really matter if this was the intention of "Aristophanes-as-author," or if the play is a parody, a satire, a mocking of the strange utopian schemes circulating in Athens at the beginning of the fourth century BCE, after its defeat by the Spartans in the Peloponnesian War.[27] If the democracy, after several oligarchic coups, and humiliation in war, attempted to reconfigure itself after it had executed Socrates, if in the moment of confusion or opening that followed their defeat, the Athenians had tried to remake themselves, refashion their democracy, then this play presents a fascinating intervention in the field of possibilities or impossibilities.

Once again, I look in particular at the collective, at the ways in which the comic utopian impulse can inhabit another temporality, another spatiality, another order of identity, and in which comic collective practice takes on a life of its own. In this play the chorus is made up of "Attic women," *gynaikon Attikon*. The role of the chorus is somewhat reduced from that which we have seen in other plays, such as the *Birds*, where the chorus plays an active role, establishing a sort of alternative sequence to a plot dependent on the characters and resolution of their dramatic issues. In *Women at the Assembly* the Attic chorus members enter separately, without the procession typical of some comedies. They are often absent from the action, which takes place between various principal women and others in supporting roles. The play, unusually, lacks a parabasis, the address directly to the audience, sometimes in what seems to be the voice of the playwright himself. And songs that typically divided the episodes from one another also are lacking in this play.

Can these elements be explained by the fact that the premise of the entire play is the collective enfranchisement of all the Attic women? Or that the parabasis would seem misplaced in the mouth of the chorus leader here, or of a revolutionary, communist and utopian woman, the central character Praxagora? Her imaginative, strong-willed assertions and plans may themselves express a swarming potential in the collective of Attic women, an atmosphere, a *Stimmung* of solidarity between chorus and character. Or is relative diminution of the chorus due to the fact that the play, dated tentatively to about 390 BCE, was written after the defeat of the Athenians in the Peloponnesian War, in a period of questioning of political arrangements, and in a moment when the collective voice of the *demos* has been called into question by the collapse of its hegemony and empire? As elsewhere, we can see comedy registering a political crisis, like that experienced in the United States after the presidential election of 2016, the assault on the Capitol by the former president's mob, and a desire to rethink, to reformulate, politics in light of that crisis.

The chorus leader speaks early in *Women at the Assembly*, calling her allies into action. Several women enter separately, in an atypical arrival of the chorus. The citizen-class woman Praxagora addresses the crowd, some of whom have speaking roles; they are dressed as men with sticks and in Laconian boots and men's cloaks, wrapped tight and sporting beards. After some planning they are urged to lean on their sticks, to sing a rural elders' song. And the chorus leader addresses them as "men," *andres* (285), and reminds the chorus members that they must say "men," and never forget their transvestism and their disguise.

The complexities of the conventional cross-dressing of ancient Athenian drama are exaggerated here, for comic effect, in a strange set of reversals. The women, dressed as men to pass for men in the assembly, are in fact male chorus members pretending to be women pretending to be men to pass for assemblymen. And the chorus leader rouses them to action: "Let's go to the Assembly, men! (*ondres = o andres*)" (285). (S)he addresses them with men's names, errs in calling them women, and then corrects herself as they dance together, as they dance off.

One of the actual men actually attending describes the arrival of an unusually large crowd at the assembly's gathering, but notes that "we thought they all looked like shoemakers; really, the Assembly was awfully pale faced to behold" (385–87). Women, as on Attic vases, were conventionally thought to have pale skin, painted in white on vases, and cobblers, because they spent their days inside, were thought to resemble them. Shoemakers appear in Plato's work, and in the reflections of Jacques Rancière on workers. Here they may represent a line of flight, a way of understanding the presence of women in the assembly as an incommensurable, anomalous, disruptive category among the heterogeneous population of the city. As Robert Sobak argues in his fascinating essay on social interaction in the democracy, "Does the shoemaker's knowledge then not go beyond the sandal? . . . One way to begin to answer this question is to recognize that discrete, strictly bounded expertise does not exist in the world of lived experience, which is made up of individual and group relationships, and is where epistemic indiscretion helps define humans as social animals."[28] These shoemaker-like women, social animals if not literally animal, represent inhabitants of the city, part of the *demos*, a line of flight into the reality of the *demos*, the *polis*, which contained far more than the citizen body and its exclusive assembly. As Sobak further notes, "The fact that metics, slaves, and women, for example, had no formal political agency did not render them superfluous to the epistemic functioning of the city."[29] Sobak points to the network of associations, of knowledges, that exceeds a traditional analysis based on the city's formal institutions and their representations in elite sources.

Some of the most salient work of the French theorist Jacques Rancière comes in engagement with the populace, with ancient democracy, and in critiques of the utopian Plato, as in *The Philosopher and His Poor*. Considering the noble lie of the *Republic*, Rancière points to the impossible and troubling presence of the artisan in the city. In the division of labor in the ideal *polis*, the artisan, the poor man, is required not to think: "The rights of philosophic virtue depend upon their strict separation from the virtue of shoemaking."[30] The artisan "is not a free man sharing in the virtue of the city, but neither is he a slave. . . . A false free man and part-time slave, the artisan belongs neither to his trade nor to the one who assigns him work. . . . The artisan is not simply a lowly being to be kept away from the government of the city. Properly speaking, he is an impossible being, an unthinkable nature."[31]

In the *Women at the Assembly* the character Khremes gives a messenger's speech describing the activities of the chorus members, the women disguised as men, looking like shoemakers, who had come to what he assumed was a special meeting to deliberate concerning the "salvation . . . of the city" (*soterias tes poleos*). Was the *polis*, then, in a crisis mode, and is the communist proposal of the women a speculation about that salvation, rather than a satire, as most readers assume? Khremes describes a "pale, nice-looking youth" who rose and addressed the *demos*, and who advocated giving the city (*polin*) over to the women (427–30). The mass of "shoemakers" made a lot of noise, and applauded this plan. This youth had also noted on their behalf that the women, sworn to secrecy about their rites, never reveal the mysteries of their festival, the Thesmophoria. The assembled group ended by voting to give the city over to the women. "That seemed to be the only thing that hasn't been tried" (456–57). The observation seems to suggest a period of reinvention and experiment in the city, or at least of speculation about how to go forward in this time of difficulty for Athens. The extremity of this choice may be emphasized here, its ludicrousness, its hilarious impossibility. But there is also a utopian thrust, a leap into the void that has been created by the loss of empire and the exhaustion of the city in a time of political turmoil and rivalry among various states concerning the hegemony of the mainland. The male character Blepyros, husband of Praxagora, consoles himself concerning the prospect of these changes, including forced sex, with an evocation of ancient wisdom: "There *is* an ancestral saying, that however brainless or foolish our policies, all our affairs will turn out for the best" (473–75).

The chorus enters, stealthily approaching, urging caution lest the women and their deception be exposed. They re-equip themselves, returning to what they were before (499a–b). Praxagora addresses them as they all return to normal, readying themselves for new responsibilities in their former garments, now beardless. The metatheatricality of all this is quite apparent, actors, young men, pretending to be women pretending to be young men and then taking off their beards, as part of theatrical costume, and returning to their pretense of being women. Greek drama, saturated as it was with transvestism, reaches new such heights here, and calls attention to the polymorphous mutability of gender roles.[32] Such mutability is exploited in the plot that follows, where the chorus recedes and the characters interact in ways that stress the revolutionary possibilities and dangers of female rule. Other references to gynaecocracy stress the dangers of the rule of women, in the form of Lemnian women who murder their husbands, or the Amazons who appear in many works of art, vases and sculpted friezes, in combat with the Greeks.[33] These women were seen as monstrous, violating the codes of gender difference, and supporting the general Athenian view that women should not be given weapons. Here, in Aristophanes' comedy, the women use their domestic skills and economic power to govern benignly, and to gratify their sexual desires, notoriously excessive and unsatisfied in the gender ideology of the Athenians.

Praxagora lists the benefits that will flow from the women's rule, among them "no more poor people" (*me peneta medena*, 566). The chorus supports her plans, asking her to have a "philosophical mind" (*phrena philosophon*), in language that foreshadows the utopianism of Plato:

> For it's to the prosperity of all alike
> that from your lips comes a bright idea
> to gladden the lives of the city's people (*demon*)

with countless benefits;
now's the time to reveal its potential.
Yes, our city (*polis*) needs
some kind of sage scheme;
describe it in full, making sure only
that none of it's ever been
said or done before;
they hate to watch the same old stuff
over and over again!
(574–80)

If we consider the reading of Alain Badiou of Plato's *Republic*, and its implicit utopianism, then this comic vision of the future, the willingness to entertain radically new arrangements, a commune-ism of property and daily life, anticipate or echo the innovations proposed in the philosopher's text. The novelty that the crowd, the spectators, demand in comic presentation is transferred, or linked, or asserted in relation to the novelty required of political ideas in this time of searching in the city.

Praxagora's speeches that follow emphasize this novelty, which continues to refer ambiguously to both the ideas on governance that she proposes, and the comic situation in which women dominate. Although she expresses anxiety about the audience's reception of her plan, so unconventional, a neighbor reassures her: "Don't worry about quarrying new veins: for us, indifference to precedent takes precedence over any other principle of government" (586–87). This reaction seems more like a moment of political theory than a comic speech. And Praxagora goes on to set forth a communist agenda: everyone will own everything in common, and have a living from the same source. She will get rid of the rich and the poor. Her revolutionary plan does not extend explicitly to slaves: "No more rich man here, poor man there, or a man with a big farm and a man without land enough for his own grave, or a man with many slaves and a man without even an attendant (*akoloutho*). No, I will establish one and the same standard of life for everyone" (591–95). The plan of leveling the *bioton*, the standard of living, to include all may suggest that everyone, the common, will have the same number of slaves; as is most frequently the case, with the rarest of exceptions, slaves are excluded, or ambiguously not counted among those who make the "common," the *koinon*.

Praxagora declares that her first act will be to "communize," that is, make "common," *koinon* again, the land, the silver or money, and everything else that belongs separately to each of them. The women will administer this commonalty, and those who own movable property such as coins will contribute it to this common fund. And in a startling prefiguration of the demand for "communal luxury," as Kristin Ross designates the aims of the Paris Commune of 1871, Praxagora announces that all will share in the bounty of the common possessions: "No one will be doing anything as a result of poverty, because everyone will have all the necessities: bread, salt fish, barley cakes, cloaks, wine, garlands, chickpeas" (605–7). Although these may not seem like luxury goods to us, they made up the diet of most of the people of ancient Athens, many of whom seemed to have eaten meat only when it was distributed after the sacrificing of animals, rarely consuming expensive rare fish or other delicacies. Wine is clearly, it seems, a necessity, taken for granted as a basic ingredient of a common diet.

The communist, communalist, egalitarian plan realizes the egalitarianism, the *isonomia*, potential in democratic ideology, the advantages of which are discussed in a famous passage in Herodotus's *Histories*. Herodotus puts the argument concerning the best form of government in the mouths of Persian nobles, who, after deposing various contenders for the role of emperor, seem to conduct a seminar in Greek political theory. Otanes, one of the nobles who conspired to defeat the Magi who threatened them, presents the case against monarchy: "A monarch subverts a country's customs, takes women against their will, and kills men without trial. What about majority rule, on the other hand? In the first place, it has the best of all names to describe it—-equality before the law (*isonomie*). It is government by lot, it is accountable government, and it refers all decisions to the common people" (3.80, trans. Waterfield).[34] The arguments concerning the relative merits of monarchy, oligarchy, and democracy had already been introduced in the work of Pindar (*Pythian* 2), and would be rehearsed later by others, including Plato, Aristotle, and Isocrates. Otanes, who loses the debate to those who prefer monarchy, exempts himself and his family from future domination by the emperor. But his arguments, especially the concepts of equality before the law, the selection of officers of the government by lottery, the accountability of the officers of the democracy, their exposure to an audit at the end of their service, and the practice of voting in the assembly on actions of the *polis*, make a strong case for the values of Athenian and other democracies in the fifth century BCE, practices that Praxagora wants to extend beyond male citizens, to their female counterparts, who will rule as a "majority," a *plethos*.

A problem arises when the question of sexual equality looms; Praxagora wants to give the women resources "common to all" as well. "Equality," *koinonia*, extends to sexual rights, and the old and ugly women, the ugly and runtish men, will have as much access to sexual pleasure as the beautiful. The question of offspring is settled neatly: a man will not claim children as his own, but the children "will regard all older men of a certain age to be their fathers" (636–37). This radical notion is taken up, with some limitations, not only by Plato in his description of Kallipolis in the *Republic*, but by other subsequent utopian communities. Praxagora suggests that this practice will protect older men from assault by the younger, since each will assume the other to be a near relation.

Although comedy may have advanced the possibility of freedom for slaves in the utopia of the *Birds*, where even the tattooed slave bird, the francolin, could find refuge, in Praxagora's utopia the slaves are not free, and they will do the work. Her husband Blepyros asks: "Who will there be to farm the land?" And she replies: "The slaves (*hoi douloi*)" (651). It's as simple as that, in a response that prefigures Aristotle's reflections on automata, and Herbert Marcuse's utopian projection of a world in which robots, automata again, will do the labor, allowing for a rich and gratifying cultural and erotic life for human beings. In Praxagora's fantasy, other human beings take on this role, liberating her and her kind for all manner of pleasures.[35]

Theft will be eliminated under the new regime, which will be well regulated, like a well-regulated household overseen by a competent mistress. Praxagora will set up ballot boxes in the *agora*, near Harmodius, one of the two heroes, lovers, mentioned earlier, who were credited with the abolition of the sixth-century Athenian tyranny through their assassination of one of the tyrant's sons, Hipparchus, in 514. The allusion to this great moment of democratic revolutionary liberation aligns Praxagora's reforms with those of the Athenian experiment that followed the end of tyranny.

Praxagora also plans to have all the Athenians draw lots, receiving numbers that assign them to different collective dining halls. And women will stop the men on the way home from dining, to offer them lovely girls but requiring them first to gratify those women: "The inferior men (*hoi phauloteroi*) will chase after the handsome lads, . . . the law says that the pug-nosed and the ugly get first fuck" (702b–6). Rather than a misogynist gesture that condemns the ugly and old women, the law requires all the young to permit the older citizens first choice of sexual partners. As noted, the slaves remain a separate class in this ideal polity; the suggestion is that they are wont to steal away the affections of the free. Therefore, says Praxagora, "slave girls will no longer be allowed to wear makeup (*kosmoumenas*) and steal away the fond hearts of the free boys. They'll be allowed to sleep only with slaves, with their pussies trimmed like a woolen barn jacket" (721–24). Free women will be nicely depilated, while the slave women (*doulas*) will have a clumsy, rustic look.

After these pronouncements comes the first sign of a serious decline in the role of the chorus in this play, and others. The text indicates *chorou*, that is, a song of the chorus, but does not preserve it before the entrance of a neighbor, and his two male slaves. We cannot know what the indication "chorus" means; is it a sign of a standard, generic song and dance, not composed by the playwright himself, or of a failure in the transmission of the text? In any case, in the fourth century, in the transition from Middle to New Comedy, the role of the chorus, so intensely present in the comedies of the high democratic period of the fifth century, has declined. As K. J. Dover noted some years ago, with respect to the *Women at the Assembly* and the later play *Wealth*, "[The] bare indication of a choral song becomes more familiar to us in *Wealth*, where the total number of lines sung by the chorus is only a dozen, and of those spoken by the chorus-leader only thirty, while one or more manuscripts present *khoro* no less than seven times. We may—indeed, we must—make allowance for some erroneous insertion of *khoro* in late antiquity, but even when such allowance has been made it is clear the *Ass.* and *Wealth* show a rapid progress in the direction of the 'uninvolved chorus.'"[36] The chorus is beyond "uninvolved."

In New Comedy of the fourth century BCE, as in Menander's *Dyskolos*, noted by Dover, "it seems a fair inference that the comic poet no longer regarded it as part of his own job to write the songs which served simply as entertainment during breaks in the action."[37] Some scholars have disputed the designations "Old," "Middle," and "New" for these different moods of comic presentation, arguing that they reflect not historical development, but rather different comic aims. But the differences, this breaking apart of the structure of Old Comedy, does suggest that the chorus comes to be understood as a separate entity in the progress of the drama, that is, as Aristotle argued in relation to tragedy, the plot, and its characters.[38] The comedy of the fourth century resembles the Aristotelian reduction of the genre's essential elements, in a centripetal swerve consistent with the end of the radical democracy of the fifth century. Dover attributes these developments also to "an awareness on his [Aristophanes'] part that comedy could expect much wider popularity in the Greek world—such as tragedy was coming to enjoy—if the elements of Athenian topicality, associated especially with the parabasis, were greatly reduced."[39]

In the case of *Women at the Assembly*, there is no parabasis. It may be that the theme of the play itself, the seizure of power by women and their institution of a radical, communist democracy, inhibited the role of the chorus. The women have become the democracy, and the address to the audience has fallen away. The scenes that follow this diminution of the chorus's role emphasize the results of the great reforms, which include the material objects of everyday life. Kitchen implements are summoned and line up animatedly, in a parody of a ritual procession, ready to be surrendered to the state in compliance with the new laws, a silent object chorus until some refuse to obey. Bounteous feasts are prepared for all, and another chorus goes missing.

Attention shifts from possessions and communal dining to the sex question, subject of much humor and mockery; the women are libidinous, as always, and eager to set in motion the new plan of equal distribution of *eros*. A spat between young and old women reveals perhaps not so much concerning the erotic life of women in this society, but rather men's fantasies about *eros*, especially that the sex act must figure a penis, or a simulacrum thereof. In any case, the humor, for some, lies in the cat fight between women, and between generations of women, all of whom are seen to rely on dildos for their pleasure. The women in this scene proceed to fight over a young man who enters, as an older woman insists on her right, according to the new law, to possess him first. Although he claims his rights as a free man (*eleuthero*, 942), she stresses the link between the reforms and the democracy, saying: "If we still are democratizing (*ei demokratoumetha*), according to the law, to do this is the right thing" (944–45, trans. modified; not Henderson). They are still "doing democracy," and this time the democracy includes all the citizen-class persons, women as well as men. The women have outvoted the men, and established the new *nomoi*, new laws, a new version of sexual equality.

The play ends with the invitation to the feast. The comic interlude with the old women is over, and the festivities begin. Blepyros, Praxagora's husband, relishes the prospect of sex with one of the girls, so perhaps we are meant to assume that he has paid his dues with the older women. Instead of the chorus, the chorus leader speaks to the judges of the dramatic festival, in a parabasis-like speech, asking them to remember the "smart," *sophon*, parts of the comedy, and the jokes. And he reminds them to keep their pledge, to judge the choruses (*khorous*) fairly, to keep in mind, then, all the competitors in the dramatic contest, not acting like *hetairas*, who remember only their most recent customers.

We haven't seen much of the chorus, nothing of the chorus's dancing of course, few of their words in this play, but it now chimes in, and describes the menu with the longest word ever, a fabulous dish, a description of the feast, fit for a hungry, war-weary audience, all its elements strung together:

> limpets saltfish sharksteak dogfish
> mullets oddfish with savory pickle sauce
> thrushes blackbirds various pigeons
> roosters pan-roasted wagtails larks

nice chunks of hare marinated in mulled wine
all of it drizzled with honey silphium
vinegar oil spices galore.
> (1169–75, trans. modified; Henderson)

This is a feast worthy of the land of Cockaigne, or the Big Rock Candy Mountain, and the chorus, after launching this word picture of paradise, dances off the scene, *euai, hos epi nike, euai, euai, euai,* "hurray, to victory, hurray, hurray" (1182–83). They will be victors, are victorious, they have changed the city, they have not surrendered, not gone back on their reforms, and although there was a rough spot when the men resisted the new sexual regulations, the play ends ecstatically with this celebration of a luxurious, new, democratic, communist utopia ruled democratically by its women.

The feasting at the end of comic plays like this one, in part a response to food shortages in times of war and siege, can point outside the frame of the dramatic performance, to the festival that contains it. The Dionysiac celebrations incorporated abundance and plenty, a rejoicing at the opening of the new wine, for example, and these scenes have a metatheatrical dimension. The victory hailed at the end of *Women at the Assembly* can refer simultaneously to the playwright's or producer's victory in the dramatic contest, to the women's victory over the forces that want to suppress their participation in the city's life, political and erotic, and to a victory of the play's radical, communist politics, a response to the needs of the city's poor.

The misogyny and unconcealed hilarity concerning the sexual regulations of this new regime should not detract from the radical innovation of Praxagora's proposals. In fact, the reforms set forth in her speeches, and endorsed by the women in the assembly, might be seen to extend what I would call the logic of democracy. That is to say, the implicit *telos*, the "final cause," of the idea of rule by the *demos*, the people, all the people of the *polis*, all the city's and the country's inhabitants, male and female, free and slave, Athenian and not, is rule by *all, isonomia,* equality under the law, just as the call for *parrhesia* implicates saying, *speaking all.* The women prefigure a new extension, a new definition of the *demos*.

POLITICS AND THE *DEMOS*

As a counter to what I see as a contemporary, interested attempt to label white supremacy and nativism "populism," or to replace a fuller democracy with "epistocracy," rule by the learned, I return to the work of Jacques

Rancière, who has written extensively about democracy.[40] Rancière's book *Hatred of Democracy*, first published in 2006, returns to themes of an earlier book called in translation *Disagreement*, although the title *La mésentente* might be better rendered as *Misunderstanding*, or *Dissension*. In contrast to Jason Brennan, who is "against democracy," conceived as the right or privilege of voting, Rancière bases his arguments on the question of *equality* as revealed through the lottery system of ancient democracy. In *Disagreement*, he makes a distinction between what he calls "politics" and "the police": "The police is . . . first an order of bodies that defines the allocation of ways of doing, ways of being, and ways of saying, and sees that those bodies are assigned by name to a particular place and task; it is an order of the visible and the sayable that sees that a particular activity is visible and another is not, that this speech is understood as discourse and another as noise" (29). In contrast to all that is police, Rancière describes politics as "an extremely determined activity antagonistic to policing: whatever breaks with the tangible configuration whereby parties and parts or lack of them are defined by a presupposition that, by definition, has no place in that configuration" (29–30). As an example, Rancière cites Jeanne Deroin, who, as a woman, "in 1849, . . . presents herself as a candidate for a legislative election in which she cannot run. In other words she demonstrates the contradiction between a universal suffrage," that is, the declaration of the rights of human beings, and the governing, policing system that excludes her gender from that universality. "This is the staging of the very contradiction between police logic and political logic" (41).

Rancière relies in this book and subsequently on the distinction I mentioned earlier, between the *demos* defined as all the people, and the *demos* as the poor, or, as he puts it, "the part that has no part," that is, those whose speech, or claims, or demands, or shouts are heard not as discourse, but as *noise*. For Rancière, democracy *is* politics. In his view, ancient conservatives, antidemocratic thinkers, invented political theory, political "science," so called, to control the *demos*, the people, the poor, and we see this ambition in the work of Plato, who argued for geometric, rather than arithmetic rule, rule by the best, those most deserving of power. That is to say, precisely what we see in the US Senate and the Electoral College—weighting the process in favor of the "best," the few, the elder, the blest, the wealthiest, as opposed to a one-person, one-vote process. Rancière sees republican government, French and American, as "pastoral rule," governing through what we might call biopolitics, the managing of the population. And he emphasizes the role of the lottery, the drawing of lots in Athenian democracy, which broke up the presumed naturalness of aristocratic domination, the geometricity of rule by the best, whether senators or epistocrats.

Democracy according to Rancière is "the dissolving of any standard by which nature could give its law to communitarian artifice via the relations of authority that structure the social body. The scandal [of democracy] lies in the disjoining of entitlements to govern from any analogy to those that order social relations, from any analogy between human convention and the order of nature" (*Hatred of Democracy*, 41). Sortition removes the entitlements to govern of kinship and wealth, puts into practice a radical equality, giving voice to those who have been voiceless. For Rancière, democracy, politics, would be Rosa Parks refusing to sit in the back of the bus, Occupy around the world, in Hong Kong as well as on Wall Street, Diamond Reynolds livestreaming the police murder of Philando Castile, or Black Lives Matter and the weeks of protest around the world after the murder of George Floyd. Democracy, then, is not an established system of governance for Rancière: "Egalitarian society is only ever the set of egalitarian relations that are traced here and now through singular and precarious acts" (96–97). Democracy is singular, and precarious, and comedy can bring it into being on stage.

Although the playwright Aristophanes is often considered to be a reactionary, a conservative at best, Mark Griffith concludes: "There is no evidence at all to suggest that Aristophanes was a radical reactionary, a Spartan sympathizer (Laconizer), a secret oligarch, or anything other than a staunch supporter of the democracy. But democracy of course could be practiced—and imagined—in several different ways among the Athenians, and Aristophanes' own opinions may well have shifted from time to time during the turbulent years of the Peloponnesian War, especially its later stages."[41] As for democracy, especially as discussed by Jacques Rancière in his work on "disagreement," or "misunderstanding," and on the *hatred* of democracy, we can interpret several of these comedies as exemplifying what he defines as "politics," the claims of "the part that has no part."[42] Remarkably, the comedies of Aristophanes depict swarms of disenfranchised, unenfranchised actors, and include not just *parrhesia*, saying it all, the free speech of the citizens ridiculing and insulting the powerful and corrupt, utopian fantasies of the redistribution of wealth, but also the rupture of the social codes that kept women, even citizen women, in their place, in their houses.

And one can imagine the extension of the rights of the *demos* to include slaves, preeminently those who have "no part." In the communal, communist redistribution of all that the city possesses in *Women at the Assembly*, the collection of private property so that it can be shared among all the inhabitants of the city, including the women, there is a radical program that moves toward equality, toward *isonomia*, equality in the law. The Greek political notions of "the middle," *to meson*, and of the "common," *koinon*, are relevant to the assemblywomen's radical reconfiguration of the *polis*. As potent, and less ambiguous, is the call for *koinonia*, that is, commonness, communality, communalism, communism, in the giving voice to those who have no part.[43] The comic communalism performed in *Women at the Assembly* draws in its audience, past and present, to a joyful, sometimes hilarious and ecstatic process of egalitarian political *praxis*.

[CHAPTER 7]

Epilogue
The Politics of the Present

> Only that historian will have the gift of fanning the spark of hope in the past who is firmly convinced that *even the dead* will not be safe from the enemy if he wins.
>
> Walter Benjamin, *Theses on the Philosophy of History* VI

What does ancient Greek comedy have to offer to politics in the present? I have suggested that its potential lies in its representations of women's power, of *parrhesia*, or free speaking, which includes ridicule and mockery of the powerful, in the possibilities inherent in utopianism, often itself dismissed in the present day, and in the potential of the swarm, the collective, the commune, the anonymous group, exemplified in the ancient Athenian democracy by the chorus of comedy.[1] I look in this epilogue at some of its reception over many centuries, and at ways in which the reading of ancient comedy can come together with the work of contemporary theorists and activists to enable a politics that goes beyond the tragic individual. The comic potential of the swarm finds its echoes in the swarm of recent performance, in the idea of autopoiesis, in the utopian concept of communal luxury, in the politics of Occupy and Black Lives Matter.

MODERN TRANSFORMATIONS OF ANCIENT COMEDY

The dramas of ancient Athens have had a long afterlife, finding a voice even in nineteenth-century India. Phiroze Vasunia has brilliantly traced the engagement of British colonialism in India with the classical tradition in his now classic *The Classics and Colonial India*.[2] His chapter "Aristophanes' *Wealth* and Dalpatram's *Lakshmi*" shows the reach of ancient comedy beyond the specific circumstances of classical Athens. Dalpatram Dahyabhai (1820–98) published a Gujarati translation of Aristophanes' *Wealth*, with the assistance of Alexander Kinloch Forbes, in 1850. "By the late 1860s," Dalpatram's translation "had sold almost a thousand copies . . . , and it went into four editions" (279). Vasunia notes that "from the middle of the seventeenth century to the early twentieth century, Aristophanes' plays were edited, annotated, and translated, but seldom acted out on the live theatrical stage" (280). Dalpatram was "one of a number of reformers who were trying to modernize the social behaviour of Indians in the second half of the nineteenth century" (280), and he considered the translation and presentation of *Wealth* to be part of this mission.

Stephen Halliwell claims that *Wealth* "requires much less historical exegesis than any other surviving Aristophanic play."[3] In the ancient comedy, Chremylos, and his slave Cario, take home the character Wealth, *Ploutos*, a god, who is old and blind. The premise of the comedy is, and this is the basis of the utopianism projected there, that if Wealth regained his sight, he would "redistribute" the resources of the world, giving money to the good, not the bad. Chremylos and Cario restore his eyesight at the temple of Asclepius, god of healing, and try to set Wealth up on the Acropolis of Athens in order to protect the city's treasury.

As Vasunia describes, in the Indian version of the play, set in a new context by Dalpatram and named for the Hindu goddess Lakshmi, Dhirsinh and his servant Bhima take home the goddess, who has become old and blind. They bring back her sight in the temple of Dhanvantri (the physician of the gods) and try to install her in a temple. The play incorporates "several stock characters of Indian, and specifically Gujarati, folk theatre" (284), using the "language of modern social reform" (284). Dalpatram followed the Swaminarayan group, a reform movement. A narrator in this version of ancient comedy emphasizes Dalpatram's moral message: "People must 'not earn wealth through injustice, immorality, and slander.'" Vasunia notes jokes about caste, about the greed of Brahman priests, and about the infanticide of girls, and he shows that "the play attempts to work contrapuntally: it simultaneously campaigns for reform along modern lines and relies on a nostalgic and impossible vision of the simple village" (284). Dalpatram's *Lakshmi* includes "popular language and humour" (286), "a version of the popular that was stylized, carefully demarcated, and often moralizing in its intent" (287). The Gujarati playwright avoided the local *bhavai* drama's obscenity, for example. And, "in his version, Dalpatram takes out much of the flatulence, the sexual banter, and the scatological references of Aristophanes' play" (287). He "sets aside the male-male lovers and redirects the sexual valence of the original" (288); Dalpatram uses the ethnic or religious distinctions of his own context to mark characters within the play: an old woman and her adulterous young lover are Muslims, not Hindu; a Muslim slave also speaks Hindi. In a sense, Dalpatram's version of the ancient Athenian comedy maintains the Greek democratic recognition of cultural heterogeneity, with others marked as slaves or as linguistically defined strangers, even as he conceives of "the village in *Lakshmi* as a Hindu community" (289).

Alexander Kinloch Forbes's *Ras Mala* (*A Garland of Chronicles*), a study of Gujarati culture and history, was translated into Gujarati in 1869 by another scholar, Ranchodbhai Udayaram (294). "In *Ras Mala*, Forbes himself had compared the lament of Gujarati women to the laments of Greek tragedy and had thereby demarcated them as alien and archaic," according to Vasunia (295). "His [Dalpatram's] knowledge of the Aristophanic play came from Forbes, who studied from 1840 to 1843 at Haileybury, the training college for civil servants of the East India Company" (296).

Here is Vasunia's translation of the song that ends the comedy:

The wasp is flying in the celebration hall,
The drum-beats are rolling
In the procession of Lakshmi.
(286)

Vasunia concludes, concerning this reconceptualization of ancient comedy: "What is notable ... is the transformation of the conservative Aristophanes in a colonial context" (297), the context "shaped by mercantile and political elites" (298).

Although Dalpatram was fluent in neither English nor Greek, he "understood the singular authority given to the ancient Athenians by modern Europeans" (299). What is most telling here is that Dalpatram chose not Greek tragedy, perhaps a more elite genre in the modern European context, but rather comedy, and in particular Aristophanes' *Wealth*, with its potential for mockery, condemnation, attacks on the powerful, and an implicitly utopian call for redistribution of worldly goods, none of which emerges from Greek tragedy.[4] As in Deleuze and Guattari's discussion of "minority discourse," using the work of Franz Kafka as an example, Dalpatram rewrites the ancient Greek play in the language of the hegemonic British, while decentering it. "A minor literature doesn't come from a minor language; it is rather that which a minority constructs within a major language," according to Deleuze and Guattari.[5] And they add: "The third characteristic of minor literature is that in it everything takes on a collective value."[6] Dalpatram turns ancient Greek comedy into English, in his own way.

Modern Greek audiences saw performances of Aristophanic comedy, as noted earlier, but perhaps the most politically pointed examples of comedies presented in the twentieth and twenty-first centuries were those featuring female characters. Even though these roles were played by male actors in ancient Athens, actors who specialized in female characters and were appreciated for their skills in transvestism, the presence of strong characters in the comedy *Lysistrata*, especially, have spoken to feminist theater producers and antiwar activists in modernity. In the US and the UK, in particular at the time of the Iraq War, there were several notable performances of this play.[7] Strangely enough, although the ancient comedy *Lysistrata* contained a wide range of political references, to alliance between Spartans and Athenians, to the power of the priestess of Athena in the city of Athens, to various forms of radical politics, it has become known almost exclusively as an antiwar play in the present.

In *Sex and War on the American Stage* (2014), Emily Klein traces the many performances of *Lysistrata* in the United States from 1930 to 2012.[8] Ranging from the Federal Theater's 1936 Negro Repertory production of the play to those of the international Lysistrata Project organized in protest of the Iraq War in 2003, she recounts the complexities of American theater's engagement with the issues of feminism and pacifism as presented in this comedy. Klein concludes: "The old *Lysistratas* under investigation suggest that during the Depression, American audiences were curious to recall a resplendent Greek empire on the verge of ruination. During the Cold War, we became more invested in reflections of an untamed Western frontier. And in the 1970s, idealized feminine figures from the 1940s, 1950s and 1980s became the subjects of a production that sought to articulate new approaches to gender and sexuality."[9] Klein predicts "a rich futurity" for *Lysistrata*.[10]

COMMUNAL, COMMUNIST UTOPIA

One of the promising and intriguing topics of Old Comedy, besides its celebration of strong women, both central characters and members of the chorus, its calls for *parrhesia*, and for utopia, is its representation of communeism, of communalism. Some of these plays, among them *Wealth* and the *Ecclesiazusae*, and including the *Birds*, seem to give the lie to the deeply embedded idea in classical scholarship that Aristophanes was a right-wing conservative. Even if we acknowledge that he presents impossibilities, worlds upside down, and that these are exposed as impossible in the course of the plays, we can also see them as representing tentative explorations of impossibilities, in the sense of Niklas Luhmann's description of such practices.

In *Social Systems*, Luhmann presented his notion of autopoiesis, the manner in which a "system" continually produces itself, always in motion, always defining itself in relation to a past and present, toward a horizon of possibility. Such a model for understanding an entity like Athenian democracy illuminates the many ways in which experimentation with possibilities occurs constantly as systems make and remake themselves in time. Luhmann defined "meaning" in an idiosyncratic way, as "the hypothesis of the *closure of self-referential system formations*."[11] Meaning is "a processing according to differences," and "the auto-agility of meaning occurrences is autopoiesis par excellence."[12] That is, a system constantly creates meaning through its mobility, orienting itself to differences, and selecting from among an established set of these. In this structural analysis of systems, there is no stasis: "The difference between meaning and world is formed for this process of the continual self-determination of meaning as the difference between order and perturbation, between information and noise."[13] Although Luhmann here relied on the model of an apparently closed system, his work casts light on the antisystematic, often incoherent, amorphous, and open-ended thing that is ancient comedy. And his observations are intriguing in relation to Sean Gurd's recent discussion in *Dissonance: Auditory Aesthetics in Ancient Greece*, of the role ancient Greek song played in creating dissonance, an interface between social order and disorder: "Greek auditory artworks clear an unsettling space for the vibrations that we call 'sound' but that are, at base, one front along which human bodies interface passionately with the world."[14] The choruses of Old Comedy make song, make order/disorder that inhabits the speculative boundary between animacies, the human and the not-human, and between reality and the imaginable.

Objections have been raised to the notion of autopoiesis, especially with regard to current thinking about the distinction between the Anthropocene as descriptive of our current global or planetary calamities, and what Donna Haraway has called the Chthulucene. She prefers the term "sympoiesis," "making with," to signify interdependence and co-creation: "Nothing makes itself; nothing is really autopoietic or self-organizing. In the words of the Inupiat computer 'world game,' earthlings are *never alone*. That is the radical implication of sympoiesis. *Sympoiesis* is a word proper to complex, dynamic, responsive, situated, historical systems. It is a word for worlding-with, in company. Sympoiesis enfolds autopoiesis and generatively unfurls and extends it."[15] Although these debates are generated in ecological circles, especially in relation to the Gaia hypothesis, they have some relevance for thinking about literary texts. Is an ancient comedy "autopoietic," or sympoietic? Haraway clarifies: "As long as autopoiesis does not mean self-sufficient self-making, autopoiesis and sympoiesis, foregrounding and backgrounding different aspects of systemic complexity, are in generative friction, or generative enfolding, rather than opposition."[16] If we open the text to lines of flight, to include audience, city, countryside, environment, other animals, birds, wasps, clouds, frogs, how does our understanding of ancient comedy alter?

Taking Luhmann's insights lightly, with sympathy for the immense effort involving in translating his work into comprehensible English, absent the pleasure principle, and accepting too that autopoiesis is unfurled and extended in sympoiesis, we might see comic speculation as a process, as the creation of disturbances, as a system making meaning for itself by constant motion and selection, extending beyond the autocracy of the author, the genre, the festival, the city itself, the history of ancient comedy, the boundaries established by classical literary studies. The limit between human and animal is one such site. Take slavery as another instance: the plays accept slavery as an institution without question, they promulgate communism, which would seem to include all persons in communal sharing, but exclude slaves, but then at another moment include a freed slave, the tattooed francolin, in the paradise of Cloudcuckooland. Rather than seeing all these instances of speculation as contradicting one another, catching the author Aristophanes in contradiction and failure to state his political views clearly, we could interpret these moves as part of the autopoiesis-sympoiesis of comedy and its relation to the Athenian democracy, proposing differences such as slave and free, sometimes accepting this distinction, sometimes moving through, perhaps abandoning the disturbance, the disorder, the noise that would be implicit in the call to abolish slavery.[17]

Can we not interpret some of Old Comedy's representations of collectives, swarms of animals, birds, insects, clouds, and women, as speculative fictions about changing the world of the ancient Athenian democracy? And these might affect our own desires for the future as, to cite Fredric Jameson again, "the past will itself become an active agent in the process . . . as a radically different life form which rises up to call our own form of life into question and to pass judgment on us, and through us, on the social formation in which we exist."[18]

Note that the communalist speculative fictions of Old Comedy are not impeded by the hierarchical class divisions we find in Plato's utopian scheme. Perhaps we need to detoxify the notion of communalism, of what Kristin Ross has called "communal luxury."[19] In her tracing of the legacy of the aspirations of the Paris Commune of 1871, Ross describes what she calls its "centrifugal effects" (2). Acknowledging the failure of the Commune in the nineteenth century, she nonetheless follows the subsequent dissemination of its goals and ambitions well into the twentieth and even twenty-first. She notes how the present shaped the account she gives of these processes, that is, "the concerns that dominate today's political agenda—the problem of how to refashion an internationalist conjuncture, the future of education, labor, and the status of art, the commune-form and its relationship to ecological theory and practice" (2). Reading the impact of the Paris Commune's utopian demands and ideals on those who came after, such as Karl Marx, Kropotkin, and William Morris, Ross shows how the brief moment of the Paris Commune lives on in theory and practice.

The Commune itself has been seen as conforming to the rules of tragedy laid out by Aristotle: unity of place, of time, of action. That is, the rebellion of the communards falls into expectations of genre, limited to a local event, compressed in its duration, with terrible numbers of deaths. These are among the elements of "the tragic" that have colored modernity's sense of resistance as limited, brief, doomed to failure, without consequences. And she insists: "Thinking of the Paris Commune in terms of the classic unities of tragedy risked isolating it from its conceptual and political after-lives" (122). This is a particularly telling observation, given the emphasis on the tragic individual that I've pointed to in the philosophical and political theoretical tradition's appropriations and interpretations of classical antiquity. If we see only the tragic, only tragedy, only the tragic individual, especially as handed down in modernity, a partial, limited, interested version of tragedy, then what remains is mourning, melancholy, and isolation in a private, subjective world of loss.

But in our contemplation of ancient Athenian drama, there is also a remainder of comedy, of pleasure, of community. Ross detects in the afterlives of the Paris Commune a persistent commitment to what she calls "communal luxury": "Communal luxury countered any notion of the sharing of misery with a distinctly different kind of world: one where everyone, instead, would have his or her share of the best" (65). This ideal, utopian and still profoundly radical, can be traced backward, not just to the nineteenth century, with its struggles for workers' rights and control of their own labor and production, but further back, to the slave revolts of ancient history, and to the utopianism of ancient comedy.[20]

Conservative opinion today generally dismisses the possibility of a more anarchist, open, parrhesiast communalism that would incorporate some of the aspects of ancient Athenian democracy. But groups like the militants of Occupy, on Wall Street and in the US, as well as in Asia, and groups like Black Lives Matter, which have inspired massive international groups to demonstrate against repression and racism, have striven to avoid the pitfalls of collective action that depends too much on charismatic leadership, on hierarchies and what Jacques Rancière might call "policing." Instead, they have sought to make decisions collectively, to resist allowing traditionally privileged sectors of their movements to dominate.[21]

Chantal Mouffe, in *For a Left Populism*, argues against the Left's surrender to centrism, which Mouffe sees as having enabled the nativist, nationalist, often racist populism of contemporary right-wing movements in the UK, Europe, and US. Rather than giving up on "populism," she urges: "By acknowledging the crucial role played by the democratic discourse in the political imaginary of our societies, and by establishing around democracy as the hegemonic signifier, a chain of equivalence among the manifold struggles against subordination, a left populist strategy resonates with the aspirations of many people."[22]

Some modes of resistance, of politics in this sense in the present, echo the ancient metaphor of the swarm, insist on the anonymity of the collective, or labor to avoid past errors of elevating individuals to positions of absolute power in attempting to ameliorate the world. In *When They Call You a Terrorist: A Black Lives Matter Memoir*, Patrisse Khan-Cullors and Asha Bandele discuss the politics of the movement they helped to found.[23] Khan-Cullors begins with a message to a friend, Alicia Garza, who had said: "I continue to be surprised at how little Black lives matter."[24] She responds with the hashtag #BlackLivesMatter (180). Khan-Cullors recounts the suffering and struggles in her life, public and private, since that time. And she describes the accomplishments of this collective:

> Since Black Lives Matter was born in 2013 we have done some incredible work. We have built a decentralized movement that encourages and supports local leaders to name and claim the work that is needed in order to make their communities more just. This is monumentally difficult in a world that has made even activism a celebrity pursuit. But we have more than 20 chapters across the United States, in Canada and the UK, all autonomous but all connected and coordinated. We have centered and amplified the voices of those not only made most vulnerable but most unheard, even as they are on the front lines at every hour and in every space: Black women—all Black women. (249)

These accomplishments now include the rallying of massive international protests against racist murder and police brutality against people of color. This is a remarkable set of achievements, realizing Rancière's "politics," the making audible, and visible, of those "who have no part."[25] And as Angela Davis insists in her foreword to Patrisse Khan-Cullors's memoir, the comrades in the Movement for Black Lives "call for an inclusiveness that does not sacrifice particularity" (xiv).

In *The Undercommons*, Stefano Harney and Fred Moten present a related agenda, an exhilarating set of premises that urge "black study" and "fugitive planning," and undermine many of the pieties of the university, of "governance," of policy, of incarceration: "We plan. We plan to stay, to stick and move. We plan to be communist about communism, to be unreconstructed about reconstruction, to be absolute about abolition, here, in that other, undercommon place, as that other, undercommon thing, that we preserve by inhabiting. Policy can't see it, policy can't read it, but it's intelligible if you got a plan."²⁶ This is a utopianism that refuses to call itself to order, to present bureaucratic solutions to problems generated by the state, that urges "hacking concepts and squatting terms as a way to help us do something."²⁷ A toybox, not a toolbox.

Although dystopic fictions may predominate in the present, especially in so-called speculative fiction, there is still room for a comic undermining of the status quo and for the imagining of better ways of life that include luxury for all. Such aspects of democracy, its emphasis on equality and particularity, as we look back to the multicostumed chorus of birds, can be overshadowed by currents of political theory that emphasize the vote, the homogeneity of the citizen body, its potential to be hijacked by charismatic demagogues who become tyrants, or totalitarian dictators. But I insist here on this other quality of the ancient democracy, in deliberations on sovereignty and political bodies, that private life, the multifarious differences among democratic citizens, are not the target of a democratic communalism.

Present-day politics might benefit from attention to ancient Athenian comedy, which put on stage the contradictory and sometimes utopian drives of human community, and forms part of a long genealogy of resistance to inequality. Rather than an emphasis on the *tragic* state of the world, and the *tragic individual* stranded in its midst, comedy offers another paradigm for thinking about politics. Exhibiting female agency, freedom of speech, the capacity to mock and ridicule and insult corrupt leaders, as well as an intense attachment to democracy, and an erotic, joyous, comic, utopian pleasure in celebration of the collective, ancient Old Comedy provides a contrast to the alternative, a politics derived from a tragic perspective.²⁸ The choruses of Old Comedy, made up of swarms of dancing, singing citizens of the democracy, dressed as wasps, clouds, birds, frogs, letters, cities, or even women, present an alternative to endless meditations on Antigone and Oedipus, on the tragic individual in the tragic nuclear family. These choruses embody a libidinal, often ecstatic, pastoral commitment to equality, to communal festivity, bodily pleasures of food and drink and *eros*, and finally a redistribution of wealth that benefits all, including those who have had no part.

Acknowledgments

This book has emerged out of a swarm of friends, colleagues, and adversaries. I am grateful to Melissa Browne and Ryan Warwick, who invited me to give the Poultney Lecture at Johns Hopkins University in 2018. And at Hopkins, to Emily Anderson, Silvia Montiglio, Josh Smith, Dimitrios Yatromanolakis, Christopher Cannon, Alex Lewis, and Giacomo Loi, for their engagement with my arguments. I thank Susan Lape, Daniel Richter, Greg Thalmann, and their colleagues and students in the Classics Department at USC, and Jody Valentine, of Pomona College, for their generosity. Aimee Bahng, David Roselli, and Ellen Finkelpearl, when I gave the Harry Carroll Lecture at Pomona College, shared stimulating questions and responses. Ellen O'Gorman and Ahuvia Kahane invited me to a meeting at Royal Holloway in London to discuss the work of Jacques Rancière, where I met with generous hospitality and some bracing resistance. Even though we sometimes disagree, Edith Hall, who has done so much to further the politics of the study of the classics, and comedy, has my profound gratitude and admiration. I thank her, Henry Stead, and Tom Geue for their kind invitation to confer about the sublime at a stimulating event at King's College London. My visit to Dalhousie University in Halifax, Nova Scotia, gave me a chance to present my work in progress, and I acknowledge Christopher Grundke, Eli Diamond, and Hilary Ilfak for their generosity. Princeton University's Classics Department invited me to deliver the Faber Lecture in 2019, and I very much appreciated the hospitality and responses of Johannes Haubold, Andrew Feldherr, Barbara Graziosi, Kay Gabriel, and Dan-El Padilla Peralta. The warm welcome of Donald Ainslie, Victoria Wohl, and Kenny Yu at the University of Toronto, when I was invited to present the Stubbs Lecture in 2019, gave me the impetus to pursue new questions. I thank Ken Reinhard for his generous invitation to present this work, in progress, at the UCLA Program in Experimental Critical Theory, and for his and his students' responses to my presentation. I'd like to express, too, my thanks to Clara Boesak-Schroder of the University of Illinois at Urbana-Champaign, and her colleagues, for inviting me to speak there. And I am indebted to the audience for a wonderfully timely question that helped me rethink my orientation to the climate of public opinion about classical studies in the present. The graduate students of the Classics Department of UCLA gave me the honor of asking me to speak to them, and I thank them and Alex Purves, Amy Richlin, and Bryant Kirkland for their hospitality and challenging contributions to my work on this book.

The kernel of ideas for this book came with the opportunity to contribute to "The Future of the Human," special issue, *Differences* 20, nos. 2–3 (2009), edited by Warren Montag and my dear friend Nancy Armstrong; I am grateful to her for support, friendship, and exemplary resistance for decades.

I thank my colleagues Jacobo Myerston Santana and Sara Johnson for collegiality and generous contributions to my thinking, and my former colleague Tony Edwards, who knows more about comedy than I ever will, but who graciously conversed with me when I was beginning this project. Denise Demetriou has given me the gift of her friendship, for which I am most grateful. I learned much from Patrick Anderson. I thank my dear friend Lisa Lowe. Bruce Lincoln has my gratitude for his inspiring work, and for his support. I appreciated and continue to thank the challenging and engaged and committed members of my seminar "Swarm Theory" in the Literature Department at UCSD: Zachary Bushnell, Jing Chen, Tina Hyland, Sang Eun Lee, Grant Leuning, Jesus "Eddy" Miramontes, Matt Moore, Yanqin Tan, Maria Vlahaki, Stacie Vos, Xiaojiao Wang, and Jeanine Webb. I am grateful for pleasure and inspiration and support from former students Eunsong Kim and Reema Rajbanshi. My friends William Fitzgerald, Susan Smith and Sheldon Nodelman, Michael Meranze and Helen Deutsch, Edmond Chang and Esther Hsiao, Kate Harper and Harper Page Marshall, Melvyn Freilicher and Joe Keenan, are all part of a generative and kindly swarm. My gratitude extends to the late Tom Habinek and to Hector Reyes. And I thank Mary Kelly for dearest friendship and generosity. The anonymous reader of my manuscript proved extraordinarily lavish with commentary and suggestions, and I thank you, too, whoever you are. Susan Bielstein is a brilliant editor, and I am so appreciative of her talents and support for this project. Thank you, Susan.

I thank Suzanne Mathews for her guidance and empathy. I am forever grateful to the late Antonia Meltzoff. And to my beloved, John Daley.

Notes

PREFACE

1. M. L. Nestel, "Veteran Posts Signs at Colleges Telling Whites to Be 'Great Again,'" *The Daily Beast*, October 16, 2016, www.thedailybeast.com/veteran-posts-signs-at-colleges-telling-whites-to-be-great-again.

2. See, for example, the online journal *Eidolon*, which tracked many of these interventions.

3. Page duBois, *A Million and One Gods: The Persistence of Polytheism* (Cambridge, MA: Harvard University Press, 2014).

4. Nick Montgomery and Carla Bergman, *Joyful Militancy: Building Thriving Resistance in Toxic Times*, Anarchist Interventions 7 (Chico, CA: AK Press, 2017).

5. Mark Payne, "Teknomajikality and the Humanimal in Aristophanes' *Wasps*," in *Brill's Companion to the Reception of Aristophanes*, ed. Philip Walsh (Leiden: Brill, 2016), 129–14.

6. The collective noun for a group of wombats is a "mob," or a "wisdom." Jay Sacher, *A Compendium of Collective Nouns: From an Armory of Aardvarks to a Zeal of Zebras* (San Francisco: Chronicle Books, 2013), 213.

7. Rutger Bregman points out that while people take for truth the inevitability of group degeneration into the bullying, tyranny, and murder of the novel *The Lord of the Flies*, a fiction from 1954, a real event that paralleled its story of descent, of a uninhabited island into a smoldering wasteland, was a story of cooperation, generosity, and survival concerning shipwrecked Tongan schoolboys. Rutger Bregman, "The Real *Lord of the Flies*," in *Humankind: A Hopeful History*, trans. E. Manton and E. Moore (New York: Little, Brown, 2019), 22–40. Bregman cites the Nobel Prize–winning William Golding, author of *The Lord of the Flies*: "Man produces evil as a bee produces honey" (Bregman, 23).

INTRODUCTION

1. For reflections on comedy in the form of comics, see "Comics & Media," ed. Hillary Chute and Patrick Jagoda, special issue, *Critical Inquiry* 40, no. 3 (2014). Articles include discussion of transmedia, ludic movement, ballet, games and interplay among them, with contributions from Joe Sacco, Alison Bechdel, R. Crumb and Aline Kominsky-Crumb, among others. For modern(ist) discussions of "comedy," see, in a vast bibliography, Charles Baudelaire, "On the Essence of Laughter" (1855); Henry

Bergson, *Laughter* (1900): "Our laughter is always the laughter of a group" (6); on comic drama: 163–69; Sigmund Freud: *Jokes and Their Relation to the Unconscious* (1900); Northrop Frye: *Anatomy of Criticism* (1957), and *A Natural Perspective: The Development of Shakespearean Comedy and Romance* (1965); Alenka Zupancic, *The Odd One In: On Comedy* (Cambridge, MA: MIT Press, 2008).

2. Barbara Ehrenreich, *Dancing in the Streets: A History of Collective Joy* (New York: Henry Holt, 2006), 29.

3. On reading against "the whole," see Stephen Harrison, Stavros Fragoulidis, and Theodore D. Papanghelis, eds., *Intratextuality and Latin Literature* (Berlin: De Gruyter, 2018), with an emphasis on the reading of texts; and Alison Sharrock and Helen Morales, eds., *Intratextuality: Greek and Roman Textual Relations* (Oxford: Oxford University Press, 2001).

4. On these plays, see the brilliant Amy Richlin, *Slave Theater in the Roman Republic: Plautus and Popular Comedy* (Cambridge: Cambridge University Press, 2017).

5. Mario Telò, *Aristophanes and the Cloak of Comedy: Affect, Aesthetics, and the Canon* (Chicago: University of Chicago Press, 2016). S. Douglas Olson offers a valuable survey of "modern," that is, twentieth- and twenty-first-century arguments about the politics, or the intentions, of Aristophanes: S. Douglas Olson, "Comedy, Politics, and Society," in *Brill's Companion to the Study of Greek Comedy*, ed. G. W. Dobrov (Leiden: Brill, 2010), 35–69, especially 46–59. He concludes: "It is difficult to discover precisely whose views the genre articulated and to what end. An effective analysis of the question must account simultaneously for comedy's appeal to a broad popular audience and for the scathing criticism Aristophanes' plays in particular direct against the contemporary democratic government. It must also explain why, despite the overt political content of many of the plays and the poet's own claim that his purpose is to educate the citizenry, the genre had so little obvious impact on day-to-day life in the city" (59). See also Ian Ruffell, *Politics and Anti-Realism in Athenian Old Comedy: The Art of the Impossible* (Oxford: Oxford University Press, 2011), which focuses in part on the humor of Aristophanic comedy, and also on what Ruffell calls "impossibility": "drawing together three parallel strands—metatheatre, metafiction, and related forms of self-reflexivity ('breaking of the illusion'); the use of jokes to create the fictional world and its narrative structures; and finally parody, intertextuality, and other productive, foregrounded relationships with contemporary cultural forms" (18). He notes further: "Comic form, with its absurdist, comparative, and self-reflexive moves, anchors itself in the political and cultural context, even as it constructs and develops anti-realist worlds, scenarios, and motivations. The result is an absurdist dialectic. . . . In order to process the jokes and construct such impossibilities, the audience are exploring ideological and political positions" (429). I share his emphasis on impossibility without regarding it as "absurdist."

6. On this question, see Mary Depew and Dirk Obbink, eds., *Matrices of Genre: Authors, Canons, and Society* (Cambridge, MA: Harvard University Press, 2000).

7. In his important book *Making Mockery: The Poetics of Ancient Satire* (Oxford: Oxford University Press, 2007), Ralph Rosen comes at this question from a slightly different angle: "[Classicists] have generally trained their eye on one poet at a time, or a cluster of poets working in the same tradition, and when all is said and done, despite a toolkit of sophisticated critical methodologies, they have often found it difficult— claims to the contrary notwithstanding—to resist treating a satirical work as anything other than thinly veiled autobiography" (xi). His answer is to present a complex,

diachronic analysis of "poetic mockery" that treats Aristophanes along with Homer, Euripides, Callimachus, Juvenal, and other poets, including Archilochus.

8. Roland Barthes, "The Death of the Author," in *The Rustle of Language*, trans. Richard Howard (1984; New York: Hill and Wang, 1986), 49–55, here 49–50. Barthes here refers to the work of Jean-Pierre Vernant, on Greek tragedy, of course: "Recent investigations (J.-P. Vernant) have shed some light on the constitutively ambiguous nature of Greek tragedy, whose text is 'woven' of words with double meanings, words which each character understands unilaterally (this perpetual misunderstanding is precisely what we call the 'tragic'); there is, however, someone who understands each word in its duplicity" (54). Barthes refers, inaccurately but productively, to Vernant's essay "Ambiguity and Reversal: On the Enigmatic Structure of Oedipus Rex," trans. Page duBois, *New Literary History* 9, no. 3 (1976): 475–501. See also Michel Foucault, "What Is an Author?," in *Language, Counter-Memory, Practice: Selected Essays and Interviews*, ed. D. F. Bouchard, trans. D. F. Bouchard and S. Simon (Ithaca, NY: Cornell University Press, 1977), 113–38.

9. Mary Lefkowitz, *The Lives of the Greek Poets*, 2nd ed. (Bristol: Bristol Classical Press, 2012).

10. Pierre Macherey, *A Theory of Literary Production*, trans. Geoffrey Wall (London: Routledge, 2006).

11. Macherey, *Theory*, 106.

12. Macherey, 168.

13. For an invaluable resource on all eras of comedy, see Alan Sommerstein, ed., *The Encyclopedia of Greek Comedy*, 3 vols. (Hoboken, NJ: Wiley-Blackwell, 2019).

14. See Peter Wilson, *The Athenian Institution of the Khoregia: The Chorus, the City, and the Stage* (Cambridge: Cambridge University Press, 2000), 144. On the contradictory identification of the khoregos with the collective, vis-à-vis J. P. Vernant's description of tragedy's archaic heroes and citizen chorus, see also Wilson, 111. Wilson points out the importance to Athens of its "leitourgic system," the institution through which the wealthy paid for significant aspects of the city's welfare: "Operated with such a high degree of care and investment by the Athenians in the fifth and fourth centuries, it put the security of the city's choral culture on the same footing as that of its naval power, which was the backbone of its empire" (4). On the "granting of choruses," which had political and aesthetic dimensions, see Wilson, 61–70. The story of Alcibiades the khoregos is recounted in Andokides 4, *Against Alcibiades*; Demosthenes, *Against Meidias*; and Plutarch's *Life of Alcibiades*.

15. Macherey, *Theory*, 363.

16. Foucault, "What Is an Author?," 119, 123.

17. *Texts for Nothing*, trans. Samuel Beckett (London: Calder & Boyars, 1974), 16; cited by Foucault, 115 and 138.

18. Francesco Orlando, *Obsolete Objects in the Literary Imagination: Ruins, Relics, Rarities, Rubbish, Uninhabited Places, and Hidden Treasures*, trans. Gabriel Pihas, Daniel Seidel, and Alessandra Grego (1994; New Haven, CT: Yale University Press, 2006), 5: "Literature, both through its texts and through its codes, is irreplaceable as a testimony of the past . . . , the imaginary site of a return of the repressed. . . . Literature is either openly or secretly concessive, indulgent, partial, favorable, or complicit toward everything that encounters distancing, diffidence, repugnance, refusal, or condemnation outside of the field of fiction. . . . Literature possesses the permanent value of a

photographic negative of the positive cultural reality from which it emanates, and as a historic archive it is unequalled by the sum of all the other, more fortuitous and less organic documents that can bear witness to past rebellions, infractions, and frustrations."

19. Elaine Freedgood, *The Ideas in Things: Fugitive Meaning in the Victorian Novel* (Chicago: University of Chicago Press, 2010).

20. Fredric Jameson, *Allegory and Ideology* (London: Verso, 2019), 34.

21. Gilles Deleuze and Félix Guattari, *A Thousand Plateaus: Capitalism and Schizophrenia*, trans. Brian Massumi (1980; Minneapolis: University of Minnesota Press, 1987), 3–4, 9. See also Deleuze and Guattari, chap. 10, "1730: Becoming-Intense, Becoming Animal, Becoming Imperceptible," 232–309.

22. Deleuze and Guattari, *Thousand Plateaus*, 1, 9. Although Fredric Jameson is dismissive of Deleuze and Guattari's methodology, Deleuze himself says: "I think Félix Guattari and I have remained Marxists, in our two different ways, perhaps, but both of us. You see, we think any political philosophy must turn on the analysis of capitalism and the ways it has developed. . . . First, we think any society is defined not so much by its contradictions as by its lines of flight, it flees all over the place, and it's very interesting to try and follow the lines of flight taking shape at some particular moment or other. . . . There's another direction in *A Thousand Plateaus* which amounts to considering not just lines of flight rather than contradictions, but minorities rather than classes. . . . Then, . . . finding a characterization of 'war machines' that's nothing to do with war but to do with a particular way of occupying, taking up space-time, or inventing new space-times"; Gilles Deleuze, "Control and Becoming," *Negotiations: 1972–1990* (1990; New York: Columbia University Press, 1995), 169–76 ("conversation with Toni Negri"), here 171–72. On his use of the concept of transversality in Guattari and Deleuze, which Jameson associates with "that war on Marxism or totality declared by Jean-François Lyotard," see Jameson, *Allegory and Ideology*, xviii.

23. Lefkowitz, *Lives*, 4. Lefkowitz presents the biography of Aristophanes in her appendix 6; it also appears in Jeffrey Rusten, ed., *The Birth of Comedy: Texts, Documents, and Art from Athenian Competitions, 486–280*, trans. Jeffrey Henderson, David Konstan, Ralph Rosen, Jeffrey Rusten, and Niall W. Slater (Baltimore: Johns Hopkins University Press, 2011), 274–75.

24. See, for example, work on the corpus associated with the name Theognis: Hendrik Selle, *Theognis und die Theognidea* (Berlin: De Gruyter, 2008); Andrew Lear, "The Pederastic Elegies and the Authorship of the Theognidea," *Classical Quarterly* 61 (2011): 378–93. See also Barbara Graziosi, *Inventing Homer: The Early Reception of Homer* (Cambridge: Cambridge University Press, 2002), who traces the centuries of effort to establish a "biography" for the supposed author of the *Iliad* and the *Odyssey*: "Contemporary scholars offer a united front concerning the biographical tradition: currently, the consensus is that it should be ignored" (15). See also Graziosi's discussion of Barthes and Foucault on the death of the author (17–18). Graziosi offers a more nuanced historical account of how ancient audiences created the author Homer. See also Gregory Nagy, "Homeric Questions," *Transactions of the American Philological Association* 122 (1992): 28–31. On the "reinvention" of Euripidean biography in the 330s BCE, long after the poet's death, see Johanna Hanink, *Lycurgan Athens and the Making of Classical Tragedy* (Cambridge: Cambridge University Press, 2014). See also David Kawalko Roselli, "The Theater of Euripides," in *A Companion to Euripides*, ed. Laura K. McClure (Malden, MA: John Wiley & Sons, 2017), 390–411 ("Euripides' increased openness to new performance styles is the flipside of the agency of actors, musicians, stage-hands,

public officials, entrepreneurs, khoregoi, and audiences with increasing confidence in their ability to express judgment about theatrical performance. To a certain degree, these agents were able to destabilize authorial agency in Euripidean drama" [404–5]); and Roselli, "Vegetable-Hawking Mom and Fortunate Son: Euripides' Tragic Style, and Reception," *Phoenix* 59 (2005): 1–49. Roselli argues that Aristophanes' representation of Euripides is evidence for the reception of the tragic poet's work. On Aristophanes' own creation of a "brand," see Donald Sells, *Parody, Politics, and the Populace in Greek Old Comedy* (London: Bloomsbury Academic, 2018). In Sells's argument, Aristophanes emulates the tragic hero Telephos, in his own play *Acharnians*: "By modelling the comic projects of his hero and himself on that of a popular but culturally and generically ambivalent tragic hero, Aristophanes attempts what amounts to a crude form of 'product placement' in the highly competitive festivals of Dionysus in the fifth century." This is the "strategic launch of his comic brand" (24). Sells considers in detail the Aristophanic corpus's relationship to other contemporary genres of classical Athens, including not just tragedy, but also satyr play, lyric poetry, and prose treatises such as Xenophon's *Oikonomikos*.

25. See Wilson, *Khoregia*.

26. Eric Csapo, Hans Rupprecht Goette, J. R. Green, Peter Wilson, eds., *Greek Theatre in the Fourth Century BC* (Berlin: De Gruyter, 2014).

27. Ian C. Storey, *Eupolis: Poet of Old Comedy* (Oxford: Oxford University Press, 2004). Storey translates the frustratingly limited and allusive passages that remain of *Demoi*, Eupolis's most celebrated play, including such fragments as these from a Cairo codex: "And indeed they say that Peisandros was screwed yesterday while having breakfast, after he said he wouldn't feed a stranger. And Pauson, standing beside Theogenes dining to his heart's content off one of his merchant-ships, thrashed and screwed him good, and the beaten Theogenes lay there, farting all night" (frag. 99; Storey, 12); "Chorus or Character: I think I see seated these men who they say have come from the dead . . . from friends at . . . since Pyronides is standing upright in front of them, let us ask him. Tell me . . . you came . . . to the citizens' . . . tell us what . . ." (Storey, 13). An unassigned fragment reads: "Have you ever seen a more tight-fisted choregos than him?" (Storey, 27). Here we have sex, violence, scatology, hunger, and the seeking of advice from the dead, all elements found also in the works of Aristophanes.

28. See the recent commentary of Christian Orth, *Strattis: Die Fragmente; Ein Kommentar* (Heidelberg: Verlag-Antike, 2009); Mario Telò, *Eupolidis Demi*, Biblioteca Nazionale, Serie dei Classici Greci e Latini, n.s. 14 (Florence: Felice le Monnier, 2007); Emmanuela Bakola, *Cratinus and the Art of Comedy* (Oxford: Oxford University Press, 2010).

29. See the fragment of a plot summary, *POxy*. 663, in Rusten, *Birth*, 182.

CHAPTER 1

1. See Victor Caston and Silke-Maria Weineck, eds., *Our Ancient Wars: Rethinking War through the Classics* (Ann Arbor: University of Michigan Press, 2016), esp. Nancy Sherman, "Moral Injury, Damage, and Repair," 121–54, and Silke-Maria Weineck, "Epilogue: Distances," 275–81.

2. Joshua Billings, *Genealogy of the Tragic: Greek Tragedy and German Philosophy* (Princeton, NJ: Princeton University Press, 2014), 2. Billings argues that "since Peter Szondi's 1961 'An Essay on the Tragic,' it has been proverbial that 'since Aristotle,

there has been a poetics of tragedy. Only since Schelling has there been a philosophy of the tragic'" (8); Peter Szondi, *An Essay on the Tragic*, trans. Paul Fleming (Stanford, CA: Stanford University Press, 2002). See also Vassilis Lambropoulos, *The Tragic Idea* (London: Duckworth, 2006). Comedy in Billings's book is mentioned only in relation to Hegel's discussion of it, comedy contrasted with tragedy "animated by insubstantial drive," Hegel locating it on the side of "fatelessness" (156–57).

3. See, for example, the Simons: Simon Critchley, *Tragedy, the Greeks, and Us* (New York: Vintage, 2020); Simon Goldhill, *Love, Sex & Tragedy: How the Ancient World Shapes Our Lives* (Chicago: University of Chicago Press, 2004); and Simon Perris, *The Gentle, Jealous God: Reading Euripides' "Bacchae" in English*, Bloomsbury Studies in Classical Reception (London: Bloomsbury Academic, 2016), which considers seven twentieth- and twenty-first-century translations of Euripides' *Bacchae*, from Gilbert Murray's (1902) to Anne Carson's (2016). The *BMCR* reviewer, Michael Kochenash, writes:

> Published in 1991, Irish poet Derek Mahon's "parodic translation" of the *Bacchae*, titled *The Bacchae: after Euripides*, renders the tragedy using conventions more familiar to comedies. Of particular prominence is his use of "heroic couplets." Mahon's tragicomedy mocks, in Perris's judgment, a number of targets: from Irish language to the political appropriation of Greek tragedies by his contemporaries. Chapter Six features another Irishman's translation, Colin Teevan's *Euripides: Bacchai* (2002). Perris is nearly unequivocal in his criticism of this translation and production, contrasting it unfavorably with a 1981 production of Aeschylus's *Oresteia* featuring the same director, composer, and lead actor. Teevan's translation is largely prosaic, despite various attempts at poeticizing the text, and—in contrast to Mahon's apolitical translation—explicitly draws from Teevan's sociopolitical (post-9/11) environment. Scottish playwright David Greig's translation, *Euripides: The Bacchae* (2007), prioritizes dynamic equivalence (or "radical authenticity"), bringing out elements of humor—in the tradition of Mahon's translation—and assonance. In contrast to his evaluation of Teevan, Perris largely approves of Greig's work. Nevertheless, he critiques Greig's *Bacchae* as lacking emotional depth: "Greig locates the Dionysiac in neoliberal bourgeois hedonism."

See also Julian Young, *The Philosophy of Tragedy: From Plato to Zizek* (Cambridge: Cambridge University Press, 2013).

4. Miriam Leonard, *Tragic Modernities* (Cambridge, MA: Harvard University Press, 2015).

5. Jean-Pierre Vernant and Pierre Vidal-Naquet, *Myth and Tragedy in Ancient Greece*, trans. Janet Lloyd (1972, 1986; New York: Zone Books, 1990).

6. On the many varieties of historicism, see Fredric Jameson, "Marxism and Historicism," *New Literary History* 11, no. 1 (1979): 41–73; reprinted in Jameson, *The Ideologies of Theory* (London: Verso, 2009), 451–82. Jameson remarks on the "curious destiny" of the term *historicism* (*Ideologies*, 453), and traces its history.

7. John J. Winkler and Froma Zeitlin, eds., *Nothing to Do with Dionysos?: Athenian Drama in Its Social Context* (Princeton, NJ: Princeton University Press, 1990).

8. Terry Eagleton, *Sweet Violence: The Idea of the Tragic* (Oxford: Wiley-Blackwell, 2002); see George Steiner, *The Death of Tragedy* (London: Faber and Faber, 1961); also Steiner, *Antigones: How the Myth of Antigone Has Endured in Western Literature, Art, and Thought* (New Haven, CT: Yale University Press, 1996).

9. On Hegel and ancient drama, see Mark William Roche, *Tragedy and Comedy:*

A Systematic Study and a Critique of Hegel (Albany: State University of New York Press, 1998).

10. *Hegel: On Tragedy*, ed. Anne Paolucci and Henry Paolucci (New York: Harper and Row, 1962), 68. The passage cited comes from *The Philosophy of Fine Art*, vol. 4, trans. F. P. B. Osmaston (London: G. Bell and Sons, 1920).

11. See Roche, *Tragedy and Comedy*, 136: "The strength of Hegel's discussion of comedy is not his typology, which is both brief and undialectical, but his insight into subjectivity and particularity as the distinguishing features of the genre.".

12. Steiner, *Death of Tragedy*. Tragedy may have seemed inconceivable in 1960. But see Helen Morales, *Antigone Rising: The Subversive Power of the Ancient Myths* (New York: Bold Type Books, 2020). Morales describes the performance of Antigone in Ferguson after the killing of African American Michael Brown Jr. (x–xi), and *Antígona González* by Sara Uribe, set in contemporary Mexico: "The book draws on a long Latin American tradition that identifies Polynices with the marginalized, the separated and the lost" (149–50).

13. Friedrich Nietzsche, *The Birth of Tragedy*, trans. Clifton P. Fadiman (New York: Dover, 1995). See James Porter, *The Invention of Dionysus: An Essay on the Birth of Tragedy* (Stanford, CA: Stanford University Press, 2000).

14. Nietzsche, *Birth of Tragedy*, 27.

15. Billings, *Genealogy*, 3.

16. For the seminal argument concerning the emergence of the individual in the West, which in fact goes back to ancient Athenian emphases on private life, see C. B. Macpherson, *The Political Theory of Possessive Individualism: Hobbes to Locke* (Oxford: Clarendon Press, 1962); see also Joel Fineman, *Shakespeare's Perjured Eye: The Invention of Poetic Subjectivity in the Sonnets* (Berkeley: University of California Press, 1986).

17. Sigmund Freud, *The Interpretation of Dreams*, trans. James Strachey (New York: Avon Books, 1965), 296.

18. Bernard Knox, *Oedipus at Thebes: Sophocles' Tragic Hero and His Time* (New Haven, CT: Yale University Press, 1957), 14.

19. Billings, *Genealogy*, 11, 12.

20. Judith Butler, *Antigone's Claim: Kinship between Life and Death* (New York: Columbia University Press, 2002). See also the extraordinary account of the fate of Antigone in Bonnie Honig's *Antigone, Interrupted* (Cambridge: Cambridge University Press, 2013).

21. Hanif Kureishi, introduction to Slavoj Zizek, *Antigone* (London: Bloomsbury Academic, 2016), viii.

22. Zizek, *Antigone*, xxiv.

23. For another view, see Sophie Wahnich, *In Defence of the Terror: Liberty or Death in the French Revolution*, trans. David Fernbach (2003; London: Verso, 2012).

24. Honig, *Antigone Interrupted*; Tina Chanter, *Whose Antigone? The Tragic Marginalization of Slavery* (Albany: State University of New York Press, 2011); Anne Carson, *Antigo nick* (New York: New Directions, 2015).

25. Kamila Shamsie, *Home Fire* (New York: Riverhead Books, 2017).

26. Aristotle, *Poetics*, "Longinus," *On the Sublime*, Demetrius, *On Style*, trans. W. Hamilton Fyfe (Aristotle), Loeb Classical Library (Cambridge, MA: Harvard University Press, 1932).

27. Florence Dupont, *Aristote ou le vampire du théâtre occidental* (Paris: Flammarion, 2007); all translations my own.

28. Dupont (*Aristote*, 10n1) quotes Hegel, cited by Ulrich Willamowitz-Müllendorf, "Was ist eine attische Tragödie?," *Einleitung in die attische Tragödie* (Berlin: Weidmannsche Buchhandlung, 1889), 43–119.

29. Simon Goldhill, "The Great Dionysia and Civic Ideology," in Winkler and Zeitlin, *Nothing to Do with Dionysos?*, 97–129.

30. Wilson, *Khoregia*, 67–80.

31. Goldhill, "Great Dionysia." And in fact Winkler and Zeitlin's volume takes its impetus as a response to Oliver Taplin, who notoriously wrote: "There is nothing intrinsically Dionysiac about Greek tragedy"; Oliver Taplin, *Greek Tragedy in Action* (London: Routledge, 1978), 162. On festivals and the drama, with bibliography, see Edith Hall, "Comedy and Athenian Festival Culture," in *The Cambridge Companion to Greek Comedy*, ed. M. Revermann (Cambridge: Cambridge University Press, 2014), 306–21. The ancient phrase "nothing to do with Dionysos" comes from Polybius (39.2.1–3).

32. Barbara Goff and Michael Simpson, *Crossroads in the Black Aegean: Oedipus, Antigone, and Dramas of the African Diaspora* (Oxford: Oxford University Press, 2008).

33. Richard Janko, *Aristotle on Comedy: Toward a Reconstruction of Poetics II* (London: Duckworth, 2002).

34. W. Koster, *Scholia in Aristophanem, Pars 1, Fasc. 1A: Prolegomena de Comoedia* (Groningen: Bouma's Boekhuis, 1975).

35. Janko cites in boldface "the portions of the reconstruction that are in the text and translation constituted" in the previous chapter; he adds fragments of the *Poetics* when pertinent, and then "a construct whose details are endlessly debatable, which possesses no independent authority whatsoever, but is intended only to present in a convenient form a summary of the conclusions reached in [his] Commentary, as to how the interstices between the terse entries are to be filled" (*Aristotle on Comedy*, 91). Cautious as he is, this reconstruction is immensely valuable in helping us to imagine how Aristotle may have written a second part of the *Poetics* on comedy.

36. *The Complete Greek Tragedies*, Centennial Edition, ed. David Grene and Richmond Lattimore, vol. 1, Aeschylus, *The Suppliant Maidens*, trans. Seth G. Benardete, and *Prometheus Bound*, trans. David Grene; vol. 2, Aeschylus, *The Oresteia*, trans. Richmond Lattimore (Chicago: University of Chicago Press, 1992).

37. Nicole Loraux, *The Mourning Voice: An Essay on Greek Tragedy*, trans. Elizabeth Trapnell Rawlings (Ithaca, NY: Cornell University Press, 2002); and Loraux, *Mothers in Mourning, with the Essay "Of Amnesty and Its Opposite,"* trans. Corinne Pache (Ithaca, NY: Cornell University Press, 1998).

38. Loraux, *Mourning Voice*, 59.

39. Loraux, 59, citing Charles Segal, "Song, Ritual, and Commemoration in Early Greek Poetry and Tragedy," *Oral Tradition* 4 (1989): 339–40; 339: "Weeping is in itself a kind of song."

40. Billings, *Genealogy*, 224.

41. For a brilliant and wide-ranging commentary on Sophocles' *Antigone*, see Sophocles, *Antigone*, ed. Mark Griffith (Cambridge: Cambridge University Press, 1999).

42. On comic aspects of tragedy, see Bernd Seidensticker, *Palintonos Harmonia: Studien zu komischen Elementen in der griechischen Tragödie*, Hypomnemata, vol. 72 (Göttingen: Vandenhoeck and Ruprecht, 1982). On what is called the "New Music," deployed by Euripides here, see Eric Csapo, "The Politics of the New Music," in *Music and the Muses: The Culture of Mousikê in the Classical Athenian City*, ed. Penelope Murray and Peter Wilson (Oxford: Oxford University Press, 2004), 230: "The elite theorists

characterized New Music and its practitioners as effeminate, barbarous, and vulgar, and likely to produce these same qualities in its audiences." Csapo elaborates on Plato's hostility to such musical trends (235 and following) and notes: "Far from contesting the critics' charges about the ethos of music, New Music cultivated its womanly and barbarian associations, its reputation for high-emotion, and Dionysiac hysteria" (247). After *Heracles* (418?), Euripides used female choruses. And Csapo adds: "From the late 420s onwards the choruses tend not only to be women, but frequently Asiatic women, or if not Asiatic, then Greek captives in Eastern lands. The greatest New Musical monodies of the era, in Timotheus [sic] *Persians*, and Euripides' *Orestes*, used delirious, panic-stricken Persians and Phrygian eunuchs. . . . Such characters and situations maximized music's potential for expressing powerful and raw emotion" (247).

43. Sean Alexander Gurd, *Dissonance: Auditory Aesthetics in Ancient Greece* (New York: Fordham University Press, 2016), 55.

44. Eduardo Viveiros de Castro, *Cannibal Metaphysics: For a Post-Structural Anthropology*, trans. Peter Skafish (2009; Minneapolis: University of Minnesota Press, 2017), 72.

45. Aristophanes, *Frogs, Assemblywomen, Wealth*, ed. and trans. Jeffrey Henderson, Loeb Classical Library (Cambridge, MA: Harvard University Press, 2002). Henderson's translation of these plays is used throughout unless otherwise indicated.

46. *A Greek-English Lexicon, Compiled by Henry George Liddell and Robert Scott, Revised and Augmented throughout by Sir Henry Stuart Jones with the Assistance of Roderick McKenzie and with the Cooperation of Many Scholars, with a Revised Supplement* (Oxford: Clarendon [Oxford University Press], 1996); hereafter LSJ.

47. Marcel Detienne and Jean-Pierre Vernant, *Cunning Intelligence in Greek Culture and Society*, trans. Janet Lloyd (Chicago: University of Chicago Press, 1991).

48. Gurd, *Dissonance*, 12.

49. As Henderson notes, ad loc., the reference to tattooing may accompany the naming of Adeimantus, accused of treachery in the battle of Aegospotami, and that "he had unsuccessfully opposed an Assembly motion to mutilate all enemy prisoners," citing Xenophon's *Hellenica* 2.1.32.

50. Edith Hall and Amanda Wrigley, eds., *Aristophanes in Performance, 421 BC–AD 2007* (London: Routledge, 2007).

51. Jeffrey Henderson, *The Maculate Muse: Obscene Language in Attic Comedy*, 2nd ed. (Oxford: Oxford University Press, 1991).

52. See Richlin, *Slave Theater*.

CHAPTER 2

1. Kristin Ross, *The Emergence of Social Space: Rimbaud and the Paris Commune* (Minneapolis: University of Minnesota Press, 1989), 105.

2. Michael Hardt and Antonio Negri, *Multitude: War and Democracy in the Age of Empire* (New York: Penguin, 2004), 91–92.

3. Michael Hardt and Antonio Negri, *Assembly* (New York: Oxford University, 2017).

4. Hardt and Negri, *Assembly*, 295.

5. Hardt and Negri, *Assembly*, xxi.

6. Rosi Braidotti, *Nomadic Theory* (New York: Columbia University Press, 2011).

7. On insects, see also Steven Shaviro, "Two Lessons from Burroughs," in *Posthuman Bodies*, ed. Judith Halberstam and Ira Livingston (Bloomington, Indiana: In-

diana University Press, 1995), 38–54. Jacques Derrida, *The Politics of Friendship*, trans. George Collins (London: Verso, 2006).

    8. Deleuze and Guattari, *Thousand Plateaus*, 308.

    9. Karl Marx, *Grundrisse: Foundations of the Critique of Political Economy*, trans. Martin Nicolaus (London: Penguin, 2005), Notebook VII, p. 706.

    10. See Max Horkheimer and Theodor W. Adorno, *Dialectic of Enlightenment*, trans. Edmund Jephcott (1947; Stanford, CA: Stanford University Press, 2002), esp. 26–27: "The servant is subjugated in body and soul, the master regresses" (27); "Excursus I: Odysseus or Myth and Enlightenment," 35–60; and "The Culture Industry: Enlightenment as Mass Deception," 94–136. In the allegory of Odysseus and the Sirens, the bee-like sirens, insectoid female singers, represent a danger that Odysseus, "the prototype of the bourgeois individual" (35), alone can tolerate, while the laboring crew must be protected from their song: "It is impossible to hear the Sirens and not succumb" (46).

    11. See, for example, Lauren Wilcox, "Drones, Swarms, and Becoming-Insect: Feminist Utopias and Posthuman Politics," *Feminist Review* 116 (2017): 25–45: "Posthuman warfare . . . contains the possibilities of both appropriating and rewriting antagonisms of masculine and feminine in the embodiment of the subject of war in the swarm. This piece seeks to analyse new ways of feminist theorising of the relations of power and violence in the embodiment of war as the swarm" (1). See also the sex workers site, SWARM Collective (swarmcollective.org).

    12. Achille Mbembe, "Necropolitics," trans. Libby Meintjes, *Public Culture* 15 (2003): 11–40, here 22.

    13. Mbembe, "Necropolitics," 23.

    14. Mbembe extends the metaphor of the swarm in subsequent work, discussing migration, especially to Europe and the US: "The ordeal of these new international movements is yielding—little by little and across the entire planet—diverse assemblages of mosaic territories. This new swarming—which adds to the previous waves of migration from the South—blurs criteria of national belonging." And he points out the swarming of "water, air, dust, microbes, termites, bees, insects," the move from "the human condition to the terrestrial condition." Achille Mbembe, *Necropolitics*, trans. Steven Corcoran (2016; Durham, NC: Duke University Press, 2019), 12–13.

    15. Nick Dyer-Witheford, *Cyber-Marx: Cycles and Circuits of Struggle in High-Technology Capitalism* (Urbana: University of Illinois Press, 1999), 238.

    16. Claire Preston, *Bee* (London: Reaktion Books, 2006), 11.

    17. Preston cites Les Murray's poem "The Swarm," published in 1977, which condemns the English bees, enslaved to their sovereign, contrasting monarchy with Australian republicanism (*Bee*, 63).

    18. On the racial allegory, the swarm of zombies, in *Night of the Living Dead*, see Jeffrey Stewart, "Toward the New Commons: A Meditation on *Night of the Living Dead* and 1968," *Kalfou: A Journal of Comparative and Relational Ethnic Studies* 2 (May 2015): 206–24.

    19. Gabriel Germain, *Genèse de l'Odyssée, le fantastique, le sacré* (Paris: Presses universitaires de France, 1954). The epinician poet Pindar calls one of the priestesses at the oracle of Delphi *melissa*, "bee" (*Pythian* 4.60). Bees are a particularly fascinating group in the insect world, as we learn from Claude Lévi-Strauss's work in *From Honey to Ashes, Introduction to a Science of Mythology*, vol. 2, trans. Doreen Weightman and John Weightman (New York: Harper and Row, 1973).

20. Horkheimer and Adorno, *Dialectic*, 35.

21. Preston, *Bee*, 108–12.

22. In his *Oikonomikos*, a treatise on household management, Xenophon instructs his wife to behave like "the (female) leader of the bees," *he ton melitton hegemon*, and to remain indoors (7.35).

23. Ovid, *Metamorphoses*, trans. D. Raeburn (London: Penguin, 2004), 280.

24. Homer, *The Iliad*, trans. R. Fagles (New York: Viking, 1990), 421. Fagles's translation of the *Iliad* is used throughout unless otherwise indicated.

25. Aristotle, *On the Soul, Parva Naturalia, On Breath*, trans. W. S. Hett, Loeb Classical Library (Cambridge, MA: Harvard University Press, 1973), 413b20.

26. Michael Shanks, *Art and the Early Greek State: An Interpretive Archaeology* (Cambridge: Cambridge University Press, 1999), 211.

27. Shanks uses the terminology of Gilles Deleuze and Félix Guattari in describing the human/animal forms on some vases: "Deleuze and Guattari (1988) propose a distinction between the molecular and the molar (comparable with Canetti's distinction between pack, and mass or crowd). The form of the molecular is multiplicity; it is constantly becoming something else through non-genetic or non-structural transformation, affinity, contagion and infection, flowing beyond boundaries. In contrast, the molar is a stability of identities and forms, and involves relations of conjugality and reproductive filiation. Korinthian are of the molecular, forming a (heterogeneous) assemblage—lion, bird, person, monster. Monsters, in their Korinthian variety, are different from the animals which appear clearly speciated, posed and identifiable, painted in lines" (*Art*, 104). "Wild animals are painted in great numbers, but in stylised 'tamed' poses. . . . The hoplite's shield shows him as bird, sometimes wild and sometimes domesticated, where the reference seems to be a link with the (wild) feline. Birds are also the link between domesticated dogs and men" (136).

28. Shanks refers to the work of Klaus Theweleit in his two-volume *Male Fantasies* (1987), on twentieth-century Germany, to elucidate his understanding of the soldier society: "A primary motivation is towards bodily and social unity. This will to wholeness arises because of the perceived threat of its opposite: those wild and disorderly powers which break down barriers, setting off floods and waves of lower and sordid elements; there is fear of dissolution, commingling with these base elements, fear of engulfment" (Shanks, *Art*, 127).

29. For reflection on the appeal of bodily discipline and the tendencies toward "fascist" dispositions, and a call for a complex communitarianism in resistance, see William E. Connolly, *Aspirational Fascism: The Struggle for Multifaceted Democracy under Trumpism* (Minneapolis: University of Minnesota Press, 2017). "Multifacetedness" extends beyond democracy to a variety of expression of interests and desires, a Habermasian type of listening and resolution of differences, attentiveness to others, and creativity without a command center.

30. Thanks to Alex Purves for this reference.

31. *The Homeric Hymns*, trans. A. Athanassakis, 2nd ed. (Baltimore: Johns Hopkins University Press, 2004).

32. See Ellen Greene and Marilyn Skinner, eds., *The New Sappho on Old Age: Textual and Philosophical Studies* (Washington, DC: Center for Hellenic Studies, 2010).

33. Sean Gurd begins his fascinating book on sound, noise, and song in ancient Greece with a list of the cries emitted by creatures and recorded in ancient literature,

all footnoted in his text: "Cicadas sing, as do birds: you can hear the cries of eagles, the song of the nightingale, and the singing, shouting, and noise of cranes, herons, hawks, falcons." Gurd, *Dissonance*, 1.

    34. *Greek Lyric Poetry*, trans. M. L. West (Oxford: Oxford University Press, 1993), Semonides 7, p. 18.

    35. Plato, *The Last Days of Socrates: Euthyphro, Apology, Crito, Phaedo*, trans. H. Tredennick and H. Tarrant (London: Penguin, 2003).

    36. On this question, see Jacques Rancière, *The Philosopher and His Poor*, trans. A. Parker, C. Oster, and J. Drury (1983; Durham, NC: Duke University Press, 2004).

    37. Aristotle, *On the Soul*, trans. Hett; see also 413b20.

    38. Aristotle, *Historia Animalium*, vol. 1, trans. A. L. Peck, Loeb Classical Library (Cambridge, MA: Harvard University Press, 1965). For a brilliant study of Aristotle's corpus, see Emmanuela Bianchi, *The Feminine Symptom: Aleatory Matter in the Aristotelian Cosmos* (New York: Fordham University Press, 2014).

    39. Aristotle, *Parts of Animals*, trans. A. L. Peck, *Movement of Animals, Progression of Animals*, trans. E. S. Forster, Loeb Classical Library (London: Heinemann, 1961).

    40. Aristotle, *Generation of Animals*, trans. A. L. Peck, Loeb Classical Library (Cambridge, MA: Harvard University Press, 1963).

    41. See Page duBois, *Slaves and Other Objects* (Chicago: University of Chicago Press, 2003), 170–88; and Leslie Kurke, *Aesopic Conversations: Popular Tradition, Cultural Dialogue, and the Invention of Greek Prose* (Princeton, NJ: Princeton University Press, 2011).

    42. Gilles Deleuze and Felix Guattari, *Kafka: Toward a Minor Literature*, trans. D. Polan, foreword by Reda Bensmaia (1975; Minneapolis: University of Minnesota Press, 1986), 13.

    43. Deleuze and Guattari, *Kafka*, 12; "Kafka's animals never refer to a mythology or to archetypes but correspond solely to new levels, zones of liberated intensities where contents free themselves from their forms as well as from their expressions, from the signifer that formalized them. There is no longer anything but movements, vibrations, thresholds in a deserted matter: animals, mice, dogs, apes, cockroaches are distinguished only by this or that threshold, this or that vibration, by the particular underground tunnel in the rhizome or the burrow. Because these tunnels are underground intensities. . . . In the becoming-insect, it is a mournful whining that carries along the voice and blurs the resonance of words" (13).

    44. Deleuze and Guattari, *Kafka*, 15.

    45. On the chorus of wasps, in *Wasps*, see especially Cécile Corbel-Morana, *Le bestiaire d'Aristophane* (Paris: Les Belles Lettres, 2012), 136–70. Corbel-Morana suggests that the notion of autochthonous wasps, promulgated by the chorus, may owe something to the cicadas, born of the earth (*Anacreontea*, 34 West, and elsewhere), which the Athenians in the archaic period took as the emblem of their autochthony, wearing golden cicadas in their hair. Authentic Athenians resembled the cicada; the warriors of the Marathon age, like the chorus of the comedy, also had waspishly fought on the city's behalf against the Persians (Corbel-Morana, 157). Corbel-Morana cites Herodotus 8.50, as well as verses from Aeschylus's *Persians*. The warriors' lances are likened to the insects' stingers: "Pour créer son chœur, Aristophane s'est inspiré du bestiaire symbolique traditionnel de la poésie archaïque . . . et de l'imagerie populaire" (167). Corbel-Morana argues that the comparisons between human beings, the chorus of Athenians and their audience, and animals, serve as a moralizing discourse critical of the citizens,

negative in its representation of the bestialization of the city. See also her reading of the *Birds*, 171–207 and 249–303: "Les contradictions de l'État de nature créé dans les Oiseaux permettent par ailleurs de formuler le constat d'une rémanence de la sauvagerie au sein de la Cité . . ." (207). My interpretation of this bestiary is, obviously, more positive, seeing an energy and a "line of flight" in the analogy with animals.

46. Aristophanes, *Clouds, Wasps, Peace*, ed. and trans. Jeffrey Henderson, Loeb Classical Library (Cambridge, MA: Harvard University Press, 1998). Henderson's translation of these plays is used throughout unless otherwise indicated.

47. Aristophanes, *Wasps*, ed., with an introduction and commentary, Douglas M. MacDowell (Oxford: Clarendon Press, 1971), 3. For a more recent edition of the *Wasps*, see Aristophanes, *Wasps*, ed. Z. Biles and S. D. Olson (Oxford: Oxford University Press, 2016).

48. Aristophanes, *Wasps*, ed. MacDowell, 4.

49. On the inscription of the tablet as a metaphor for the female body, see Page duBois, *Sowing the Body: Psychoanalysis and Ancient Representations of Women* (Chicago: University of Chicago Press, 1988), 130–66.

50. Thebes as well as Athens claimed autochthony for its citizens, a god-given right to their lands, citing the sowing of the dragon's teeth, when their founder, Kadmos, encountered and killed this dragon son of Ares defending a spring whose water was needed for the performance of a sacrifice. From the sowing sprang up warriors, who fought until only five remained, the Spartoi, or "sown men," from whom the Thebans traced their origin.

51. Hesiod, *Theogony, Works and Days, Shield*, trans. Apostolos N. Athanassakis, 2nd ed. (Baltimore: Johns Hopkins University Press, 2004).

52. See Kurke, *Aesopic Conversations*. The first, diachronic, half of this book focuses on the figure of Aesop himself, and demonstrates with great care and convincing attention to detail that much of the *Life of Aesop* called Vita G, of uncertain late date, not only preserves very ancient traditions, but can be read backward into moments of the classical period, to confirm or illuminate insights Kurke untangles from the welter of material concerning Aesop. She considers the story of his engagement with the Delphic oracle and the Delphians, and shows how an opposition between Apollo and Aesop serves to demystify the claims and privileges of the oracular site. She lays out the characteristics of a prephilosophical or even antiphilosophical, popular tradition of *sophia* that includes the Seven Sages, some pre-Socratics, and religious figures such as Epimenides. This enduring system features forms of competition, a typical life trajectory that moves from rhetorical and verbal skill deployed for political effects, often in a competitive context, to religious expertise and to journeys of *theoria*. Aesop emerges as a critical or parodic figure in relation to the high wisdom traditions, moving between sage and parodist, and this ambiguity persists even into the late biography of Vita G, which reveals many historical strata.

53. Aristophanes, *Clouds*, ed., with introduction and commentary, K. J. Dover (Oxford: Clarendon Press, 1968), xxiv.

54. See Jacques Rancière, *Disagreement: Politics and Philosophy*, trans. Julie Rose (1995; Minneapolis: University of Minnesota Press, 2004), 15–17.

55. Deleuze and Guattari, *Thousand Plateaus*, 3.

56. Ross, *Emergence of Social Space*, 107, 108.

57. Ross, 120.

CHAPTER 3

1. On the *ekphrasis*, the rhetorical description of Achilles' shield, see Page duBois, *History, Rhetorical Description, and the Epic* (Cambridge: Boydell and Brewer, 1983).

2. Homer, *The Iliad: A New Translation*, trans. Peter Green (Berkeley: University of California Press, 2015), 18.561–72 (354). On women's work songs and their relationship to choral traditions, see Andromache Karanika, *Voices at Work: Women, Performance, and Labor in Ancient Greece* (Baltimore: Johns Hopkins University Press, 2014).

3. For a thorough and enlightening study of the ancient chorus, see Barbara Kowalzig, *Singing for the Gods: Performances of Myth and Ritual in Archaic and Classical Greece* (Oxford: Oxford University Press, 2007)

4. Yana Zarifi, "Chorus and Dance in the Ancient World," in *The Cambridge Companion to Greek and Roman Theatre*, ed. Marianne McDonald and Michael Walton (Cambridge: Cambridge University Press, 2007), 227–46.

5. See the foundational work of Claude Calame, *Choruses of Young Women in Ancient Greece: Their Morphology, Religious Role, and Social Functions*, trans. Derek Collins and Janice Orion, rev. ed. (Lanham, MD: Rowman and Littlefield, 2001).

6. On the important presence of metics, non-Athenians resident in Athens, see Demetra Kasimis, *The Perpetual Immigrant and the Limits of Athenian Democracy* (Cambridge: Cambridge University Press, 2018).

7. Louis Althusser, "The Piccolo Teatro: Bertolazzi and Brecht; Notes on a Materialist Theatre," in *For Marx*, trans. Ben Brewster (New York, Vintage, 1970), 129 and following.

8. Althusser, "Piccolo Teatro," 137–38, 141.

9. Althusser, 142.

10. See also Wilson, *Khoregia*.

11. Joshua Billings, Felix Budelmann, and Fiona Macintosh, eds., *Choruses, Ancient and Modern* (Oxford: Oxford University Press, 2013), 263, 264, 266, 271, 273, 275, 276 (*Frogs*).

12. Edith Hall, "Mob, Cabal, or Utopian Commune? The Political Contestation of the Ancient Chorus, 1789–1917," in Billings, Budelmann, and Macintosh, *Choruses*, 281–307.

13. Citing C. Hughes, "Music of the French Revolution," *Science & Society* 4 (1940): 193–210, here 194.

14. Hall discusses various deployments of the ancient chorus in modernity, mentioning James Robertson's 1846 adaptation of Aristophanes' *Birds* and calling him "by far the most conservative writer of burlesque, [who] used the Greek chorus to deride advocates of social reform and universal suffrage" ("Mob," 286). But elsewhere she stresses the "connection between chorality and discourse on revolution" (287). Aeschylus's *Prometheus Bound* stimulated progressive thinkers; Prometheus fettered triggered connections with slaves, for abolitionists. Marx was represented as Prometheus chained, in 1842, comforted by Oceanid-Rhine-maidens, in *Die rheinische Zeitung* (296). In his version of the myth, Shelley's Spirits call for a new world: "The dew of our wings is a rain of balm, / And, beyond our eyes, / The human love lies, / Which makes all it gazes on Paradise." In various choruses, Hall identifies the "chorus as vehicle for emancipatory sentiments" (299).

15. Martin Revermann, "Brechtian Chorality," in Billings, Budelmann, and Macintosh, *Choruses*, 151–69, here 164.

16. Claude Calame, *La tragédie chorale: Poésie grecque et rituel musical* (Paris: Les Belles Lettres, 2017).

17. See the articles of Mark Griffith: "Brilliant Dynasts: Power and Politics in the Oresteia," *Classical Antiquity* 14 (1995): 62–129, and "The King and Eye: The Rule of the Father in Greek Tragedy," *Proceedings of the Cambridge Philological Society* 44 (1998): 22–86.

18. For a thorough presentation of satyr drama, see Ralf Krumeich, Nikolaus Pechstein, and Bernd Seidensticker, *Das griechische Satyrspiel*, Texte zur Forschung, Bd. 72 (Darmstadt: Wissenschaftliche Buchgesellschaft, 1999); and Pierre Voelke, *Un théâtre de la marge: Aspects figuratifs et configurationnels du drame satyrique dans l'Athènes classique* (Bari: Levante, 2001).

19. Euripides, *Cyclops, Alcestis, Medea*, ed. and trans. David Kovacs, Loeb Classical Library (Cambridge, MA: Harvard University Press, 1994).

20. See Horkheimer and Adorno, *Dialectic*, 35; and Paul Lafargue, *The Right to Be Lazy*, ed. Bernard Marszalek (1880, 1883; Chico, CA: AK Press, 2011), a response to "the right to work."

21. Mark Griffith, *Greek Satyr Play* (Berkeley: California Classical Studies, 2015), 8. The book, principally a collection of previously published essays, provides an invaluable survey of the history of scholarship on the satyr play, and an extensive bibliography on this form.

22. Eric Lott, *Love and Theft: Blackface Minstrelsy and the American Working Class* (Oxford: Oxford University Press, 1993).

23. See also Ralph Rosen, who discusses Euripides' *Cyclops* in the context of poetic mockery: "For our purposes, the most significant change from Homer's version [of the Cyclops episode in the *Odyssey*] lies in the portrait of Odysseus as an essentially blameless victim" (*Making Mockery*, 144). For his analysis of the satyr play, see 143–54. He notes: "Euripides is able to clarify the moral and generic ambiguity we find in Homer's version of the story by constructing his own version that draws more straightforwardly on a well-established poetics of satire" (153). It is interesting that Rosen cites "the final lines of the *Cyclops*" (153) as the words of Odysseus in triumph over Polyphemos, omitting the final song of the enslaved satyr chorus, who will still be slaves of Dionysos.

24. David Kawalko Roselli, *Theater of the People: Spectators and Society in Ancient Athens* (Austin: University of Texas Press, 2011).

25. Ralph M. Rosen, "The Greek 'Comic Hero,'" in Revermann, *Cambridge Companion to Greek Comedy*, 222–40.

26. Rosen, "Greek 'Comic Hero,'" 226.

27. As Jeffrey Henderson remarks in an essay on the chorus and the demagogue in Aristophanes' plays, "In Aristophanes' time, officially and theatrically, the chorus was the main event, as it had always been, long before the ascendancy of actors. Its size (24 dancers for comedy), prominent placement, and spectacular activity aside, the chorus was what the poet had 'asked for' and been 'granted' for the competition and what determined victory or failure for the production." Jeffrey Henderson, "The Comic Chorus and the Demagogue," in *Choral Mediations in Greek Tragedy*, ed. Renaud Gagné and Marianne Govers Hopman (Cambridge: Cambridge University Press, 2013), 278–96, here 280.

28. Athenaeus provides excerpts from a comedy by a Kallias entitled *The Alphabetic Tragedy*, in which each female chorus member represented one of the twenty-four letters of the Greek alphabet (Athenaeus 10.453). For more on this, see R. Gagné, "Danc-

ing Letters: The Alphabetic Tragedy of Kallias," in Gagné and Hopman, *Choral Mediations*, 297–316. Gagné suggests tentatively that the figure of the teacher in the play may have been modeled on the poet Sappho, or Psappho, who appeared in other comedies.

29. Rothwell emphasizes the orderly, stratified characteristics of wasp collectivity, but acknowledges as well their "belligerence" when aroused: "They are simultaneously irascible and social"; Kenneth Rothwell, *Nature, Culture, and the Origins of Greek Comedy: A Study of Animal Choruses* (Cambridge: Cambridge University Press, 2007), 107–8. See also K. Reckford, *Aristophanes' Old-and-New Comedy* (Chapel Hill: University of North Carolina Press, 1987), 236.

30. Mark Griffith, *Aristophanes' Frogs* (Oxford: Oxford University Press, 2013), 5.

31. Mel Chen, *Animacies: Biopolitics, Racial Mattering, and Queer Affect* (Durham, NC: Duke University Press, 2012). See also the work of the brilliant critic Mark Payne; for example, his essay "Aetna and Aetnaism: Schiller, Vibrant Matter, and the Phenomenal Regimes of Ancient Poetry," *Helios* 43, no. 2 (Fall 2016): 89–108.

32. See Page duBois, *Centaurs and Amazons: The Prehistory of the Great Chain of Being* (Ann Arbor: University of Michigan Press, 1982).

33. See again duBois, *Centaurs and Amazons*.

34. Aristotle, *Politics*, trans. H. Rackham (London: William Heinemann, 1944).

35. See especially Rothwell, *Nature, Culture*.

36. On the importance of ritual in comedy, see Anton Bierl, *Ritual and Performativity: The Chorus of Old Comedy*, trans. Alexander Hollmann (2001; Washington, DC: Center for Hellenic Studies [Harvard University Press], 2009).

37. Getty Villa 82.AE.83; for discussion of the image see Eric Csapo, "The Iconography of Comedy," in Revermann, *Cambridge Companion to Greek Comedy*, 95–127, esp. 102–4, with illustrations. See also Eric Csapo and W. J. Slater, eds., *The Context of Ancient Drama* (Ann Arbor: University of Michigan Press, 1995); and Martin Revermann, *Comic Business: Theatricality, Dramatic Technique, and Performance Contexts of Aristophanic Comedy* (Oxford: Oxford University Press, 2006).

38. Csapo, "Iconography of Comedy," 103. He makes this observation in relation to the speculation that the previously mentioned vase might show the confrontation between the Greater and Lesser Arguments in Aristophanes' play *Clouds*.

39. On drama in the fourth century BCE, see Csapo et al., *Greek Theatre in the Fourth Century BC*; and Ingo Gildenhard and Martin Revermann, eds., *Beyond the Fifth Century: Interactions with Greek Tragedy from the Fourth Century BCE to the Middle Ages* (Berlin: De Gruyter, 2010).

40. On Roman comedy, see the groundbreaking study of Plautus by Richlin, *Slave Theater*.

41. Susan Lape, *Reproducing Athens: Menander's Comedy, Democratic Culture, and the Hellenistic City* (Princeton, NJ: Princeton University Press, 2003).

42. On further effects of Old Comedy in antiquity, see Anna Peterson, *Laughter on the Fringes: The Reception of Old Comedy in the Imperial Greek World* (Oxford: Oxford University Press, 2019); see also Richlin, *Slave Theater*.

43. Jean-Pierre Vernant, "Tensions and Ambiguities in Greek Tragedy," in Vernant and Vidal-Naquet, *Myth and Tragedy*, 29–48, here 34.

44. Vernant and Vidal-Naquet, *Myth and Tragedy*.

45. See Nicole Loraux, *Tragic Ways of Killing a Woman*, trans. Anthony Foster (Cambridge, MA: Harvard University Press, 1991); and Loraux, *Mothers in Mourning*.

46. See Roland Champagne, *The Methods of the Gernet Classicists: The Structuralists on Myth* (London: Routledge, 2016).

47. Pierre Vidal-Naquet, "Oedipus in Athens," in Vernant and Vidal-Naquet, *Myth and Tragedy*, 301–27, here 311, 312.

48. David Konstan, *Greek Comedy and Ideology* (New York: Oxford University Press, 1995).

49. Simon Goldhill, *The Poet's Voice: Essays on Poetics and Greek Literature* (Cambridge: Cambridge University Press, 1991), 200.

50. This does not mean that Konstan ignores the chorus, but rather that it is secondary to his focus on narrative plot, and character. But see, for example, his astute commentary (19–24) on the chorus of jurymen in the *Wasps*: "Philocleon and the jurors stand not for antinomianism or some abstract state of nature but for an anterior social order" (21); "In *Wasps*, the overdetermined status of the chorus—the conflation of class and generational characteristics—enables a semantic slide by which a problem of class tension is illusorily resolved by the prospect of comfortable retirement, even though this possibility can be realized by only one of the jurors, namely Philocleon" (23). Konstan concurs with G. E. M. de Sainte-Croix that Aristophanes promulgated political views in his plays, and that he saw the system of jury courts as "a form of popular tyranny"; G. E. M. de Sainte-Croix, *The Origins of the Peloponnesian War* (Ithaca, NY: Cornell University Press, 1972), 362. In concluding his analysis of the *Wasps*, Konstan includes a most welcome acknowledgment of the dimensions of class difference, and of the presence of slaves in Athens: "The collapse of the class distinction between Philocleon and his fellow jurors reflects the ideological solidarity among citizens of all classes in Athens as against slaves or resident aliens" (27).

51. Angus Fletcher, *Comic Democracies: From Ancient Athens to the American Republic* (Baltimore: Johns Hopkins University Press, 2016), 6–7.

52. The features that constitute the inheritance Fletcher analyzes include "the comic slave trick of impetuoso," imitatio, indolentia, "Quixotic governance," and "comic self-revision." Fletcher, *Comic Democracies*, 13, 34–135.

53. Fletcher, *Comic Democracies*, 29.

54. Fletcher, 22. Other scholars consider the genre of comedy: Mario Telò, in *Aristophanes and the Cloak of Comedy*, an innovative and provocative analysis of Aristophanes' intentions as playwright, focuses on aesthetics and affect in the *Wasps* and *Clouds* to identify a political desire on the part of the writer to comfort and heal as a "paternal son." His approach, although productive and enriching of our understanding of Aristophanic comedy, differs from mine in its attribution of intention to a version of authority, or authorship, that I find problematic in the context of ancient Greek performance, and especially in relation to the role of the chorus in ancient comedy.

In an analysis of Old Comedy that mines the work of Mikhail Bakhtin for what it can offer to this genre, Charles Platter goes beyond a simple inversion, an interpretation relying on the Saturnalia, the world upside down that some scholars have used to discuss Aristophanic practices; Charles Platter, *Aristophanes and the Carnival of Genres* (Baltimore: Johns Hopkins University Press, 2007). Pointing to what he terms the "carnivalization" of genres, Platter demonstrates the densities of intertextuality, generic reference, and appropriation, in the texts of Aristophanes. He notes that 'the competitive pressures on Aristophanic comedy did not allow it to be complacently in the service of a single ideology" (184n7). Platter traces allusions and borrowings and parody in the comedies of tragedy, other comedians' works, of epic, of lyric, all producing a hybrid and complex artifact: "Views concerning the specific socio-political orientation of Aristophanic comedy benefit from an approach predicated on the notion that the work of Aristophanes lies at the nexus of conflicting forces and that it stages their intense, if unstable interaction" (37). I share Platter's sense of the conflict and instability in the plays, although my emphasis is somewhat different from his, relying as it does on a sense of the chorus in particular as providing a collective presence that undermines the purported intention or message of the plays, or of their comic heroes.

Platter insists on the inconsistency of the comedies: "Although it is generally conceded that Aristophanic humor works on multiple levels, criticism of the plays nevertheless often assumes a consistent trajectory and treats the plays' cultural meanings, their various political affiliations and literary allegiances, as fixed and knowable.... Monolithic theses about Aristophanic comedy are impossible to maintain with consistency" (179). Relying on such varied philological dating as the presence of "lyric" alphas in the chorus of the *Clouds*, Platter usefully undermines a version of the work of Aristophanes that finds "authorial" intention and stability in the plays.

55. G. M. Sifakis, *Parabasis and Animal Choruses: A Contribution to the History of Attic Comedy* (London: Athlone Press [University of London], 1971).

56. Csapo, "Iconography of Comedy."

57. Bierl, *Ritual and Performativity*, x.

58. Richard Seaford, "The Politics of the Mystic Chorus," in Billings, Budelmann, and Macintosh, *Choruses*, 261–79, discusses a very different aspect of the chorus, focusing on Aristophanes' *Frogs*, again a comedy about tragedy: "The political significance of the ancient Greek χορος (a group that sings and dances) is based in part on its implicit claim to public space" (261); "In *Frogs*, ... the mystic chorus seems to embody the whole polis" (275); "The singing and dancing group had in the classical polis an importance that is entirely unknown in mainstream monotheism"; "based on the implicit claim of the group to space (and time)"; the mystic chorus "a transcendent model of happy cohesion" (279).

Sifakis argues with regard to the parabasis that it does not entail a breaking of the dramatic "illusion" of the plays, but rather there is no "illusion" involved in their production: "My contention is that illusion as a psychological phenomenon was entirely alien to Greek theatrical audiences and that the use of the term with reference to Greek drama is an anachronism" (*Parabasis*, 7). Contemporary theater audiences, accustomed to realistic stage presentations, mistake the nature of the dramatic performances of antiquity. Sifakis notes, for example, that the ancient dramas were performed outdoors, in sunlight (10). And Greek drama was what Sifakis terms "conventional," that is, entailing a sort of contract between audience and actors, making the drama by definition "unrealistic and, in consequence, anti-illusionistic": "The spectators are constantly aware that the actors represent, that is, pretend to be, the characters of a play" (11). There is constant interaction in comedy between the audience and the actors, jokes and speeches addressed to the spectators, incorporation of audience reaction into the performance. Sifakis calls this a "dialogue," the performance a "game," based on direct communication (11–12). Sifakis makes these points in part to critique interpretations of the parabasis that link it as a particular, archaic element of the comedies, based on ancient ritual practices.

Sifakis analyzes the specific nature of the comic chorus, which, because it is a group standing between the actors and the audience, is enabled "to identify sometimes with the characters of the play, sometimes with the group of performers, and at other times with the public" (23). In the earlier parts of the comedies, the choruses exhibit their specific character; after the parabasis these characteristics are played down to enable the identification of the chorus with the Athenian spectators before them: "In none of the comedies does the chorus have a consistent and unalterable dramatic character" (32). And the parabasis is demonstrably not an archaic, vestigial part of the comedies, in Sifakis's view.

59. Roselli, *Theater of the People*; see also Roselli, "Social Class," in Revermann, *Cambridge Companion to Greek Comedy*, 241–58, with additional bibliography.

60. Euripides, vol. 3, *Hecuba, Andromache, The Trojan Women, Ion*, ed. David Grene and Richmond Lattimore, *Hecuba*, trans. William Arrowsmith (Chicago: University of Chicago Press, 1958).

61. For speculation and reconstruction concerning the end of this play, the lines of which are full of lacunae, see Richard Seaford, ed., Euripides, *Bacchae* (Liverpool: Aris and Phillips, 1996).

62. Aristophanes, *Birds, Lysistrata, Women at the Thesmophoria*, ed. and trans. Jeffrey Henderson, Loeb Classical Library (Cambridge, MA: Harvard University Press, 2000). Henderson's translation of these plays is used throughout unless otherwise indicated.

63. See duBois, *Sowing*, 39–85.

64. Aristophanes, *Lysistrata*, ed. and trans. Henderson, 383n83.

65. Konstan, *Greek Comedy and Ideology*, 60.

66. On the question of female and other excluded groups, as characters, enacting politics in tragedy, see Edith Hall, "The Sociology of Athenian Tragedy," in *The Cambridge Companion to Greek Tragedy*, ed. P. E. Easterling (Cambridge: Cambridge University Press, 1997), 93–126: "Non-Athenians, women, and slaves were in reality excluded from the assembly and normally had to be represented by a citizen in the lawcourts.... Yet, paradoxically, the fictional representatives of these groups, silenced in the public discourse of the city, are permitted by the multivocal form of tragedy to address the public in the theatre as they never could in reality" (93); "Greek tragedy does its thinking in a form which is vastly more politically advanced than the society which produced Greek tragedy" (125).

67. See duBois, *Sowing*, 65–85.

68. See Sean Gurd's discussion in *Dissonance*, 56–57; "Both Aristophanes and his demagogic targets evince the same uneasy ability to seem both the safeguards of civic order and a dangerous, destabilizing force. Noise occurs on both sides of this 'opposition'" (57).

69. Page duBois, *Torture and Truth* (1991; repr., London: Routledge, 2016).

70. Vincent Azoulay and Paulin Ismard, *Athènes 403: Une histoire chorale* (Paris: Flammarion, 2020). Along with statesmen, orators, and Socrates, they also include "Le chœur domestique" of the wife Hegeso, and the slave Gerys, "marchand de legumes," part of the polyphony of the city.

CHAPTER 4

1. See Rusten, *Birth*, 158–60, here 158–59.

2. Douglas M. MacDowell, *Aristophanes and Athens: An Introduction to the Plays* (Oxford: Oxford University Press, 1995).

3. On slaves in combat, see Peter Hunt, *Slaves, Warfare, and Ideology in the Greek Historians* (Cambridge: Cambridge University Press, 1998).

4. MacDowell takes these proposals with some seriousness, but also notes that "the enfranchisement of all slaves volunteering for naval service, if it had been made a permanent arrangement . . . would have produced a big drop in the number of slaves, and it is not surprising that the Athenians did not adopt this suggestion" (*Aristophanes and Athens*, 287). It is noteworthy that although this is a utopian suggestion, potentially eroding the reliance on slave labor in the *polis*, female slaves would of course not be eligible for this release from slavery.

5. Cited by Kishani Witnaratya, Verso blog post 10/11/2014, with video. See Judith Butler, *Notes Toward a Performative Theory of Assembly* (Cambridge, MA: Harvard University Press, 2015), for further deliberation on the concept of "the people": "Acting in concert can be an embodied form of calling into question the inchoate and powerful dimensions of reigning notions of the political" (9).

6. Gregory Claeys and Lyman Tower Sargent, *The Utopia Reader*, 2nd ed. (New York: New York University Press, 2017), 528.

7. Claeys and Sargent, *Utopia Reader*, 528.

8. See, for example, during the protests over the murder of George Floyd in Minneapolis, John Eligon and Kimiko de Freytas-Tamura, "Today's Activism: Spontaneous, Leaderless, but Not without Aim," *New York Times*, June 4, 2020: "Social media is the strongest organizer. At the core is an egalitarian spirit, a belief that everyone's voice matters"; "The absence of organized leadership does not mean the movements—from the Arab Spring to Occupy Wall Street to Black Lives Matter—are rudderless." Note that this article was published on the thirtieth anniversary of the Tian an Men demonstrations, and massacre, which was marked also by memorial protests forbidden by the Chinese government in 2020.

9. Darko Suvin, an important theorist of utopia, and of science fiction, uses "Utopia" to refer only to More's text, and a lowercase "utopia" for all other references. For a useful survey of his views on utopia, see Suvin, "Defining the Literary Genre of Utopia: Some Historical Semantics, Some Genology, a Proposal, and a Plea," in *Defined by a Hollow: Essays on Utopia, Science Fiction, and Political Epistemology* (Bern: Peter Lang, 2010), 17–48: utopia is "a literary genre, induced from a set of man-made books within a man-made history" (43). Suvin notes that utopia is always aimed at human relations, but its characters do not have to be human or even outwardly anthropomorphic (41).

10. In a vast bibliography, see Fredric Jameson, *Archaeologies of the Future: The Desire Called Utopia and Other Science Fictions* (London: Verso, 2007).

11. Rhiannon Evans, *Utopia Antiqua: Readings of the Golden Age and Decline at Rome* (New York: Routledge, 2008). See also Edward J. Watts, *The Eternal Decline and Fall of Rome: The History of a Dangerous Idea* (Oxford: Oxford University Press, 2021).

12. Evans, *Utopia Antiqua*, 2–3.

13. Doyne Dawson, *Cities of the Gods: Communist Utopias in Greek Thought* (Oxford: Oxford University Press, 1992).

14. Claeys and Sargent, *Utopia Reader*, 39.

15. Claeys and Sargent, *Utopia Reader*, 68.

16. Athenaeus 6.267E, describing life without work; cited with translation in Rusten, *Birth*, 139.

17. Herbert Marcuse, *Eros and Civilization: A Philosophical Inquiry into Freud* (Boston: Beacon Press, 1955); Aaron Bastani, *Fully Automated Luxury Communism: A Man-

ifesto (London: Verso, 2019), esp. chap. 4, "Full Automation: Post-Scarcity in Labour," 69–93. And "the return of 'the people' as the main political actor is inevitable, whether as the rabble who patrician elites defend from their own desires, the Volk grounded in land, blood and soil, as witnessed in the revival of the far right, or the masses as a potentially transformative subject which makes history" (Bastani, 191). See also Rutger Bregman, *Utopia for Realists: How We Can Build the Ideal World*, trans. Elizabeth Manton (New York: Back Bay [Little, Brown], 2018), who ends his book with this advice: "Cultivate a thicker skin. Don't let anyone tell you what's what. If we want to change the world, we need to be unrealistic, unreasonable, and impossible" (264).

18. See Mario Telò and Melissa Mueller, eds., *The Materialities of Greek Tragedy: Objects and Affect in Aeschylus, Sophocles, and Euripides* (Oxford: Bloomsbury Academic, 2019).

19. Rusten, *Birth*, 144–45.

20. Tom Moylan, *Demand the Impossible: Science Fiction and the Utopian Imagination* (London: Methuen, 1986); reprinted with additions and commentary, ed. Rafaelle Baccollini (Oxford: Peter Lang, 2014), 1. In the reprinted edition of this much-cited text, Moylan quotes his own earlier formulation, generated by speculative fiction novels of the 1970s: "A central concern in the critical utopia is the awareness of the limitations of the utopian tradition, so that these texts reject utopia as a blueprint while preserving it as a dream. Furthermore, the novels dwell on the conflict between the originary world and the utopian society opposed to it so that the process of social change is more directly articulated. Finally, the novels focus on the continuing presence of difference and imperfection within utopian society itself and thus render more recognizable and dynamic alternatives" (10–11).

21. Claeys and Sargent, *Utopia Reader*, 1–2.

22. Moylan, *Demand the Impossible* (2014), xv.

23. Ernst Bloch, in the second volume of his *Principle of Hope*, calls the *Birds* Aristophanes' "malicious comedy." Writing of the Greek hedonist conceptions of the golden age, Bloch explains: "The image of pleasure became a rebellious one in the play in so far as it was never accommodated, never remained undisturbed. After all, the heroes of the comedy . . . decided to remain in the clouds with the birds and to propose that they found a new state in the air. Yet the different, considerably more earthly and actually existing utopia of that time is also already cited in the comedy" (2:484). Aristophanes in Bloch's view is satirizing the democratic betrayal of the hedonist ideal. He also sees Aristophanes as mocking the women of the *Ecclesiazusae* (591), and in general "rebelling" against his own times (432).

24. Robert C. Elliott, "The Nature of Satire," *Encyclopædia Britannica* (2004).

25. Tom Moylan, *Dark Horizons: Science Fiction and the Dystopian Imagination* (New York: Routledge, 2003).

26. See Froma Zeitlin, "Travesties of Gender and genre in Aristophanes' *Thesmophoriazusae*," in *Playing the Other: Gender and Society in Classical Greek Literature* (Chicago: University of Chicago Press, 1996), 375–416.

27. Alan Sommerstein, "The Politics of Greek Comedy," in Revermann, *Cambridge Companion to Greek Comedy*, 298. In his essay in *The Imaginary Polis*, Sommerstein argues concerning the two "imaginary" *poleis* of Aristophanes, in the *Birds* and *Ecclesiazusae*: "Both in Nephelokokkygia and in Gynaikopolis, effective rulership is in the hands of one person"; Sommerstein, "Nephelokokkygia and Gynaikopolis: Aristophanes' Dream Cities," in *The Imaginary Polis*, ed. M. H. Hansen (Copenhagen: Royal

Danish Academy of Arts and Sciences, 2005), 73–99, here 76. He continues: "All in all, then, we find that just as Peisetairos took sole power in the name of the birds and used it to benefit men (and especially himself), so Praxagora, taking sole power in the name of the women, has used it mainly to benefit men (and perhaps, to a limited extent, herself).... Old Comedy presents its audiences with fantasies of felicity for people like themselves.... the answer to our question 'who for whom?' turns out to be: one person (the comic hero) rules for the benefit of the average male citizen" (87–88).

28. Ian Ruffell, "Utopianism," in Revermann, *Cambridge Companion to Greek Comedy*, 206–21, here 206.

29. Fredric Jameson, *The Seeds of Time* (New York: Columbia University Press, 1994), pt. 2, "Utopia, Modernism, and Death," 73–128.

30. See William Fitzgerald, *Variety: The Life of a Roman Concept* (Chicago: University of Chicago Press, 2016).

31. François Hartog, *The Mirror of Herodotus: The Representation of the Other in the Writing of History*, trans. Janet Lloyd (Berkeley: University of California Press, 2009).

32. On ancient utopian thinking, see the brilliant and underappreciated book by Doyne Dawson, *Cities of the Gods: Communist Utopias in Greek Thought* (Oxford: Oxford University Press, 1992).

33. Alain Badiou, *Plato's Republic: A Dialogue in Sixteen Chapters*, trans. Susan Spitzer, intro. Kenneth Reinhard (New York: Columbia University Press, 2012). Badiou's republic emphasizes education and a communism that will come to include all.

34. Alain Badiou, *The Communist Hypothesis*, trans. David Macey (London: Verso, 2010), 278, emphasis mine.

35. Plato, *The Republic*, vol. 1, trans. Paul Shorey, Loeb Classical Library (Cambridge, MA: Harvard University Press, 1969).

36. He also cites an article he published in 1906, in the *Independent*, vol. lx, 253–56: "Plato and His Lessons for Today."

37. Dawson, *Cities of the Gods*, 63.

38. Cited in Badiou, *Plato's Republic*, 361–62n7.

39. Stewart M. Cameron, "Cinderella Revisited," *British Medical Journal* 331 (7531), December 24–31, 2005, 1543–44.

40. Jameson, "The Politics of Utopia," *New Left Review* 25 (2004): 35–54, here 42. Citing Louis Marin on utopia, he thinks: "Utopia is somehow negative.... It is most authentic when we cannot imagine it. Its function lies not in helping us to imagine a better future but rather in demonstrating our utter incapacity to imagine such a future—-our imprisonment in a non-utopian present without historicity or futurity—so as to reveal the ideological closure of the system in which we are somehow trapped and confined" (47).

41. Roselli, "Social Class," 241–58. See also Roselli, *Theater of the People*.

42. Roselli, "Social Class," 246.

43. But see Peter Wilson, "The Glue of Democracy? Tragedy, Structure, and Finance," in *Why Athens?: A Reappraisal of Tragic Politics*, ed. D. M. Carter (Oxford: Oxford University Press, 2011), 19–43, esp. 39–43. Wilson explains: "To my mind the most likely scenario is that at least some distributions were in fact made in the fifth century, probably as the result of one-off decrees that individual politicians managed to author in their own names. The silence of Old Comedy has seemed significant to many, but we should remember that no comedies survive from the 440s–430s. And I think there is still a good case to make that 'those two obols that have such power everywhere' that

Dionysos is surprised to hear of from Heracles in the Underworld on his katabasis in the *Frogs* (140–42) may have one layer, among others, of theatrical-theoric reference" (41).

44. Raymond Williams, *Marxism and Literature* (Toronto: Oxford University Press, 1977).

45. Roselli, "Social Class," 253.

46. See especially Rothwell, *Nature, Culture*.

47. Getty Villa 82.AE.83; for discussion on the image, see Csapo, "Iconography of comedy," 95–127, esp. 102–4, with illustrations. See also Csapo and Slater, *Context of Ancient Drama*; Revermann, *Comic Business*; and the extended discussion by Gwendolyn Compton-Engle, *Costume in the Comedies of Aristophanes* (Cambridge: Cambridge University Press, 2015), 129–43, with illustrations including cloaked bird figures in early comedy.

48. See Carol Dougherty, *The Poetics of Colonization: From City to Text in Ancient Greece* (Oxford: Oxford University Press, 1993); Denise Demetriou, *Negotiating Identity in the Ancient Mediterranean: The Archaic and Classical Greek Multiethnic Emporia* (Cambridge: Cambridge University Press, 2013).

49. Gurd, *Dissonance*, 134.

50. See Gurd, *Dissonance*, 55: the cry of the frogs "derives much of its significance from the fact that it comes from the outside of human language: it paradoxically embodies both a pure music and a pure sound or noise."

51. Compton-Engle, *Costume*, 129. Compton-Engle comments further: "*Birds* presents the reverse dynamic from that of choral stripping or weakened choral identity: rather than the chorus losing its costume or identity, virtually everyone else in the play wants to gain those items of costume (wings in particular) and the powers that come with them" (129). Compton-Engle comments on the beaks, which "most often signify danger and hostility" (130), and the wings of the chorus and actors.

52. Kristin Ross, *Communal Luxury: The Political Imaginary of the Paris Commune* (London: Verso, 2015).

53. Aristophanes, *Birds*, ed. and trans. Henderson, 123n61.

54. Aristophanes, *Fragments*, ed. and trans. Jeffrey Henderson, Loeb Classical Library (Cambridge, MA: Harvard University Press, 2008); Koster, *Prolegomena*, 5.

55. Koster, *Prolegomena* (XXXa).

56. On tattooed slaves, see duBois, *Slaves*, 3, 4–5, 106–9, 122.

57. See duBois, *Slaves*, passim.

58. See, for example, Jane Bennett, *Vibrant Matter: A Political Ecology of Things* (Durham, NC: Duke University Press, 2010); and Chen, *Animacies*, with their extensive bibliographies mapping the extent of this new tendency in thinking about matter. As to the classics and the new materialism, see Telò and Mueller, *Materialities of Greek Tragedy*.

59. Mark Payne, *The Animal Part: Human and Other Animals in the Poetic Imagination* (Chicago: University of Chicago Press, 2010); Donna Haraway, *The Companion Species Manifesto: Dogs, People, and Significant Otherness* (Chicago: PricklyParadigm Press, 2003).

60. Ashley Clements, "Divine Scents and Presence," in *Smell and the Ancient Senses*, ed. Mark Bradley (London: Routledge, 2015), 46–59, here 53.

61. On the metic, see Demetra Kasimis, *The Perpetual Immigrant and the Limits of Athenian Democracy* (Cambridge: Cambridge University Press, 2019).

62. See Carol Dougherty, *The Poetics of Colonization: From City to Text in Archaic Greece* (Oxford: Oxford University Press, 1993).

63. David Konstan concludes concerning the *Birds*: "The city of the birds . . . is . . . simultaneously a token of the golden age, in which people lived in harmony and the earth spontaneously yielded its bounty, and a well-ordered civic community from which the tensions and litigiousness of Athens . . . are banished. But the inscription of a restrospective [*sic*] ideal of complete sufficiency into the differentiated and competitive structure of a civic polity offers the promise of fulfillment to an unlimited desire for mastery. . . . The city of the birds is contradictory" (*Greek Comedy*, 43–44).

64. Althusser, "Piccolo Teatro," 142.

65. For a fascinating and beautiful account of the place of birds in antiquity, see Jeremy Mynott, *Birds in the Ancient World* (Oxford: Oxford University Press, 2018); Mynott lists all the birds named in Aristophanes' works, many of which also appear in Aesop. The francolin (*attagas*) is offered among the wares of a Boeotian trader in the *Acharnians* (878); Mynott cites Pliny's *Natural History* 10.133–35: "The francolin is a very famous Ionian bird. It is normally very vocal but when captured falls silent" (Mynott, 101). Rather than this exotic fare, Horace would rather eat olives from his own trees (*Epodes* 2.53–56).

66. Eduardo Viveiros de Castro, *Cannibal Metaphysics: For a Post-structural Anthropology*, trans. Peter Skafish (Minneapolis: University of Minnesota Press, 2014 [2009]), 72. On the "New World," see the thought-provoking work by Mark Payne, *Hontology: Depressive Anthropology and the Shame of Life* (Alresford, Hants.: Zero Books, 2018).

67. Payne, *Animal Part*, 88.

68. Payne, 99.

69. See, for examples, Helene Foley, *Reimagining Greek Tragedy on the American Stage* (Berkeley: University of California Press, 2012).

70. Gonda Van Steen, "From Scandal to Success Story: Aristophanes' Birds as Staged by Karolos Koun," in Hall and Wrigley, *Aristophanes in Performance*, 154–78, here 157.

71. P. Mitchell in *The Argus*, August 22, 1980, cited by Betine van Zyl Smit, "Freeing Aristophanes in South Africa," in Hall and Wrigley, *Performances of Aristophanes*, 232–46, here 236.

72. Francesca Schironi, "A Poet without 'Gravity': Aristophanes on the Italian Stage," in Hall and Wrigley, *Aristophanes in Performance*, 267–75, here 267–68.

73. Sean O'Brien, "A Version of the *Birds* in Two Productions," Hall and Wrigley, *Aristophanes in Performance*, 276–86, here 283.

74. Martina Treu, "Poetry and Politics, Advice and Abuse: The Aristophanic Chorus on the Italian Stage," in Hall and Wrigley, *Aristophanes in Performance*, 255–66, here 263. See also Martina Treu, *Undici cori comici: Aggressività, derisione et techniche drammatiche in Aristofane* (Genoa: Universita di Genova, 1999).

75. Treu, "Poetry and Politics," 262.

76. Bill McKibben, *Radio Free Vermont: A Fable of Resistance* (New York: Blue Rider Press, 2017), 219.

CHAPTER 5

1. For a rich and detailed examination of the question of "free" speech in the ancient world, see Ineke Sluiter and Ralph M. Rosen, eds., *Free Speech in Classical Antiquity*,

Mnemosyne Supplement 254 (Leiden: Brill, 2004). The introduction contains information on the semantics of *parrhesia* (4–8), and includes examples of disapprobation of "free" or "frank" speech, including passages in Plato (*Phaedrus* 240e6) and in the orator Isocrates. "In democratic ideology," the authors observe, "parrhēsia is a positive value, and again this positive evaluation is mostly emphatically reinforced by the context: people 'flourish' in their parrhêsia, it is associated with the courageous expression of one's beliefs, however unpopular they may be. It always involves frankness, and the full disclosure of one's thoughts—in that sense it is opposed to dissimulation, hiding one's real thoughts or the unpleasant truth, or to silence applied as a discourse strategy to get one's way, as the strategy of a 'moderate politician', or as the despicable attitude of someone lacking in political commitment" (6–7). On free speech in Old Comedy, see, in this volume, especially Stephen Halliwell, "Aischrology, Shame, and Comedy" (115–45), and Alan H. Sommerstein, "Harassing the Satirist: The Alleged Attempts to Prosecute Aristophanes" (145–74). Kurt Raaflaub, in "Aristocracy and Freedom of Speech," also in this volume (41–62), discusses the development of the concept of free speech, from *eleutheros legein* (to speak "freely," that is, as a free person as opposed to a slave) to *isegoria* (equal freedom of speech) to *parrhesia* (frankness, saying it all, license to speak), and why the aristocracy of the Greek *polis* did not produce a counter term, an aristocratic version of *parrhesia*, which remained a democratic concept: "For aristocrats the crucial issue was not freedom, which only described a necessary precondition of their high status and the absence of oppressive authoritarian power. What mattered to them was that they were part of an exclusive group who shared power and government and in that sense were equal—even if within this framework they competed fiercely for primacy. Excellence, power, and equality thus were prime aristocratic values" (57–58). See also the essay by D. M. Carter in this volume, "Citizen Attribute, Negative Right" (197–220), and that of Robert W. Wallace, "The Power to Speak—and Not to Listen—in Ancient Athens" (221–32). See also S. Sara Monoson, "Frank Speech, Democracy, and Philosophy: Plato's Debt to a Democratic Strategy of Civic Discourse," in *Athenian Political Thought and the Reconstruction of American Democracy*, ed. J. P. Euben, J. R. Wallach, and J. Ober (Ithaca, NY: Cornell University Press, 1994), 172–197; and Arlene Saxonhouse, *Free Speech and Athenian Democracy* (Cambridge: Cambridge University Press, 2008), especially 134–38, on the *Thesmophoriazusae*: "The contest in the *Thesmophoriazusae* is between comedy and tragedy as to who owns the franchise to beneficial parrhesia" (138). For a later ancient reflection on *parrhesia*, see Philodemos (110–35 BCE), *On Frank Criticism*, trans. David Konstan et al. (Atlanta: Society of Biblical Literature, 1998).

2. There is an immense bibliography on this question, including Stanley Fish's *There's No Such Thing as Free Speech . . . and It's a Good Thing Too* (Oxford: Oxford University Press, 2004).

3. Michel Foucault, *The History of Sexuality*, vol. 1, *An Introduction*, trans. R. Hurley (1976; New York: Vintage, 1990); vol. 2, *The Use of Pleasure*, trans. R. Hurley (1984; New York: Vintage, 1990); vol. 3, *The Care of the Self*, trans. R. Hurley (1984; New York: Vintage, 1988).

4. Michel Foucault, *The Hermeneutics of the Subject: Lectures at the Collège de France 1981–1982*, ed. Frédéric Gros, trans. Graham Burchell (2001; New York: Palgrave Macmillan, 2005).

5. Foucault, *Hermeneutics*, 406.

6. See Arnaldo Momigliano, "La libertà di parola nel mondo antico," *Rivista storica italiana* 83 (1971): 499–524.

7. Michel Foucault, *Fearless Speech*, ed. Joseph Pearson (Los Angeles, CA: Semiotext(e), 2001), 27. This book consists of the record of tape-recorded lectures made at UC Berkeley in 1983, part of the seminar "Discourse and Truth." On the parrhesiast: "The one who uses *parrhesia*, the *parrhesiastes*, is someone who says everything he has in mind" (12).

8. Foucault, *Fearless Speech*, 19–20; see also Michel Foucault, *The Government of Self and Others*, ed. F. Gros, trans. Graham Burchell (2008; New York: Palgrave Macmillan, 2010), lectures of 1983; Foucault, *The Courage of Truth: The Government of Self and Others II*, ed. F. Gros, trans. Graham Burchell (2008; New York: Palgrave Macmillan, 2011), a record of the lectures of 1983–84, in which Foucault recounts the "genealogy of the study of *parrhesia*," reminds the reader of the political origin of the term, and lists its "structural features," i.e., "truth, commitment, and risk," and goes on to discuss its appearance in tragic and philosophical works. He notes that *parrhesia* can be found "used in a pejorative sense, first in Aristophanes, and afterward very commonly, even in Christian literature. Used in a pejorative sense, *parrhesia* does indeed consist in saying everything, but in the sense of saying anything (anything that comes to mind, anything that serves the cause one is defending, anything that serves the passion or the interest driving the person who is speaking). The parrhesiast then becomes and appears as the impenitent [*sic*] chatterbox, someone who cannot restrain himself or, at any rate, someone who cannot index-link his discourse to a principle of rationality and truth" (9–10).

9. In *Courage of Truth*, as noted above, Foucault mentions Aristophanes in passing: "I think we find it [*parrhesia*] used in a pejorative sense, first in Aristophanes, and afterwards very commonly, even in Christian literature" (9).

10. "In the Greek conception of *parrhesia* . . . there does not seem to be a problem about the acquisition of the truth since such truth-having is guaranteed by the possession of certain moral qualities" (*Fearless Speech*, 15). The parrhesiast is moral, courageous, takes a risk, is in all likelihood a philosopher, perhaps an orator, speaking to a superior, to someone more powerful and in extreme cases, risking death (18). And "telling the truth is regarded as a duty" (19).

11. Euripides, *Children of Heracles, Hippolytus, Andromache, Hecuba*, ed. and trans. David Kovacs, Loeb Classical Library (Cambridge, MA: Harvard University Press, 1995).

12. On this play, see Zeitlin, "Travesties," 375–416.

13. Euripides, vol. 3, *Hecuba, Andromache, Trojan Women, Ion*, ed. David Grene and Richmond Lattimore, *Ion*, trans. Ronald Frederick Willetts (Chicago: University of Chicago Press, 1958).

14. See duBois, *Slaves*; and duBois, *Slavery: Antiquity and Its Legacy* (London: I.B. Tauris, 2009).

15. Euripides had a fondness for this word, and for the concept; he uses it in the *Phoenician Women* 391. The queen of Thebes, Oedipus's mother and wife, interrogates her son Polyneices:

> Jocasta: What is it like? What annoys the exile? [390]
> Polyneices: One thing most of all; he cannot speak his mind.
> Jocasta: This is a slave's lot you speak of, not to say what one thinks.

Once again, the discourse of *parrhesia* is implicated in the language of slavery and freedom, this defining opposition. One stays in one's own city because it is there that one has the freedom to speak, to say all, something that is denied to a slave, or to an exile living in a foreign city. For the Greeks, it is not only Hellenicity that comes to matter, but also, perhaps most, the free citizenship of one's own particular *polis*. *Parrhesia* forms part of the network of rights and privileges that define a citizen's political identity.

Parrhesia is mentioned again in the *Bacchae* (668), and here it is probably a slave, the messenger who brings to the king of Thebes, Pentheus, news of the ecstatic celebrations of the bacchantes on Mount Parnassos, who asks to speak with *parrhesia*, fearing the wrath and vengeance of his ruler:

> Having seen the holy Bacchae, who [665] goaded to madness have darted from this land with their fair feet, I have come to tell you and the city, lord, that they are doing terrible things, beyond marvel. I wish to hear whether I should tell you in free speech (*parrhesia*) the situation there or whether I should repress my report, [670] for I fear, lord, the quickness of your mood, your keen temper and your too imperious disposition. (trans. Arrowsmith)

The messenger's apprehension, characteristic of such scenes, which border sometimes on comedy, here shows the limits of *parrhesia*, those to whom it is allowed, those to whom it is customarily forbidden; a slave could not appeal to the right to *parrhesia*.

16. A frustrating aspect of Foucault's work on Greek antiquity, characteristic also of his book *The Use of Pleasures*, concerning the management of the self in classical Greece, is that is conceived not immanently, not focused on the mentality of the world he is describing, but always with a gaze toward the future, the Hellenistic, Roman, Christian, then psychoanalytic present. A gravitational pull marks his careful, meticulous readings of the classical Greek texts, toward the observations and interventions he desires to make concerning the twentieth century, that seems at times to mark his understanding of the classical material. He tends to privilege the philosophical works of the fourth century, Plato's, and Aristotle's, and to neglect the historical writings of Herodotus, for example, and the forensic orators whose speeches are invaluable sources for everyday life in the democratic city. Some of the anecdotal evidence he presents, even for the fifth century, comes from much later thinkers, such as Plutarch, who is a citizen of the Roman Empire, remote from the experimentation and radicalism of fifth-century Athenian democracy. And I detect a strong tide toward an idealization of Socrates, who emerges in the *Courage of Truth* as an avatar of Foucault himself, but also as a saint, a martyr. There is an aspect of denegation, of paradoxical denial in Foucault's description of Socrates, dependent on Georges Dumézil's discussion of Socrates' last words in the *Phaedo*: "No doubt Socrates—without, of course, having been the victim of temptation (*tentation*), it is not a question of that—might to some extent also have been persuaded by Crito and could have decided to escape" (108). "Victim of temptation," the term echoes a Christian vocabulary. Foucault also refers to Socrates' followers: "As death approaches, what does Socrates say to his disciples (*disciples*) in his next to last words?" (111). The rhyming with the martyrdom of Jesus is for me an insistent undercurrent in Foucault's view of Socrates. The fifth century BCE, the age of Socrates rather than Plato, is inevitably being drawn into another history, that of the development of Roman philosophy and its integration into Christian theology. The politics of the fifth-century democracy is enlisted for this narrative of longer duration.

17. Isocrates, *On the Peace, Areopagiticus, Against the Sophists, Antidosis, Panathenaicus*, trans. George Norlin, Loeb Classical Library (Cambridge, MA: Harvard University

Press, 1929), 8.14, pp. 14–15. The word translated here as "the comic poets" is *komoidodidaskalois*, the maker of comedies who had to train the choruses and the actors.

18. Aristophanes, *Acharnians, Knights*, ed. and trans. Jeffrey Henderson, Loeb Classical Library (Cambridge, MA: Harvard University Press, 1998). Henderson's translation of these plays is used throughout unless otherwise indicated.

19. Telò, *Aristophanes and the Cloak of Comedy*.

20. Henderson, *Maculate Muse*, 213–14.

21. On the question of Aristophanes' liability to prosecution, see Sommerstein, "Harassing the Satirist," 145–74.

22. One aspect of this question is treated by Paulin Ismard, *Democracy's Slaves: A Political History of Ancient Greece*, trans. Jane Marie Todd (Cambridge, MA: Harvard University Press, 2017). See also Hunt, *Ancient Greek and Roman Slavery*, and *Slaves, Warfare, and Ideology*.

23. See Mark Griffith on the relationship of the classical Greeks to cherished horses and their kind: "Horsepower and Donkeywork: Equids in the Ancient Greek Imagination," pt. 1, *Classical Philology* 101, no. 3 (2006): 185–246; pt. 2, 101, no. 4 (2006): 307–58.

24. On this comic poet, see Bakola, *Cratinus and the Art of Comedy*. Sean Gurd discusses this scene in *Dissonance*, 54–55.

25. Fredric Jameson, "Reification and Utopia in Mass Culture," *Social Text* 1 (1979): 141.

26. Later, in the fourth century it seems, and perhaps already in some "Old" comedies, *parrhesia* comes to be seen as a negative, a reckless, verbally violent, and destructive practice that undermines civility. Plato uses it in the *Phaedrus* (240e), where it is shaded with disapproval, connoting, according to LSJ "licence of tongue," and Isocrates deploys it in a critical phrase, "loose talk, perhaps, or unseemly frankness concerning the gods" (11.40). In the *Republic*, at 557b, Plato seems to deplore the fact that Athens is "stuffed" with *parrhesia*.

27. Halliwell, "Aischrology," 135.

28. Halliwell, 137.

29. Halliwell, 140.

30. Sommerstein, "Harassing the Satirist," 167.

31. Wallace, "Power to Speak," 221–32.

32. Wallace, "Power to Speak," 227. Sean Gurd implicitly alludes to class difference in *Dissonance*: "The culture in which Greek poets and composers operated consistently aligned the presence of sound with the over-turning of order. . . . Society, culture, and peace were on the side of silence (or at least of radically controlled, 'cooked' sound), while monsters, the wilds, and war roared with raw noise. But song violated this opposition, countering social expectation with auditory disruption and creating a vital dissonance" (11). The songs of the comic chorus are especially dissonant. See also the description of the passage in the *Acharnians* recording the sounds of war preparation (50). Gurd characterizes Aristophanes' ambivalence toward the noisiness of democracy and its "populist" leaders: "Aristophanes's diagnosis of the noisiness of populist politics . . . may not be simply a conservative attack on democratic politics, but an acknowledgment of the auditory investments of rhetorical craft. Cleon and Paphlagon are noisy not because they are unscrupulous leaders of the demos but because they are artists" (52). But of course the choruses of comedy are noisy, sounding, artful as well. Gurd

notes "Aristophanes's own uneasy position between the noise of power and the noise of critique. At once a sophisticated form of abuse and a partisan form of advocacy for peace and the polis, Aristophanic comedy might be said to both thunder in the name of Olympian order and to caw like crows at its opponents" (53–54).

33. Butler, *Excitable Speech*, 163.

CHAPTER 6

1. Rancière, *Disagreement*; and Rancière, *Hatred of Democracy*, trans. Steve Corcoran (2005; London: Verso, 2006).

2. Jason Brennan, *Against Democracy* (Princeton, NJ: Princeton University Press, 2016).

3. Garett Jones, *10% Less Democracy: Why You Should Trust Elites a Little More and the Masses a Little Less* (Stanford, CA: Stanford University Press, 2020), 1. Jones describes the storm of internet hatred that came upon him after "misreporting" of his ideas. Jones is the author of *Hive Mind: How Your Nation's IQ Matters So Much More Than Your Own* (Stanford, CA: Stanford University Press, 2014), a book on swarm intelligence that argues for a national IQ, the notion that your neighbors may have higher IQs than you, be therefore more patient, informed, and cooperative, contributing to a hive mind that can be trained and the training of which will improve economic and social conditions for all.

4. Robert Sobak, "Sokrates among the Shoemakers," *Hesperia* 84 (2015): 669–712, here 669.

5. Sobak, "Sokrates," 708.

6. Mogens Herman Hansen, ed., *The Imaginary Polis* (Copenhagen: The Royal Danish Academy of Sciences and Letters, 2005), and *Polis: An Introduction to the Greek City State* (Oxford: Oxford University Press, 2006).

7. For this conception of status difference in the ancient *polis*, see, for example, Ian Morris, "The Strong Principle of Equality and the Archaic Origins of Greek Democracy," in *Demokratia: A Conversation on Democracies, Ancient and Modern*, ed. J. Ober and C. Hedrick (Princeton, NJ: Princeton University Press, 1996), 19–48; and Leslie Kurke, *Coins, Bodies, Games, and Gold: The Politics of Meaning in Archaic Greece* (Princeton, NJ: Princeton University Press, 1999).

8. On slave participation in war and ancient historians' failure to acknowledge such participation, see Hunt, *Slaves, Warfare, and Ideology*.

9. Greg Anderson, *The Realness of Things Past: Ancient Greece and Ontological History* (New York: Oxford University Press, 2018), 143. Anderson observes: "In mainstream modernist social theory, the state tends to be objectified as a kind of autonomous command structure, an agency with its own distinct mind, will, and interests which rules over its corresponding 'society,' as it were, from without or above.... In our standard accounts of Athenian 'democracy,' Demos of course tends to be defined in similarly modernist terms" (194).

10. See Josine H. Blok and André P. M. H. Lardinois, eds., *Solon of Athens: New Historical and Philological Approaches*, Mnemosyne Supplement 272 (Leiden: Brill, 2006).

11. Vincent Azoulay, *The Tyrant-Slayers of Ancient Athens: A Tale of Two Statues*, trans. Janet Lloyd (Oxford: Oxford University Press, 2017).

12. See William T. Loomis, *Wages, Welfare Costs, and Inflation in Classical Athens* (Ann Arbor: University of Michigan Press, 1998).

13. See the earlier chapter on the chorus for discussion of the *khoregos*, the wealthy benefactor who funded dramatic performances.

14. See Kasimis, *Perpetual Immigrant*; Hunt, *Slaves, Warfare, and Ideology*; Hans van Wees, *Greek Warfare: Myth and Realities* (Bristol: Bristol Classical Press, 2004); and van Wees, *War and Violence in Ancient Greece* (Swansea: Classical Press of Wales, 2000).

15. DuBois, *Slaves*; duBois, *Slavery*; duBois, *Torture and Truth*; Keith Bradley and Paul Cartledge, eds., *The Cambridge World History of Slavery*, vol. 1, *The Ancient Mediterranean World* (Cambridge: Cambridge University Press, 2011); Hunt, *Ancient Greek and Roman Slavery*.

16. On the question of a de facto oligarchy, see Lape, *Race*; on Aristophanes and other comic writers, see especially, in Lape's chap. 2, the section "Old Comedy and the City's 'Foreign' Leaders," 64–71: "Comic poets usually malign citizens for having the specifically non-Greek origins associated with slaves" (65); "Targeting his ancestry was an ideologically safe way to malign a democratic leader before a popular audience" (70). There were other ways of denigrating comedy's targets: "By bringing an Athenian citizen or his mother on stage speaking in a flawed Attic dialect or in an altogether foreign language, the comic poets had their characters act out or perform their foreign ancestry. With this move, they lent credence or substance to what might otherwise have seemed unsupported allegations of bad birth" (71).

17. On imperialism, see Kenneth DeLuca, "Aristophanes' Herodotean Inquiry: The Meaning of Athenian Imperialism in the *Birds*," in *The Political Theory of Aristophanes: Explorations in Poetic Wisdom*, ed. Jeremy J. Mhire and Bryan-Paul Frost (Albany: State University of New York Press, 2014), 161–82.

18. John Ma, "Afterword: Whither the Athenian Empire?," in *Interpreting the Athenian Empire*, ed. John Ma, Nikolaos Papazarkadas, and Robert Parker (London: Duckworth, 2009), 223–31, here 227. The work of Josiah Ober presents a generally more favorable view of Athenian democracy; see, for example, Josiah Ober, *Mass and Elite in Democratic Athens: Rhetoric, Ideology, and the Power of the People* (Princeton, NJ: Princeton University Press, 1991).

19. See duBois, *Slaves*.

20. Lisa Lowe, *The Intimacies of Four Continents* (Durham, NC: Duke University Press, 2015).

21. Orlando Patterson, *Slavery and Social Death: A Comparative Study*, 2nd ed. (Cambridge, MA: Harvard University Press, 2018).

22. Douglas Blackmon, *Slavery by Another Name: The Re-Enslavement of Black Americans from the Civil War to World War II* (New York: Doubleday, 2008). I discuss the difficulties of pedagogy concerning the history of slavery, ancient and modern, in "Teaching the Uncomfortable Subject of Slavery," in *From Abortion to Pederasty: Addressing Difficult Topics in the Classics Classroom*, ed. N. Rabinowitz and F. McHardy (Columbus: Ohio State University Press, 2015), 187–98.

23. Juleyka Lantigua-Williams, "A Digital Archive Documents Two Decades of Torture by Chicago Police," *the atlantic.com*, October 26, 2016.

24. Kristine Phillips, "Thousands of ICE Detainees Claim They Were Forced into Labor, a Violation of Anti-Slavery Laws," *Washington Post*, March 5, 2017, www

.washingtonpost.com/news/post-nation/wp/2017/03/05/thousands-of-ice-detainees-claim-they-were-forced-into-labor-a-violation-of-anti-slavery-laws.

25. Sobak, "Sokrates," 709.

26. On this play and Plato, see Robert Tordoff, "Aristophanes' *Assembly Women* and Plato, *Republic* book 5," in *Debating the Athenian Cultural Revolution: Art, Literature, Philosophy and Politics, 430–380 BC*, ed. Robin Osborne (Cambridge: Cambridge University Press, 2007), 242–63. Discussing Plato, Tordoff writes: "The cumulative effect of all these passages gives the distinct impression that, as Plato systematically constructs philosophy as an authoritative intellectual practice and systematically excludes rival types of intellectual discourse, drama, and in particular a drama like *Assembly Women*, is very much in his sights. In summary, there are two important points here. First, the evidence of *Republic* book 5 shows marked Platonic anxiety about the sort of intellectualising comedy that Aristophanes' *Assembly Women* represents. Secondly, that anxiety points very clearly to an Aristophanic strategy of presenting comic poetry as more than just a few laughs, but as an important and authoritative political and philosophical voice" (261).

27. Alan Sommerstein argues in *Talking about Laughter and Other Studies in Greek Comedy* (Oxford: Oxford University Press, 2009) that Aristophanes offers "a twofold model of an alternative political system," especially in his *Knights* (204–22, 206). Its features would include the abolition of public pay for civic functions, that is, jury service, and assembly attendance; repression of sycophancy, that is, malicious prosecution; rejection of leaders of low social status; peace with Sparta (206–9). Sommerstein is "tempted to call [Lysistrata's sexual and financial coercions] a political reverse rape" (215)—an unhappy choice of words, in my view.

28. Sobak, "Sokrates," 672. Sobak considers the active participation of the many in the city's institutions, including the assembly, as evidenced by discussions in Plato and Xenophon, while noting that "if we choose to adopt the terminology introduced by Plato, we must strive to avoid the many antidemocratic entailments that lurk in such vocabulary" (681).

29. Sobak, "Sokrates," 695.

30. Rancière, *Philosopher and His Poor*, 23.

31. Rancière, 24.

32. See Zeitlin, "Travesties," 375–416.

33. See duBois, *Centaurs and Amazons*; Adrienne Mayor, *The Amazons: Lives and Legends of Warrior Women across the Ancient World* (Princeton, NJ: Princeton University Press, 2014); Walter Penrose, *Postcolonial Amazons: Female Masculinity and Courage in Ancient Greek and Sanskrit Literature* (Oxford: Oxford University Press, 2017).

34. Herodotus, *The Histories*, trans. Robin Waterfield (Oxford: Oxford University Press, 1998).

35. Herbert Marcuse, *Eros and Civilization: A Philosophical Inquiry into Freud* (Boston: Beacon Press, 1974).

36. K. J. Dover, *Aristophanic Comedy* (Berkeley: University of California Press, 1972), 194.

37. Dover, *Aristophanic Comedy*, 194.

38. On the anachronistic division, and evolution from "Old" to "Middle" and "New Comedy," see Eric Csapo, "From Aristophanes to Menander? Genre Transformation in Greek Comedy," in Depew and Obbink, *Matrices of Genre*, 115–34; he writes: "Our ideas

about the evolution of comedy are based on the partial remains of two authors [Aristophanes and Menander], each surviving by separate processes and canons of preservation" (115).

39. Dover, Aristophanic Comedy, 195.

40. See also Chantal Mouffe, *For a Left Populism* (London: Verso, 2018).

41. Griffith, *Aristophanes' Frogs*, 31.

42. There is a vast bibliography on the question of Aristophanes and his politics. See Mhire and Frost, *Political Theory of Aristophanes*, with bibliographies for each essay. See especially in this volume Arlene W. Saxonhouse, "Boundaries: The Comic Poet Confronts the 'Who' of Political Action," 89–108, and Stephanie Nelson, "Aristophanes and the Polis," 109–36. Nelson provides a good survey of prevailing opinion on the question of Aristophanes' engagement with politics (126–27n6).

43. The Greek word *koinos* means "common," and is the word used for the evolved classical Greek language in the Hellenistic period, the commonly used demotic form of Greek that people spoke in the communities of the post-Alexandrian world, and that is the language of the Christian "New" Testament. An interesting question, one that can't be pursued here, is the degree of "communism" of early Christian groups, comprising the followers of Jesus. A recent translator of the New Testament claims to have found "communism" in the text. Could we trace a lineage, a genealogy of communist utopianism, of democracy, from ancient Greek comedy, including the reforms of Aristophanes' assemblywomen, to the works of the early church fathers, to the kibbutzim of early socialist Israel, and of course, into the present?

CHAPTER 7

1. Griffith, *Aristophanes' Frogs*, 251.

2. Phiroze Vasunia, *The Classics and Colonial India* (Oxford: Oxford University Press, 2013).

3. Stephen Halliwell, *Aristophanes: Birds, Lysistrata, Assembly-Women, Wealth* (Oxford: Oxford University Press, 1998), 210.

4. On this comedy, see also Francisco Barrenechea, *Comedy and Religion in Classical Athens: Narratives of Religious Experience in Aristophanes' "Wealth"* (Cambridge: Cambridge University Press, 2018). Barrenechea shows how the play draws on a variety of religious institutions in the ancient city, including divination and cure through incubation, divine epiphany, and the importation into the city of new gods. Barrenechea proposes that "the comedy is structured upon a rich and largely unexplored religious framework, based on traditional narratives of religious experiences that permeate the plot and underlie its comic fantasy" (1). Barranchea also points out that other plays, including the *Peace*, and surviving fragments of other comic writers, engage with religious themes (6–7); then notes: "*Wealth* . . . offers a celebratory and hopeful vision of an efficacious mortal and divine relationship, particularly in the action of philanthropic, savior deities" (162). Barrenchea also includes an extensive bibliography of scholarship on this play.

5. Deleuze and Guattari, *Kafka*, 16. They note: "Prague German is a deterritorialized language, appropriate for strange and minor uses. (This can be compared in another context to what blacks in America today are able to do with the English language.)" (17).

6. Deleuze and Guattari, *Kafka*, 17.

7. Tony Harrison reset the play as *The Common Chorus*, at the women's years-long encampment in protest against the Greenham Common nuclear missile base in Britain. Tony Harrison, *The Common Chorus: A Version of Aristophanes' Lysistrata* (London: Faber and Faber, 1992). Harrison recalls that "a women's peace magazine produced from Brighton in the 1980s called itself *Lysistrata*" (xii).

8. Emily Klein, *Sex and War on the American Stage: Lysistrata in Performance 1930–2012* (London: Routledge, 2014). See also the volume of essays on this play entitled *Looking at Lysistrata: Eight Essays and a New Version of Aristophanes' Provocative Comedy*, ed. David Stuttard (London: Bristol Classical Press, 2011).

9. Klein, *Sex and War*, 145.

10. Klein, 144.

11. Niklas Luhmann, *Social Systems*, trans. John Bednarz Jr., with Dirk Baecker (1984; Stanford, CA: Stanford University Press, 1995), 62.

12. Luhmann, *Social Systems*, 66.

13. Luhmann, 83.

14. Gurd, *Dissonance*, 6.

15. Donna Haraway, *Staying with the Trouble: Making Kin in the Chthulucene* (Durham, NC: Duke University Press, 2016), 58.

16. Haraway, *Staying*, 61.

17. Perry Anderson, *A Zone of Engagement* (London: Verso, 1992), 7.

18. Jameson, "Marxism and Historicism," 70. Revivifying Marx, Fredric Jameson lists several permutations of the "dilemma of historicism," the alternation between Identity and Difference in encountering the past, including "antiquarianism, existential historicism, structural typology, and Nietzschean antihistoricism" (45). With "simple antiquarianism, . . . the past does not have to justify its claim of interest upon us"; "this position . . . solves the problem of the relationship between present and past by the simple gesture of abolishing the present as such" (45). Jameson sees this as the equivalent of the ideology of empiricism. After analyzing this and the other possibilities, Jameson offers the Marxist concept of the mode of production, which encompasses all other forms of historicism; he includes in his list "the Asiatic mode of production, the polis, slavery, feudalism, capitalism, and communism" (67). His Marxist historicism seeks to resolve the problem of an alternation between Identity and Difference. The Marxist position is "the partisan commitment to that future or utopian mode of production which seeks to emerge from the hegemonic mode of production of our own present" (71). Such an approach would not project backward "into radically different social formations [of] a concept of 'production' drawn from capitalism, any more than a dialectical perspective can accept the ahistorical assumption of certain psychoanalytic schools that the constituted subject, the unconscious, the Oedipus complex, desire, and the like—all theorized from modern or bourgeois psychic materials—remain constant throughout history" (67–68). To encounter a historically distant society, one might attempt to understand the categories that defined mental and social and economic life in that society, rather than finding our identity in the past, recognizing that we are bound within the horizon of our own historical moment, framing our encounter with the past through interested, conscious and unconscious desires, and also, most importantly, imagining a future (70).

19. Ross, *Communal Luxury*.

20. See Page duBois, "Histories of the Impossible," in *Out of Athens: The New Ancient Greeks* (Cambridge, MA: Harvard University Press, 2010), 114–29.

21. Most recently, see Jacques Rancière, "Les fous et les sages—réflexions sur la fin de la présidence Trump," in *AOC* (*Analyse, Opinion, Critique*), January 14, 2021, https://aoc.media/opinion/2021/01/13.

22. Mouffe, *For a Left Populism*, 6.

23. Patrisse Khan-Cullors and Asha Bandele, *When They Call You a Terrorist: A Black Lives Matter Memoir* (New York: St. Martin's Griffin, 2020).

24. Note that there is a long tradition of African American and Black resistance to the Marxist tradition, especially as exemplified in the form of the Communist Party of the US, which was seen by Ralph Ellison as "the Brotherhood," opportunistic and exploitative of black suffering, betraying class politics as well during World War II. See Ralph Ellison, *Invisible Man* (1952); and more recently, Cedric Robinson, *Black Marxism: The Making of the Black Radical Tradition*, 2nd ed. (1983; Chapel Hill: University of North Carolina Press, 2000); and Frank B. Wilderson III, *Afropessimism* (New York: Liveright, 2020).

25. Rancière continues: "This break is manifest in a series of actions that reconfigure the space where parties, parts, of lack of parts have been defined. Political activity is whatever shifts a body from the place assigned to it or changes a place's designation. It makes visible what had no business being seen, and makes heard a discourse where once there was only place for noise; it makes understood as discourse what was once only heard as noise" (*Disagreement*, 29–30).

26. Stefano Harney and Fred Moten, *The Undercommons: Fugitive Planning & Black Study* (Wivenhoe: Minor Compositions/Autonomedia, 2013), 82.

27. Harney and Moten, *Undercommons*, 105.

28. "Marxians are conservative, we want to conserve some good old bourgeois—or indeed medieval and Hellenic and Buddhist—values destroyed by the rotting bourgeoisie." Darko Suvin, "Afterword: With Sober, Estranged Eyes," *Learning from Other Worlds: Estrangement, Cognition, and the Politics of Science Fiction and Utopia*, ed. Patrick Parrinder (Durham, NC: Duke University Press, 2001), 242.

Selected Bibliography

Althusser, Louis. *For Marx*. Translated by Ben Brewster. 1968. New York: Vintage, 1970.
Anderson, Greg. *The Realness of Things Past: Ancient Greece and Ontological History*. New York: Oxford University Press, 2018.
Anderson, Perry. "The River of Time." *New Left Review* 26 (2004): 67–77.
Aristophanes. *Clouds*. Edited by K. J. Dover. Oxford: Clarendon Press, 1968.
———. *Wasps*. Edited by Douglas M. Macdowell. Oxford: Clarendon Press, 1988.
———. *Birds*. Edited by Nan Dunbar. Oxford: Oxford University Press, 1995.
———. *Wasps*. Edited by Z. Biles and S. D. Olson. Oxford: Oxford University Press, 2016.
Azoulay, Vincent. *The Tyrant-Slayers of Ancient Athens: A Tale of Two Statues*. Translated by Janet Lloyd. Oxford: Oxford University Press, 2017.
Azoulay, Vincent, and Paulin Ismard. *Athènes 403: Une histoire chorale*. Paris: Flammarion, 2020.
Bahng, Aimee. "Plasmodial Improprieties: Octavia E. Butler, Slime Molds, and Imagining a Femi-Queer Commons." In *Queer Feminist Science Studies: A Reader*, edited by Cyd Cipolla, Kristina Gupta, David A. Rubin, and Angela Willey, 310–25. Seattle: University of Washington Press, 2017.
Bakhtin, Mikhail. "Epic and Novel." In *The Dialogic Imagination: Four Essays*, edited by Michael Holquist, translated by Caryl Emerson and Michael Holquist, 3–40. Austin: University of Texas Press, 1983.
Bakola, Emmanuela. *Cratinus and the Art of Comedy*. Oxford: Oxford University Press, 2010.
Bakola, Emmanuela, Lucia Prauscello, and Mario Telò, eds. *Greek Comedy and the Discourse of Genres*. Cambridge: Cambridge University Press, 2013.
Barker, Elton T. E. "'Possessing an unbridled tongue': Frank Speech and Speaking Back in Euripides' *Orestes*." In Carter, *Why Athens?*, 145–63.
Barrenechea, Francisco. *Comedy and Religion in Classical Athens: Narratives of Religious Experience in Aristophanes' "Wealth."* Cambridge: Cambridge University Press, 2018.
Bastani, Aaron. *Fully Automated Luxury Communism: A Manifesto*. London: Verso, 2019.
Bennett, Jane. *Vibrant Matter: A Political Ecology of Things*. Durham, NC: Duke University Press, 2010.
Bergson, Henri. *Laughter: An Essay on the Meaning of the Comic*. Translated by Cloudesley Brereton and Fred Rothwell. New York: Macmillan, 1912.

Bierl, Anton. *Ritual and Performativity: The Chorus of Old Comedy*. Translated by Alexander Hollmann. 2001. Washington, DC: Center for Hellenic Studies (Harvard University Press), 2009.
Billings, J., F. Budelmann, and F. Macintosh, eds. *Choruses, Ancient and Modern*. Oxford: Oxford University Press, 2013.
Billings, Joshua. *Genealogy of the Tragic: Greek Tragedy and German Philosophy*. Princeton, NJ: Princeton University Press, 2014.
Bloch, Ernst. *The Principle of Hope*. Translated by Neville Plaice, Stephen Plaice, and Paul Knight. Vols. 1–3. Cambridge, MA: MIT Press, 1995.
———. *The Spirit of Utopia*. Translated by A. Nassar. 1923. Stanford, CA: Stanford University Press, 2000.
Boedeker, Deborah, and K. Raaflaub, eds. *Democracy, Empire, and the Arts in Fifth-Century Athens*. Cambridge, MA: Center for Hellenic Studies (Harvard University Press), 1998.
Bonnamour, Jacqueline, and S. Delavault, eds. *Aristophane, les femmes et la cité*. Fontenay-aux-Roses: École normale supérieure, 1979.
Boschung, Dietrich, Alan Shapiro, and Frank Wascheck, eds. *Bodies in Transition: Dissolving the Boundaries of Embodied Knowledge*. Paderborn: Wilhelm Fink, 2015.
Braidotti, Rosi. *Nomadic Theory*. New York: Columbia University Press, 2011.
Bregman, Rutger. *Utopia for Realists: How We Can Build the Ideal World*. Translated by Elizabeth Manton. New York: Back Bay (Little, Brown), 2018.
———. *Humankind: A Hopeful History*. Translated by E. Manton and E. Moore. New York: Little, Brown, 2019.
Brooks, Gwendolyn. *Riot*. Detroit: Broadside Press, 1969.
Brown, Adrienne Maree. *Pleasure Activism: The Politics of Feeling Good*. Chico, CA: AK Press, 2019.
Butler, Judith. *Excitable Speech: A Politics of the Performative*. New York: Routledge, 1997.
———. *Notes toward a Performative Theory of Assembly*. Cambridge, MA: Harvard University Press, 2015.
Calame, Claude. *La tragédie chorale: Poésie grecque et rituel musical*. Paris: Les Belles Lettres, 2017.
Carter, D. M., ed. *Why Athens? A Reappraisal of Tragic Politics*. Oxford: Oxford University Press, 2011.
Cartledge, Paul. *Aristophanes and His Theatre of the Absurd*. Bristol: Bristol Classical Press, 1991.
Caston, Victor, and Silke-Maria Weineck, eds. *Our Ancient Wars: Rethinking War through the Classics*. Ann Arbor: University of Michigan Press, 2016.
Cavarero, Adriana. *For More Than One Voice: Toward a Philosophy of Vocal Expression*. Translated by P. A. Kottman. 2003. Stanford, CA: Stanford University Press, 2005.
Champagne, Roland A. *The Methods of the Gernet Classicists: The Structuralists on Myth*. London: Routledge, 2016.
Chen, Mel. *Animacies: Biopolitics, Racial Mattering, and Queer Affect*. Durham, NC: Duke University Press, 2012.
Chute, Hillary, and Patrick Jagoda, eds. "Comics & Media," special issue, *Critical Inquiry* 40, no. 3 (2014).
Compton-Engle, Gwendolyn. *Costume in the Comedies of Aristophanes*. Cambridge: Cambridge University Press, 2015.

Connolly, William E. *Aspirational Fascism: The Struggle for Multifaceted Democracy under Trumpism*. Minneapolis: University of Minnesota Press, 2017.
Corbel-Morana, Cécile. *Le bestiaire d'Aristophane*. Paris: Les Belles Lettres, 2012.
Critchley, Simon. *Tragedy, the Greeks, and Us*. New York: Vintage, 2020.
Csapo, Eric. "From Aristophanes to Menander? Genre Transformation in Greek Comedy." In Depew and Obbink, *Matrices of Genre*, 115–34.
———. "The Politics of the New Music." In *Music and the Muses: The Culture of Mousikê in the Classical Athenian City*, edited by Penelope Murray and Peter Wilson, 207–48. Oxford: Oxford University Press, 2004.
Csapo, Eric, Hans Ruprecht Goette, J. R. Green, and Peter Wilson, eds. *Greek Theatre in the Fourth Century BC*. Berlin: De Gruyter, 2014.
Csapo, Eric, and Margaret Miller. "Democracy, Empire, and Art: Toward a Politics of Time and Narrative." In Boedeker and Raaflaub, *Democracy, Empire, and the Arts in Fifth-Century Athens*, 87–126.
Csapo, Eric, and W. J. Slater. *The Context of Ancient Drama*. Ann Arbor: University of Michigan Press, 1995.
Dawson, Doyne. *Cities of the Gods: Communist Utopias in Greek Thought*. New York: Oxford University Press, 1992.
Deleuze, Gilles. *Negotiations, 1972–1990*. Translated by Martin Joughin. 1990. New York: Columbia University Press, 1995.
———. "Plato, the Greeks." In *Essays Critical and Clinical*, translated by D. W. Smith and M. A. Greco, 136–37. 1993. Minneapolis: University of Minnesota Press, 1997.
Deleuze, Gilles, and Félix Guattari. *Kafka: Toward a Minor Literature*. Translated by Dana Polan. 1975. Minneapolis: University of Minnesota Press, 1986.
———. *A Thousand Plateaus: Capitalism and Schizophrenia*. Translated by Brian Massumi. Vol. 2. 1980. Minneapolis: University of Minnesota Press, 1987.
Depew, Mary, and Dirk Obbink, eds. *Matrices of Genre: Authors, Canons, and Society*. Cambridge, MA: Harvard University Press, 2000.
De Sousa Santos, Boaventura. *Epistemologies of the South: Justice against Epistemicide*. London: Routledge, 2016.
Dobrov, G. W., ed. *The City as Comedy: Society and Representation in Athenian Drama*. Chapel Hill: University of North Carolina Press, 1997.
———, ed. *Brill's Companion to the Study of Greek Comedy*. Leiden: Brill, 2010.
Dover, K. J. *Aristophanic Comedy*. Berkeley: University of California Press, 1972.
duBois, Page. *Centaurs and Amazons: Women and the Pre-History of the Great Chain of Being*. Ann Arbor: University of Michigan Press, 1982.
———. *History, Rhetorical Description, and the Epic from Homer to Spenser*. Cambridge: Boydell and Brewer, 1983.
———. *Sowing the Body: Psychoanalysis and Ancient Representations of Women*. Chicago: University of Chicago Press, 1988.
———. *Torture and Truth*. 1991. Reprint, London: Routledge, 2016.
———. *Slaves and Other Objects*. Chicago: University of Chicago Press, 2003.
———. "Toppling the Hero: Polyphony in the Tragic City." In *Rethinking Tragedy*, edited by Rita Felski, 127–47. Baltimore: Johns Hopkins University Press, 2008.
———. *Slavery: Antiquity and Its Legacy*. Oxford: I.B. Tauris, 2009.
———. "Histories of the Impossible." In *Out of Athens: The New Ancient Greeks*, 114–29. Cambridge, MA: Harvard University Press, 2010.
Dué, Casey. "'Get in Formation, This Is an Emergency': The Politics of Choral Song and

Dance in Aristophanes' *Lysistrata* and Spike Lee's *Chi-Raq*." *Arion: A Journal of Humanities and the Classics* 24, no. 1 (2016): 111–44.
Dutsch, Dorota. "Projecting *Lysistrata*: Aristophanes and Political Activism." In *The Oxford Handbook of Greek Drama in the Americas*, edited by Kate Bosher, Justine McConnell, and Patrice Rankine, 575–94. New York: Oxford University Press, 2015.
Dyer-Witheford, Nick. *Cyber-Marx: Cycles and Circuits of Struggle in High-Technology Capitalism*. Urbana: University of Illinois Press, 1999.
Eagleton, Terry. *Sweet Violence: The Idea of the Tragic*. Oxford: Wiley-Blackwell, 2002.
Edwards, Anthony. "Aristophanes' Comic Poetics: Τρυξ, Scatology, Σκωμμα." *Transactions of the American Philological Association* 121 (1991): 157–79.
———. "Historicizing the Popular Grotesque: Bakhtin's *Rabelais and His World* and Attic Old Comedy." In *Bakhtin and the Classics*, edited by B. Branham, 27–55. Evanston, IL: Northwestern University Press, 2002.
Ehrenberg, Victor. *The People of Aristophanes*. 1943. New York: Schocken, 1962.
Ehrenreich, Barbara. *Dancing in the Streets: A History of Collective Joy*. New York: Henry Holt, 2006.
Euripides. *Bacchae*. Edited by Richard Seaford. Liverpool: Aris and Phillips, 1996.
———. *Cyclops*. Edited by R. A. S. Seaford. London: Bristol Classical Press, 1998.
Evans, Rhiannon. *Utopia Antiqua: Readings of the Golden Age and Decline at Rome*. New York: Routledge, 2008.
Fields, Dana. *Frankness, Greek Culture, and the Roman Empire*. New York: Routledge, 2020.
Fletcher, Angus. *Comic Democracies: From Ancient Athens to the American Republic*. Baltimore: Johns Hopkins University Press, 2016.
Foley, Helene. "The 'Female Intruder' Reconsidered: Women in Aristophanes' *Lysistrata* and *Ecclesiazusae*." *Classical Philology* 77, no. 1 (1982): 1–21.
Foucault, Michel. *Fearless Speech*. Edited by Joseph Pearson. Los Angeles: Semiotext(e), 2001.
———. *The Hermeneutics of the Subject: Lectures at the Collège de France, 1981–1982*. Edited by F. Gros. Translated by Graham Burchell. 2001. New York: Palgrave Macmillan, 2005.
———. *The Government of Self and Others: Lectures at the Collège de France, 1982–1983*. Edited by F. Gros. Translated by Graham Burchell. 2008. New York: Palgrave Macmillan, 2010.
———. *The Courage of Truth: The Government of Self and Others II: Lectures at the Collège de France, 1983–1984*. Edited by F. Gros. Translated by Graham Burchell. 2008. New York: Palgrave Macmillan, 2011.
———. *Wrong-Doing, Truth-Telling: The Function of Avowal in Justice*. Edited by Fabienne Brion and Bernard E. Harcourt. Translated by Stephen W. Sawyer. Chicago: University of Chicago Press, 2014.
Freud, Sigmund. *The Joke and Its Relation to the Unconscious*. Translated by Joyce Crick. 1905. London: Penguin, 2003.
Frye, Northrop. *Anatomy of Criticism*. Princeton, NJ: Princeton University Press, 1957.
———. *A Natural Perspective: The Development of Shakespearean Comedy and Romance*. New York: Columbia University Press, 1965.
Fuller, Roslyn. *Beasts and Gods: How Democracy Changed Its Meaning and Lost Its Purpose*. London: Zed Books, 2015.

Gagné, Renaud. "Dancing Letters: The *Alphabetic Tragedy* of Kallias." In Gagné and Hopman, *Choral Mediations*, 297–316.
Gagné, Renaud, and Marianne Govers Hopman, eds. *Choral Mediations in Greek Tragedy*. Cambridge: Cambridge University Press, 2013.
Gamel, Mary-Kay. "Sondheim Floats Frogs." In Hall and Wrigley, *Aristophanes in Performance*, 209–30.
Germain, Gabriel. *Genèse de l'Odyssée, le fantastique, le sacré*. Paris: Presses universitaires de France, 1954.
Giovanelli, Maddalena. *Aristofane nostro contemporáneo: La commedia antica in scena oggi*. Rome: Carocci, 2018.
Goff, Barbara, and M. Simpson. *Crossroads in the Black Aegean: Oedipus, Antigone, and Dramas of the African Diaspora*. Oxford: Oxford University Press, 2007.
Goldhill, Simon. "The Great Dionysia and Civic Ideology." In Winkler and Zeitlin, *Nothing to Do with Dionysos?*, 97–129.
———. *Love, Sex & Tragedy: How the Ancient World Shapes Our Lives*. Chicago: University of Chicago Press, 2004.
Griffith, Mark. *Aristophanes' Frogs*. Oxford: Oxford University Press, 2013.
———. *Greek Satyr Play: Five Studies*. Berkeley: California Classical Studies, 2015.
Guattari, Félix, and Toni Negri. *Communists Like Us: New Spaces of Liberty, New Lines of Alliance*. Translated by Michael Ryan. New York: Semiotext(e), 1990.
Gurd, Sean. *Dissonance: Auditory Aesthetics in Ancient Greece*. New York: Fordham University Press, 2016.
Hall, Edith. "The Sociology of Athenian Tragedy." In *The Cambridge Companion to Greek Tragedy*, edited by P. E. Easterling, 93–126. Cambridge: Cambridge University Press, 1997.
———. "The Many Faces of Lysistrata." In *Looking at Lysistrata*, edited by David Stuttard, 29–36. London: Bristol Classical Press, 2010.
———. "The English-Speaking Aristophanes, 1650–1914." In Hall and Wrigley, *Aristophanes in Performance*, 66–92.
———. "Comedy and Athenian Festival Culture." In Revermann, *The Cambridge Companion to Greek Comedy*, 306–21.
Hall, Edith, and P. Vasunia, eds. *India, Greece, and Rome, 1757–2007*. London: Institute of Classical Studies, 2010.
Hall, Edith, and A. Wrigley, eds. *Aristophanes in Performance, 412 BC–AD 2007: Peace, Birds, and Frogs*. Oxford: Legenda, 2007.
Halliwell, Stephen. *Aristophanes: Birds, Lysistrata, Assembly-Women, Wealth*. Oxford: Oxford University Press, 1998.
———. "Aischrology, Shame, and Comedy." In Sluiter and Rosen, *Free Speech in Classical Antiquity*, 115–44.
Han, Byung-Chul. *In the Swarm: Digital Prospects*. Translated by Erik Butler. Cambridge, MA: MIT Press, 2017.
Hansen, Mogens Herman, ed. *The Imaginary Polis*. Copenhagen: The Royal Danish Academy of Sciences and Letters, 2005.
———. *The Polis: An Introduction to the Ancient Greek City-State*. Oxford: Oxford University Press, 2006.
Haraway, Donna. *The Companion Species Manifesto: Dogs, People, and Significant Otherness*. Chicago: Prickly Paradigm Press, 2003.

———. *Staying with the Trouble: Making Kin in the Chthulucene.* Durham, NC: Duke University Press, 2016.

Hardwick, Lorna, and S. Harrison, eds. *Classics in the Modern World: A Democratic Turn?* Oxford: Oxford University Press, 2013.

Harney, Stefano, and Fred Moten. *The Undercommons: Fugitive Planning & Black Study.* Wivenhoe: Minor Compositions/Autonomedia, 2013.

Harris, Edward M. *Democracy and the Rule of Law in Classical Athens.* Cambridge: Cambridge University Press, 2006.

Harrison, Tony. *The Common Chorus.* Cambridge: Proquest, 2004.

Henderson, Jeffrey. "The Demos and the Comic Competition." In Winkler and Zeitlin, *Nothing to Do with Dionysos?*, 271–313.

———. *The Maculate Muse: Obscene Language in Attic Comedy.* 2nd ed. New York: Oxford University Press, 1991.

———. "Women and the Athenian Dramatic Festivals." *Transactions of the American Philological Association* 121 (1991): 133–47.

———. "Attic Old Comedy, Frank Speech, and Democracy." In Boedeker and Raaflaub, *Democracy, Empire, and the Arts in Fifth-Century Athens,* 255–73.

——— "The Comic Chorus and the Demagogue." In Gagné and Hopman, *Choral Mediations,* 278–96.

Horkheimer, Max, and Theodor W. Adorno. *Dialectic of Enlightenment.* Translated by Edmund Jephcott. 1947. Stanford, CA: Stanford University Press, 2002.

Horvat, Srecko. *The Radicality of Love.* Cambridge: Polity, 2016.

Hubbard, T. K. "Utopianism and the Sophistic City in Aristophanes." In Dobrov, *The City as Comedy,* 23–50.

Hunt, Peter. *Slaves, Warfare, and Ideology in the Greek Historians.* Cambridge: Cambridge University Press, 1998.

Jameson, Fredric. "Marxism and Historicism." *New Literary History* 11, no. 1 (1979): 41–73.

———. "Reification and Utopia in Mass Culture." *Social Text* 1 (1979): 130–48.

———. "The Politics of Utopia." *New Left Review* 25 (2004): 35–54.

———. *Archaeologies of the Future: The Desire Called Utopia and Other Science Fictions.* London: Verso, 2005.

———. *Allegory and Ideology.* London: Verso, 2019.

Janko, Richard. *Aristotle on Comedy: Towards a Reconstruction of Poetics II.* London: Bristol Classical Press, 2002.

Jones, Garett. *Hive Mind: How Your Nation's IQ Matters So Much More Than Your Own.* Stanford, CA: Stanford University Press, 2014.

———. *10% Less Democracy: Why You Should Trust Elites a Little More and the Masses a Little Less.* Stanford, CA: Stanford University Press, 2020.

Kasimis, Demetra. *The Perpetual Immigrant and the Limits of Athenian Democracy.* Cambridge: Cambridge University Press, 2018.

Khan-Cullors, Patrisse, and Asha Bandele. *When They Call You a Terrorist: A Black Lives Matter Memoir.* New York: St. Martin's Griffin, 2020.

Khitrova, Daria. "'This Is No Longer Dance': Media Boundaries and the Politics of Choreography in *The Steel Sky.*" In Chute and Jagoda, *Critical Inquiry* 40, no. 3 (2014): 134–49.

Kidd, Stephen. *Nonsense and Meaning in Ancient Greek Comedy.* Cambridge: Cambridge University Press, 2017.

Knox, Bernard. *Oedipus at Thebes: Sophocles' Tragic Hero and His Time*. New Haven, CT: Yale University Press, 1957.
Konstan, David. "The Classics and Class Conflict." *Arethusa* 27 (1994): 47–70.
———. *Greek Comedy and Ideology*. New York: Oxford University Press, 1995.
———. "The Two Faces of *parrhêsia*: Free Speech and Self-Expression in Ancient Greece." *Antichthon* 46 (2012): 1–13.
Koster, W. J. W. *Scholia in Aristophanem Pars I, Fasc. 1A: Prolegomena de Comoedia*. Groningen: Bouma's Boekhuis, 1975.
Kowalzig, Barbara. *Singing for the Gods: Performances of Myth and Ritual in Archaic and Classical Greece*. Oxford: Oxford University Press, 2007.
Kozak, L. A., and J. W. Rich, eds. *Playing Around: Aristophanes, Essays in Honour of Alan Sommerstein*. Liverpool: Liverpool University Press, 2006.
Krumeich, Ralf, Nikolaus Pechstein, and Bernd Seidensticker. *Das griechische Satyrspiel*. Texte zur Forschung, Bd. 72. Darmstadt: Wissenschaftliche Buchgesellschaft, 1999.
Kurke, Leslie. *Aesopic Conversations: Popular Traditions, Cultural Dialogue, and the Invention of Greek Prose*. Princeton, NJ: Princeton University Press, 2011.
Lafargue, Paul. *The Right to Be Lazy*. Edited by Bernard Marszalek. 1880, 1883. Chico, CA: AK Press, 2011.
Lape, Susan. *Reproducing Athens: Menander's Comedy, Democratic Culture, and the Hellenistic City*. Princeton, NJ: Princeton University Press, 2003.
———. *Race and Citizen Identity in the Classical Athenian Democracy*. Cambridge: Cambridge University Press, 2010.
Lee, Spike, dir. *Chi-Raq*. Amazon Studios, 2015.
Leonard, Miriam. *Tragic Modernities*. Cambridge, MA: Harvard University Press, 2015.
Long, Timothy. *Barbarians in Greek Comedy*. Carbondale: Southern Illinois University Press, 1986.
Loraux, Nicole. "Aristophane, les femmes d'Athènes, et le théâtre." In Reverdin and Grange, *Aristophane*, 203–44.
MacDowell, Douglas M. *Aristophanes and Athens: An Introduction to the Plays*. Oxford: Oxford University Press, 1995.
Macherey, Pierre. *A Theory of Literary Production*. Translated by Geoffrey Wall. With a New Introduction by Terry Eagleton and a New Afterword by the Author. 1966. London: Routledge, 2006.
Mee, Erin, and Helene Foley. *Antigone on the Contemporary World Stage*. Oxford: Oxford University Press, 2011.
Mhire, Jeremy J., and Bryan-Paul Frost, eds. *The Political Theory of Aristophanes: Explorations in Poetic Wisdom*. Albany: State University of New York Press, 2014.
Minnema, Lourens. *Tragic Views of the Human Condition: Cross-Cultural Comparisons between Views of Human Nature in Greek and Shakespearean Tragedy and the Mahabharata and Bhagavadgita*. London: Bloomsbury, 2013.
Momigliano, Arnaldo. "La libertà di parola nel mondo antico." *Rivista storica italiana* 83 (1971): 499–524.
Morales, Helen. *Antigone Rising: The Subversive Power of the Ancient Myths*. New York: Bold Type Books, 2020.
Mouffe, Chantal. *For a Left Populism*. London: Verso, 2018.
Murnaghan, Sheila. "*Choroi achoroi*: The Athenian Politics of Tragic Choral Identity." In Carter, *Why Athens?*, 245–68.

Mynott, Jeremy. *Birds in the Ancient World*. Oxford: Oxford University Press, 2018.
Nelson, Stephanie. "Aristophanes and the Polis." In Mhire and Frost, *The Political Theory of Aristophanes*, 109–36.
O'Brien, Sean. "A Version of *The Birds* in Two Productions." In Hall and Wrigley, *Aristophanes in Performance*, 276–86.
Olson, S. Douglas. "Comedy, Politics, and Society." In Dobrov, *Brill's Companion to the Study of Greek Comedy*, 35–69.
Orth, Christian. *Strattis: Die Fragmente; Eine Kommentar*. Heidelberg: Verlag-Antike, 2009.
Osborne, Robin, ed. *Debating the Athenian Cultural Revolution: Art, Literature, Philosophy, and Politics, 430–380 BC*. Cambridge: Cambridge University Press, 2007.
O'Sullivan, P., and C. Collard, eds. *Euripides: Cyclops and Major Fragments of Greek Satyric Drama*. Liverpool: Aris and Phillips, 2013.
Parrinder, Patrick, ed. *Learning from Other Worlds: Estrangement, Cognition, and the Politics of Science Fiction and Utopia*. Durham, NC: Duke University Press, 2001.
Patterson, Orlando. *Slavery and Social Death: A Comparative Study*. 2nd ed. Cambridge, MA: Harvard University Press, 2018.
Payne, Mark. *The Animal Part: Human and Other Animals in the Poetic Imagination*. Chicago: University of Chicago Press, 2010.
———. "*Aetna* and Aetnaism: Schiller, Vibrant Matter, and the Phenomenal Regimes of Ancient Poetry." *Helios* 43, no. 2 (Fall 2016): 89–108.
———. *Hontology: Depressive Anthropology and the Shame of Life*. Alresford: Zero Books, 2018.
Perris, Simon. *The Gentle, Jealous God: Reading Euripides' "Bacchae" in English*. London: Bloomsbury Academic, 2016.
Perusino, F., and M. Colantonio, eds. *Dalla lirica corale alla poesia drammatica: Forme e funzioni del canto corale nella tragedia e nella commedia greca*. Pisa: Edizioni ETS, 2007.
Peterson, Anna. *Laughter on the Fringes: The Reception of Old Comedy in the Imperial Greek World*. Oxford: Oxford University Press, 2019.
Platter, Charles. *Aristophanes and the Carnival of Genres*. Baltimore: Johns Hopkins University Press, 2007.
Postclassicisms Collective (Blanchard, Alistair, et al.). *Postclassicisms*. Chicago: University of Chicago Press, 2020.
Preston, Claire. *Bee*. London: Reaktion Books, 2006.
Raaflaub, Kurt. "Aristocracy and Freedom of Speech in the Graeco-Roman World." In Sluiter and Rosen, *Free Speech in Classical Antiquity*, 41–61.
Rancière, Jacques. *Disagreement: Politics and Philosophy*. Translated by Julie Rose. 1995. Minneapolis: University of Minnesota Press, 2004.
———. *Hatred of Democracy*. Translated by Steve Corcoran. 2005. London: Verso, 2006.
Reverdin, Olivier, and Bernard Grange, eds. *Aristophane*. Entretiens sur l'Antiquité classique, vol. 38. Geneva: Fondation Hardt, 1991.
Revermann, Martin. *Comic Business: Theatricality, Dramatic Technique, and Performance Contexts of Aristophanic Comedy*. Oxford: Oxford University Press, 2006.
———, ed. *The Cambridge Companion to Greek Comedy*. Cambridge: Cambridge University Press, 2014.

Rheingold, Howard. *Smart Mobs: The Next Social Revolution*. Cambridge, MA: Basic Books, 2002.
Richlin, Amy. *Slave Theater in the Roman Republic: Plautus and Popular Comedy*. Cambridge: Cambridge University Press, 2017.
Robinson, Cedric. *Black Marxism: The Making of the Black Radical Tradition*. 1983. 2nd ed. Chapel Hill: University of North Carolina Press, 2000.
Robson, James. *Aristophanes: An Introduction*. London: Bloomsbury Academic, 2009.
Roche, M. W. *Tragedy and Comedy: A Systematic Study and a Critique of Hegel*. Albany: State University of New York Press, 1998.
Roselli, David. *Theater of the People: Spectators and Society in Ancient Athens*. Austin: University of Texas Press, 2011.
———. "Social Class." In Revermann, *The Cambridge Companion to Greek Comedy*, 241–58.
———. "The Theater of Euripides." In *A Companion to Euripides*, edited by Laura K. McClure, 390–411. Malden, MA: John Wiley & Sons, 2017.
Rosen, Ralph. *Old Comedy and the Iambographic Tradition*. American Classical Studies 19. New York: Oxford University Press, 1988.
———. *Making Mockery: The Poetics of Ancient Satire*. Oxford: Oxford University Press, 2007.
Rosen, Ralph, and Helene P. Foley, eds. *Aristophanes and Politics: New Studies*. Leiden: Brill, 2020.
Ross, Kristin. *Communal Luxury: The Political Imaginary of the Paris Commune*. London: Verso, 2015.
Rothwell, K. *Nature, Culture, and the Origins of Greek Comedy: A Study of Animal Choruses*. Cambridge: Cambridge University Press, 2007.
Ruffell, I. A. *Politics and Anti-Realism in Athenian Old Comedy: The Art of the Impossible*. Oxford: Oxford University Press, 2011.
Rusten, Jeffrey, ed. *The Birth of Comedy: Texts, Documents, and Art from Athenian Competitions, 486–280*. Translated by Jeffrey Henderson, David Konstan, Ralph Rosen, Jeffrey Rusten, and Niall W. Slater. Baltimore: Johns Hopkins University Press, 2011.
Said, Suzanne. "L'assemblée des femmes: Les femmes, l'économie, et la politique." In Bonnamour, *Aristophane*, 33–70.
Saxonhouse, Arlene W. *Fear of Diversity: The Birth of Political Science in Ancient Greek Thought*. Chicago: University of Chicago Press, 1992.
———. "Boundaries: The Comic Poet Confronts the 'Who' of Political Action." In Mhire and Frost, *The Political Theory of Aristophanes*, 89–108.
———. *Free Speech and Athenian Democracy*. Cambridge: Cambridge University Press, 2008.
Schironi, Francesca. "A Poet without 'Gravity': Aristophanes on the Italian Stage." In Hall and Wrigley, *Aristophanes in Performance*, 267–75.
Segal, E., ed. *Oxford Readings in Aristophanes*. Oxford: Oxford University Press, 1996.
Seidensticker, Bernd. *Palintonos Harmonia: Studien zu komischen Elementen in der griechischen Tragödie*. Hypomnemata, vol. 72. Göttingen: Vandenhoeck and Ruprecht, 1982.
Sells, Donald. *Parody, Politics, and Populace in Greek Old Comedy*. London: Bloomsbury Academic, 2018.

Shanks, Michael. *Classical Archaeology: Experiences of the Discipline*. London: Routledge, 1996.
———. *Art and the Early Greek State: An Interpretive Archaeology*. Cambridge: Cambridge University Press, 1999.
Shapiro, H. Alan. "Autochthony and the Visual Arts in Fifth-Century Athens." In Boedeker and Raaflaub, *Democracy, Empire, and the Arts in Fifth-Century Athens*, 127–52.
Shaw, C. A. *Satyric Play: The Evolution of Greek Comedy and Satyr Drama*. Oxford: Oxford University Press, 2014.
Sidwell, Keith. *Aristophanes the Democrat: The Politics of Satirical Comedy during the Peloponnesian War*. Cambridge: Cambridge University Press, 2009.
Sifakis, G. M. *Parabasis and Animal Choruses: A Contribution to the History of Attic Comedy*. London: Athlone Press (University of London), 1971.
———. "The Structure of Aristophanic Comedy." *Journal of Hellenic Studies* 112 (1992): 123–42.
Silk, M. S. *Aristophanes and the Definition of Comedy*. Oxford: Oxford University Press, 2000.
Slater, Niall. *Spectator Politics: Metatheater and Performance in Aristophanes*. Philadelphia: University of Pennsylvania Press, 2001.
Sluiter, Ineke, and Ralph M. Rosen, eds. *Free Speech in Classical Antiquity*. Mnemosyne Supplement 254. Leiden: Brill, 2004.
Sobak, Robert. "Sokrates among the Shoemakers." *Hesperia* 84 (2015): 669–712.
Sommerstein, Alan H. "Harassing the Satirist: The Alleged Attempts to Prosecute Aristophanes." In Sluiter and Rosen, *Free Speech in Classical Antiquity*, 145–74.
———. "Nephelokokkygia and Gynaikopolis: Aristophanes' Dream Cities." In Hansen, *The Imaginary Polis*, 73–99.
———. *Talking about Laughter and Other Studies in Greek Comedy*. Oxford: Oxford University Press, 2009.
———. "Slave and Citizen in Aristophanic Comedy." In *Talking about Laughter*, 136–54.
———, ed. *The Encyclopedia of Greek Comedy*. 3 vols. Hoboken, NJ: Wiley-Blackwell, 2019.
Sophocles. *Antigone*. Edited by Mark Griffith. Cambridge: Cambridge University Press, 1999.
Storey, Ian C. *Eupolis: Poet of Old Comedy*. Oxford: Oxford University Press, 2004.
Strauss, Leo. *Socrates and Aristophanes*. New York: Basic Books, 1966.
Suvin, Darko. "Afterword: With Sober, Estranged Eyes." In Parrinder, *Learning from Other Worlds*, 233–71.
———. *Defined by a Hollow: Essays on Utopia, Science Fiction, and Political Epistemology*. Bern: Peter Lang, 2010.
———. "Defining the Literary Genre of Utopia: Some Historical Semantics, Some Genology [sic], a Proposal and a Plea." In *Defined by a Hollow*, 17–48.
Taaffe, L. K. *Aristophanes and Women*. London: Routledge, 1993.
Telò, Mario. *Eupolidis Demi*. Biblioteca Nazionale, Serie dei Classici Greci e Latini, n.s. 14. Florence: Felice le Monnier, 2007.
———. *Aristophanes and the Cloak of Comedy: Affect, Aesthetics, and the Canon*. Chicago: University of Chicago Press, 2016.
Telò, Mario, and Melissa Mueller, eds. *The Materialities of Greek Tragedy: Objects and Affect in Aeschylus, Sophocles, and Euripides*. Oxford: Bloomsbury Academic, 2019.

Tordoff, Robert. "Aristophanes' *Assembly Women* and Plato, *Republic* Book 5." In Osborne, *Debating the Athenian Cultural Revolution*, 242–63. Cambridge: Cambridge University Press, 2007.
Treu, Martina. "Poetry and Politics, Advice and Abuse: The Aristophanic Chorus on the Italian Stage." In Hall and Wrigley, *Aristophanes in Performance*, 256–75.
Van Steen, Gonda. "From Scandal to Success Story: Aristophanes' *Birds* as Staged by Karolos Koun." In Hall and Wrigley, *Aristophanes in Performance*, 155–78.
van Zyl Smit, Betine. "Freeing Aristophanes in South Africa: From High Culture to Contemporary Satire." In Hall and Wrigley, *Aristophanes in Performance*, 232–46.
Vasunia, Phiroze. "Aristophanes' *Wealth* and Dalpatram's *Lakshmi*." In Hall and Wrigley, *Aristophanes in Performance*, 117–34.
———. *The Classics and Colonial India*. Oxford: Oxford University Press, 2013.
Vernant, Jean-Pierre, and Pierre Vidal-Naquet. *Myth and Tragedy in Ancient Greece*. Translated by Janet Lloyd. 1972, 1983. New York: Zone Books, 1990.
Viveiros de Castro, Eduardo. *The Inconstancy of the Indian Soul: The Encounter of Catholics and Cannibals in 16th-Century Brazil*. Translated by Gregory Duff Morton. Chicago: Prickly Paradigm Press, 2011.
———. *Cannibal Metaphysics: For a Post-Structural Anthropology*. Translated by Peter Skafish. 2009. Minneapolis: University of Minnesota Press, 2014.
Wallace, Robert W. "The Power to Speak—and Not to Listen—in Ancient Athens." In Sluiter and Rosen, *Free Speech in Classical Antiquity*, 221–32.
Whitman, Cedric. *Aristophanes and the Comic Hero*. Cambridge, MA: Harvard University Press, 1964.
Wilcox, Lauren. "Drones, Swarms, and Becoming-Insect: Feminist Utopias and Posthuman Politics." *Feminist Review* 116 (2017): 25–45.
Wilderson, Frank, III. *Afropessimism*. New York: Liveright, 2020.
Willi, Andreas, ed. *The Language of Greek Comedy*. Oxford: Oxford University Press, 2002.
———. "Languages on Stage: Aristophanic Language, Cultural History, and Athenian Identity." In Willi, *Language of Greek Comedy*, 111–49.
Williams, Raymond. *Marxism and Literature*. Toronto: Oxford University Press, 1977.
Wilson, Peter. *The Athenian Institution of the Khoregia: The Chorus, the City, and the Stage*. Cambridge: Cambridge University Press, 2000.
Winkler, J. J., and F. Zeitlin, "The Ephebes' Song: Tragoidia and Polis." In Winkler and Zeitlin, *Nothing to Do*, 20–62.
———, eds. *Nothing to Do with Dionysos?: Athenian Drama in Its Social Context*. Princeton, NJ: Princeton University Press, 1990.
Wright, Matthew. *The Comedian as Critic: Greek Old Comedy and Poetics*. London: Bloomsbury Academic, 2012.
Zarifi, Yana. "Chorus and Dance in the Ancient World." In *The Cambridge Companion to Greek and Roman Theatre*, edited by Marianne McDonald and Michael Walton, 227–46. Cambridge: Cambridge University Press, 2007.
Zeitlin, Froma. *Playing the Other: Gender and Society in Classical Greek Literature*. Chicago: University of Chicago Press, 1996.
———. "Travesties of Gender and Genre in Aristophanes' *Thesmophoriazusae*." In Zeitlin, *Playing the Other*, 375–416.
Zupancic, Alenka. *The Odd One In: On Comedy*. Cambridge, MA: MIT Press, 2008.

Index

Acharnians (Aristophanes), ix, 163–68
Adorno, Theodor, 50, 53, 117, 126, 220n10
Aeschylus, 36–37, 42–44, 85, 118, 131
Aesop, 49, 64, 74
Alcibiades, 5
Alcman, 57–58, 81, 111
Althusser, Louis, 81–83, 90, 148
Amazons, 109
anarchism, xii
Anderson, Greg, 179–80, 239n9
Andromeda, 113
animacy, 91–92, 193–94
animals, 2, 47, 56, 91–92, 100
Antigone, x, 20, 23–27, 37, 46, 97, 207
Antigone (Sophocles), 20, 23–24, 38
ants, 53–55
Aphrodite, 58–59
Archilochus, 22
Ariphrades, 172
Aristero-phanes, 151
Aristophanes, life of, 9–12, 121. *See also individual plays*
Aristotle, 1, 14, 18, 57–58, 92, 121, 134, 177, 191; on drama, 27–28, 205; on natural history, 61–64; on slavery, 182–83, 192
Artemis, 110, 113
Athena, 59, 114
Athens, 13, 29–30, 33, 57, 59, 65–66, 68, 102; in *Acharnians*, 163–68; in *Birds*, 134, 142; *Birds* performance (1959), 150–51; coins of, 144; democracy in, 178–83; empire of, 72, 104, 125–26, 132, 142, 182, 188; jury system of, 67–69, 72, 118; in *Lysistrata*, 108–11; *parrhesia* in, 156, 159; population of, 181–82

autopoiesis, 202–4
Azoulay, Vincent, 116, 229n70

Babylonians (Aristophanes), 105
Badiou, Alain, 127–31, 190
Baptist, Edward, 184
Barthes, Roland, 3–4
Bastani, Aaron, 122
bees, 51–52, 60–61, 62–63, 69
Benjamin, Walter, 199
Bierl, Anton, 100–102
Big Rock Candy Mountain, 195
Billings, Joshua, 17, 22, 83
birds, 56, 126–27, 234n65
Birds (Aristophanes), 1, 2, 15, 118, 121, 126–27, 133–50, 186, 202; reception of, 150–53
Black Lives Matter, xii, xiv, 119, 175, 197, 205–6
Blackmon, Douglas, 184
Bloch, Ernst, 231n23
Braidotti, Rosi, xii, 48–50
Bregman, Rutger, 211n7, 231n17
Brennan, Jason, *Against Democracy*, 175–76
Brooks, Gwendolyn, 175
Burke, Kenneth, 1
Butler, Judith, xii, 23, 25, 49, 118–19, 174

Calame, Claude, 84–85
Carson, Anne, 25
catharsis, 31–32, 34, 63
Chanter, Tina, 25
Chen, Mel, xii, 91–92
Childs, Dennis, 184

chorus, 2, 15, 79–86; animal, 91–93; in Aristotle, 28, 34–35; comic, 92–93; diminution of, 11, 192–93; Dupont on, 31; satyr, 86–89; tragic, 83–86; Zizek's, 24
Christianity, 158
cicadas, 58–60, 143, 172
cinderology, 130
Claeys, Gregory, and L. T. Sargent, *Utopia Reader*, 118, 120–22
Clements, Ashley, 144
Cleon, 10, 11, 67–68, 74, 140, 164–68, 169–70
Clouds (Aristophanes), 105–7
Colbert, Stephen, 174
colonies, 134, 146
comedy, 211n1 (intro.); costumes of, 69, 93, 134, 136; engagement with tragedy, 18, 39–44; gender in study of, 45–46; Hegel on, 20–21
communal luxury, 16, 191, 204–5
communism, 131, 133, 191, 195, 198, 206
Compton-Engle, Gwendolyn, 136, 233n51
Corbel-Morana, Cécile, 222n45
Corinth, 55–56
crabs, 75
Crates, 120, 121, 132
Cratinus, 13, 132
Csapo, Eric, 93, 218n42
Cyclops (Euripides), 15, 86–89, 115

Dalpatram, Dahyabhai, translation of *Wealth*, 199–201
dance, 1–2, 29, 57, 75–76, 80–81, 207
Dawson, Doyne, 120
Deleuze, Gilles, xii, 8–9, 48–49, 51, 56, 64–65, 76, 201, 214n22
Demeter, 111–16
democracy, 76, 99, 102–5, 114, 120, 125, 132, 136, 146, 162–63, 167–68, 174; antidemocracy discourses, 175–77, 185–86; as "Demokratia" in *Acharnians*, 165–66; in *Ecclesiazusae*, 186–95; Rancière on, 195–97
demos, 173, 178–80, 183, 185, 188, 195; as "Demos" in *Knights*, 170–72
Derrida, Jacques, 49
dildos, xv, 107

Dionysia, Great, 13, 29–30, 33, 84, 173
Dionysus, 13, 22, 32–34, 39–42, 46, 81, 86, 97, 106, 138, 164; in *Bacchae*, 104–5; theater of, 102–3, 133
Dover, K. J., 75–76, 193
Dupont, Florence, 28–32
Dyer-Witheford, Nick, 51

Ecclesiazusae (*Women at the Assembly*; Aristophanes), 16, 100, 112, 120–21, 125, 186–95, 202
Ehrenreich, Barbara, 1
Elliott, Robert, 122–23
epistocracy, 176
Eros, 138–39, 147, 194
Eupolis, 12
Euripides, 15, 28, 38–39, 42–44, 85, 86–89, 108, 157–58; in *Acharnians*, 165; *Bacchae*, 104–5, 158; *Hecuba*, 103, 115; *Hippolytus*, 160–61; *Ion*, 161–62; in *Thesmophoriazusae*, 112–15, 168–69
Evans, Rhiannon, 120

Fitzgerald, William, ix, 232n30
Fletcher, Angus, 99–100
Foucault, Michel, 237n16; on the author, 3–8, 13–14; on *parrhesia*, 16, 156–60, 168, 171, 236nn8–10
Freedgood, Elaine, 7
free speech, 155
Freud, Sigmund, 19, 22
Frogs (Aristophanes), ix, 18, 39–44, 77, 83, 97, 117, 135, 139, 141

Galen, 157
Gbowee, Leymah, 111
Golden Age, 120
Goldhill, Simon, 29, 33–34
Gramsci, Antonio, 133
Graziosi, Barbara, 214n24
Griffith, Mark, 88–89, 103, 123, 197
Guattari, Félix, ix, xii, 8–9, 48–49, 51, 56, 64–65, 76, 201
Gurd, Sean, 40, 43, 135, 203, 221n33, 229n68, 238n32

Hall, Edith, 45, 83–84, 224n14, 229n66
Halliwell, Stephen, 173, 200

INDEX › 259

Haraway, Donna, 141, 203
Hardt, Michael, 47–48
Harney, Stefano, and Fred Moten, *The Undercommons*, 206–7
Harrison, Tony, 243n7
Hegel, G. W. F., 19–21, 23, 49, 97
Heidegger, Martin, 125
Henderson, Jeffrey, xiii, 40, 45, 109, 110, 140, 167, 225n27
Hephaistos, 59
Heraclitus, 57–58
Herodotus, 57–58, 127, 191
Hesiod, 53, 73, 113, 138
Homer, 53–55, 59, 79–80, 127, 139
Honig, Bonnie, 25

Identity Evropa, xi
impossible, 118–19, 140
insects, 50–65. *See also individual insects*
Isocrates, 162–63, 191
isonomia, 55, 71, 76, 136, 181, 191, 195, 197

Jameson, Fredric, 7–8, 124–27, 131–32, 173, 204, 232n40, 243n18
Janko, Richard, 34–35, 218n35
Jim Crow, 177
Jones, Garett, 177, 239n3

Kafka, Franz, 64–65, 201, 222n43
Khan-Cullors, Patrisse, and Asha Bandele, *When They Call You a Terrorist*, 206
khoregos, 4, 11, 13
Klein, Emily, 202
Knights (Aristophanes), 16, 155, 163, 169–72
koinonia, 179–80, 190–92, 197–98, 242n43
Konstan, David, 98–99, 111, 227n50, 234n63
Kureishi, Hanif, 23–24
Kurke, Leslie, 223n52

Lacan, Jacques, 19, 22, 25, 32
Lakshmi, 199–201
Lape, Susan, 94, 240n16
laughter, 17, 34–35, 38, 76, 153, 241n27

Lee, Spike, 26, 111
Lefkowitz, Mary, 3, 9–10
Le Guin, Ursula, 126
Lenaia, 163
Leonard, Miriam, 18–19
lice, 57–58
line of flight, 1, 65, 76, 116, 141, 152, 156
Loraux, Nicole, xii, 37–38
Lowe, Lisa, 184
Luhmann, Niklas, 202–3
Lysistrata (Aristophanes), 15, 34, 90, 100, 107–11, 115, 121, 201–2

Ma, John, 182
MacDowell, Douglas, 67–68, 117–18, 230n4
Macherey, Pierre, 4–6, 98, 132
Mao Zedong, 127, 129, 131
Marcuse, Herbert, 122, 192
Marx, Karl, xii, 19, 50, 204
Marxism, xii, 244n24
Mbembe, Achille, 51, 220n14
Meleager of Gadara, 60
Melos, 104, 182
Menander, 93–95, 98, 132, 193
metics, 145, 181
Milesians, 182
military, 33, 56, 68, 70–72, 92, 116, 150–51, 170–71, 179
More, Thomas, 119–20
Mouffe, Chantal, 205–6
mourning, 37–38
Moylan, Tom, 122–23, 231n20
Mynott, Jeremy, 234n65

Negri, Antonio, 47–48, 51
new materialism, 141
Nietzsche, Friedrich, 19, 21–22
nomadism, 8, 49

obscenity, xiii
Occupy, 118–19, 175, 197, 205
Odysseus, 53, 86–88
Oedipus, x, 22–23, 46
Olson, S. Douglas, 212n5
Orlando, Francesco, 7, 213n18
Otanes, 191
Ovid, 54

Paris Commune, 204–5; as tragedy, 205
Park Chan-wook, 25–26
parrhesia, 15–16, 40, 112, 156, 195; in Euripides, 236n15; Foucault on, 156–60
Patterson, Orlando, 182, 184
Payne, Mark, 141, 149–50
Peace (Aristophanes), 125, 152
Pericles, xii, 22, 105, 107, 136, 182
Persian Empire, 30, 32, 65, 68, 71–72, 125, 165, 166, 179
Persians (Aeschylus), 36
Pherecrates, 117
Pherecydes, 57
Plato, 5, 51, 59, 60–61, 78, 105, 107, 124, 127–31, 185, 188–92, 204
Platonov, Andrei, 124–27
Platter, Charles, 227n54
Ploutos (*Wealth*; Aristophanes), 11, 13, 95, 133, 152, 193, 199–201, 202, 242n4
Plutarch, 5, 105, 159, 182
Praxagora, 187–95
Presley, Elvis, ix
pre-Socratics, 125
Preston, Claire, 51–52

Rancière, Jacques, 78, 173, 175, 180–81, 187–88, 195–97, 205, 244n25
Reinhard, Ken, 130
Revermann, Martin, 84
Roman comedy, 2
Roselli, David Kawalko, 89, 102–3, 132–33
Rosen, Ralph, 89–90, 212n7, 225n23
Ross, Kristin, 16, 47–48, 77, 139, 204–5
Ruffell, Ian, 123–24, 212n5

Sappho, 3, 59, 79, 114–15, 170
satire, 122–23
satyr play, 15, 86–89, 116
Saxonhouse, Arlene, 234–35n1
Schironi, Francesca, 151
Scriabin, Alexander, 84
Seaford, Richard, 228n58
Segal, Charles, 38
Shakespeare, William, 2, 19, 35–36, 124
Shamsie, Kamila, 25
Shanks, Michael, 55–57, 221nn27–28
Shorey, Paul, 130

Sifakis, G. M., 100, 228n58
slaves, 36–37, 38, 39, 40, 41–42, 44, 66–68, 70, 74, 77, 81, 85, 86–89, 92, 94, 100, 102–4, 105, 109, 113–16, 117, 161–62, 164, 178, 179–83, 188, 190, 204; in *Birds*, 140; city of, 132; in *Ecclesiazusae*, 192; in *Knights*, 170, 172; in United States, 183–84
Sluiter, Ineke, and Ralph M. Rosen, *Free Speech in Classical Antiquity*, 234n1
Sobak, Robert, 178–79, 186, 188, 241n28
Socrates, 44, 59, 60, 105–7, 129, 160, 178, 185
Solon, 159–60, 180
Sommerstein, Alan, 123, 173, 231n27, 241n27
Sondheim, Stephen, 45
Sophocles, 17, 20, 22–23, 26, 28, 85, 134, 157
Sparta, 57–58, 81, 111, 115, 164–68, 186
Spartacus, 129
Spinoza, Baruch, xii, 49
Storey, Ian, 12, 215n27
Strattis, 12–13
suture, 2
Suvin, Darko, 230n9
swarm, 14–15, 40, 134, 141, 173; intelligence, x; menace of, 47, 49, 50–51; positive aspects, 47–50; *Swarm* (film), 52
sympoiesis, 203–4

Teleclides, 122
Telò, Mario, 3, 227n54
Thebes, 223n50
Them (film), 51
Thesmophoriazusae (Aristophanes), 100–102, 111–16, 121, 168–69
Tithonos, 58
Tordoff, Robert, 241n26
torture, 184–85
tragedy, 14, 17–34, 118
Treu, Martina, 152

utopia, 15, 48, 111, 117–32, 149, 205

Van Steen, Gonda, 150–51
van Zyl Smit, Betine, 141

vases, 55–57, 93, 100, 134, 187
Vasunia, Phiroze, 199–201
Vernant, Jean-Pierre, xii, 95–97
Vidal-Naquet, Pierre, 97–98
Viveiros de Castro, Eduardo, 40, 148–49

Wallace, Robert W., 173
wasps, 52, 54, 63–64, 109, 167

Wasps (Aristophanes), 65–77, 100, 181
Whitman, Cedric, 89–90
Wilcox, Lauren, 220n11
Williams, Raymond, 19, 125, 133
Wilson, Peter, 4–5, 213n14, 232n43

Zeitlin, Froma, ix, 218n31
Zizek, Slavoj, 23–25